THE ILLUSTRATED ENCYCLOPEDIA OF THE
OLD WEST

THE ILLUSTRATED ENCYCLOPEDIA OF THE
OLD WEST

PETER NEWARK

BROCKHAMPTON PRESS

This edition printed in 1998 under license from
André Deutsch Limited by
Brockhampton Press Limited
20 Bloomsbury Street, London WC1B 3QA
A member of the Hodder Headline Group of companies

First Published in 1980 by André Deutsch Limited
Reprinted in 1984

Design by Arena Design Workshop & Oxford Publishing Services
from a conception by John Maxwell Enterprises

Cover Design by Open Door Ltd

Printed in Indonesia

ISBN: 1-86019-935-6

NOTE ON THE ILLUSTRATIONS

All illustrations researched and compiled by Peter Newark and the
Western Americana Picture Library,
86 Park Road, Brentwood, Essex, England.

Author's Note

The Old West described in this book embraces the history, topography, and wildlife of the United States west of the Mississippi River during the whole of the nineteenth century.

Certain exceptions have been made, with particular regard to the Spanish entry into North America in the sixteenth century and the Spanish influence on the history and culture of the South-west and California. Certain aspects of Canadian history have also been included.

The Old West is a vast and varicoloured canvas and the items selected for this single volume were chosen for their importance in the general concept of the Old West.

Cross references are indicated by the use of small capitals.

For the purposes of further reading, the books listed below each entry are suggested as the best and most accessible on the subject dealt with.

Acknowledgements

The author wishes to express his special thanks to the following persons and organizations for providing information and illustrations used in this book:

American Quarter Horse Association
Amoco Oil Company
Appaloosa Horse Club
Arizona Historical Society
Department of the Army
Atchison, Topeka and Santa Fe Railway
    Company
Association of American Railroads
Buffalo Bill Historical Center, Cody, Wyoming
Bureau of Indian Affairs, U.S. Department of
    the Interior
W. A. McKenzie, Burlington Northern
State Historical Society of Colorado
Colt Industries, Firearms Division
Library of Congress
Custer Battlefield National Monument
Death Valley Natural History Association
English Westerners' Society
Sylvia and Joe Hammersly
Barney Hubbs
Hudson's Bay Company
Justin Boot Company
Kansas State Historical Society
Levi Strauss and Company
Robin May
National Archives
National Park Service, U.S. Department of the
    Interior

New Hampshire Historical Society
University of Oklahoma Library
Oregon Trail Museum
Remington Arms Company
Rodeo Cowboys Association
Theodore Roosevelt National Memorial Park
Royal Canadian Mounted Police
C. M. Russell Museum, Great Falls, Montana
Saguaro National Monument
Smith & Wesson
Smithsonian Institution
Southern Pacific Transportation Company
Springfield Armory Museum
St Joseph Museum and Pony Express Stables
    Museum
John B. Stetson Company
Francis B. Taunton
Texas Ranger Hall of Fame
The Daughters of the Republic of Texas
Ken Ulyatt
Barry C. Combs, Union Pacific Railroad
    Company
Utah State Historical Society
Wells Fargo Bank History Room
Whitman Mission National Historic Site
Winchester-Western Division
Woolaroc Museum, Bartlesville, Oklahoma
Oliver Yates.

The following books dealing with the history of the American West in broad and general terms are recommended as introductory reading:

The West in American History by D. E. Clark (New York, 1947)
The Look of the Old West by F. Harris (New York, 1955)
America Moves West by R. E. Riegel (New York, 1955)
The Far Western Frontier, 1830-1860 by R. A. Billington (New York, 1956)
The Book of the American West edited by J. Monaghan (New York, 1963)
The American West by D. Lavender (New York, 1965)
The American West by J. A. Hawgood (London and New York, 1967)
Westward Expansion: A History of the American Frontier by R. A. Billington (New York, 1974)
A Short History of the American West by J. A. Stout Jr and O. B. Faulk (New York, 1974)
The Conquest of the American West by J. Selby (London, 1975)

Introduction

Historical Outline of the Trans-Mississippi West during the Nineteenth Century.

When the United States gained independence in 1783, the western boundary of the new nation was established at the Mississippi River. Only a few trail-blazers and pioneers had crossed the Appalachian Mountains at that time, but soon legions of land-hungry settlers began to fill this fertile area. Floating down the Ohio River or travelling overland through the Cumberland Gap on the Wilderness Road, they entered the Old North-west (Ohio, Illinois, Indiana, Michigan, Wisconsin), Kentucky and Tennessee. By 1800 they had reached the banks of the Mississippi.

Recognizing the essential need for American possession of the port of New Orleans, and the Mississippi River, a vital transportation artery, President Thomas Jefferson seized the opportunity to purchase the immense French empire of Louisiana from Napoleon in 1803. This vast acquisition doubled the land area of the young republic and assured the United States of a major role in the settlement of North America.

In 1804-6 the Lewis and Clark Expedition explored part of the Louisiana Purchase — a great wilderness stretching from the Mississippi River to the Rocky Mountains — travelling up the Missouri River to the Rockies, then on to the Pacific Ocean.

Commercial fur trappers followed, searching for the lucrative beaver and other fur-bearing animals to satisfy the demands of fashion in the eastern U.S. and in Europe; these hardy mountain men, such as Jedediah Smith, Jim Bridger, and Joe Walker, also explored the wilderness and blazed trails in the Far West.

Steamboats soon made St Louis, Missouri, on the banks of the Mississippi, the headquarters of the fur trade and one of the gateways to the West. As the westward migration got under way, thousands of covered wagons rolled over the trails to Oregon and California, long journeys fraught with danger and hardships. In 1847 the Mormons headed into the empty West from Illinois and settled in Utah.

The settlement of the disputed Oregon country (in which Britain had an interest) and other U.S. territorial ambitions brought into vogue the chauvinist American phrase 'Manifest Destiny'. In 1845 an article in *The United States Magazine and Democratic Review* , an expansionist organ, declared that foreign governments were trying to obstruct the annexation of Texas (a former province of Mexico) by the U.S. in order to restrain 'the fulfilment of our manifest destiny to overspread the continent allotted by Providence for the free development of our yearly multiplying millions'.

Twenty years later Horace Greeley, founder and editor of the New York *Tribune* and propagator of Western settlement, made popular another phrase when he wrote: 'Go West, young man, and grow up with your country.'

Texas joined the United States in 1845 and this resulted in the Mexican War of 1846-8, a disastrous happening for Mexico but a fortunate one for the U.S. Defeated Mexico relinquished all claims to Texas above the Rio Grande and ceded to the U.S. the lands of New Mexico (including the present states of Arizona, New Mexico, Utah, Nevada, and parts of Wyoming and Colorado) and the present State of California.

The discovery of gold in 1848 at Sutter's Mill in California transformed the steady westward migration into the great, hectic Gold Rush of 1849, during which 'Forty-Niners' in many thousands from all parts of the world flocked to the American Eldorado. In the following years other rich gold and silver discoveries in Colorado, Nevada, Montana, and the Dakotas attracted further rushes and gave birth to new towns and cities in the West. Some became permanent communities, others declined into derelict ghost towns.

Speeding the process of Western development were the railroads. The first transcontinental line was completed in 1869, when the rails of the Union Pacific Railroad from the East joined the rails of the Central Pacific from the West, at Promontory Point in Utah. By 1884 four great railroads linked the Mississippi Valley area with the Pacific coast.

In 1867 Texas cattlemen began to drive herds of their native longhorns north over the Chisholm Trail to Kansas, from where the railroad took the live beef to markets in the East. The long trail drives became a regular event; the colourful Texas cowboy became a national (then international) figure and the Kansas railhead cowtowns of Abilene, Wichita, and Dodge City flourished in the cattle boom.

Cattle ranching spread north and west from Texas and immense ranches appeared in Colorado, Wyoming, Kansas, Nebraska, Montana, New Mexico, Arizona, and the Dakota Territory. Conflicts of interest between cattlemen, sheep raisers, farmers, homesteaders, and Indians, the lure of quick riches from gold and silver strikes, all combined to create the turbulence of the 'Wild West' and triggered the legendary fame of gunfighters, bandits, and lawmen such as Wild Bill Hickok, Billy the Kid, Jesse James, and Wyatt Earp.

The Indians resisted the white advance across the Western lands as best they could. Some tribes made treaties, some waged war, others were friendly and readily accepted reservation life. The fiercest resistance came from the Plains Indians — the Sioux, Cheyennes, Comanches, and Kiowas — proud, horse-riding nomads who hunted the buffalo and lived in tipis.

In June 1876 the Indian Wars reached a climax when the Sioux and their allies defeated the Seventh Cavalry, killing General Custer and some 200 of his men in the celebrated Battle of the Little Bighorn in Montana. Thereafter the hostile Plains tribes were scattered, subdued, and confined to reservations. By the mid 1880s the buffalo, which only fifty years before had roamed the Great Plains in millions, had been exterminated to the edge of extinction by professional white hunters in the cause of commercial profit.

The Western cattle boom reached its peak about 1885. By then the hitherto open ranges were being settled by homesteaders, who staked their claims under the Homestead Act, fenced them in with barbed wire and ousted the big cattlemen from extensive lands they had possessed without legal title. The cattle ranges became overstocked, the price of beef fell, and the terrible winter of 1886-7 wiped out great herds on the open ranges. The ranchers that survived the disaster reorganized the cattle industry to suit the changing conditions.

In 1889 a section of the Indian Territory (which later became Oklahoma) was opened to white settlement and thousands of homesteaders raced in to stake claims in the last of the free land; other Oklahoma land rushes followed. In 1890 the U.S. Census Director stated in his report that 'there can hardly be said to be a frontier line'. The frontier days were over. By the turn of the century the Old West was fast giving way to the new.

Table of Major Events

1803
Louisiana purchased by United States from France.

1804-6
Lewis and Clark western expedition to the Pacific.

1806-7
Zebulon M. Pike explored Colorado and New Mexico.

1807
John Colter credited as first white man to enter present Wyoming.

1811
First steamboat (the *New Orleans*) on the Mississippi River.

1819
First steamboat (the *Independence*) on the Missouri River.

1821
Mexico gained independence from Spain.
Santa Fe Trail established by trader William Becknell.
Hudson's Bay Company merged with rival North West Company.

1823
Origin of Texas Rangers (formally organized in 1835).

1824
Great Salt Lake region explored by Jim Bridger and Étienne Provost.

1826-30
Jedediah Smith led expeditions to California and Pacific North-west.

1830
Indian Removal Bill passed by Congress; empowered President to remove any Eastern tribes to trans-Mississippi regions.

1831
Cyrus McCormick invented mechanical reaper.

1832
Black Hawk Indian War in Illinois.
Fight at Pierre's Hole (Idaho); Indians v. fur trappers.

1833-4
Joe Walker led expedition to California; found Walker Pass in Sierra Nevada Mountains.

1834
Fort Laramie trading post (Wyoming) established by Sublette and Campbell; military post 1849-90.

1835
Texans revolted against Mexican rule.

1836
Battle of the Alamo; Mexicans defeated Texans.
Battle of San Jacinto; Texans defeated Mexicans.
Texas declared a Republic.
First Colt revolver.
Narcissa Whitman and Eliza Spalding are first white women to pass over Oregon Trail to Far West.

1838
Trail of Tears; forcible removal of Cherokees to Indian Territory.

1841
Battle of Bandera Pass; Texas Rangers v. Comanches.

1842
John C. Frémont explored the Far West (1842-4).
Beginning of the Great Migration to Oregon country (1842-3).

1843
Fort Bridger (Wyoming) established by Jim Bridger and Louis Vasquez; military post 1858-90.

1845
Texas annexed by United States.

1846
Oregon Treaty between Britain and United States

established present border between U.S. and Canada.
Donner Party; ill-fated caravan to California (1846-7).
Mexican War (1846-8); defeated Mexico cedes vast area of West to United States.

1847
Initial Mormon migration to Utah; Salt Lake City founded.
Marcus Whitman killed by Cayuse Indians; Cayuse War (1847-50).

1848
Gold discovered at Sutter's Mill, California.

1849
Great Gold Rush to California.

1850
Allan Pinkerton established Pinkerton National Detective Agency in Chicago.

1851
San Francisco's first Vigilance Committee formed to fight crime (second formed in 1856).

1852
Wells Fargo and Company organized; opened office in San Francisco.

1856
Lawrence, Kansas, sacked in Border War over slavery issue.

1857
Mountain Meadows Massacre perpetrated by Mormons.

1858
Inauguration of the Butterfield Overland Mail service.
Discovery of gold in Colorado and Nevada.

1859
Virginia City, Nevada, founded on Comstock Lode discovery.

1860
Pony Express (1860-1).
Paiute Indian War (1860-1).

1861
Transcontinental telegraph completed.
American Civil War (1861-5).

1862
Sioux uprising in Minnesota.
Homestead Act passed by Congress.

1863
Bozeman Trail established.
Montana gold rush.
Mangas Coloradas, Apache chief, killed.
Kit Carson campaigned against Navajos.

1864
Henry Plummer hanged by Montana vigilantes.
First Battle of Adobe Walls; Indians v. U.S. troops.
Sand Creek Massacre of Cheyennes by Colorado Volunteers.

1865
Union Stockyards opened in Chicago.

1866
Fort Phil Kearny established on Bozeman Trail.
Red Cloud's War (1866-8).
Fetterman Massacre near Fort Phil Kearny.
Wells Fargo purchased Ben Holladay's Overland Mail Company.
First train robbery in U.S. committed by Reno brothers.
First Winchester repeating rifle, Model 1866.

1867
Wagon Box Fight near Fort Phil Kearny.
Hayfield Fight near Fort C. F. Smith (Montana).
Dominion of Canada established.
Abilene, Kansas, became first railhead cattle town; start of cattle drives from Texas to Kansas.

1868
Bozeman Trail closed by U.S. Government.

Fort Phil Kearny abandoned and destroyed.
Red Cloud signs Fort Laramie Treaty; establishment of great Sioux Reservation.
Battle of Beecher Island (Colorado); death of Roman Nose.
Battle of the Washita; Custer destroyed Cheyenne village.

1869
First transcontinental railroad completed; joining of Union Pacific and Central Pacific railroads at Promontory, Utah.

1872
Yellowstone National Park established; first national park in U.S.
Modoc Indian War (1872-3).

1873
North West Mounted Police formed in Canada

1874
Barbed wire patented by J. F. Glidden.
Second Battle of Adobe Walls; Indians v. buffalo hunters.
Battle of Palo Duro Canyon; Indians v. U.S. troops.
Custer's expedition to Black Hills of Dakota; gold deposits reported.

1875
Gold rush in Black Hills.

1876
Battle of the Rosebud; Indians v. U.S. troops.
Battle of the Little Bighorn; death of Custer.
Sitting Bull led his people to refuge in Canada.
Wild Bill Hickok killed by Jack McCall.
Jesse James - Younger brothers gang routed at Northfield, Minnesota.

1877
Nez Percé Indian War; surrender of Chief Joseph.

1878
Bannack Indian War.
Lincoln County (cattle) War, New Mexico.

Leadville, Colorado, boomed on silver strike.

1879
Nathan Meeker, Indian agent, killed by Ute Indians, Colorado.

1880
Victorio, Apache chief, killed.

1881
Billy the Kid killed by Pat Garrett.
Gunfight at the O.K. Corral, Tombstone, Arizona.
Sitting Bull returned to U.S. and surrendered.

1882
Jesse James killed by Bob Ford.

1883
Northern Pacific Railroad completed.
Buffalo Bill Cody organized his first Wild West Show.

1885
Buffalo slaughtered to edge of extinction.

1886
Geronimo, Apache leader, surrendered; end of Apache Wars.
Disastrous winter blighted the cattle country (1886-7).
End of open range cattle industry.

1889
Indian Territory (Oklahoma) opened to white settlement.
Ghost Dance movement established among Dakota Sioux.

1890
Sitting Bull killed by Indian police.
Massacre of band of Sioux by U.S. troops at Wounded Knee Creek, South Dakota.

1892
Johnson County (cattle) War, Wyoming.
Dalton gang wiped out during bank raid at Coffeyville, Kansas.

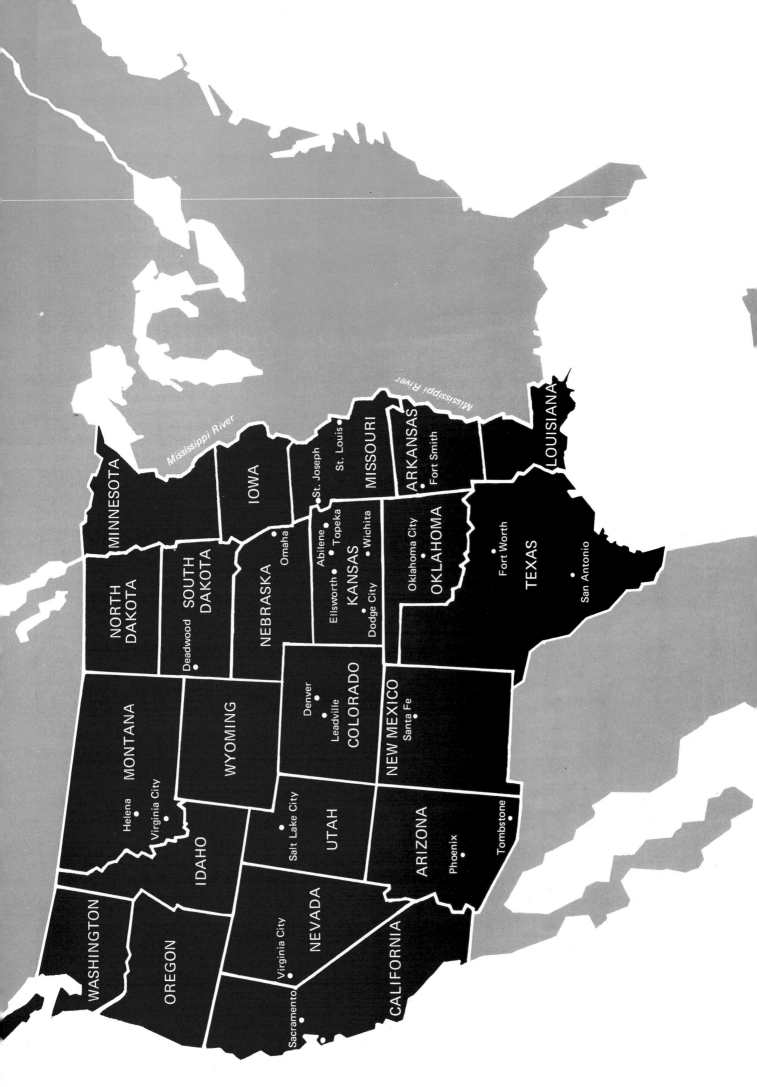

Trans-Mississippi West: Territorial Status & Statehood

State	Created a Territory		Entered Union	
Arizona	24 February	1863	14 February	1912
Arkansas	2 March	1819	15 June	1836
California	No Territorial status		9 September	1850
Colorado	28 February	1861	1 August	1876
Idaho	4 March	1863	3 July	1890
Iowa	12 June	1838	28 December	1846
Kansas	30 May	1854	29 January	1861
Louisiana	26 March	1804	30 April	1812
Minnesota	3 March	1849	11 May	1858
Missouri	4 June	1812	10 August	1821
Montana	26 May	1864	8 November	1889
Nebraska	30 May	1854	1 March	1867
Nevada	2 March	1861	31 October	1864
New Mexico	9 September	1850	6 January	1912
North Dakota	2 March	1861	2 November	1889
Oklahoma	2 May	1890	16 November	1907
Oregon	14 August	1848	14 February	1859
South Dakota	2 March	1861	2 November	1889
Texas	No Territorial status		29 December	1845
Utah	9 September	1850	4 January	1896
Washington	2 March	1853	11 November	1889
Wyoming	25 July	1868	10 July	1890

ABILENE, Kansas

First of the major railhead cattle towns, Abilene set the pattern for the other celebrated 'cowtowns' of the Old West. From 1867 to 1872 it was a booming depot, shipping some 1½ million Texas LONGHORNS by railroad to Kansas City and Chicago and meat markets in the East. Abilene (a biblical name meaning 'City of the plains') was settled in 1856. It remained a quiet hamlet of some dozen log cabins until livestock promoter Joseph McCOY selected the place as a terminus for Texas cattle drives in 1867; that year the railroad had reached Abilene. McCoy chose the town because the area was virtually unsettled, was well watered, had excellent grass, and was ideally suited for holding large numbers of cattle. He bought 250 acres on the edge of the settlement, built the big Drover's Cottage hotel, erected cattle pens, loading chutes, barns, and livery stables. Then the long drives began from Texas over the CHISHOLM TRAIL. At trail's end in Abilene the rowdy, free-spending cowboys attracted saloon keepers, gamblers, brothels, and all types of frontier riff-raff; the town became notorious for its lawlessness and vice. Wild Bill HICKOK was hired for a time to keep the peace in Abilene. As the town grew, prospered, and stabilized, its law-abiding citizens decided to discourage the troublesome cattle trade with its uncouth, transient cowboys and early in 1872 requested the Texas cattlemen to drive their herds elsewhere, which they soon did, and Abilene's role as a wild cow town came to an abrupt end.

Prairie Trails and Cow Towns by F. B. Streeter (Boston, 1936);
Early Days in Abilene by J. B. Edwards (Abilene, 1938);
The Cattle Towns by R. R. Dykstra (New York, 1968).

1 ▼

ADAMS & COMPANY

A banking and express delivery service founded by Alvin Adams (1804-77), as the Western branch of the Adams Express Company, that competed with WELLS FARGO in California during the GOLD RUSH years of the early 1850s, carrying valuables and other securities. Following the 'great express panic' which involved the financial affairs of several such companies, Adams & Company went out of business in 1855; Wells Fargo survived and flourished. In the East, however, the Adams Express Company continued in business and remained a leading firm until 1918, when it merged into the American Railway Express Company.

Express and Stagecoach Days in California by O. O. Winther (Stanford University Press, 1936);
Wells Fargo by N. M. Loomis (New York, 1968).

ADAMS 'Grizzly' 1812-60

John Capen Adams, better known as 'Grizzly' Adams, was a remarkable mountain man who captured and tamed grizzly BEARS. Born in Massachusetts, Adams was a shoemaker until he was twenty-one. He then became a hunter in the forests of New England, trapping wildcats and wolves for a local menagerie. After being savaged to the point of death by a tiger in the menagerie,

1 *Loading cattle on to rail cars at Abilene for shipment east.*

he returned to shoemaking for another fifteen years. He then headed for the gold fields of CALIFORNIA. Failing to find his fortune, he went up into the SIERRA NEVADA Mountains to trap animals for their furs. He began catching and training giant grizzly bears; his reputation spread and he turned to capturing bears for zoos. Later, he went to the ROCKY MOUNTAINS on bear-hunting expeditions. He reared two bear cubs, named Lady Washington and Benjamin Franklin, and trained them as companions and pack animals. Once, when Adams was attacked by an angry female grizzly, Ben Franklin rushed to his master's rescue and saved his life. In 1855 Adams took his bears and other wild animals to SAN FRANCISCO and opened an exhibition at the Mountaineer Museum, which attracted wide attention. The gray-bearded Adams, always dressed in buckskins, became a celebrated figure, strolling the city streets with his grizzly pets. Early in 1860 he took his zoo to New York and became a partner of the famous showman Phineas T. Barnum in his American Museum. In the opening parade down Broadway, the mountain man was the centre of attraction, riding a big bear and holding two on chains. Adams had survived a number of fights with grizzly bears but the terrible injuries he had suffered shortened his life. He died on 25 October 1860, aged forty-eight.

The Legend of Grizzly Adams by R. Dillon (New York 1966).

ADOBE

A sun-dried brick made of clay mixed with straw or grass. Houses built of adobe bricks were used principally in the arid south-western region of the U.S. and Mexico. Adobe comes from the Spanish *adobar,* meaning 'to plaster'. When the Spanish explorers first discovered Indians living in well-planned towns built of adobe, they named the sedentary natives PUEBLOS, meaning 'village dwellers'. Adobe was widely used by the Spanish to build missions, forts and trading posts. The wet clay was mixed with fibrous material and trampled on with the bare feet, then moulded into bricks and dried in the sun for a week or two. The walls, usually plastered over with more clay, were thickly built and this made the interior cool. The word adobe was corrupted to 'dobie' by the Americans.

2 ∨

ADOBE WALLS, Battles of 1864 and 1874

The first Battle of Adobe Walls was fought between a force of soldiers commanded by Colonel Christopher (Kit) CARSON and several thousand KIOWA and COMANCHE warriors near the abandoned trading post called Adobe Walls, or Adobe Fort, on the north side of the Canadian River in the Texas Panhandle in late November 1864. Carson's two mountain howitzers and their explosive shells saved his column from defeat and he managed to destroy a Kiowa village. The second Battle of Adobe Walls took place on 27 June 1874 when a combined force of Comanche, CHEYENNE and Kiowa braves attacked a party of white buffalo-hide hunters at the newly-built trading post near the ruins of the old one. The Comanches were led by noted chief QUANAH PARKER; the defending hunters included Bill DIXON and Bat MASTERSON. The Indians had a special enmity for the professional BUFFALO HUNTERS who were destroying their main source of food, clothing and shelter. (Of the 3,700,000 BUFFALO

3 ∨

slaughtered between 1872 and 1874, the Indians killed only 150,000.) The Indians attacked at dawn, and strangely enough, charged to the signals of a bugle, played some say by a renegade Negro cavalryman. But the marksmanship and the big SHARPS buffalo rifles of the stalwart hunters proved too much for the Indians. The main fighting ended at four in the afternoon when the Indians, after suffering heavy casualties, abandoned the attack. Three hunters were killed in the battle.

Kit Carson's Fight with the Comanche and Kiowa Indians by G. H. Pettis (Santa Fe, 1908);
The Life of Billy Dixon by O. K. Dixon (Dallas, 1927);
Great Western Indian Fights by Members of the Potomac Corral of the Westerners (Lincoln, 1970).

ALAMO, Battle of 1836

In 1835 the Anglo-American colonists in the Mexican province of Texas made armed rebellion against Mexican rule with the intention of proclaiming Texas a republic. In December 1835 the revolutionaries captured the fortified mission of the Alamo in San Antonio. On 23 February 1836 a Mexican army of 5,000 commanded by General Antonio Lopez de SANTA ANNA, President of Mexico, entered San Antonio. When Santa Anna demanded the surrender of the Alamo, Colonel William Barret Travis, commander of the small garrison of some 180 men, answered with a cannon shot. So began the thirteen-day siege that ended with the Mexicans storming the fortress; the defenders, to a man, fought on until death. The stubborn defenders included James BOWIE of 'Bowie knife' fame, and Davy CROCKETT of Tennessee. Crockett, in sympathy with the Texans' cause, had arrived in San Antonio early in February 1836 with a dozen Tennessee volunteers. Bowie held joint command of the Alamo with Travis until stricken with typhoid-pneumonia. Santa Anna launched his final assault at dawn on 6 March. With bugles sounding the 'Deguello' (signifying no quarter to the defenders) the Mexicans attacked the adobe walls from all four sides and broke through. Travis was shot dead over his cannon. Crockett, using his rifle as a club, fell under a swarm of the enemy. Bowie fought to the last from his sickbed. The Mexicans had won a Pyrrhic victory, suffering more than 1,500 casualties. 'Another such victory and we are ruined,' declared Colonel Juan Almonte. Santa Anna spared the life of Mrs Dickinson (widow of a defender), her infant

2   *Adobe house in Arizona in 1880s.*

3   *Grizzly Adams and his pet bear 'Ben Franklin.'*

18

daughter, and fourteen other non-combatants. On 21 April, forty-six days after the fall of the Alamo, less than 800 Texans and American volunteers led by General Sam HOUSTON defeated Santa Anna and his army of 1,300 at San Jacinto. Shouting 'Remember the Alamo!' Houston's men completely routed the Mexicans in a matter of minutes, killing 630 while losing only 8. Santa Anna was captured, and the Republic of Texas was born. Today, the chapel of the Alamo, the only remaining part of the building of 1836, is maintained by the Daughters of the Republic of Texas as a shrine and a museum.

The Alamo by F. Chabot (San Antonio, 1936);
13 Days to Glory by L. Tinkle (New York, 1958);
A Time to Stand by W. Lord (New York, 1961).

ALLISON, Clay
1841-87

A rancher and gunman of some notoriety whose capricious violence was mostly triggered by his heavy drinking. Born in Tennessee, Robert Clay Allison served for a short time in a Confederate regiment during the Civil War, his unstable character bringing him a medical discharge. After the war he went to Texas and worked as a cowboy; by 1870 he had his own ranch in Colfax County, New Mexico. Instead of the fifteen men he supposedly killed, the record shows only three dying in the gunfight situation for which Allison earned his reputation; they were John 'Chunk' Colbert, Francisco Griego, and deputy sheriff Charles Faber. Legend has it that he also tangled with noted lawmen Wyatt EARP and Bat MASTERSON. In 1880 Allison was living near Mobeetie, Texas, and Bill Oden who knew him then described him as 'a quiet, unassuming man with no element of the desperado about him. He

4 ∇

never killed anyone except in self defence.' Legend also has it that Allison in his cups was a roaring, swaggering braggart. In 1886 Allison made his home in Pecos, Texas, and his neighbour Mr R. D. Gage wrote of him: 'When sober he was a quiet, pleasant, affable man, but under the influence of liquor he was a very dangerous man. He was never boisterous or loud spoken. In fact, the drunker he became, the softer became his speech.' Allison did not die by a bullet. On 3 July 1887 he was driving a wagonload of supplies to his ranch when he fell off (some say in a drunken state) and one of the wagon wheels ran over his neck or fractured his skull, killing him. No one witnessed the accident.

Clay Allison of the Washita by O. S. Clark (Houston, Texas, 1920);
Robert Clay Allison, Gentleman Gun Fighter by C. Parsons (Pecos, Texas, 1977).

AMERICAN FUR COMPANY

Fur trapping and trading company founded in 1808 by John Jacob Astor (1763-1848), a poor immigrant born in Germany, to challenge the powerful North West and HUDSON'S BAY companies of Canada, which at that time controlled the fur trade in North America. In 1810 he established Fort Astoria at the mouth of the Columbia River, in OREGON, and carried out profitable trade with the Indians. In the war of 1812 Fort Astoria was sold to the North West Company for the bargain price of $58,000 and renamed Fort George. The American Fur Company continued trading in the ROCKY MOUNTAINS and by 1828 had a virtual monopoly of the United States fur trade. In 1834 Astor sold his interests in the company in order to deal in other things. He died in 1848, leaving $20 million. The American Fur Company continued trading until 1847.

The American Fur Trade of the Far West by H. M. Chittenden (New York, 1902, 1935);
Furs by Astor by J. U. Terrell (New York, 1963).

AMERICAN HORSE

A chief of the Oglala SIOUX, he fought with CRAZY HORSE against the U.S. Army in the Battle of the ROSEBUD and the Battle of the LITTLE

4 *John Jacob Astor, founder of the American Fur Company.*

5 Λ

6 V   7 V

5   *Mexican troops storm the Alamo.*

6   *Clay Allison recovering from a shooting incident in 1870.*

7   *The Alamo building today, flying the Texas flag.*

8 ∧

9 V

11 V

10 ∧

BIGHORN. After their great victory at the Little Bighorn the Sioux scattered, with the army determined to hunt them down. On 9 September 1876 near Slim Buttes, South Dakota, soldiers of General George CROOK attacked the village of American Horse and trapped the chief, four warriors and some fifteen women and children in a canyon cave. Crook requested the chief to surrender but he refused and fought back in the face of heavy fire. Finally, when mortally wounded in the stomach, American Horse gave up and emerged from the cave biting on a piece of wood to keep him from showing the pain caused by his dreadful wound. He died soon after.

Death on the Prairie by P. I. Wellman (New York, 1934);
Bury My Heart at Wounded Knee by D. Brown (New York, 1970).

ANTELOPE, Pronghorn
Antilocapra americana

Before the West was settled, the pronghorn antelope was as numerous as the BUFFALO and ranged the Great Plains in herds of thousands. Endowed with remarkable vision, endurance and speed (a scientist once clocked a pronghorn running over a short distance at 60 m.p.h.) it could easily out-distance its natural enemies. Indians hunted them with some success. With the coming of the railroads and the settlers the pronghorn was slaughtered, almost to extinction, for its meat. Happily, protective legislation and wild life management has increased the pronghorn numbers to some 200,000.

APACHE INDIANS

Fierce nomads of the Athapascan linguistic family. By the time the Spanish arrived around 1540 the Apaches were feared as raiders and killers among the peaceful, settled PUEBLO INDIANS and other tribes of the area that is now Arizona and New Mexico. For the Apaches, masters of combat and concealment, war and plunder were a way of life. They were incredibly cruel and incredibly brave. Their name comes from the Zuni word '*Apachu*' or 'enemy'. They travelled in small raiding bands or clans which

8 *Apaches armed for war in 1880s.*

9 *Chief American Horse.*

10 *The Apache Kid.*

11 *Pronghorn antelope.*

could easily be hidden in the mountains and canyons. They lived in brush shelters called 'wickyups' built by the women; these were simple to construct and easy to take down for quick decampment; they were also satisfactory shelter in the arid climate. There were six main tribal divisions — Jicarilla Apaches, Mescalero Apaches, Chiricahua, Mimbrenos, San Carlos, and Coyotero — each subdivided into bands, and bands into groups made up of families related through the mother. There was little tribal solidarity. As white immigration increased into the South-west, so did widespread Apache attacks on the settlers. The mid-nineteenth century saw many years of warfare between Apache bands and the U.S. Army, settlers, and Mexicans. This was the period that produced notable warrior-chiefs such as MANGAS COLORADAS and COCHISE. In 1875 most hostile bands were rounded up and placed on reservations. But some Apache groups, under GERONIMO and other leaders, refused to stay on the reservations and continued to raid settlements in New Mexico, Arizona and Chihuahua (Mexico) until Geronimo's surrender in 1886. Most members of the various Apache bands today occupy reservations in Arizona and New Mexico.

The Apache Indians by F. C. Lockwood (New York, 1938);
Apacheland by R. Santee (New York, 1947);
Life Among the Apaches by J. C. Carey (San Francisco, 1954);
Death In the Desert by P. I. Wellman (London, 1972).

APACHE KID
c. 1867-94

An outlaw Indian of Arizona. While serving as a sergeant of Apache scouts under Al SIEBER in the 1880s the Kid killed a man to avenge the murder of his father, and then went on the run. When he was later brought to trial and convicted, President Grover Cleveland granted him a pardon, but the local authorities charged the Kid with another crime; he was found guilty and sent to the penitentiary at Yuma in November 1889. On the way to Yuma he managed to escape from his escort and thereafter lived the life of a hunted outlaw, killing and stealing, with a reward on his head. His depredations suddenly ceased in 1894. He just vanished. It is believed that he was mortally wounded by a gunshot during a night raid and that he crawled away to die in a hiding place. Apparently his body was never found. Others say that he crossed into Mexico and lived to old age.

Lone War Trail of Apache Kid by E. R. Forrest and E. B. Hill (Pasadena, California, 1947).

APPALOOSA HORSE

A distinctive breed of spotted horse historically associated with the NEZ PERCÉ INDIANS of the North-west. A similar type of spotted horse was known to ancient man in Europe and China. The Spaniards brought such horses to the Americas in the sixteenth century and by about 1730 the Nez Percé had them. During the exploration of the West by LEWIS AND CLARK the Nez Percé were found to be the only tribe to have Appaloosas in large numbers; they prized their intelligence, stamina and colourful markings and chose to breed them in preference to other horses. They bred only their best animals and gelded or traded the poorer ones. The land inhabited by the Nez Percé was ideal for horse production: lush summer range in the hills and meadows and abundant winter range in the sheltered canyons of the Snake, Clearwater, and Palouse rivers. The name 'Appaloosa' derives from 'a Palouse' horse from the Palouse River country. The breed nearly disappeared after the Nez Percé War of 1877; the horses bred to perfection by the tribe were sold and began to become assimilated into other breeds. In 1938 the Appaloosa Horse Club was formed to keep the breed from extinction. Some descendants of the Nez Percé horses made up the foundation stock. Since then the growth of the Appaloosa Horse Club, the official breed registry, has been rapid. Today there are more than 150,000 registered Appaloosas in the U.S.

Appaloosa: the Spotted Horse in Art and History by F. Haines (Livingstone, Montana, 1950);
Horse Breeds of the West by F. S. Harris (Houston, Texas, 1973).

APPLEGATE, Jesse 1811-88

A leading figure in the Great Migration from INDEPENDENCE, Missouri, to OREGON in 1843, the trek which established the OREGON TRAIL in the nation's awareness. Having one of the largest herds, Jesse Applegate was elected captain of the 'cow column', comprising nearly 2,000 cattle, the last and slowest of the 1843 companies. He later wrote a classic account of this journey, *A Day with the Cow Column,* published in 1876. Born in Kentucky, he later moved to Missouri. On bringing his column safely to the Columbia River, he established a farm in the Willamette Valley. Applegate entered politics, became a member of Oregon's provisional government in 1845, and was influential in securing Abraham Lincoln's election as President in 1860. In 1849 he moved to southern Oregon, set up a large ranch in the Umpqua Valley and raised cattle. He was a leading promoter in the construction of the Oregon and California railroad.

Westward Vision: The Story of the Oregon Trail by D. Lavender (New York, 1963).

ARAPAHO INDIANS

An important branch of the Algonquin linguistic family; their name probably derives from the Pawnee term *tirapihu* or 'trader'. Once an agricultural people living near the Red River in Minnesota, they migrated south-westward and became a Plains tribe. Like other PLAINS INDIANS, Arapaho life centred on the hunt for the BUFFALO. Tribesmen were valorous and contemplative. The SUN DANCE was extremely important to them. The main enemies of the Arapaho were the SHOSHONI, UTES, COMANCHES, KIOWAS, PAWNEES, CROWS and SIOUX. By 1840 the Southern Arapahos had made peace with the Sioux, Kiowas, and Comanches. In 1851 they participated in the treaty council at FORT LARAMIE, Wyoming, but persisted in attacks on other tribes and white settlers. The Northern Arapahos resisted forcible settlement longer than

12 ▼

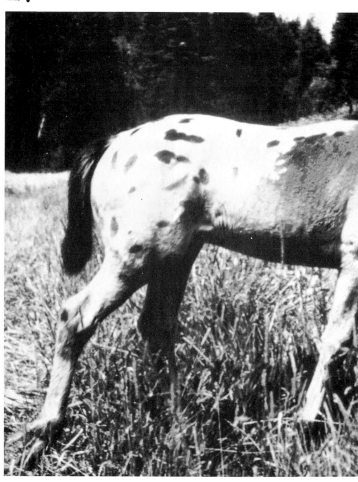

the Southern group, and were involved with the Oglala Sioux and Northern CHEYENNES in frontier raids and the Battle of the LITTLE BIGHORN in 1876. The 1867 treaty of Medicine Lodge with the U.S. Government — where Arapaho chief Little Raven distinguished himself by his intelligence and oratorical skill — placed the Southern Arapahos and the Southern Cheyennes on reservation lands in the central and western part of INDIAN TERRITORY, now Oklahoma. While on the way south the Arapahos stopped on the Platte River, insisting that the U.S. President be informed they wanted a reservation in Wyoming. The Government obtained reluctant consent from Chief WASHAKIE of the Shoshoni tribe to place the Arapahos on the Wind River Reservation, and there, despite Shoshoni protests, they remained. Arapahos and Shoshonis became neighbours but not friends. Both tribes were chagrined when one of Washakie's sons married an Arapaho girl. Although ancient enmity has faded, the tribes generally continue to live apart. An Arapaho claim against the U.S. for land cessions, settled in

1963, netted the tribe approximately $3 million. Other Arapahos live in Oklahoma.

The Arapaho by A. L. Kroeber (New York, 1902); *Early Days Among the Cheyenne and Arapaho Indians* by J. H. Seger (Norman; Oklahoma, 1934, 1956).

ARIKARA INDIANS

A tribe forming the northern group of the Caddoan linguistic family and differing only dialectically from the PAWNEE. The name comes from the Skidi Pawnee word *ariki* or 'horn', referring to the Arikara method of wearing the hair with two pieces of bone standing up like horns on each crest. The agricultural Arikara lived in earth-lodge villages along the MISSOURI RIVER, Nebraska, until driven north about 1750 by an invading band of western SIOUX. In 1804 LEWIS AND CLARK found the Arikara occupying three villages between the Grand and Cannonball Rivers, Dakota. They grew crops of corn, beans

13 ▼

12 *Young Appaloosa horse.*

13 *General Custer and his Arikara scouts in 1873; Bloody Knife points at map.*

14 *'The Skirmish Line' by Charles Schreyvogel.*

and pumpkins; in the winter they hunted the BUFFALO. They caught fish in basket traps, and were expert swimmers. The Arikara became close neighbours and allies of the MANDAN and HIDATSA tribes of the Missouri River. All three tribes were greatly reduced in numbers by the terrible smallpox epidemic of 1837 which swept the Missouri and over the plains, killing thousands of Indians. In 1870 survivors of the Arikara, Mandan and Hidatsa were placed on a reservation at the junction of the Missouri and Little Missouri rivers of North Dakota. In the Sioux campaign General George A. CUSTER used Arikara and CROW scouts. Bloody Knife, Arikara chief and one of Custer's favourite scouts, was killed in the Battle of the LITTLE BIGHORN. Although reduced in size through the years by land sales, the present Fort Berthold Reservation, North Dakota, is still the home of the Arikara, Mandan, and Hidatsa tribes.

Five Indian Tribes of the Upper Missouri by E. T. Denig (Norman, Oklahoma, 1961);
Indian Life on the Upper Missouri by J. C. Ewers (Norman, Oklahoma, 1968).

ARIZONA

This ruggedly beautiful cowboy territory of the South-west did not achieve Statehood within the Union until 1912. Here in the wild frontier days important mining strikes were made, ranchers raised cattle, the U.S. Army campaigned against hostile APACHES, and Wyatt EARP engaged in the celebrated Gunfight at the O.K. CORRAL, in TOMBSTONE. Arizona has a rich variety of climate and scenery, green cattle country and arid desert; its natural wonders include the GRAND CANYON, the PETRIFIED FOREST, and MONUMENT VALLEY. Arizona is the ancient home of the NAVAJO INDIANS and a number of other tribes. The first Europeans to come to Arizona were the Spanish in the sixteenth century. In 1692 Jesuit missionaries established the first white settlement at Geuvavi, eight miles north of Nogales. During the GOLD RUSH of 1849 the Gila River route across Arizona was a principal overland trail to CALIFORNIA. In 1858 gold was found on the Gila, and later silver and copper were mined. Arizona was organized as a Territory in 1863 and attained Statehood in 1912, with Phoenix as its capital city.

Pioneer Days in Arizona by F. C. Lockwood (New York, 1932);
Arizona: The Last Frontier by J. Miller (New York, 1956);
Arizona: The History of a Frontier State by R. K. Wyllys (Phoenix, 1950).

ARKANSAS RIVER

One of the great western branches of the MISSISSIPPI, the Arkansas River features largely in the history of the West. From its source in the ROCKY MOUNTAINS of central COLORADO, it traverses through canyons to the plains. Flowing out of Colorado it crosses KANSAS, OKLAHOMA, and Arkansas on its 1,450 mile journey to the Mississippi. The principal tributaries of the Arkansas are the Cimarron, Canadian and Neosho rivers.

ARMY OF THE WEST

The U.S. Army that fought in the INDIAN WARS from 1865 to 1890 was composed of regular soldiers. This period saw thirteen different campaigns and at least 1,067 separate engagements with the Indians. In July 1866 the strength of the Regular Army was set at 54,302 officers and enlisted men, with provision for 1,000 INDIAN SCOUTS. In 1869 Congress cut the strength to 45,000, and in 1876 to a total force of 27,442. During the Indian Wars from 1865 to 1876 some 15,000 soldiers were stationed in the West, scattered over a vast area in isolated forts. In 1866 the general command and administrative structure for frontier defence comprised the Division of the Missouri, containing the Departments of Arkansas, Missouri, Dakota, and the Platte; the Division of the Pacific, consisting of the Departments of California and the Columbia; and the independent Department of the Gulf, whose area included Texas. The Army used infantry, cavalry, and artillery units against the Indians, who used traditional weapons and modern rifles and revolvers. Indeed, the Army repeatedly found itself outclassed by Indian warriors using superior firearms, such as the WINCHESTER repeating rifle. Up till the adoption of the SPRINGFIELD Model 1873 breech-loading rifle, the Indian-fighting Army was using Civil War muzzle-loaders converted to breech-loaders. The new Springfield was a single-shot; it was not until 1892 that the Army adopted a repeating rifle, the Danish Krag-Jorgensen. The Gatling machine gun was issued to the Army but was seldom used because of its tendency to jam. In 1873 the U.S. CAVALRY was issued with the COLT Single Action Army revolver, Model 1872. The most effective piece of artillery used in the Indian Wars was with the twelve-pounder mountain howitzer which could be carried in parts on pack mules and swiftly assembled for action. Soldiers serving in the West were paid every two months by a travelling paymaster. For most of the Indian campaigns pay for enlisted men ranged from $13 a month for a private to $22 for a first sergeant. The soldiers' food was poor, mainly beans, hardtack, salt pork and beef, with little fresh fruit or vegetable; scurvy was rampant. Men enlisted for an initial five-year term, but campaigning against the Indians was such an arduous and unpleasant assignment that desertions from the Army were frequent.

Indian-Fighting Army by F. Downey (New York, 1944);
Forty Miles a Day on Beans and Hay by D. Rickey, Jr. (Norman, Oklahoma, 1963);
The Soldiers by Time-Life Books (New York, 1973);
Frontier Regulars by R. M. Utley (New York, 1973).

ASHLEY, William 1778-1838

An influential fur trader who organized the first association of free trappers that came to be known as the ROCKY MOUNTAIN FUR COMPANY, William Henry Ashley gave a number of famous MOUNTAIN MEN their start in the fur trade and in legend. Not a mountain man himself, although he made several expeditions to the Rockies, Ashley entered the fur trade to make money in order to pursue a political career. Born in Virginia, he moved to MISSOURI in 1802, becoming a general of the militia and Lieutenant-governor of the State. In March 1822, in partnership with Andrew Henry, he published his celebrated advertisement in the Missouri newspapers:

To
Enterprising Young Men

The subscriber wishes to engage ONE HUNDRED MEN, to ascend the river Missouri to its source, there to be employed for one, two or three years. — For particulars, enquire of Major Andrew Henry, near the Lead Mines, in the County of Washington, (who will ascend with, and command the party) or to the subscriber at St. Louis.

Wm. H. Ashley

Among the young adventurers subsequently engaged were Jim BRIDGER, Jedediah SMITH, Bill SUBLETTE, and Hugh GLASS. Because he was short of funds, Ashley did not hire the trappers at a fixed wage, as was the normal custom, but in return for outfitting them and transporting them to the ROCKY MOUNTAINS, he would take a share of the furs they acquired. Ashley's company was the first to depend primarily upon trapping the beaver directly rather than obtaining the furs from Indians by trade. And it was Ashley who initiated the rendezvous system of trading — an arranged meeting place in the wilderness where trappers sold their furs instead of taking them to an established trading post. Ashley retired from the fur business in 1826, selling his interests to Jedediah Smith and two partners, and continued his political career, serving as a Whig in Congress from 1831 to 1837.

A Majority of Scoundrels: An Informal History of the Rocky Mountain Fur Company by D. Berry (New York, 1961); *The West of William H. Ashley, 1822-1838* edited by D. L. Morgan (Denver, 1964).

ASSINIBOIN INDIANS

A large Siouan tribe originally part of the Yanktonai SIOUX, which scattered and ranged over the great plains from Saskatchewan in Canada to the MISSOURI RIVER in the U.S. They also lived in the Lake Winnipeg region. Their name derives from the Chippewa words *usini upwawa* — 'one who cooks by the use of hot stones'. Their dress, tents, customs and life-style were similar to other buffalo-hunting PLAINS INDIANS; they were constantly at war with other tribes of the Dakotas. Today, several thousand Assiniboins live on the Fort Peck and Fort Belknap reservations in MONTANA.

ATCHISON, TOPEKA AND SANTA FE RAILROAD

One of the great transcontinental railroads that spanned the Western states and territories in the latter half of the nineteenth century. Organized by Cyrus K. Holliday, founding father of Topeka, Kansas, who first intended only to link Atchison with Topeka, the state capital; but generous Federal land grants encouraged him to extend track to Santa Fe, capital of New Mexico Territory. Construction on the Atchison, Topeka and Santa Fe began in October 1868 and was completed in February 1880; then track was pushed on through Arizona and California. By 1888 the A.T. & S.F. extended from Chicago to the Pacific Coast and to the Gulf of Mexico. In 1873 the line stretched from Topeka to the Colorado state line, but there were very few people along the railroad and little freight to be carried. The young road needed traffic but without settlers there could be little business. So agents were appointed in the new towns, the East, and in Europe to encourage settlers to the lands

granted to the company. In 1874 the railroad managed to entice nearly 2,000 Mennonites (a Protestant religious sect) from Russia, and these excellent farmers introduced the hardy red Turkey wheat that made KANSAS one of the world's great granaries. In 1878 the A.T. & S.F. was involved in a 'railroad war' with the rival Denver and Rio Grande line over the use of two strategic passes in the Rocky Mountains of Colorado. Armed hostilities broke out between the construction crews of both companies. The Santa Fe hired a group of gunmen from DODGE CITY, Kansas, which included Bat MASTERSON, Doc HOLLIDAY, and Ben THOMPSON. The Rio Grande also used armed mercenaries. In one encounter the Santa Fe had two men killed and several wounded in a shoot-out with the Rio Grande. The fighting proved costly to both sides; a truce was called and compromise arrangements made to end the war.

The Story of the Western Railroads by R. E. Riegel (New York, 1926); *Rebel of the Rockies: A History of the Denver and Rio Grande Western Railroad* by R. G. Athearn (New Haven, 1962); *Steel Rails to Santa Fe* by L. L. Waters (Lawrence, 1950); *Bat Masterson* by R. O'Connor (New York, 1957).

AUSTIN, Stephen
1793-1836

The founding father of TEXAS, Stephen Fuller Austin was born in Virginia and moved with his family to Missouri in 1798. In 1820 his father,

15 V

15 *Stephen Austin.*

16 *Assiniboin Indian (left) and Yanktonai Indian by Karl Bodmer.*

17 *Atchison, Topeka & Santa Fe Railroad, New Mexico, 1880.*

16 ∧

17 ∨

Moses Austin, was granted permission by the Spanish authorities to establish a colony of 300 Anglo-American families in the virtually uninhabited Mexican province of Texas. Moses Austin died before he could carry out his plans and his son, Stephen, set out to complete the task. In January 1822 he established the first legal Anglo-American colony in Texas, on the Brazos River. In the meantime, Mexico had won independence from Spain. Until the forming of an elected government in 1828, Stephen Austin was the undisputed leader of the growing colony, being law-maker, chief judge, and military commander. He retained continuing influence and worked hard to develop the infant colony; he dealt with the Indians, charted the province, encouraged industry and promoted commerce with the U.S., and kept a steady flow of immigrants to Texas. But Mexico, alarmed at the numbers of Anglo-Americans pouring in, tried to stop the tide in 1830. This action and other repressive measures brought about the Texas War of Independence. Austin was imprisoned for a year by the Mexicans and released in 1835. Later that year the Texans rose in revolt and Austin was called to command the volunteer army. He led a campaign against San Antonio. In December 1835 he was sent to the U.S. on a diplomatic mission to enlist aid and volunteers. He returned to Texas in June 1836 and, defeated for the presidency of the Republic of Texas by Sam HOUSTON, accepted office as Secretary of State. He died on 27 December 1836, aged forty-three.

The Life of Stephen F. Austin by E.C. Barker (Nashville, 1925); *Stephen F. Austin* by W. F. McCaleb (San Antonio, 1974).

B

BADLANDS OF DAKOTA

These desolate regions in both North and South DAKOTA were so-named not because they were the refuge of outlaws, but because they were difficult to traverse. French-Canadian trappers in search of BEAVER were probably the first white men to see the Badlands — a raw, arid landscape of eroded ridges and rocks and treacherous, crumbly soil — and described the region appropriately as *les mauvaises terres à traverser* ('bad lands to travel across'). The Indians called it *mako sica*, which means roughly the same. This barren wasteland supports little wildlife. Temperatures on sunny days frequently soar into the nineties and higher; chilly winter days may quickly become bitterly cold. Nevertheless they are strangely beautiful places with weirdly-shaped rock formations carved by the weather and buttes and mesas striped with horizontal bands of delicate colours. In 1939 Congress established the Badlands National Monument in South Dakota in order to preserve the region in its natural state. The Badlands of North Dakota form part of the Theodore ROOSEVELT National Memorial Park.

History of Dakota Territory by G. W. Kingsbury (Chicago, 1915);
Roosevelt in the Badlands by H. Hagedorn (Boston & New York, 1921).

BAKER, Jim
1818-98

A famous trapper and army scout, Jim Baker was one of the most colourful of MOUNTAIN MEN; he wore Indian dress, adopted Indian customs and manners, and married six Indian squaws. Born in Illinois, he went West at the age of nineteen, joining a company of trappers in ST LOUIS, MISSOURI, that Jim BRIDGER was recruiting for the AMERICAN FUR COMPANY. He spent the following years trapping BEAVER in the ROCKY MOUNTAINS and took part in the fierce fight in 1841, on the Colorado-Wyoming border, in which a small band of trappers beat off a large force of Indians. On the decline of the fur trade, Baker became chief of scouts for General Harney at FORT LARAMIE and in 1857 guided an army column against the MORMONS. He served as guide on other expeditions, tried his hand at gold prospecting, and in 1873 made a permanent log cabin home in the valley of the Little Snake River, WYOMING, where he raised livestock and lived till he died. By most accounts he was a fine man; Captain Marcy of the U.S. Army described him as 'a generous, noble-hearted specimen of the trapper type who would peril his life for a friend at any time or share his last morsel of food'.

The Life of Jim Baker by N. Mumey (New York, 1972).

18 *Badlands of Dakota.*

19 *Jim Baker.*

20 *Riding the line of the barbed wire fence, by Frederic Remington.*

21 *Sam Bass at sixteen.*

20 ∨ 19 ∧

BANNOCK INDIANS

The Bannock (or Bannack) tribe, a branch of the Shoshonean family, once roamed in IDAHO and WYOMING and along the Snake River into OREGON. The Camas Prairie, which provided the nutritious camas root, was a primary source of food for the Bannocks. And when white settlers came to the Camas Prairie, their livestock eating the roots, the Indians tried to drive them out. This resulted in the Bannock War of 1878 in which some 1,500 Indians (Bannocks and PAIUTES) under chiefs Buffalo Horn and Egan fought a number of skirmishes with the U.S. Army. After the death of Buffalo Horn in June 1878 the Bannocks were subdued and settled on the Fort Hall Reservation.

The Bannock Indian War of 1878 by G. F. Brimlow (Caldwell, Idaho, 1938);
The Bannock of Idaho by B. D. Madsen (Caldwell, 1958).

BARBED WIRE

The introduction of barbed wire fences on the hitherto open ranges in the 1870s was a major factor in improving cattle breeds and agriculture on the Western plains, where the traditional fence materials of wood and stone were scarce. Before the coming of barbed wire fencing, untamed cattle roamed free, making it difficult to breed the best beef stock; the scrawny, native Texas LONGHORN was not the ideal meat producer. In 1874 Joseph F. Glidden, an Illinois farmer, patented his particular type of homemade barbed wire which proved the most

21 V

practical and effective of the many kinds that had been devised; his improvement over the previous types was in the special barbed spur twisted through the double-strand wire. Glidden's wire went into cheap mass production (other types followed) and the open range was doomed. The initial use of barbed, or 'bob' wire as it was also called, by farmers and ranchers to protect their private land upset the free-ranging cattlemen, who called it 'devil's rope'. And big cattle outfits fenced in large tracts of public land and watering places to which they had no legal right. All this resulted in 'fence wars' in which opposing factions cut fences and many men were killed. But barbed wire had come to stay and by 1890 most of the private range land had been fenced, making it possible to breed fine cattle such as Herefords, Durhams, and Shorthorns. Barbed wire gave the cowboy a new job, fence riding, patrolling the many miles of line to keep it in good order and repair. The widespread use of barbed wire also helped bring law and order to the Old West. It encouraged hard-working settlers to farm the land without fear of milling cattle trampling their crops, and it reduced the crime of RUSTLING.

The Wire that Fenced the West by H. H. and F. T. McCallum (Norman, Oklahoma, 1965);
The Great Plains by W. P. Webb (Boston, 1931).

BASS, Sam
1851-78

A bandit of the 1870s who was eventually shot and killed by TEXAS RANGERS. Born in Indiana, Sam Bass went to TEXAS in 1870 and worked as a farmhand and teamster for five years. He then turned to horse stealing and robbing stagecoaches. In 1877 he and his gang held up a UNION PACIFIC train at Big Springs, NEBRASKA, stealing 60,000 dollars from the express car and money and valuables from the passengers. The gang was pursued and three of them killed. Bass formed a new gang and in 1878 held up and robbed four trains in Texas. The Rangers chased them, killing one and capturing three of the bandits. One of the prisoners, Jim Murphy, offered to betray Bass in exchange for his freedom; he was released and rejoined Bass. During an attempt to rob the bank at Round Rock, Williamson County, Texas, Murphy alerted the Rangers and in the ensuing gunfight Bass was mortally wounded. He died two days later on his birthday, 21 July, aged twenty-seven. Folklore soon made Bass a 'noble bandit', a good cowboy gone wrong.

Sam Bass by Wayne Gard (Boston & New York, 1936);
Triggernometry, a Gallery of Gunfighters by E. Cunningham (London, 1967).

BEAR, Grizzly
Ursus horribilis

A huge and powerful carnivore that once roamed widely throughout North America. With an average size of eight feet in length and a weight of 800 pounds, the grizzly was indeed a frightening sight to encounter and a terrible opponent. Possessed of amazing strength it can kill a full grown ELK or a man with a single blow of its heavy paw. It has been known to carry a 200 pound deer under its arm. In old Spanish California fierce bulls were pitted against grizzlies at fiestas, and many a bull's neck was broken with the first swipe of the bear's paw. The grizzly was so-named because its greyish-brown fur, sprinkled with silver-tipped hairs, give it a grizzled appearance. The Indians revered the animal for its great strength, courage, and endurance and often used the bear symbol as a totem, or sacred guardian spirit, on their lodges, shields, and dress; many warriors painted red bear-claw marks on their faces before battle. When aroused by a hunter the grizzly would attack ferociously, slapping, clawing, and biting; contrary to popular belief, it did not indulge in the rib-cracking 'bear hug'. Only a rare few, such as mountain man Hugh GLASS, have survived such a mauling. Although the flesh-eating grizzly would kill a man it would not eat him. Because the grizzly also preyed on domestic livestock, bounties were paid for killing them. Hunters also considered this magnificent bear the ultimate trophy — thus the grizzly was hunted almost to extinction. A rare sight today, they live under government protection in the national parks or in remote mountain regions. The Black Bear, also much hunted in the Old West for its hide, is smaller and much less ferocious than the grizzly.

American Wild Life by W. G. Van Name (New York, 1961); *Wild Animals of North America* by National Geographic Society (Washington, D.C., 1960),

BEAVER
Castor canadensis

A bulky river rodent with an average weight of 30 to 50 pounds. Its silky-smooth fur undercoat was much prized for its commercial use in making fashionable hats and trimming in the early nineteenth century. The large scale hunting of beaver skins by professional trappers and MOUNTAIN MEN spurred the exploration and conquest of the Old West. In their search for the profitable animal, hunters blazed trails which others were to follow. The trappers usually caught the beavers in steel traps placed under water. The cured pelt of an adult beaver would fetch the trapper about five or six dollars at the annual rendezvous or trade meeting. The beaver was hunted to such an extent that by 1840 it was scarce in the West. Today, beavers range through most of the woodlands of North America and are rapidly increasing. The beaver is renowned for its engineering ability; it cuts down river-bank trees with its big, gnawing teeth, builds dams to create a beaver pond, and in the pond constructs a dome-shaped lodge.

BEAN, Judge Roy
c. 1825-1903

A near-illiterate frontier justice of the peace who ran a combined courtroom-saloon in the tiny railroad hamlet of Langtry in the west Texas desert, between the Pecos River and the RIO GRANDE, Judge Roy Bean was known as the 'Law west of the Pecos'. Born in Kentucky, he became a trader and saloon-keeper in the Southwest; early in 1882 he was running a saloon in a tent-town for railroad builders called Vinegaroon. It was a wild and lawless camp and Bean, backed by the TEXAS RANGERS and the railroad, was appointed justice of the peace, although he had never studied law. He managed to keep the peace with a strange brand of rough justice and common sense, often basing his ruling on a single law book. He was always supported by the Rangers. The stories about him are legion, mostly apocryphal. At one inquest he found forty dollars and a gun on the dead man; he promptly fined the corpse forty dollars for carrying a concealed weapon. The fines usually stayed in his pocket. When a drinking companion was brought in for killing a Chinaman, Bean studied his tattered law book and concluded that, although it was homicide to kill a human being, 'I'm damned if I can find where it says it's illegal to kill a Chinee', and acquitted the accused on condition that he buy a round of drinks for the boys. When Vinegaroon folded up he moved to another infant railroad town near the Rio Grande, which he named Langtry after the woman he most admired, the English actress Lillie Langtry, known as the 'Jersey Lily'. By fair means and foul, sometimes rigging the votes, he got himself elected Langtry's justice of the peace, holding court in his crude saloon called the 'Jersey Lily', where he lived till his death in 1903. The Law west of the Pecos was a law unto himself. In 1896 he brought fame to Langtry by staging the Bob Fitzsimmons-Peter Maher heavyweight boxing championship on a sandy flat in the Rio Grande Canyon in defiance of both state and federal

22 ∧   23 ∨   24 ∨

22   *Grizzly bear shot dead by hunters.*

23   *Grizzly bear and victim.*

24   *Beavers at work.*

25 *Judge Roy Bean.*

26 *Jim Beckwourth.*

27 *Bent's Fort.*

27 V

25 Λ   26 V

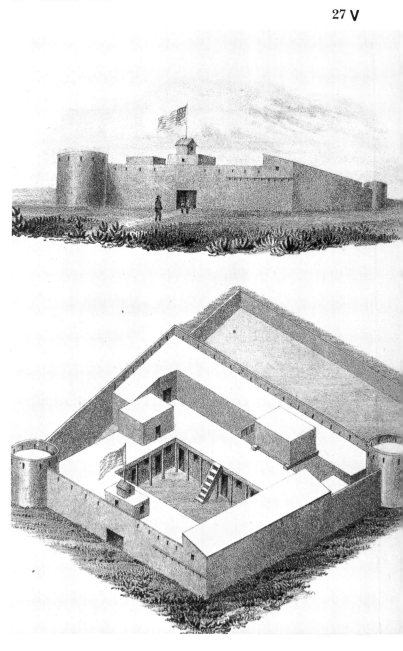

authority. He also performed marriages, ending the short ceremony with the words 'I, Roy Bean, Justice of the Peace of this district, hereby pronounce you man and wife. May God have mercy on your souls.' Bean's 'Jersey Lily' has been preserved by the Texas Highway Department and is now a tourist attraction.

Roy Bean, Law West of the Pecos by C. L. Sonnichsen (New York, 1943).

BECKWOURTH, Jim
c. 1798-1867

A Mulatto trapper, frontiersman and, if we are to believe him, a war chief of the CROW INDIANS; for James Pierson Beckwourth (or Beckwith) was an extravagant story-teller. Born in Virginia of a white planter and a Negro slave, he spent all his adult life in the Far West. In the early 1820s he was a member of the ASHLEY fur trading expedition to the ROCKY MOUNTAINS; then in 1829 he went to live with the Crows. According to his autobiography, his strength and courage in battle with the Crows against the BLACKFEET INDIANS earned him membership of the Dog Soldiers, the elite military society, and later elevation to war chief. He lived with the Crows for about six years, marrying a number of squaws. In 1846 he is believed to have served as guide and courier to Colonel Stephen W. KEARNY in the war with Mexico. He settled down in the DENVER, Colorado area and in 1864 became involved in the SAND CREEK MASSACRE, a notorious atrocity committed against the Indians, in which Colonel John M. Chivington and his Colorado Volunteers attacked a friendly Cheyenne-Arapaho camp and slaughtered some 300 men, women and children. The blood-thirsty Chivington conscripted Beckwourth, then old and with failing eyesight, and threatened to hang him if he refused to guide the column to the Indian camp. After 200 miles on the trail the infirm Beckwourth was replaced by a half-breed Cheyenne, Jack Smith. Jim is believed to have returned to the Crows in 1866 and died among them a year later.

The Life and Adventures of James P. Beckwourth an autobiography edited by T. D. Bonner (New York, 1931); *Breeds and Half-Breeds* by G. Speck (New York, 1969); *Jim Beckwourth, Negro Mountain Man* by H. W. Felton (New York, 1970).

BEECHER ISLAND
Battle of, 1868

A fierce nine-day fight between a small group of scouts commanded by Major George A. Forsyth and a large combined force of SIOUX, CHEYENNE and ARAPAHO warriors on the Arickaree Fork of the Republican River in COLORADO. Forsyth had been directed by Major-General Philip H. SHERIDAN to 'employ fifty first-class hardy frontiersmen to be used against the hostile Indians', and the column clashed with the hostiles on the Arickaree Fork at dawn on 17 September 1868. About 600 braves attacked the scouts, who had hurriedly dug themselves into a shallow defensive position on a small island in the low river. The scouts were armed with excellent weapons: the seven-shot SPENCER repeating carbine and the COLT army percussion revolver. After several unsuccessful charges the Indians settled to a siege. Forsyth was wounded, his second-in-command, Lieutenant F. H. Beecher was killed, as was the surgeon; three scouts were killed and more than twenty wounded. The Indian losses included the influential war chief ROMAN NOSE. Forsyth sent two pairs of scouts for help and they slipped past the Indians. The first rescue force to appear on the morning of 25 September was Captain Carpenter's company of Negro troopers of the all-black Tenth U.S. Cavalry. The dead officers and scouts were buried on the island, which was named after Lieutenant Beecher.

The Story of the Soldier by G. A. Forsyth (New York, 1900); *The Fighting Cheyennes* by G. B. Grinnell (New York, 1915); *Great Western Indian Fights* by the Potomac Corral of the Westerners (Lincoln, Nebraska, 1970).

BENT'S FORT

Situated on the SANTA FE TRAIL, on the north bank of the upper Arkansas River in south-eastern Colorado, some 100 miles from the foot of the ROCKY MOUNTAINS, Bent's Fort was an important post in the fur trade and for wagon trains. Built with strong walls of ADOBE by the brothers Charles and William Bent in 1833, this massive fortress-trading post, one of the largest in the trans-Mississippi West, dominated the fur trade of COLORADO for fifteen years.

Bent's Fort by D. Lavender (New York, 1954).

BIGHORN SHEEP
Ovis canadensis

A wild mountain sheep of the West, ranging from Canada to New Mexico, that has never been domesticated. The typical bighorn is the tawny-coloured, white-rumped Rocky Mountain variety, standing about three feet high at the shoulder and five feet in length. The enormous horns of the male sweep back in a spiral up to forty inches long. In the mating season the rams fight for the females by battering their horns together. The Indians hunted the bighorn for its meat and skin; they fashioned the huge horns into a number of implements and dressed the hide to make a fine BUCKSKIN for clothes. White hunters regarded the magnificent spiral horns as a splendid trophy. The bighorn's chief means of protection are keen eyesight and a remarkable agility in high, precipitous places.

Mammals of North America by V. H Cahalane (New York, 1947);
America Wild Life by W. G. Van Name (New York, 1961).

BILLY THE KID
1859-81

The most famous outlaw-gunfighter of the South-west, Billy the Kid was known by several names, Henry McCarty, William Antrim, but mostly as William Bonney; historians still argue as to which is the correct one. Believed to have been born in New York City, Billy moved west with his family and eventually became a cowboy in Lincoln County, NEW MEXICO, for cattleman J. H. Tunstall. In February 1878 Tunstall was killed by a rival cattle outfit and this started the LINCOLN COUNTY WAR, in which Billy played a leading part and was one of the group that shot dead Sheriff Brady. He became an outlaw with a price on his head. In 1880 Pat GARRETT, a former friend of the Kid, was elected sheriff of Lincoln County and set out to capture the young outlaw. He caught him and Bill was convicted of killing Sheriff Brady and sentenced to be hanged on 13 May 1881. But Bill, although shackled hand and foot, managed to escape from jail by shooting dead the two deputies guarding him. Garrett went after him again and on 15 July 1881 tracked him to the home of Pete Maxwell at Fort Sumner, New Mexico, and there shot him dead by surprise in a darkened room. Legend says that Billy killed twenty-one men in his twenty-one years of life; the exact figure is not known but is thought to be much less. A slightly-built fellow, Billy was said to be a likeable, agreeable youth with a quiet manner and a favourite with women, albeit a callous killer.

The Authentic Life of Billy the Kid by P. Garrett (Santa Fe, 1882 and Norman, Oklahoma, 1954);
The True Story of Billy the Kid by W. L. Hamlin (London, 1965);
Billy the Kid by C. W. Breihan and M. Ballert (Seattle, 1970).

28 *Battle of Beecher Island, by Robert Lindneux.*

28 V

29 *Billy the Kid.*
31 *Bighorn sheep.*

30 V

29 Λ

REWARD
($5,000.00)
Reward for the capture, dead or alive,
of one Wm. Wright, better known as
"BILLY THE KID"
Age, 18. Height, 5 feet, 3 inches.
Weight, 125 lbs. Light hair, blue
eyes and even features. He is
the leader of the worst band of
desperadoes the Territory has
ever had to deal with. The above
reward will be paid for his capture
or positive proof of his death.
JIM DALTON, Sheriff.
DEAD OR ALIVE!
"BILLY THE KID"

31 V

BLACK BART

There were several bandits known as 'Black Bart' in the Old West but the most noted was Charles E. Bolton (or Boles), a mild-mannered fellow with a penchant for writing doggerel. He plagued WELLS FARGO for eight years with his robberies and liked to leave pieces of verse after his hold-ups, his most celebrated effort being this:

> Here I lay me down to sleep
> To wait the coming morrow
> Perhaps success, perhaps defeat
> And everlasting sorrow
> I've labored long and hard for bread
> For honor and for riches
> But on my corns too long you've tred
> You fine-haired sons of bitches
> Let come what will, I'll try it on
> My condition can't be worse
> And if there's money in that box
> Tis munney in my purse.

He signed himself 'Black Bart the Po8' (meaning poet). He robbed twenty-eight Wells Fargo stagecoaches single-handed before he was captured by the company's chief of detectives James B. Hume in 1883. Hume tracked him down to SAN FRANCISCO by the clue of a laundry mark on a handkerchief left by Bolton at the scene of a hold-up. Black Bart, who it is said never killed or injured anyone during his robberies, was sentenced to six years in San Quentin. He was released in 1888 and then vanished.

U.S. West, the Saga of Wells Fargo by L. Beebe and C. Clegg (New York, 1949);
Wells Fargo by N. M. Loomis (New York, 1968).

BLACK HILLS OF DAKOTA

Lying mainly in South Dakota and spreading into south-eastern Wyoming, the Black Hills, so-called because they are clad darkly with thick ponderosa pines, were regarded as sacred by the SIOUX. Under the FORT LARAMIE Treaty of 1868 the Black Hills formed part of the Great Sioux Reservation and white people were not permitted to settle upon, or pass through the territory without the consent of the Indians. The treaty was soon violated by the Americans. The hills were thought to be rich in gold and in 1874 General George A. CUSTER led an expedition there and reported that gold had been found among the roots of the grass. This provocative report started a gold rush. At first the Federal government tried to protect the rights of the

32 ∧

32 *Black Bart (Charles E. Bolton).*

33 *Gold miners in the Black Hills of Dakota in 1870s.*

Sioux, then relaxed its efforts and gold hunters invaded the hills. In 1875 government agents tried to buy the Black Hills for six million dollars but the Indians refused to sell. The aggravation of the gold seekers, and other related issues, resulted in the war in which the Sioux and allied tribes wiped out Custer and his immediate command in the Battle of the LITTLE BIGHORN in June 1876. The army exacted revenge for

33 ∧

Custer and the government relinquished the treaty of 1868 and gold miners flooded into the Black Hills. The town of DEADWOOD was established and the Black Hills became a major gold-producing area. The hills are also famous for the giant sculptured heads of four American presidents — Washington, Jefferson, Lincoln, and Theodore ROOSEVELT — carved out of Mount Rushmore by Gutzon Borglum; and the gigantic mounted figure of Sioux chief CRAZY HORSE, begun in 1948 by Korczak Ziolkowski and now nearing completion.

The Black Hills by R. Peattie (New York, 1952);
Pioneer Years in the Black Hills by R. B. Hughes (Glendale, California, 1957);
Gold in the Black Hills by W. Parker (Norman, Oklahoma, 1966);
Custer's Gold: the U.S. Cavalry Expedition of 1874 by D. Jackson (New Haven, Connecticut, 1966).

BLACKFEET INDIANS

Members of the Algonquian linguistic family, the Blackfeet seem to have been the vanguard in the movement of Indian groups from the north-eastern forests to the north-western plains. In the eighteenth century the Blackfeet had already begun to acquire, through trade, the horses and weapons which were to make them the strongest military power on the north-western buffalo plains. The semi-nomadic buffalo culture of the Blackfeet was that of the PLAINS INDIANS generally. Their name probably originated from their black-coloured leggings and moccasins. The Blackfeet were famous horsemen and hunters; brave and savage warriors, of middle height, with broad shoulders and great expansion of chest, they were feared and respected by their enemies, who included the SIOUX, the CROWS and the FLATHEAD tribes. The Blackfeet confederacy was made up of three subtribes: the Piegan, the Bloods, and the Siksika proper. Until confined to reservations in the late nineteenth century, Blackfeet held most of the immense territory from the North Saskatchewan River in Canada to the southern headstreams of the MISSOURI RIVER in MONTANA, and from the eastern border of Montana to the base of the ROCKY MOUNTAINS. They became hostile to the white Americans as early settlers increasingly threatened their lands and buffalo. They made a treaty with the U.S. Government in 1855 when part of their land was designated Blackfeet Hunting Territory, but this peace treaty was ruined by unscrupulous white traders, gold prospectors, and land-hungry settlers. This resulted in Blackfeet attacks on stagecoaches, ranches, and forts; and retaliatory destruction of Indian villages and camps. In January 1870 some 170 Blackfeet, many of them women and children, were massacred at Piegan chief Red Horn's camp. At about the same time, the decline of the BUFFALO, as well as starvation and disease, greatly reduced the tribe both in number and spirit. By 1888 all United States Blackfeet were gathered on to a reservation in north-west Montana.

Blackfeet Indians by F. B. Linderman (St Paul, Minnesota, 1935).
The Blackfeet, Raiders on the Northwestern Plains by J. E. Canfield (Norman, Oklahoma, 1958).

34 *Karl Bodmer (extreme right) and Prince Maximilian meet Minnetaree Indians, by Karl Bodmer.*

35 *Blackfeet Indians by George Catlin.*

BODMER, Karl
1809-93

Karl Bodmer, a French-trained Swiss artist, accompanied the German naturalist Maximilian, Prince of Wied-Neuwied on his famous expedition into the Far West in 1833-4. The prince and his party left St Louis in April 1833 and travelled up the MISSOURI RIVER, first by steamboat then on a keelboat. Their journey took them to Fort Pierre in South Dakota, through the land of the MANDAN INDIANS, on to Fort Union in North Dakota, then through the country of the BLACKFEET INDIANS to Fort McKenzie, outpost of the AMERICAN FUR COMPANY on the eastern slope of the ROCKY MOUNTAINS. On this long journey Bodmer produced many magnificent paintings of wildlife and landscapes, and captured for posterity the life, customs, dress, and ceremonies of the Indians, realistically recorded in watercolour. Prince Maximilian's notable two-volume work on the expedition was accompanied by a separate portfolio containing eighty-one of Bodmer's paintings. Today, these historic illustrations are highly regarded as a significant and accurate record of the Old West.

Travels in the Interior of North America by Maximilian of Wied-Neuwied (London, 1844);
Across the Wide Missouri by B. Devoto (New York, 1947);
A Gallery of Dudes by M. Sprague (London, 1967).

BOONE, Daniel
1734-1820

Long hunter, Indian fighter, trail-blazing pioneer, and first of the frontier folk heroes, Daniel Boone was born in Pennsylvania. Moving to North Carolina he settled in the Yadkin Valley, supporting his family by hunting, often making long trips for profitable animal skins. The 'Long hunters' were so called because their long wilderness hunts might last more than a year. Boone was impressed by the Indian hunting grounds of Kentucky (from the Indian word *Ken-ta-kee* meaning 'among the meadows') and determined to make his home in this unsettled, fertile land rich with game. In 1773 he left the Yadkin Valley with his own and several other families and headed West. The journey was thwarted by hostile Indians who killed six of the party including Boone's eldest son, James. Boone, however, vowed to complete the emigration at the first favourable opportunity. In 1775 Richard Henderson of the Transylvania Company, having made a deal with the Indians, chose Boone to establish an emigrant path into Kentucky. With a band of hardy woodsmen, Boone set forth and blazed a trail — known as the Wilderness Road

36 ∧

37 ∧   38 ∨

36 *Daniel Boone.*

37 *A Justin cowboy boot circa 1900.*

38 *James Bowie.*

— through the Cumberland Gap of the Appalachian Mountains to the Kentucky River, where they built a fort named Boonesborough, to which Boone later brought his family and a group of settlers. The Wilderness Road became the main pioneer road over which poured the first waves of the great migration to the West. In January 1778 Boone was captured by Shawnee Indians and adopted into the tribe as the foster-son of Chief Blackfish. In June he escaped to warn Boonesborough of an impending Shawnee attack. Frustrated by legal nullification of his Kentucky land claims, Boone moved on to MISSOURI, then part of the Spanish territory of Louisiana, where he was granted some 8,000 acres; but the LOUISIANA PURCHASE of 1803 deprived him of this land. Even in his eighties the redoubtable Boone still hunted and trapped. He died aged eighty-six in his son's farmhouse in Missouri.

Daniel Boone by R. M. Thwaites (New York, 1902);
The Wilderness Road to Kentucky by W. A. Pusey (New York, 1921);
Daniel Boone by J. Bakeless (New York, 1939).

BOOT HILL

The name given to a cemetery in a wild cattle town or frontier settlement where cowboys, gunmen and drifters — usually victims of gunfights — were buried with their 'boots on' and little ceremony. It is claimed that cattle town DODGE City, Kansas, had the original Boot Hill and that other towns adopted the name for their rough-and-ready burial places.

Queen of the Cow Towns: Dodge City by S. Vestal (New York, 1952).

BOOTS, Cowboy

Close-fitting boots were of paramount importance to the working COWBOY. He had them custom-made, gladly paying two months' wages for the right pair. They were of functional design; the leather tops rarely less than seventeen inches high to protect the rider's legs from cactus, heavy brush, snake bites, chafing against the saddle fender, and to prevent gravel and twigs from getting inside. The narrow, pointed toe made easy entrance into the stirrup; the high, forward-sloping heel kept the foot firmly anchored in the stirrup, especially when roping an animal. Cowboy boots were made strictly for riding and discouraged walking; that suited the cowboy who spent most of his time in the saddle. Cowboys prided themselves on their small feet, which set them apart from big-footed

farmers and other 'inferior' pedestrians, and their tight-fitting, narrow boots reflected this vanity; and, with their bowed legs, produced the cowboy's curious gait. Legend tells us the traditional style of boot was first created by H. J. Justin, a young bootmaker who set himself up in business in 1879 in the little town of Spanish Fort, Texas, at the RED RIVER crossing of the CHISHOLM TRAIL; and the name 'Justin' for quaity boots became as familiar to the cowboy as the brand names COLT (revolvers), STETSON (hats), and LEVI (trousers). Today the Justin Boot Company, of Fort Worth, Texas, is a major manufacturer of cowboy boots.

The Old-Time Cowhand by R. F. Adams (New York, 1961).

BOWIE, James
*c.*1796-1836

Texas hero and knife-fighter whose name was made world famous by the type of broad-bladed knife he used and is said to have originated. Born in Georgia, Bowie made money by selling Negro slaves before going to TEXAS, where he settled in San Antonio; legend tells us he searched for and found the lost Spanish silver mine in the San Saba region. In 1830 he became a Mexican citizen (at that time Texas was a Mexican province), married the daughter of the Vice-Governor of San Antonio and became a wealthy landowner. He lost his wife and children in a cholera epidemic in 1833. When the Texans rebelled against Spanish rule, Bowie joined the rebels and was made a captain, engaging in several victories over the Mexicans. With the rank of colonel he held joint command of the ALAMO fortress with Colonel Travis until stricken down with fever; he died fighting, from his sickbed, with the rest of the garrison while defending the Alamo against an overwhelming Mexican army. Six feet tall, strong and fearless, Bowie made his reputation as a formidable knife-fighter in a number of duels, but it is not clear if he or his brother, Rezin, actually designed the original BOWIE KNIFE.

James Bowie, a Hero of the Alamo by E. Brogan (New York, 1922);
James Bowie; the Life of a Bravo by C. L. Douglas (Dallas, 1944);
Jim Bowie's Lost Mine by M. E. Francis (San Antonio, Texas, 1974).

BOWIE KNIFE

Famed as the deadliest fighting knife of the Old West, the Bowie was a vital piece of equipment for all hunters and frontiersmen for some fifty years. Apart from its use as a weapon, it was used

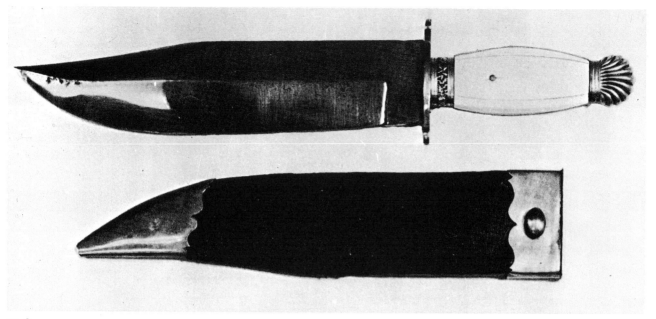

39 Λ

for skinning and cutting up meat, for shaping wood, for shaving the face, for pegging a tether to a horse on the plains, and even as a hammer. The blade was of the finest steel, anything from seven to fourteen inches long; the classic Bowie had a broad blade with a distinctive clip-point. The cutting edge of the blade was ground razor sharp, as was the back of the clip-point, giving the point a ripping edge which could easily disembowel an animal or a man. The tang or shank of the blade went all the way through the handle, making it a solid weapon indeed. It was usually carried in a leather scabbard reinforced with brass or silver. The knife's true origin is lost in legend. Some accounts say Jim BOWIE had the blade made to his pattern by James Black, the blacksmith noted for his fine knives. Some say that Black originated the blade. Others claim that Jim's brother, Rezin P. Bowie, designed the knife. In the mid nineteenth century a great many Bowie knives were made in Sheffield, England, specially for the American market.

The Bowie Knife by R. W. Thorpe (Albuquerque, New Mexico, 1948).

BOZEMAN TRAIL

A wagon road for pioneers branching north-west from the OREGON TRAIL near FORT LARAMIE, in Wyoming, to Virginia City in Montana, blazed by John Bozeman and John Jacobs in the early 1860s. In order to protect the wagon trains from hostile Indians, the army built several forts along the trail. When the SIOUX under chief RED CLOUD went to war to defend their land and destroy the Bozeman Trail, FORT PHIL KEARNY came under virtual siege; and it was near this outpost that the FETTERMAN MASSACRE (in which Captain Fetterman and eighty

39 *Sheffield-made Bowie knife, circa 1850.*

40 *Bronco-buster, by Frederic Remington.*

soldiers were annihilated) and the WAGON BOX FIGHT took place. Forced to treat with the Indians in 1868, the government agreed to Red Cloud's demand that the Bozeman Trail and the forts be abandoned, and Red Cloud did not sign the treaty until the troops had left and his warriors had burned Fort Phil Kearny to the ground. After the defeat of the Sioux in 1877, the Bozeman Trail came into use as a cattle trail for the long drives from TEXAS into WYOMING and MONTANA.

The Bozeman Trail by A. R. Brininstool and G. R. Hebard (Cleveland, Ohio, 1922);
Red Cloud's Folk: a History of the Oglala Sioux by G. E. Hyde (Norman, Oklahoma, 1937).

BRANDING

The practice of burning the owner's identifying mark on the hides of his livestock. In the time of the open range, cattle roamed freely over vast areas and brands were needed to distinguish one man's animals from another. There were thousands of different brands in the Old West and each had to be registered in the official brand book of each county. Cattle were also marked by cutting the ear in a particular way, and, like the brand, had to be registered. The most famous earmark was the 'jingle-bob' cut of cattle king John CHISUM of NEW MEXICO, in which the ear was split lengthwise so that the lower half dangled, like the jingle-bob attached to SPURS. The main calf branding was done in the spring ROUND-UP; calves born later, or overlooked the first time, were branded in the fall, or autumn round-up. The calf was roped, held down on the

40 >

41 Λ

41   *Cattle brand.*

42   *James Bridger.*

43   *A bull buffalo*

ground, and the mark made with a branding iron heated in a wood fire. Brands were formed from numbers, letters, and symbols, and the components of a brand were read from left to right, from top to bottom, or from outside to inside; thus a bar mark over the letters 'BQ' read 'Barbeque', and a 'T' inside a square reads 'Box T'. When the cattle were gathered in the fall round-up for the long drive north, it was the custom to give them an additional road brand. Unbranded cattle were known as 'mavericks' after Samuel A. MAVERICK.

Cattle Brands by A. Adams (New York, 1906);
The Old-Time Cowhand by R. F. Adams (New York, 1961);
Manual of Brands and Marks by M. R. Wolfenstein (Norman, Oklahoma, 1970).

BRIDGER, James 1804-81

One of the greatest of the MOUNTAIN MEN and a noted army guide. Born in Richmond, Virginia, Jim Bridger was orphaned at thirteen. In 1822 he joined the ASHLEY fur trapping expedition bound for the ROCKY MOUNTAINS and spent the next twenty years working for various fur trading companies in the Far West. He was the first white man to visit the GREAT SALT LAKE in Utah, and one of the first to see the natural wonders — the hot springs and spouting geysers — of what later became YELLOWSTONE NATIONAL PARK, where Bridger Lake was named after him. He discovered serveral routes later used by wagon trains, and Bridger's Pass over the Continental Divide was used by the UNION PACIFIC RAILROAD. Before he was thirty, Bridger was known as 'The Old Man of the Mountains'. When the fur trade

42 Λ

declined he established a supply-post, FORT BRIDGER, in 1843 on the Black Fork of the Green River in south-western Wyoming and serviced the emigrants of the OREGON TRAIL. Here he became known for his hospitality and for his fascinating tales of the many wonders he had seen in the Far West. In the 1860s he served as guide to various military expeditions. He was trusted and respected by all who came in contact with him, Indians and white men alike. General Grenville M. Dodge called him 'a guide without equal. . .a born topographer; the whole West was mapped out in his mind. . .a complete master of plains and woodcraft'. An illiterate in the conventional sense, Jim Bridger could speak some dozen Indian tongues, as well as English, French, and Spanish. Like most mountain men he married Indian squaws, out-living all three. In 1868 he retired to a farm in Missouri, where he died aged seventy-seven.

James Bridger by J. C. Alter (Salt Lake City, 1925);
Jim Bridger: Mountain Man by N. B. Wiltsey (Los Angeles, 1969).

43 ∧

BRONCO-BUSTING

The tough, traditional method of breaking an untamed range horse to the saddle. The name *bronco* is Spanish for 'rough', or 'peevish', and like many Spanish words used by the Mexican VAQUERO was adopted by the American COWBOY. A bronco was usually the cross-bred offspring of a wild MUSTANG and a tame horse. Every ranch had broncos in the REMUDA. A bronco would roam free on the range until he was about four, then be taken to the corral (fenced enclosure) where his wild spirit would be broken in the space of a week. Mostly professional horse-tamers, known as 'bronco-busters', were hired for the job. First, the man would rope the horse, tie the rope to a 'snubbing' post, then swing his heavy saddle on the horse's rearing back; then mount and ride the bucking bronco until he mastered it, using his quirt, or short whip, every time the horse bucked. Bronco-riding developed into a cowboy sport and today it is a standard event in a rodeo show.

Cowboy Life on the Western Plains by E. B. Bronson (New York, 1910);
The Western Pony by W. R. Leigh (New York, 1933);
The Old-Time Cowhand by R. F. Adams (New York, 1961);
The Cowboys by Time-Life Books (New York, 1973).

BUCKSKIN

The Indians, MOUNTAIN MEN and frontiersmen all wore clothing made of durable buckskin, the pliable dressed leather of the deer or elk. The long hunters like Daniel BOONE earned money out of deerskin; in those days the skin of a doe sold for about fifty cents and that of a buck for twice as much — hence the slang term 'buck' for a dollar. Indian shirts, MOCCASINS, bags, and the long dresses of the women were made of buck-skins, often decorated with porcupine quill embroidery and beads. The PLAINS INDIANS were noted for their fine white-coloured buckskins, made white by a special clay found on the prairie. The BIGHORN also provided buckskin, finer and softer in quality than the deer. George CATLIN, the artist who lived and worked among the Plains Indians, has recorded in detail the method of dressing skins and the ability of buckskin clothing 'after being ever so many times wet, to dry soft and pliant as they were before'. But wet buckskin was uncomfortable to wear as it soaked up water and became clinging and slippery. General George A. CUSTER was wearing a buckskin suit when he made his famous last stand in June 1876.

North American Indians by G. Catlin (London, 1844 and Edinburgh, 1926);
Indian Crafts and Costumes by B. S. Mason (New York, 1946)

BUFFALO
Bison bison

The American bison once roamed in millions all over the Old West. Early settlers called it the 'buffalo' and it has been the 'buffalo' to Americans ever since. It belongs to the cattle

family, is cloven-hoofed and chews the cud. Both sexes have a single set of hollow, curved horns. The bulls are immense, often weighing a ton or more and standing five to six feet high at the shoulders. The huge head and great hump covered with dark brown woolly hair contrast sharply with the small hips. Despite their great size and bulk, buffalo can wheel and change quickly. They are good swimmers and will often cross a lake or river merely to graze on the other side; they swim with the nose, forehead, and hump above the water. When the first white ranchers noted the extreme hardiness of the beast they wanted to breed this hardiness into their cattle. The hybrid resulting from crossing cattle and buffalo is know as a 'cattalo'; with few exceptions such attempts have failed, as the hybrid is usually not able to reproduce. The civilization and religion of the PLAINS INDIANS was largely based on the buffalo, which provided the Indians with meat, skins for tents and clothes, and horns and bones for weapons and tools. The Indians used every part of the buffalo: nothing was wasted. A rare white or albino buffalo was regarded by the Indians as belonging to the Sun God. Before the white man introduced horses to America, the Indians hunted the buffalo on foot, often driving them over cliffs to kill them. In the latter half of the nineteenth century the white BUFFALO HUNTERS began slaughtering the great herds for profit, mostly taking only the hide and tongue and leaving the carcass to rot on the plains. This mass slaughter was approved by the U.S. military as a ruthless means to deprive the Plains Indians of their sustenance, thus making it easy to subdue them. It has been estimated that in 1800 there were 60 million buffalo, by 1871 not more than 5½ million remained, by 1900 there were less than 300 buffalo roaming free on the North American Continent. Fortunately, during the time of the great destruction a number of people were developing small captive herds to save the animal from extinction. The American Bison Society was formed in 1905 and a number of national refuges were eventually created. Surveys of protected buffalo herds in the U.S. and Canada in recent years show a continental population of some 22,000; while this is infinitesimal compared with the great herds that once ranged North America, it is large enough to assure the future well-being of this magnificent beast.

The Border and the Buffalo by J. R. Cook (Topeka, Kansas, 1905);
The American Bison by M. S. Garretson (New York, 1938);
The North American Buffalo by F. G. Roe (Toronto, 1951).

44   *Indians wearing buckskin clothing.*

45   *Buffalo Bill Cody.*

BUFFALO BILL CODY 1846-1917

A PONY EXPRESS rider, buffalo hunter, Indian fighter, army scout, and international showman, William Frederick Cody was celebrated in his lifetime as the finest example of rugged Americanism. He did indeed have an adventurous life, but his legendary image as a frontier hero was established and promoted by sensational dime novels and his own widely successful Wild West Show. Born in Scott Country, Iowa, he moved with his family to KANSAS in 1854. A Pony Express rider at the age of fourteen, it is claimed he set an unsurpassed record by riding 322 miles in 21 hours 30 minutes, using 22 horses *en route*. After service in the Civil War with the Union forces he became an army scout. In 1867 he was hired to provide buffalo meat for workers building a railroad through Kansas (see KANSAS PACIFIC RAILWAY) and killed more than 4,000 buffalo in an eighteen month period, thus gaining his nickname 'Buffalo Bill'. Others claim that his famous sobriquet was bestowed upon him by Ned BUNTLINE, the shrewd writer of dime novels, who discovered the young scout out West in 1869 and promptly adopted him as the ideal hero for his cheap adventure books. Buntline wrote *Buffalo Bill: King of the Bordermen* for the *New York Weekly* and the fictionalized exploits of the 'greatest scout in the West' were an immediate success — Cody became a national hero. A flood of dime novels further established the fame of Buffalo Bill. Cody's meeting with Buntline changed his life; he became addicted to the limelight. In 1872 he was

45 V

awarded the Congressional Medal of Honor for bravery during a campaign against the Indians, but years later had to return the coveted medal when Congress ruled that recipients must be members of the army, not civilians. Also in 1872 Cody served as guide for Grand Duke Alexis of Russia in the 'Great Royal Buffalo Hunt'. Late that year, at the request of Ned Buntline, Cody went to Chicago to appear in the writer's successful stage play, *The Scouts of the Plains*. Then Cody organized his own stage company and continued touring in between trips out West until April 1876. In July that year, a few weeks after the stunning defeat of CUSTER in the Battle of the LITTLE BIGHORN, Cody killed and scalped the Cheyenne chief Yellow Hand in battle while serving as chief scout with Colonel Merritt and the Fifth Cavalry. This so-called 'duel' — celebrated as 'the first scalp for Custer!' — was given extensive coverage by the newspapers, mostly inaccurate as to the details. Buffalo Bill returned to the stage in a play based on the battle and drew big crowds. In 1883 he organized his Wild West Show and for the next twenty-five years toured North America and Europe; his fame spread throughout the world. In 1887 he was appointed Colonel in the National Guard and thereafter made full use of the title. He is reputed to have made a vast private fortune out of his Wild West Show but an open hand, bad investments and other financial problems in his old age left him bankrupt and in debt when he died in January 1917.

The Autobiography of Buffalo Bill by W. F. Cody (New York, 1920);
The Making of Buffalo Bill by R. J. Walsh (New York, 1928);
Buffalo Bill and the Wild West by V. Weybright and H. Sell (London, 1956);
The Lives and Legends of Buffalo Bill by D. Russell (Norman, Oklahoma, 1960);
Buffalo Bill by J. Burke (London, 1974).

BUFFALO BILL'S WILD WEST SHOW

William F. Cody is best known for his spectacular Wild West shows, full of real cowboys and Indians, in which he always played the leading role. For twenty-five years he toured North America and Europe performing before packed crowds and royalty. The show was first organized in 1883 and as it gained momentum boasted many famous westerners, including Bronco Bill Irving; Buck Taylor, 'King of the Cowboys'; crackshot Annie OAKLEY and her husband Frank Butler, and famous Indian chiefs SITTING BULL and RED CLOUD. A typical show would include rough-riding and roping by cowboys; the DEADWOOD STAGECOACH attacked by Indians and rescued in the nick of time by Buffalo Bill

himself on a white horse; a re-enactment of 'Custer's Last Stand'; sharp-shooting by Annie Oakley; the PONY EXPRESS; a horse race between cowboys and Indians, and many other events. It became the most popular and thrilling extravaganza of the period. In March 1887 Cody took the show to Europe for the first time; special performances were given before Queen Victoria and the Royal Family: the Prince of Wales saw it three times. In 1889 the show toured Britain, France, Spain, Italy and Germany. Other tours included Belgium, Austria, and the Balkan states. The travelling troupe consisted of some 500 members and 500 horses and demanded organization on military lines to transport it by railroad from city to city. The show was constantly on the move; in 1895, for example, it was presented in 131 locations in 190 days. During the tour of Germany, officers of the Kaiser's army were so impressed by Cody's organization that they recorded details of the train-loading, tent-pitching, and field kitchen operations for future military reference. In 1910 Cody went into partnership with Major Gordon W. Lillie, known as 'Pawnee Bill', in a wild west show that billed both their names. The partnership was dissolved in 1913. Cody gave his last public performance in November 1916.

Buffalo Bill from Prairie to Palace by J. M. Burke (Chicago, 1893);
Four Years in Europe with Buffalo Bill by C. E. Griffin (Aldia, Iowa, 1908);
Buffalo Bill by J. Burke (London, 1974).

BUFFALO HUNTERS

Armed with powerful, long-range rifles and motivated by commercial profit, the professional white hunters brought about the virtual extinction of the American BUFFALO. It was easy to shoot the buffalo from a safe distance. A good hunter could kill the animals faster than a skinner could remove the hides, and skinners boasted they could remove a buffalo skin in about five minutes. Hunters often killed 250 buffalo a day and many said that they killed from 2,500 to 3,000 a year. They used wagons to bring back the great loads of hides and some meat, mostly tongues. By 1870 trading in buffalo hides and tongues· reached vast numbers and buffalo hunting was the chief industry of the Plains, three million beasts being killed annually. In 1871 a single firm in St Louis bought 250,000 hides; auctions in 1873-4 in FORT WORTH, Texas, were moving 200,000 hides in a day or two. As the railroads pushed over the Plains, thousands of buffalo were shot to supply meat for the construction camps. 'Hunting' from train windows was advertised widely and passengers

46 ∧   47 ∨   48 ∨

engaged in the 'sport' of shooting from open
windows at the buffalo. Big game hunters from
Europe came to shoot the huge beasts. Having
exterminated the southern herd, the professional
hunters turned to the northern herd and,
between 1876 and 1883, destroyed that also. At
least 5,000 hunters and skinners were on the
northern range in 1882. By 1883 the buffalo,
which had numbered some 60 million in 1800,
was virtually extinct. Conservation of the buffalo
came slowly. Not until only about twenty wild
animals remained in the U.S. and 250 in Canada
was legal action taken to save the species from
extinction.

*The American Bison; Story of its Extermination and its
Restoration under Federal protection* by M. S. Garretson (New
York, 1938);
The Buffalo Hunters: The Story of the Hide Men by M. Sandoz
(New York, 1954).

46   *Buffalo skinners at work, by Frederic
Remington.*

47   *Negro regulars of the Ninth Cavalry ride to
the rescue in the Ute campaign of 1879.*

48   *Henry O. Flipper, first Negro graduate of
West Point, served with the Tenth Cavalry.*

BUFFALO BILL, SHOOTING ON HORSEBACK AT FULL SPEED.

49 ∧   50 ∨   52 ∨

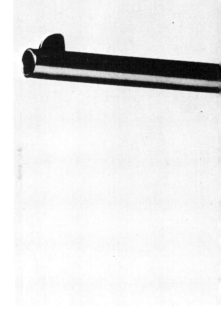

49 *Poster for Buffalo Bill's Wild West Show.*

50 *Bullwhackers on the Santa Fe Trail, by Frederic Remington.*

52 *Colt Buntline Special with 12-inch barrel.*

51 *"Dime" novel of 1896.*

Wild Bill's Last Trail.

By NED BUNTLINE.

51 ∧

BUFFALO SOLDIERS

Two Negro regiments of U.S. Cavalry played an important role in the INDIAN WARS; they were highly regarded as fighters by the Indians, who called them 'Buffalo Soldiers' because their short curly hair resembled that of the buffalo. Congress authorized the raising of the two Negro cavalry regiments — the Ninth and Tenth — in 1866, and four years later two infantry regiments — the twenty-fourth and twenty-fifth — were also formed. The infantry was mostly employed on guard duty but the cavalry took an active part in a number of hard campaigns against the SIOUX, COMANCHE, and APACHE. The Tenth accepted the sobriquet 'Buffalo Soldiers' as an honour (the courage of the buffalo was highly respected by the Indians) and adopted the animal as their regimental emblem. The blacks were steady and reliable soldiers with a desertion rate far lower than the white troops; eleven Negro soldiers received the Medal of Honor, the highest military award, for bravery in battle against the Indians. The black cavalry rode several times to the rescue of besieged white soldiers: the Tenth was the first rescue force on the scene at the Battle of BEECHER ISLAND in 1868, and the Ninth made a forced march to relieve the soldiers encircled by the UTE INDIANS on Milk Creek in 1879. These Negro regiments were usually led by white commissioned officers, one of whom was First Lieutenant John J. Pershing, who gained his famous nickname 'Black Jack' from his service with the Tenth Cavalry; Pershing later became a general and commanded the American forces in France in World War One. In 1878 Lieutenant Henry O. Flipper, the first Negro graduate from West Point, became the first black officer to serve in the Tenth Cavalry. Other black West Point graduates to serve with the Buffalo Soldiers were Lieutenant John H. Alexander, seven years with the Ninth, and Second Lieutenant Charles Young of the Tenth.

The Buffalo Soldiers: a Narrative of the Negro Cavalry in the West by W. H. Leckie (Norman, Oklahoma, 1967);
The Black Infantry in the West, 1869-1891 by A. L. Fowler (Westport, New York, 1971);
The Black Military Experience in the American West by J. M. Carroll (New York, 1971).

BULLWHACKER

For many years commercial freight and military supplies were carried over the trails of the Old West by bull trains — a number of linked wagons pulled by ox-teams. The wagon driver, called a bullwhacker, walked beside his team and carried a heavy bullwhip, up to twenty feet long, which he constantly cracked over the oxen to keep the slow-plodding beasts on the move. The tough bullwhackers were noted for their loud profanity, their drunken brawling, and their skill with the whip; they did not actually whip the oxen, but goaded them on with resounding whip-cracks and curses. If the freight train used MULES instead of oxen, the teamster was known as a mule-skinner. Oxen were slower than mules but a lot cheaper to

53 *Butterfield Overland Mail driving through a blizzard in the mountains.*

buy, and oxen being stronger than both mules and horses could pull more weight. Ox-teams were also used by emigrant wagon trains.

The Bullwhacker: Adventures of a Frontier Freighter by W. F. Hooker (New York, 1925);
The Wagonmasters: High Plains Freighting from the Earliest Days of the Santa Fe to 1880 by H. P. Walker (Norman, Oklahoma, 1966);
The Expressmen by Time-Life Books (New York, 1974).

BUNTLINE, Ned 1823-86

Ned Buntline was the pseudonym of Edward Zane Carroll Judson, an adventurer, rogue, creator and prolific writer of the 'dime novel'. Born at Stamford, New York, Judson ran away to sea as a boy and eventually became an officer in the U.S. Navy. Resigning from the navy in 1842 he served in the Seminole War, and took up writing fiction under the pen-name 'Ned Buntline' (a buntline is the rope at the bottom of a square sail). His own life was as sensational as his stories. In 1846 he killed a man over a woman, was hanged by a lynch mob but the rope was cut just in time to save his life. In New York he published a scandal sheet called *Ned Buntline's Own* and churned out a steam of cheap adventure books; he was the first of the dime novelists. The term 'dime novel' came into use when a publisher took to printing a large dime (ten cent coin) on the front of his blood-and-thunder books to prevent retailers overcharging the public; the name stuck even when the price dropped to five cents. By 1869 Buntline was America's most successful author, earning some 20,000 dollars a year. In search of fresh material for his stories he went West and at Fort McPherson, Nebraska, met the young army scout William F. Cody; dubbing Cody with the sobriquet BUFFALO BILL, Buntline promptly made him the dashing hero of a series of 'true' dime novels about Cody's supposed Western exploits. Without Buntline's promotion, Cody would have remained an unknown frontiersman, like so many others of the time. Buntline also helped to promote the fame of Wild Bill HICKOK. A short, squat man with red hair, Buntline was married four times; he loved to lecture on the virtues of temperance but this did not stop him from indulging in a drinking bout after giving his moral lecture. He died at Stamford, his birth-place.

The Life and Adventures of Ned Buntline by F. E. Pond (New York, 1919);
The Great Rascal: Life and Adventures of Ned Buntline by J. Monoghan (Boston, 1952).

BUNTLINE SPECIAL

One of the most enduring myths of the Wild West is that of Wyatt EARP and his trusty 'Buntline Special', a COLT 'Peacemaker' revolver, Model 1873, with an extra-long barrel. Standard length of a Peacemaker barrel was 7½ inches; the Buntlines had remarkable barrels 10, 12, and 16 inches long. The truth is that Earp never carried a so-called Buntline Special, a fact fully established by William B. Shillingberg's brilliant monograph *Wyatt Earp and the 'Buntline Special' Myth* published in The Kansas Historical Quarterly, Summer 1976. When the Colt Company first produced its unusual long-barrelled .45 calibre in 1876 it was known as 'Colt's pistol with carbine barrel and attachable stock', the shoulder stock being the metal skeleton type. It was not a popular model and Colt produced a very small number during the frontier years. The name and fame of the Buntline special was invented by the journalist Stuart N. Lake and published in his controversial biography *Wyatt Earp: Frontier Marshal* in 1931, a book that has been thoroughly discredited by serious historians. According to Lake the name 'Buntline Special' originated with the gun's association with Ned BUNTLINE, the dime-novelist, who ordered five special Peacemakers with twelve inch barrels and presented them in the summer of 1876 to worthy law officers in Dodge City, Kansas, including Wyatt Earp, Bat MASTERSON, and Bill TILGHMAN. Lake tells us that the Buntline became Earp's favourite gun and he often used the long barrel as a club to knock troublemakers senseless. The other recipients of the Buntlines found the long barrel inconvenient and cut them down to standard length. Lake started the legend and other writers have embellished it. The facts of the matter are that the alleged Ned Buntline purchase is not recorded in the Colt Company's carefully preserved files, no long-barrelled Peacemakers left the factory until December 1877, there is no mention of Buntline Specials in writings that predate Lake's book, and Earp's famous gun is not extant (it was said to have been lost many years ago). The Colt Company, realizing the legendary publicity value attached to the weapon, started using the official designation 'Buntline Special' for its long-barrelled Peacemaker (which is still produced today) in 1957. However, the Wyatt Earp-Buntline Special myth persists. But no amount of retelling will make it the truth.

Wyatt Earp: Frontier Marshal by S. N. Lake (Boston, 1931); *Wyatt Earp and the 'Buntline Special' Myth* by W. B. Shillingberg (Tucson, 1976).

BURROWS, Rube
1854-90

An outlaw gang leader who specialized in robbing trains in the 1880s. Reuben (Rube) Houston Burrows and his brother Jim were farm boys from Lamar County, Alabama, who took to RUSTLING in the INDIAN TERRITORY (Oklahoma). Rube was said to be a marksman who could hit a wood-knot from 100 yards. Moving to Texas, the Burrows' gang held up and robbed a number of trains, which brought the PINKERTON detectives on their trail. During a raid on a train in January 1888, Jim Burrows was caught but Rube shot his way free; Jim died in jail nine months later of fever. Back in Lamar County, Rube killed a postmaster and later another man during a train hold-up; rewards for him, dead or alive, totalled 7,500 dollars. With his gang captured one by one, Rube carried out his last train robbery single-handed, relieving a Louisville & Nashville train of several thousand dollars in September 1890. Rube Burrows met his death in October in a short-range shoot-out with a man named Carter who had planned to collect the reward on the bandit. Burrows was described in a Pinkerton reward circular as 'about 32 years of age, 6 feet in height, weighs about 160 pounds, blue eyes which do not look a person full in the face. . .light sandy hair, thin light moustache, uses Hair Vigor to darken hair. . .is a good horseman, carries a .45 calibre pistol and is a good shot'.

Badmen of the Frontier Days by C. W. Breihan (New York, 1957); *The Pinkertons* by J. D. Horan (New York, 1967).

BUTTERFIELD OVERLAND DESPATCH

At the end of the Civil War in 1865 David Butterfield (no relation to John Butterfield of the BUTTERFIELD OVERLAND MAIL) started a stage line between Atchison, Kansas, and DENVER, Colorado in competition with stagecoach king Ben HOLLADAY. But the new Butterfield Overland Despatch was soon in financial trouble, chiefly brought about by constant Indian attacks (fomented, so rumour had it, by ruthless rival Ben) with the end result that Holladay bought up the failing line in March 1866.

The Overland Mail, 1849-1869 by L. R. Hafen (Cleveland, Ohio, 1926)
Ben Holladay: The Stagecoach King by J. V. Frederick (Glendale, California, 1940).

BUTTERFIELD OVERLAND MAIL

This company, formed in 1857, ran the longest stagecoach line in America, 2,800 miles long, sweeping down from ST LOUIS in Missouri, through Arkansas, the INDIAN TERRITORY, Texas, New Mexico, Arizona, then up through southern California to Los Angeles and finally to SAN FRANCISCO. John Butterfield (1801-69) was already well established as a stage line operator when he and his partners got the six-year government contract, at 600,000 dollars a year, to provide an express U.S. Mail service between the MISSISSIPPI RIVER and San Francisco, to be made within twenty-five days for each one-way trip, in coaches suitable for passengers as well as the mail. The Butterfield line was splendidly equipped with over 100 CONCORD coaches, 1,000 horses, 500 mules, and 750 men, of whom 150 were drivers. Way stations, with food and water, were established at regular intervals on the marathon route. The fare across the continent was 100 dollars. The first trips were made on 15 September 1858; one coach leaving Tipton, Missouri on the West-bound run, and another leaving San Francisco for the East. 'Remember, boys,' said John Butterfield, 'nothing on God's earth must stop the U.S. Mail.' Both coaches reached their ultimate destinations in twenty-four days, a day inside the schedule. U.S. President James Buchanan wired Butterfield his congratulations: 'a glorious triumph for civilization and the Union'. When the Civil War split the Union in 1861 the Butterfield Overland Mail was moved northward to the Central Route in Federal controlled territory.

The Overland Mail, 1849-1869 by L. R. Hafen (Cleveland, Ohio, 1926);

C

54   *Buzzard or turkey vulture.*

The Butterfield Overland Mail, 1857-1869 by M. B. Conkling
(Glendale, California, 1947);
The Overland Stage to California by F. R. Root and W. E.
Connelley (Glorieta, New Mexico, 1970);
The Expressmen by Time-Life Books (New York, 1974).

BUZZARD
Cathartes aura

Buzzards are usually pictured hovering above a
dying traveller in the Old West, like black-winged
symbols of death, waiting to pick the body clean
to the bone. This has led to the false impression
that buzzards are evil. Actually they perform the
very necessary function of disposing of
undesirable carrion. The American buzzard,
also known as the turkey vulture, can be easily
identified at a far distance by its great upswept
wings, soaring and wheeling on rising air
currents, sweeping in wide circles and spirals,
with sharp eyes seeking out dead animals on
which to gorge. They operate in flocks and this
helps in the quick disposal of the rotting flesh they
find. The buzzard is 2½ feet long with a
wingspan of nearly 6 feet.

CALAMITY JANE
c. 1852-1903

The most famous female of the Old West, Calamity Jane was a hard-drinking character who drifted through the frontier towns creating a legend of toughness, mostly through her unruly behaviour and her own inflated accounts of her supposed exploits. She like to dress in BUCKSKIN, and worked, cursed, and acted in the manner of the rough plainsmen she mixed with. Born in Missouri as Martha Jane Cannary (there are various spellings of the surname), she is said to have worked as a BULLWHACKER, or mule-skinner, and for the army as a scout or some kind of camp follower. In 1876 she came in contact with Wild Bill HICKOK in DEADWOOD, South Dakota during the gold-mining boom, a casual relationship that she and many writers have made much of, even suggesting that they were married. How she came by her world famous sobriquet is uncertain. One version is that she saved an army officer from calamity at the hands of Indians; another version is that her own misfortunes gained her the name; another reason is that she caused a fracas wherever she went and people would say, 'Here comes Calamity!' If we are to believe Jane herself, she married Clinton Burk in Texas in 1885 and had a girl baby in 1887. Burk left her and she drifted from town to town, a legendary curiosity, drinking herself into trouble and telling tall tales of her adventures to anyone who would listen. For a short time in the 1890s she appeared on the stage, billed as 'Calamity Jane! The Famous Woman Scout of the Wild West!' She died in Terry, South Dakota, raddled by drink, aged about fifty-one and was buried in Mount Moriah Cemetery, Deadwood, near Wild Bill Hickok's grave.

Calamity Jane and the Lady Wildcats by D. Aikman (New York, 1927); *Calamity Jane* by N. Mumey (Denver, 1950); *Desperate Women* by J. D. Horan (New York, 1952); *Calamity Jane of the Western Trails* by J. L. Jennewein (Huron, South Dakota, 1953).

CALIFORNIA

The 'Golden State' of the Far West, blessed with great fortune in fine weather, fertile land and mineral wealth. Here are the world's tallest trees, the mighty redwoods (*Sequoia sempervirens*), and the largest land bird in North America, the California condor. A vast land of extreme topographic variety: dense forests, green valleys, burning deserts. Mount Whitney, 14,494 feet, in the SIERRA NEVADA Mountains is one of the highest peaks in the nation. Only sixty miles from snow-capped Mount Whitney sizzles DEATH VALLEY, the lowest, hottest place in the U.S.

55 *Calamity Jane.*

Spain started to colonize California in 1769, building twenty-one Catholic Missions throughout the land and founding SAN FRANCISCO. In 1822 the Province of California became part of Mexico, which had gained independence from Spain in 1821. Jedediah SMITH and a small band of trappers were the first Americans to complete an overland journey to California blazing a trail from the GREAT SALT LAKE in Utah. In 1842-5 John C. FRÉMONT led a U.S. government expedition into the sparsely populated land and his reports encouraged Anglo-American settlers to make the long, hard wagon journey over the CALIFORNIA TRAIL. In 1846 these settlers rebelled against Mexican rule in the Bear Flag Revolt, so called from the grizzly bear emblem on the revolutionary flag; this sparked off the U.S.-MEXICAN WAR with disastrous results for defeated Mexico, which lost

California and other vast territories to the United States. In 1848 gold was discovered at Sutter's Mill at Coloma which triggered the great GOLD RUSH. The California Gold Rush transformed the tiny settlement in San Francisco Bay into one of the world's busiest ports. In 1850 California became the Thirty-first State of the Union; by 1852 more than 200,000 gold seekers and settlers had poured into the golden state. The native Indians of California — including the MODOC, Mohave, and YUMA — were badly treated by the Spanish, Mexicans, and Americans; of the estimated 150,000 Indians in California at the time of Spanish explorations in the early sixteenth century, only about 17,000 remained by the end of the nineteenth century, a decline brought about by disease, starvation, and extermination at the hands of the white men. Between 1865 and 1868 the CENTRAL PACIFIC RAILROAD cut through the barrier of the Sierra Nevada Mountains and joined with the UNION PACIFIC in Utah, thus completing a direct rail connection between eastern U.S. and the Eldorado state.

From Wilderness to Empire: A History of California by G. S. Dumke (New York, 1959);
California: A History by A. F. Rolle (New York, 1963).

CALIFORNIA JOE
1829-76

A frontiersman and army scout described by General SHERIDAN as 'an invaluable guide and Indian fighter'. Born in Kentucky, his real name was Moses Milner, but having travelled overland to California in 1849 he became known only as 'California Joe'. After the Civil War he became an army scout in the Indian campaigns. Joe was an impressive character, over six feet tall, with long curly hair and brown beard; he was rarely seen without his pipe in his mouth, his rifle and his dog. General CUSTER was much impressed by him and appointed him chief of scouts to the Seventh Cavalry. He did not, however, hold the post for very long; he got roaring drunk, Custer put him under guard and appointed another chief scout. But a sober Joe was the best of scouts. After taking part in the Battle of WASHITA in 1868 against the CHEYENNE INDIANS, he was chosen by Custer to carry the victory news to General Sheridan, and he rode his mule (his favourite mode of transport) 100 miles through snowbound, hostile country in eighteen hours to deliver the message. In 1876 he served with the Fifth Cavalry as a guide in the SIOUX campaign; in October that year, at Fort Robinson, Nebraska, he was killed by a man called Newcomb, who bore Joe a grudge and shot him in the back.

My Life on the Plains by G. A. Custer (New York, 1874);
Heroes of the Plains by J. W. Buel (Philadelphia, 1883);
California Joe by J. E. Milner and E. R. Forrest (Caldwell, Idaho, 1935).

CALIFORNIA TRAIL

The general term applied to the various overland routes to CALIFORNIA used by emigrant settlers and gold seekers, but in particular it meant the arduous, 2,000-mile trek from the MISSOURI RIVER at INDEPENDENCE, or ST JOSEPH, or Council Bluffs. The California Trail was an offshoot of the OREGON TRAIL (the chief route West, sometimes called the Overland Trail), parting from it at two points, at FORT BRIDGER in Wyoming, or west of Fort Hall on the Snake River in Idaho. The California Trail followed the Humboldt River across Nevada, climbed the SIERRA NEVADA Mountains and ended at Sacramento. A typical WAGON TRAIN, encountering all the difficulties of the terrain, could make but fifteen to twenty miles a day over the level plains, in rough mountain country progress was even slower; thus it took perhaps four months for a train to reach California. During the initial GOLD RUSH in 1849 the trail was used by some 30,000 people, about 5,000 dying *en route*. It has been estimated, from the official register kept at FORT LARAMIE, that during the gold rush years 1850-6, some 150,000 people travelled over the California Trail. Sections of the trail were used by the PONY EXPRESS and stagecoach lines.

Journey to California by J. Bidwell (San Francisco, 1937);
The Overland Trail by J. Monaghan (Indianapolis, 1947);
The Opening of the California Trail by G. R. Stewart (Berkeley, California, 1953);
The California Trail by G. R. Stewart (London, 1964).

CAMELS IN THE WEST

During the 1850s the U.S. government engaged in an experiment in overland transport intended to demonstrate the superiority of the camel over the HORSE, MULE, and ox as the beast of burden in the Far West. It failed, largely because the American teamsters refused to understand or adapt to the strange animal. Camel transportation had been a favourite topic of speculation for years when, in 1854, Secretary of War Jefferson Davis induced Congress to appropriate 30,000 dollars for the project. Davis believed that camels would be effective against hostile Indians; he cited the use of camels by the British army and in Napoleon's Egyptian campaigns against natives resembling the COMANCHE and APACHE Indians. Davis was of the opinion that camels, drinking enough water before a journey to last 100 miles, would travel without rest at ten to fifteen m.p.h. and overtake Indian bands which eluded the horse cavalry. Camel enthusiasts also advocated a 'Lightning Dromedary Express' to carry fast and eastern newspapers to the Pacific coast in fifteen days. Thus two batches of camels (75 in total) were purchased in the Middle East and shipped to Texas in 1856 and 1857. Army packers, instructed by Egyptian camel drivers, were trained to handle the bizarre beasts. The first military trial took place in 1857 when a twenty-five camel caravan commanded by Lieutenant Beal trekked from camp Verde, Texas to California. Beale reported the camels a great success. But this initial success was doomed to failure. Mutual distrust and dislike soon developed between the camels and their American handlers. The animals balked at the rough treatment and curses meted out by their drivers, who regarded the camel as a stinking, awkward, alien beast with dirty habits. Army mules and horses also disliked the hump-backed strangers and often stampeded at the sight of them. The camels were used for several years but the experiment was judged a failure and the

58 ▼

animals were either sold or turned loose on the plains. Private freight companies which had also imported camels soon went out of business.

Uncle Sam's Camels by L. B. Lesley (Cambridge, Massachusetts, 1929);
Camels to California by H. D. Fowler (Stanford, California, 1950).

CARSON, Kit
1809-68

A frontiersman of great fame, Christopher Carson was a trapper, army scout and guide, Indian fighter and soldier. Born in Kentucky and raised on the Missouri frontier, he had no schooling and remained a near-illiterate for most of his life. He travelled the SANTA FE TRAIL and worked as a trapper for more than ten years in the ROCKY MOUNTAINS. He married an Indian girl in 1836 who died in 1842, and married a Mexican in 1843. In 1842 he served as guide to Lieutenant John C. FRÉMONT on his first government expedition to the Rockies. Frémont regarded Carson highly and took him on a second expedition in 1843-4; Carson's association with Frémont brought him national renown. He served as a guide and soldier in the MEXICAN WAR of 1846-7. In 1853 he drove 6,500 sheep from his home at Taos, New Mexico to California, making a handsome profit from their sale. On his return to Taos he was made Indian agent in charge of several tribes of UTES. During the Civil War he served as a colonel of the First New Mexico Volunteers (Federal army) in the South-west. In 1863 he waged successful campaigns against the Mescalero APACHES and NAVAJOS, ruthlessly crushing the fierce Navajos by destroying their homes, sheep, orchards and food supplies, killing some 600 Navajos and taking 8,000 prisoners. His last campaign was against the KIOWAS and COMANCHES, fighting a hard battle at ADOBE WALLS, Texas in 1864. In 1866, with the rank of brevet Brigadier-General, he took command of Fort Garland in Colorado. In his last years he developed an internal illness, caused by a fall from a horse in 1860, from which he died at Fort Lyon, Colorado on 23 May 1868. Carson was five feet eight inches tall, enjoyed smoking a pipe but never touched liquor. He was much liked and respected for his modesty and integrity.

The Life of Kit Carson by C. Burdett (New York, 1902);
Kit Carson's Autobiography edited by M. M. Quaife (Chicago, 1935);
Kit Carson Days by E. L. Sabin (New York, 1935);
The Real Kit Carson by M. Estergreen (Taos, New Mexico, 1955).

58 *Kit Carson.*

59 *Butch Cassidy.*

60 *Sioux hunting buffalo, by George Catlin.*

59 ∧

60 ∨

CASSIDY, Butch
1867-?

Celebrated leader of the WILD BUNCH gang of train robbers, Butch Cassidy was one of the last old-style bandits of the West. Born in Utah, grandson of a Mormon bishop, his real name was Robert Leroy Parker. It seems he was eager to take up a life of crime. He adopted the name 'Cassidy' in admiration of Mike Cassidy, a rustler who taught him to shoot and steal livestock; he was dubbed 'Butch' from his short time working in a butcher's shop. In 1894 he was convicted of stealing thirty horses and sentenced to two years in a Wyoming prison; he was released in January 1896. Still determined on a life of crime he formed a gang, known as the Wild Bunch, and robbed banks and trains. One of the gang was Harry Longbaugh, known as the 'Sundance Kid'. By all accounts Butch was a likeable fellow, described in a PINKERTON wanted poster as having a 'cheerful and affable manner'. It is said that, although a crack shot, he never killed anybody and disliked gratuitous violence. He had the quick wit and strength of character to dominate more desperate men. With the Pinkerton and railroad agents hot on their trail, the Wild Bunch broke up and Cassidy and Longbaugh sailed to South America in 1901 and continued their banditry there. It is believed they died in a gunfight with troops in Bolivia or Uruguay.

Triggernometry by E. Cunningham (New York, 1934);
Desperate Men by J. D. Horan (New York, 1949);
The Wild Bunch by J. D. Horan (London, 1960).

CATLIN, George
1798-1872

American artist and author who recorded in pictures and words the culture and life of the principal Indian tribes of the West in the 1830s, a way of life that was soon to vanish under the tidal wave of white civilization. Born in Pennsylvania, George Catling studied law before embarking on a new career as a self-taught painter of miniature portraits. Greatly impressed on seeing a delegation of PLAINS INDIANS *en route* to Washington, he decided to devote his life and talents, as he put it, 'in rescuing from oblivion the looks and customs of the vanishing races of native man in America'. And he succeeded brilliantly. He made his first trip West in 1832, along the MISSOURI RIVER from St Louis to the Yellowstone River in Montana, sketching and painting Indians and landscapes. In 1834 he travelled south-west; in 1835-6 to the Upper Missouri and Great Lakes. He lived an almost nomadic life among the forty-eight tribes he visited and

61   *George Catlin painted by William H. Fisk in 1849.*

painted hundreds of distinguished Indians of both sexes, the buffalo hunt, ceremonial dances and all aspects of Indian life. His *Letters and Notes on the Manners, Customs and Condition of the North American Indians,* containing some 500 of his pictures, was published in 1841. From 1837 to 1852 he took his 'Indian Gallery' (a collection of 600 portraits and paintings) on a tour of North America and Europe. In 1846, short of money and pressed by problems, Catlin offered to sell the collection to the British Museum for 35,000 dollars (7,000 pounds)! But the sale did not go through. Because of disastrous financial speculations Catlin died in debt. Joseph Harrison, one of his creditors, managed to obtain the Indian Gallery collection and it was given as a gift to the Smithsonian Institution in 1879. Catlin's style was purely documentary - no romantic imaginations, he painted exactly what he saw; hence the great historical value of his work today.

George Catlin, Painter of Indians of the West by J. C. Ewers (Washington, 1956);
George Catlin and the Old Frontier by H. McCracken (New York, 1959);
George Catlin edited by M. C. Ross (Norman, Oklahoma, 1959).

62 *Cattle drive from Texas in the 1870s.*

CATTLE DRIVES

After the Civil War cattle in the northern states had been greatly reduced. In TEXAS, however, the hardy, feral LONGHORNS had multiplied enormously and in 1865 they numbered an estimated five million head. The Americans east of the Mississippi were in the market for meat and the Texans were eager to supply it. So began the long drives north to railhead cattle towns and the colourful Texas COWBOY became a national figure. At the trail-end cattle towns of Kansas, such as ABILENE, DODGE CITY, WICHITA and NEWTON the longhorns were loaded into freight cars and taken east for slaughter. From 1866 to 1895 some ten million cattle were driven up from Texas to the railhead cowtowns, or to stock new ranges on the central and northern plains west of the Mississippi. The principal route from Texas to Kansas by way of the INDIAN TERRITORY (Oklahoma) was the CHISHOLM TRAIL, another being the Western Trail; the Sedalia Trail from Texas ran through the Indian Territory and Arkansas and ended at Sedalia in Missouri; the GOODNIGHT-LOVING TRAIL struck west through Texas, then north through New Mexico,

Colorado, and into Wyoming. These major trails stretched for 1,000 miles or more. Most Texas cowboys wanted to go on the long drives north, a chance to see new places, but only the best were chosen for the marathon journey through the wilderness; beset by all kinds of difficulties, a cattle drive was hard work and dangerous. A trail herd might number up to 3,000 head and move at the slow rate of ten to fifteen miles a day, in a column, two or three abreast, strung out nearly a mile long. A dominant steer would lead the column. The trail crew usually consisted of a trail boss, a cook and his CHUCKWAGON, a wrangler to look after the REMUDA or riding stock, and enough hands to control the herd, say one cowboy to every 250 or 300 cattle. The trail boss or his assistant would ride fifteen to twenty miles ahead of the column to scout for water, grass, and a campsite for the night. Two men rode 'point' or lead, one either side of the head of the column to keep the herd on the course, then came the 'swing riders' followed by the 'flank riders' who kept the cattle in line, and finally the 'drag riders' at the rear who looked after the calves and urged on the cows which dragged behind. A STAMPEDE usually occurred at night; something would startle the

63∧   64∨   65∨

cattle and they would run wildly for miles and the weary cowboys would have to round them up again. The arduous long drive took three or four months to complete and when the cowboys arrived at the railhead town and were paid off, they usually blew their hard-earned money in a wild spree of drinking and gambling. The age of the long drives lasted nearly thirty years; by the 1890s BARBED WIRE fencing, farmers, and the spreading railroad system closed the trails.

Prairie Trails and Cowtowns by F. B. Streeter (Boston, 1936);
We Pointed Them North by E. C. Abbott and H. Smith (New York, 1939);
The Trampling Herd by P. I. Wellman (New York, 1939);
Trail Driving Days by D. Brown and M. F. Schmitt (New York, 1952);
Great American Cattle Trails by H. S. Drago (New York, 1965);
The Old Time Cowhand by R. F. Adams (New York, 1971);
The Cowboys by Time-Life Books (New York, 1973).

CAVALRY, U.S.

The United States Cavalry helped maintain law and order in the Old West and fought in the INDIAN WARS from 1865 to 1890. In July 1866 the peacetime strength of the regular U.S. Army was set at 5 regiments of artillery, 45 of infantry, and 10 of cavalry (which included the newly-raised cavalry regiments numbered 7 and 10); in 1878 the infantry was reduced to 25 regiments. Most of the army was widely dispersed in small units along the frontier (see ARMY of the West). A garrison usually consisted of one company of infantry and one of cavalry — after 1881 a cavalry company was designated a troop — but frequently a single company was the only protection for many miles of territory. Under such conditions there could be little uniformity within regiments; for example, in 1882 the troops of the entire 10 cavalry regiments were distributed among 55 posts in the Indian country. In 1870 the First, Third and Eighth Cavalry were stationed in Arizona, Nevada and New Mexico; the Second and Fifth in Montana, Nebraska and Wyoming; the Seventh (Custer's regiment) in Kansas, and the Fourth, Sixth, Ninth and Tenth were in Texas. The Ninth and Tenth were Negro regiments — known as the BUFFALO SOLDIERS — led by white officers. A cavalry regiment rode, where it was possible, in columns of four and when dismounted for combat one man of each four would hold the horses while the others fired their weapons. A fully complemented cavalry regiment of the 1870s numbered 940 officers and men, but regiments were usually under strength. A trooper was armed with a sabre, revolver and carbine, and many carried a BOWIE KNIFE. Regulation cavalry uniform was, generally, blue tunic and trousers with yellow piping and stripes, blue kepi or wide-brimmed campaign hat; but on active service in the field dress was varied, more for comfort than military correctness, and both officers and men wore a mixture of official and civilian dress, including BUCKSKIN jackets. Patrolling and fighting on the cold Northern Plains or in the arid South-west was a hard and dirty business and those that did not desert (and many did) developed into tough, experienced horse soldiers who were often required to ride for many miles a day with little food and rest, hence the old cavalry adage 'Forty Miles a Day on Beans and Hay'.

Indian Fighting Army by D. Fairfax (New York, 1944);
Boots and Saddles by E. B. Custer (Norman, Oklahoma, 1961);
Forty Miles a Day on Beans and Hay by D. Rickey, Jr. (Norman, 1963);
The Yellowlegs: The Story of the U.S. Cavalry by R. Wormser (New York, 1966);
The Soldiers by Time-Life Books (New York, 1973).

CAYUSE INDIANS

A small tribe that lived in WASHINGTON and OREGON and were closely associated with the NEZ PERCÉ INDIANS. The Cayuse were noted for their bravery and owing to their constant fighting with other tribes were numerically weak. They were particularly noted for their fine horses, which they captured wild and bred;'cayuse' became a cowboy word for horse in the North-west. The tribe acquired wide notoriety in the early days of the white settlement of the territory. In 1838 a mission was established among the Cayuse by Marcus WHITMAN; in 1847 smallpox carried off a large part of the tribe and the warriors, believing the missionaries to be the cause, attacked them, killing Whitman and others and destroying the mission. This resulted in the Cayuse War of 1847-50 in which volunteer troops pursued the Indians without bringing about a decisive engagement. The war ended when five Cayuse surrendered, confessing to the murders; they were tried and hanged. In 1855 the Cayuse joined in the treaty by which the Umatilla Reservation was formed in Oregon and there they agreed to live.

History of Oregon by H. H. Bancroft (San Francisco, 1886);
Pacific Northwest Indian Wars by R. H. Glassley (Portland, Oregon, 1953);
The Cayuse Indians by R. H. Ruby and J. A. Brown (Norman, Oklahoma, 1972).

63 *Cattle drive, watercolour by Charles M. Russell.*

64 *Cavalry sergeant, 1890, by Frederic Remington.*

65 *Cavalry officer in campaign dress, by Frederic Remington.*

CENTRAL PACIFIC RAILROAD

In July 1862 President Abraham Lincoln signed the Pacific Railroad Act authorizing the construction of railroad between the MISSOURI RIVER and the Pacific Coast; this railroad, linked with existing track, would provide the United States with its first transcontinental railroad and open up the Far West. Two companies were organized to build it: the Central Pacific Railroad and the UNION PACIFIC RAILROAD. The Union Pacific would build westward from the Missouri to the California boundary; the Central Pacific would build eastward and connect with the Union Pacific. Government aid took the form of land grants and subsidies, and this inspired a great race between the two companies. The Central Pacific Railroad Company of California was incorporated on 28 June 1861 by four men: Collis P. Huntington, Leland Stanford, Mark Hopkins, and Charles Crocker. The latter, as president of the construction company, was the driving force. Work on the Central Pacific began at Sacramento in January 1863, and the Union Pacific broke ground at Omaha, Nebraska, in December 1863. Progress did not get properly under way until the end of the Civil War in 1865. From then till its completion in 1869 the making of the

transcontinental railroad dominated the national consciousness; it was the biggest engineering project America had ever undertaken. The country to be crossed by the Central Pacific was then almost entirely wilderness, the major obstacle being the SIERRA NEVADA Mountains. Crocker found it difficult to get white labourers so he shipped over more than 12,000 Chinese coolies, who proved excellent workers (Union Pacific had a large labour force of Irish immigrants). The Chinese, known as 'Crocker's Pets', overcame terrific problems in laying the track over the high Sierras, working only with hand tools, wheelbarrows, horsedrawn wagons, black powder; in certain sections they were lowered in baskets to cut away and blast the precipitous sides of the mountains. 'Without the Chinese', said Leland Stanford, 'it would have been impossible to complete the western portion of this national highway'. In 1866 the Central Pacific, not wishing to be restricted to the California line, gained the right from Congress to continue its track across the Nevada deserts. As the two tracks neared each other the rivalry became more energetic; when Union Pacific put down eight miles of line in one day, Central Pacific replied by laying more than ten miles in a single day, thus setting the record. After covering 1,775 miles between them the two railroads joined at

Promontory Point in Utah on 10 May 1869, where Leland Stanford and a Union Pacific official drove in the last spike, the GOLDEN SPIKE. In 1885 the Central Pacific was absorbed by the Southern Pacific Railroad.

The First Transcontinental Railroad: Central Pacific, Union Pacific by J. D. Galloway (New York, 1930);
Moguls and Iron Men: Story of the First Transcontinental Railroad by J. McCague (New York, 1964);
High Road to Promontory: Building the Central Pacific Across the High Sierra by G. Kraus (New York, 1969);
Golden Spike by R. M. Utley and F. A. Ketterson (National Park Service publication, Washington, D.C. 1969).

CHAPS

To protect his legs while riding from thick brush, cactus, rope burns, and the horns of steers the working COWBOY wore tough leather leggings, and these chaps (short for the Spanish *chaparejos*) became a conspicuous part of his outfit. The American cowboy inherited and adapted the wearing of chaps — pronounced 'shaps' — from his Mexican counterpart, the VAQUERO. There were several types of chaps. The 'shotgun' style had narrow, closed legs that resembled the double-barrel of a shotgun. The 'batwing' type had wide flapping fronts with wrap-around backs that were fastened round the legs with snap-locks;

66 *Chinese coolies working on the Central Pacific Railroad.*

67 *Cowboy chaps, or leggings.*

67 ∨

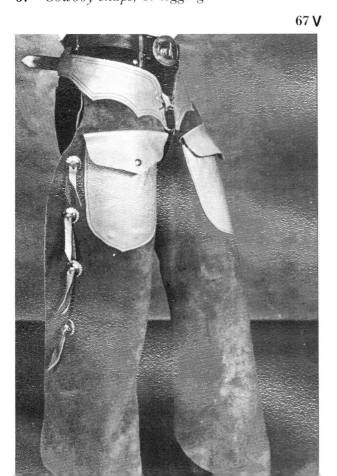

these were popular because in putting them on a cowboy need not remove his SPURS. On the cold northern ranges chaps were made of goat or bear skin, with the hair worn on the outside.

The Cowboy, His Characteristics, His Equipment by P. A. Rollins (New York, 1922);
The Look of the Old West by F. Harris (New York, 1955);
The Old Time Cowhand by R. F. Adams (New York, 1971).

CHEYENNE INDIANS

An important division of the Algonquin linguistic family, the Cheyennes were best known for many years as a horse and buffalo tribe of the PLAINS INDIANS, playing a leading role in the INDIAN WARS in the latter half of the nineteenth century. Originally natives of the Minnesota woodlands, where they built permanent villages, farmed and made pottery, the Cheyennes left their ancestral homelands and moved west to what is now North Dakota where they met, fought, and finally merged with the small Sutaio tribe, adopting the Plains Indian way of life. In time they moved farther west to the BLACK HILLS of South Dakota, where LEWIS AND CLARK met them in 1804. From there they drifted farther west and south into the Plains, pushed by the hostile SIOUX and driving the KIOWAS farther south in turn. The first treaty signed by the Cheyennes with the U.S. government in 1825 promised the tribe protection and paved the way for the building of a fort in what is now southern Colorado. In 1832 a large number of the tribe, taking up residence there, became known as the Southern Cheyenne. The rest of the tribe, continuing to roam the headwaters of the Platte and Yellowstone Rivers, was designated the Northern Cheyenne. The warriors were traditionally proud and brave and had several war societies, of which the 'Dog Soldiers' was the most noted, consisting of young braves particularly trained for war. Cheyenne men were known for their fine physiques and colourful beaded BUCKSKIN and other regalia. Cheyenne women were expected to meet unusually high standards of virtue. The Southern Cheyenne under chief Black Kettle experienced two disastrous encounters with the U.S. military in the 1860s. The first was the SAND CREEK MASSACRE of 1864 in which Colorado militia under Colonel Chivington destroyed Black Kettle's village; the second came in the so-called Battle of the WASHITA in 1868 when General CUSTER attacked Black Kettle's camp, killing the chief and many of this people. From then on the Southern Cheyenne were unrelentingly bitter and hostile to the white men. Meanwhile, the Northern Cheyenne, allied with the Sioux and Northern ARAPAHO, waged war against the white soldiers and took part in the Battle of the LITTLE BIGHORN, in which Custer and many of the Seventh Cavalry were killed.

68 *Cheyenne brave, by Frederic Remington.*

69 *Jesse Chisholm.*

70 *Cowboys eating at the chuckwagon, by Frederic Remington.*

71 *John S. Chisum.*

After the Custer fight, bands of Northern Cheyenne were taken south and put on the Cheyenne-Arapaho Reservation in INDIAN TERRITORY (Oklahoma). Many sickened in the alien climate but their pleas to return to their former homeland were refused. In September 1878 some 300 Cheyennes, men, women and children under chiefs Dull Knife and Little Wolf set out for their former homes. Thousands of troops pursued the small band of Indians, many of whom were killed in the struggle to reach the north. Dull Knife and his followers were captured and imprisoned at Fort Robinson, Nebraska. In a second attempt to escape, most of them, including Dull Knife, were killed. Little Wolf and his party reached Wyoming, where they surrendered. In 1883 the last of the Northern Cheyenne in the Indian Territory settled on a reservation on the Tongue River in Montana, where their descendants live today.

The Fighting Cheyennes by G. B. Grinnell (New York, 1956);
Cheyenne Autumn by M. Sandoz (New York, 1953);
The Cheyenne Indians, Their History and Ways of Life by G. B. Grinnell (New York, 1962).

CHISHOLM TRAIL

The Most famous of the long drive cattle trails from TEXAS over which an estimated four million LONGHORNS were driven to the railhead cattle towns of Kansas. When Joseph McCOY established ABILENE, Kansas as the first cattle town in 1867 he publicized the route pioneered by Jesse Chisholm, a half-breed trader, and it became known as the Chisholm Trail. It ran north right across central Texas, with feeder trails leading into it, traversed the INDIAN TERRITORY (Oklahoma) and halfway across Kansas to Abilene. En route the long trail crossed a number of major rivers, the Colorado, the Brazos, the RED, the Cimarron, the Canadian and the ARKANSAS. It was a popular route with the Texas cowboys, embracing the best fords and water holes, and with plenty of grass for cattle to feed on. Between 1867 and 1871 about 1½ million longhorns trod the Chisholm Trail to Abilene. After Abilene ceased to be a cattle depot the trail led to other Kansas cowtowns; when DODGE CITY became the major railhead, the Chisholm Trail branched off near Caldwell, Kansas and went direct to Dodge. The trail lost its importance in the 1880s when Texas railroads took over the task of moving cattle north.

The Chisholm Trail: A History of the World's Greatest Cattle Trail by S. P. Ridings (Guthrie, Oklahoma, 1936);
Chisholm Trail and Other Routes by T. U. Tayler (San Antonio, Texas, 1936);
The Chisholm Trail by W. Gard (Norman, Oklahoma, 1954);
Great American Cattle Trails by H. S. Drago (New York, 1965).

CHISUM, John
1824-84

A powerful cattle king of NEW MEXICO, John Simpson Chisum started with a few head of stray LONGHORNS and became one of the biggest individual cattle owners in North America, with between 60,000 and 100,000 head. Born in Tennessee, he moved with his family to Texas in 1837 where he became a building contractor and county clerk for Lamar County. In 1854 he entered the cattle business, selling beef to INDIAN RESERVATIONS. In 1867 he moved to New Mexico and established a large spread at South Spring in Old Lincoln County where he prospered greatly. He became involved in the LINCOLN COUNTY WAR of 1878-9 in which he opposed the Murphy-Dolan faction and backed cattleman J. H. Tunstall, whose gunfighter-cowboys included BILLY THE KID. It is said that Chisum paid the Kid 500 dollars for his services in the Lincoln County conflict. If Chisum was instrumental in making Billy the Kid an outlaw killer, he also figured large in his destruction; he used his considerable influence in getting Pat GARRETT elected sheriff of Lincoln County in 1880, and it was Garrett who hunted down and killed the young outlaw. Chisum's cattle brand was the Long Rail, a long, straight mark extending from shoulder to flank; he also marked his cattle with the 'jingle-bob' ear cut (see BRANDING). Chisum, who never married, died at Eureka Springs, Arkansas, leaving an estate of some 500,000 dollars.

The True Story of Billy the Kid by W. L. Hamlin (New York, 1959);
The Cattle Kings by L. Atherton (Bloomington, Indiana, 1961);
Heroes Without Glory by Jack Schaefer (London, 1968).

CHUCKWAGON

A covered wagon with an upright chuck box (a kind of kitchen cabinet) at the rear. The chuckwagon was an essential vehicle on the long CATTLE DRIVES for it not only carried food for the cowboys but also their bedrolls and other equipment. The cook was usually the second highest paid of the trail crew, the trail boss being number one. The traditional design of the chuckwagon was attributed to cattle king Charles GOODNIGHT, who in 1866 adapted an army wagon for the purpose. The chuck box was fitted with compartments to hold provisions and utensils, and its tailgate door dropped down to form a table on which the cook could work. The wagon carried a water barrel, flour box, coffee grinder, tool box and all essential implements; a leather sling under the wagon carried wood and dried buffalo 'chips' (dung) for the fire, which was made in a pit to avoid setting the prairie alight. The chuckwagon was the focal point of a trail or ROUND-UP camp and here the cowboys would eat, tell stories and sing. A favourite dish was 'son-of-a-bitch' stew of which every cook had his own version; in fact almost anything went into it. There was always plenty of beef available and it seems that cowboys liked their steak well done and their coffee strong and black. A great delicacy was the broiled testicles of a steer, which the cowboys called 'prairie oysters'.

Come An' Get it, the Story of the Old Cowboy Cook by R. F. Adams (Norman, Oklahoma, 1952);
Frontier Ways by E. E. Dale (San Antonio, Texas, 1959);
The Real Cowboy by Philip Morris Incorporated (London, 1976).

COCHISE
?-1874

Famous chief of the Chiricahua APACHES of Arizona. Little is known of his birth or early life. He was tall for an Apache; Captain Bourke describes him as, 'a fine-looking Indian, straight as a rush. . .deep-chested and roman-nosed. . . There was neither in speech or action any of the bluster characteristic of his race.' It appears there is no authentic photograph of Cochise; the one often published as Cochise (from the Arizona Historical Society) is not Cochise but Juan Rey, a Pueblo councillor. Although constantly fighting their traditional enemy, the Mexicans, Cochise and his people were friendly enough with American settlers in the 1850s. In 1861 the Chiricahuas were wrongfully accused of abducting a half-breed boy (said to be Mickey FREE) and Cochise and several relatives were seized by troops; Cochise escaped, wounded. He captured three white men and offered to exchange them for his relatives; when the offer was refused he killed his captives and the army hanged the Apaches. Cochise embarked on a campaign of revenge. With the Civil War in progress there were few troops in Arizona and they could not stop the Chiricahua depredations against white settlers. At the end of 1862 General Carleton and 3,000 California volunteers marched into south-eastern Arizona to crush the Apaches. Cochise and MANGAS COLORADAS, chief of the Mimbreno Apache, defended Apache Pass against the volunteers until forced to retreat by howitzers. With the death of Mangas, Cochise became principal chief of the Apaches when troops returned from the Civil War to mount a campaign of extermination against them. Driven into the Dragoon Mountains with 200 warriors, Cochise kept the U.S. army at bay for over ten years and continued to raid settlements. In June 1871 Lieutenant Colonel George CROOK took command of the Department of Arizona and employed Apache scouts to hunt down the hostiles, most of whom were soon brought to the reservations. Cochise surrendered in September 1871 and resigned himself to living on the Chiricahua Reservation in Arizona until his death in 1874. Arizona's Cochise County was named after him.

On the Border with Crook by J. G. Bourke (New York, 1891);
Apache Indians by F. C. Lockwood (New York, 1938);
The Conquest of Apacheria by D. L. Thrapp (Norman, Oklahoma, 1967);
Bury My Heart at Wounded Knee by D. Brown (New York, 1971).

COLORADO

In the context of the Old West, Colorado was the land of gold, silver, cowboys, and the ROCKY MOUNTAINS, the latter covering two fifths of the State. The LOUISIANA PURCHASE of 1803 brought most of eastern Colorado into the United States and victory over Mexico obtained western Colorado in 1848. Zebulon M. PIKE explored the land in 1806 and discovered the peak that bears his name. From 1800 to 1840 the MOUNTAIN MEN roamed and explored the Colorado Rockies in search of beaver and these hardy men later guided government expeditions through the mountains. BENT'S FORT, an important fur-trading post, was established on the ARKANSAS RIVER in south-eastern Colorado in the early 1830s. In 1858 gold was found in the PIKE'S PEAK region and people flocked to the new Eldorado; the Territory of Colorado was created in 1861 and Statehood came in 1876, with Denver the capital. It was good cattle country with rich pastures and in the late 1860s LONGHORNS were brought up from Texas over the GOODNIGHT-LOVING TRAIL; by 1869 Colorado had one million longhorns and ranchers began improving the breed with Hereford bulls. The mountain-dwelling UTE INDIANS seem to have been the only indigenous tribe of Colorado. The APACHES made intermittent raids into the territory; the ARAPAHOS, CHEYENNES, COMANCHES, and KIOWAS hunted and warred over parts of eastern Colorado. The discovery of silver in the San Juan Mountains brought another rush of white people, which resulted in warfare with the Utes. In 1873 the Utes abandoned the area and in 1881 were removed to reservations. Today, two groups of Utes — Southern Utes and Ute Mountain Tribes — occupy adjoining reservations in the south-west corner of Colorado.

Colorado Range Cattle Industry by O. B. Peake (Glendale, California, 1937);
Colorado and Its People edited by L. R. Hafen (New York, 1948);
The Colorado Story: A History of Your State and Mine by L. R. Hafen and A. W. Hafen (Denver, 1953);
A Colorado History by C. Ubbelohde (Boulder, Colorado, 1965).

COLT REVOLVERS

The Colt six-shooters produced by Colt's Patent Fire Arms Manufacturing Company at Hartford, Connecticut were the most popular revolvers of the Old West, used by the U.S. Army, working cowboys, pioneers and gunfighters. The most celebrated Colt, the 'Peacemaker' model of 1873 is the type usually seen in Western films; also called the New Model Army revolver it was adopted by the U.S. government for military use. The .45 calibre Peacemaker was a single-action weapon in which the hammer was hand-cocked, usually by the thumb, for each shot; in the later double-action or self-cocking revolver a single pull on the trigger both cocked and fired the gun. The Peacemaker was produced in a variety of calibres and barrel lengths; the variant with an extra long barrel and attachable shoulder stock is known as the BUNTLINE SPECIAL. The Peacemaker chambered to take the same cartridge as the .44-.40 WINCHESTER Model 1873 repeating rifle was known as the Colt 'Frontier Model'. Colt's original production revolver of 1836, a five-shot, had found particular favour with the TEXAS RANGERS, who had used the gun with devastating and surprising effect against the COMANCHE INDIANS, who were accustomed to being fired at with single-shot weapons. The first six-shot Colt was the .44 calibre 'Walker' model of 1847. Following suggestions made by Captain Samuel H. Walker of the Texas Rangers, Samuel Colt designed a new model of which the U.S. government ordered 1,000 for use in the

72 *Colt's Patent Fire Arms Manufactory, Hartford, Conn. about 1862.*

73 *Paterson Colt five-shot of 1836.*

74 *Walker Colt six-shot of 1847.*

75 *Navy Colt six-shot of 1851.*

76 *Colt 'Peacemaker' of 1873.*

72 V

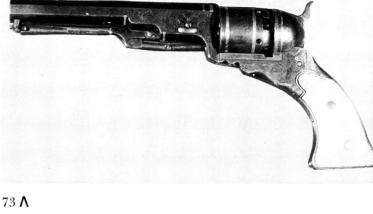

73 Λ

74 Λ

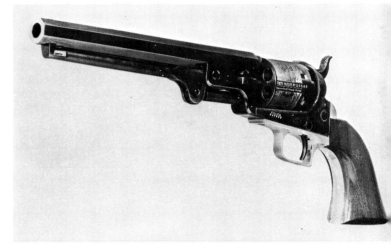

75 Λ   76 V

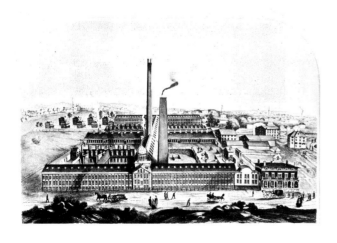

MEXICAN WAR. All Colt revolvers up to the Peacemaker model were of the percussion type, loaded with lead balls and black powder and fired by a percussion cap. The success of the Walker Colt established the reputation of Colt revolvers, of which many different models were made. Another notable type was the .36 calibre Navy Model of 1851, manufactured with variations until 1872; Wild Bill HICKOK was just one of many GUNFIGHTERS who used a Navy Colt. The Colt.44 calibre New Model Army of 1860 was the principal revolver used by Northern and Southern forces in the Civil War; over 200,000 being produced from 1860 to 1873. With the perfection of the metallic cartridge — in which cap, powder and ball were contained in a single metal case — firearms manufacture was revolutionized and a whole new line of Colt revolvers was produced, of which the Peacemaker became the most famous

and enduring; it is still in production today. The main rival revolvers of the ubiquitous Colts of the Old West were those of REMINGTON and SMITH & WESSON.

A History of the Colt Revolver by C. T. Haven and F. A. Belden (New York, 1940);
The Peacemaker and Its Rivals by J. E. Parsons (New York, 1950);
The Story of Colt's Revolver by W. B. Edwards (Harrisburg, Pennsylvania, 1957);
Guns of the Old West by C. E. Chapel (New York, 1961).

COLT, Samuel 1814-62

The American inventor of the first practical revolving pistol, Sam Colt had been interested in explosives and firearms from early boyhood. At

77 *Sam Colt.*

78 *John Colter's race for life, from Indian Anecdotes and Barbarities.*

79 *Comanche warrior, by George Catlin.*

77 V

78 V

79 V

the age of seventeen he came up with the idea, and a wooden model, of a pistol with a revolving cylinder containing several charges which could be fired through a single barrel, the genesis of the Western six-shooter. His first working model blew up when fired. In 1832 he submitted a revolving pistol and a rifle, with written descriptions, to the U.S. Patent Office in Washington. The Patent, secured on 25 February 1836, was based on three principles: (1) the cocking of the hammer rotated a multi-chambered breech in a manner which aligned each chamber in succession with a single barrel; (2) the cocking action automatically locked the cylinder in position in preparation to fire; (3) each nipple, fitted with a percussion cap, was separated by a partition, thus ensuring the discharge of only that chamber in line with the barrel. Colt established a company at Paterson, New Jersey where he produced five-shot revolvers, rifles, carbines and shotguns; the company failed through lack of business. When Sam Colt designed the new six-shot 'Walker' Model of 1847, the U.S. Government placed an order for 1,000. With no factory of his own, Colt had to sub-contract to another firearms manufacturer. Then Colt set up his own plant at Hartford, Connecticut and produced successful firearms for the U.S. and foreign markets. With business booming he built a new factory in Hartford and converted his concern into a corporation — Colt's Patent Fire Arms Manufacturing Company. In the Civil War the Colt armoury produced more than 300,000 revolvers and 100,000 muskets and rifles. Sam Colt died in January 1862; able successors carried on his enterprise and as Americans moved westward, COLT REVOLVERS went with them.

A History of the Colt Revolver by C. T. Haven and F. A. Belden (New York, 1940);
Samuel Colt, a Man and an Epoch by M. Rywell (Harriman, Tennessee, 1952).

COLTER, John
1775-1813

A beaver trapper and explorer, John Colter was described as 'a man born for hardy endurance of fatigue, privation and perils', and he is celebrated in the annals of the Old West for his amazing 'run for life' from BLACKFEET INDIANS in 1808. Born in Virginia, he was a member of the LEWIS AND CLARK EXPEDITION of 1804-6 which explored the newly acquired LOUISIANA PURCHASE. During the winter of 1807-8 he made a remarkable solo exploration through country unknown to white men; in his 500-mile journey through what is now Wyoming, Montana, and Idaho he was the first white man to see the natural wonders of YELLOWSTONE NATIONAL PARK. In the fall of 1808 Colter was trapping in Montana with a companion, John Potts, when they were attacked by a large party of Blackfeet; Potts was killed and Colter taken alive for torture. The Indians decided to make Colter run for his life, while they ran after him, intent on killing him when they caught up with him. Stripped naked and given a 400-yard start, he dashed off with 500 warriors in hot pursuit. Colter ran until the exertion caused blood to stream from his nose and mouth; he out-ran the Indians until only one pursuer remained. Colter stopped and killed the Indian with the latter's own lance, then walked for seven days until he reached the safety of a trading post. Colter spent the last years of his life on a farm in Missouri.

John Colter, Discoverer of Yellowstone Park by S. Vinton (New York, 1926);
John Colter: His Years in the Rockies by B. Harris (New York, 1952).

COMANCHE INDIANS

Famed as the finest horsemen of the West, the Comanches were an offshoot of the SHOSHONI of Wyoming. Nomadic buffalo hunters, they made little agricultural use of the land and lived entirely on the South-western Plains in the easily transported TIPI. They had a reputation for dash and courage and, although relatively few in numbers, considered themselves superior to neighbouring tribes. The name 'Comanche' comes from the Spanish *Komantcia*, a derivative of the UTE Indian word *kohmahts*, meaning 'enemy'. For nearly 200 years they waged war against the Spaniards in Mexico; they became bitter enemies of the Texans who had taken their best hunting grounds and fought them relentlessly for almost forty years. Comanche depredations in Texas and northern Mexico made their name synonymous with terror. Horses were their source of power; they either caught them wild, bought or stole them and bred them until an ordinary brave might own 250 horses and a chief more than 1,000. George CATLIN, the artist who lived among the Indians, regarded the squat, bow-legged Comanche as an ugly tribe compared with other PLAINS INDIANS; but he praised them as 'the most extraordinary horsemen I have ever seen. . .A Comanche on his feet is out of his element and comparatively almost awkward [an affinity shared with the old time COWBOY] but the moment he lays hand upon his horse he gracefully flies away like an entirely different being.' Wildest and fiercest of Comanches was the Kwahadi band; QUANAH PARKER, halfbreed son of a Comanche chief and a captured white girl, Cynthia Ann Parker, grew up to become a great Kwahadi chief. By the Treaty of Medicine Lodge in 1867 most of the Comanches agreed to go to a reservation in south-western Oklahoma, where their descendants live today.

North American Indians by G. Catlin (Edinburgh, 1926);
The Comanche Barrier to the South Plains Settlement by R. N. Richardson (Glendale, California, 1933);
The Comanches: Lords of the South Plains by E. Wallace and E. A. Hoebel (Norman, Oklahoma, 1952);
Comanches, the Destruction of a People by T. R. Fehrenbach (London, 1975).

COMANCHEROS

The Comancheros were Spanish-Mexican traders of NEW MEXICO who had special dealings with the COMANCHE INDIANS, following a peace agreement made in 1786 between Comanche chiefs and the Spanish officer Don Juan Bautista de Anza. Until de Anza's arrival in the Spanish province of New Mexico in 1779 the dreaded Comanches raided the settlements almost with impunity. With the specific intent of demonstrating his strength, de Anza led a number of successful punitive expeditions against the Comanches; having proved his point he made an offer of peace with honour and trade. The Comanches, weary of Spanish retaliation, accepted de Anza's offer as a sensible arrangement; their depredations ceased in New Mexico and traders were allowed to visit Comanche camps with various goods. These traders became known as Comancheros. However, the unyielding Anglo-Americans of the south-west failed to understand this peaceful coexistence with the Indians and viewed the Comancheros as unscrupulous renegades. The Texans, in particular, execrated the traders for supplying the Comanches with firearms (and later, repeating rifles) in exchange for stolen Texas livestock.

Forgotten Frontiers: A Study of the Spanish Indian Policy of Don Juan Bautista de Anza, Governor of New Mexico by A. B. Thomas (Norman, Oklahoma, 1932);
Comanches, the Destruction of a People by T. R. Fehrenbach (London, 1975).

CONCORD COACH

The stagecoach, carrying the U.S. Mail, passengers, gold and other valuables, played an important role in the Old West before the spreading of railroads across the land. And the most celebrated of stagecoaches was the handsome Concord coach. This four-wheeled symbol of the West was a product of the East, built by the Abbot-Downing Company of Concord, New Hampshire, founded by Lewis Downing and J. Stephens Abbot in 1826. Constructed by highly skilled craftsmen and stoutly built of the best timber, with an interior of fine leather, polished metal, and wood panelling the Concord coach earned a reputation for comfort and durability. The Concord's solidity made it possible to carry a large passenger payload: basic designs included six, nine, and twelve passenger versions and the heavier coaches seated up to a dozen men on the roof. The success of the Concord was chiefly due to its distinctive suspension; unlike other manufacturers who used metal spring-like suspensions, Abbot-Downing employed leather 'thoroughbraces'. These thoroughbraces were multi-layered leather straps of thick steerhide which supported the coach body, one on each side, running lengthwise, and functioned as shock absorbers, permitting the coach body to ride relatively smoothly over rough terrain while travelling at speed. The thoroughbraces gave a swaying motion to the coach, often causing a feeling of seasickness among the crowded passengers; Mark Twain, however, described the Concord as 'an imposing cradle on wheels'. The coach had leather boots (storage compartments) front and rear; the boot under the driver's seat usually carried the strong box with valuables, the larger boot at the rear carried passenger baggage. Curtains of leather or canvas could be rolled down to protect passengers against rain, dust and cold weather. The driver, known as the 'Whip' or 'Jehu', managed his four or six-horse team with great skill; sitting beside him would be the armed guard or 'shotgun'. Concord coaches were purchased by all the major stage lines and express companies and a total of 3,000 were built. Abbot and Downing dissolved their partnership in 1847 but continued making coaches in separate plants; in 1865 Downing's sons merged the two firms and the Abbot-Downing Company continued making Concord coaches until 1900.

The Overland Mail by L. R. Hafen (Cleveland, Ohio, 1926);
Via Western Express and Stagecoach by O. O. Winther (Stanford, California, 1945);
The Transportation Frontier: Trans-Mississippi West, 1865-1890 by O. O. Winther (New York, 1964);
Abbot-Downing and the Concord Coach by The New Hampshire Historical Society (Concord, 1965).

CONQUISTADORES

The Spanish influence in shaping the culture, geography and genetics of Mexico and the American Far West was considerable. The vanguard of this pervasive influence were the *Conquistadores* (conquerors) of the sixteenth century. These hardy soldier-frontiersmen established settlements, subdued the Indians and explored vast tracts of land; it was mostly the search for gold that drove them on into the unknown. Hernando Cortes conquered Mexico in 1519-21 and over the next 300 years Spanish

80 ∧

81 ∨

80 *Concord coach used by Wells Fargo & Company.*

81 *A Conquistador, by Frederic Remington.*

cross-breeding with the natives produced the Mexican race. In 1539 Hernando de Soto with 500 men and 200 horses marched from Tampa Bay, Florida, and in four years wandered over Georgia, the Carolinas, Tennessee, Alabama, Mississippi, Arkansas, Texas and Oklahoma; they were the first Europeans to see the MISSISSIPPI RIVER. In 1540-2 Francisco Vasquez Coronado led his famous expedition in search of the legendary 'Cibola', a place of seven cities filled with gold, which resulted in a 300-year Spanish occupation of what is now New Mexico. Coronado's party penetrated Arizona (the first white men to see the GRAND CANYON), New Mexico, Texas, Oklahoma, and probably as far east as Kansas. In New Mexico they came upon sedentary Indians living in permanent villages of stone and ADOBE houses and called them PUEBLOS (village dwellers). However, it was not until 1598 that the Spanish invaders began to influence Pueblo life; in that year Don Juan de Onate began to colonize New Mexico and gave Indian villages the Spanish saint names they have today. In 1610 the Spanish established headquarters at La Villa Real de la

82 ∧

Santa Fe de San Francisco de Assissi, which later became Santa Fe, capital of New Mexico. In 1602-3 Sebastian Vizcaino surveyed the coast of California and a Spanish colony was established at San Diego in 1769. As elsewhere, the first years of Spanish occupation of California were traumatic for the native Indians, who were subjected to *de facto* slavery to serve the settlements and the twenty-one Franciscan Missions. Although primarily established to convert the Indians to Christianity the Missions were also centres of culture and agriculture. In 1690 Alonso de León led an expedition into Texas and built the outpost of San Francisco de los Tejas on the Neches River; and some thirty years later the Spanish established the Villa of San Antonio de Béxar, which later became San Antonio. Wherever the Spanish ventured in the New World they took horses and cattle with them; indeed it was they who introduced the horse to the Americas, and horses transformed the hitherto pedestrian life of the PLAINS INDIANS. And it was Spanish cattle which evolved into the rugged Texas LONGHORN which established the great cattle industry of that cowboy State.

Spanish Exploration in the Southwest by H. E. Bolton (New York, 1916);
De Soto and the Conquistadores by M. Theodore (New York, 1930).
Coronado, Knight of Pueblos and Plains by H. E. Bolton (New York, 1950);
The Spanish Conquistadores by F. A. Kirkpatrick (New York, 1934);
Conquistadores: Men or Devils? by J. F. Bannon (New York, 1960);
Gold, Glory, and the Gospel by L. B. Wright (New York, 1970).

COWBOY

The Anglo-American cowboy originated in TEXAS in the middle of the nineteenth century. His methods of handling cattle on horseback, his practical work clothes and equipment and much

82 *Cowboy trail boss in Montana, 1887.*

83 *Cowboys preparing to stand night guard, 1890s.*

83 ∧

of his vocabulary were adopted and adapted from the VAQUERO, the Spanish Mexican cowboy who predated the Texan type. The genesis of the American cowboy and the great cattle industry of the United States of the 1870s and 1880s lay in the rugged LONGHORN cattle of Texas, which during the Civil War had roamed mostly untended over the vast plains of the south-west. At the war's end in 1865 the herds of feral longhorns had proliferated greatly to the extent of some five million head. The northern and eastern parts of the U.S. were in need of meat and prepared to pay high prices; Texas had beef on the hoof in abundance and so began the long CATTLE DRIVES north in which the hard riding Texas cowboy made his indelible mark on American history. The cattle business soon spread north and west from Texas to Kansas, Wyoming, Montana, the Dakotas, New Mexico, Colorado and Arizona; by 1880 the cattle industry had covered the great Plains of the West. The cowboy not only drove

cattle to market but worked on the big spreads where cattle was raised, taking part in the ROUND-UP and the BRANDING of the animals. A cowboy's life style was distinctive; he spent most of his long day in the saddle and his clothes and gear were fashioned for equestrian labour. He was happier on horseback than on his own feet. It was a hard life and a dirty job, often dangerous and with little reward for the ordinary cow hand, who, in the 1870s earned thirty to forty dollars a month. Mostly illiterate and without ambition, cowboys with money after a four-month trail drive would quickly blow the lot on drink and gambling in a railhead cattle town like DODGE CITY, Kansas. There were many Negro cowboys, just as skilled in handling cattle and horses as their white colleagues; Nat Love was a famous black cowboy. To the settled townsfolk and farmers of the day, the transient cowboy was a wild man who brought cattle and trouble; to city readers of dime novels he was a romantic hero on horseback; to his boss he was a loyal, hardworking hand; to himself, the cowboy was a superior being, a free spirit who acknowledged no master and looked down on people who worked on foot. The cowboy's functional dress displayed his profession. His BOOTS were made for riding not walking. He wore leather CHAPS to protect his legs when riding in thorny brush. His wide-brimmed STETSON hat was a versatile piece of headgear, as was the bandana round his neck which served as a mask against trail dust, a tourniquet in an emergency, and had various other uses. The cowboy's heavy SADDLE, Spanish in origin, had a horn in front and a high back; when he roped a cow with his LARIAT he would wrap the rope's end around the horn. A cowboy usually carried a gun as protection against wild animals, RATTLESNAKES, hostile Indians and cattle thieves. The cattle industry dominated the Great Plains from 1870 to 1885 — the heyday of the cowboy — but overstocking of the ranges brought a sharp decline in prices; the terrible winter of 1886-7 decimated the herds and brought disaster to many big cattlemen, and farmers, barbed wire, and railroads spreading over the plains ended the open range phase of the cattle industry. The cowboy of the Old West faded into legend and his modern counterpart is a different character.

The Story of the Cowboy by E. Hough (New York, 1897);
The Cowboy by P. A. Rollins (New York, 1922);
The American Cowboy: The Myth and the Reality by J. B. Frantz and J. E. Choate (Norman, Oklahoma, 1955);
The Old Time Cowhand by R. F. Adams (New York, 1961);
The Negro Cowboys by P. Durham and E. L. Jones (New York, 1965);
The American Cowboy by H. McCracken (New York, 1973);
The First Cowboy: and Those who Followed by C. Zurhorst (London, 1974).

COYOTE
Canis Latrans

The night howl of the coyote is one of the haunting wilderness sounds of the West. This cunning little prairie wolf, which resembles a small collie dog, ranges widely throughout the Western States and because it preys on small domestic livestock, man has waged relentless war against it. In the wild, coyotes exist on rodents, RABBITS, mesquite beans, fruit, nuts, and beetles. An adult coyote attains a length of about four feet and can run at forty m.p.h. Its eerie night calling has given rise to many legends and superstitions: it was the 'medicine wolf' of the Indians and MOUNTAIN MEN, harbinger of good luck or bad, fine weather or foul, depending on the time the howl was heard. Despite man's campaign to exterminate it, the coyote persists in large numbers, having learned to be wary of traps and poisoned meat; it has adapted itself to advancing civilization where other wild animals have perished to the edge of extinction. In Indian legend the coyote will be the last animal on earth.

Mammals of North America by V. Cahalane (New York, 1947);
American Wildlife by W. G. Van Name (New York, 1961);
The Clever Coyote by S. P. Young and H. H. T. Jackson (Harrisburg, Pennsylvania, 1951).

CRAZY HORSE
c. 1840-77

Eminent fighting chief of the Oglala SIOUX, Crazy Horse was an implacable enemy of the white man. An inspiring leader of considerable military skill he enjoyed a number of victories over U.S. troops and took part in the shattering defeat of General CUSTER at the Battle of the LITTLE BIGHORN. Of medium height, lithe and sinewy, he was a warrior and a mystic; in a dream his horse performed a wild and crazy dance, and so he took the name Crazy Horse. He married a CHEYENNE girl and this brought him close affiliation with the tribe. He played a leading role in the FETTERMAN MASSACRE in December 1866 in which Captain Fetterman and eighty soldiers were wiped out near FORT PHIL KEARNY during chief RED CLOUD'S War along the BOZEMAN TRAIL. Unlike Red Cloud, Crazy Horse did not settle on Sioux lands established by the 1868 FORT LARAMIE Treaty, but with his followers stayed in the unceded buffalo country to the west. In December 1875 the authority in Washington, alarmed by reports of Sioux hostilities, directed that all Indians return to government agencies by 31 January 1876. When some bands failed to meet the deadline, General George CROOK was ordered into the field against them. In June 1876 Crook's column of some 1,300 men clashed with Crazy Horse and 1,500 Sioux and Cheyenne warriors at the Rosebud River in Montana; the Battle of the ROSEBUD started in the morning and ended in the afternoon when both sides broke off and withdrew. Neither side could claim a decisive victory but Crazy Horse had given Crook a bloody nose. A week later Custer attacked a large encampment of Sioux and Cheyenne and Crazy Horse played a leading role in defeating the Seventh Cavalry. In January 1877 General Nelson A. MILES surprised Crazy Horse's winter camp, scattering the Indians without food or adequate clothing on the frozen plain. Several months later Crazy Horse and his people surrendered to General Crook at the Red Cloud Agency in Nebraska. But Crazy Horse could not endure reservation life; rumours spread that he was planning to escape and on 5 September 1877 he was placed under arrest and taken to Fort Robinson. Realizing he was to be locked up in a

84 ∧   85 ∨

84   *Crazy Horse, painted by Robert Lindneux.*

85   *Coyote.*

86   *Davy Crockett in the Battle of the Alamo.*

86 ∨

cell, Crazy Horse attempted to escape and a white soldier thrust his bayonet into the struggling chief, who died that night.

Crazy Horse, the Strange Man of the Oglalas by M. Sandoz (New York, 1945);
Crazy Horse, the Invincible Oglala Chief by E. A. Brininstool (New York, 1949);
Bury My Heart at Wounded Knee by D. Brown (New York, 1971).

CROCKETT, Davy
1786-1836

Frontiersman, army scout, Congressman, and a folk hero in his own time, David Crockett had little formal education but his native wit and

87 *General George Crook.*

88 *A Crow warrior.*

87 ∧

88 ∨

backwoods humour made him a popular representative of his people. Born in Tennessee, he grew up a skilled hunter and marksman. He ran away from home at the age of thirteen and after some years wandering settled on a farm in Lincoln County, Tennessee. After serving in the Creek Indian War of 1813-14 as a scout under Andrew Jackson, he moved to Giles County, Tennessee, where he was appointed justice of the peace, elected colonel of militia, and in 1821 voted into the legislature. Ever a restless soul, he moved to the western part of the State and spent some time in the wilderness hunting bears, claiming to have killed 105 of them in nine months. In 1823 he was again elected to the legislature and then decided to run for Congress; he won the campaign and went to Washington where he was called the 'Coonskin Congressman'. He served three terms in Congress and on losing his campaign for a fourth term decided to leave Tennessee for pastures new. Hearing of the Texans' fight for freedom against Mexico he gathered a dozen Tennessee volunteers and went to TEXAS to aid the rebels. He arrived in San Antonio early in February 1836 and died on the last day of the Battle of the ALAMO.

David Crockett by V. F. Taylor (San Antonio, 1974).

CROOK, George 1829-90

One of the U.S. Army's most distinguished frontier commanders, General George Crook fought in a number of Indian campaigns of the latter half of the nineteenth century. He had great sympathy for the Indians' hopeless struggle against white encroachment and in victory would rather pardon than punish them. Born in Ohio, he graduated from West Point in 1852 and was commissioned Lieutenant of infantry. He served with distinction in the Civil War as a fighting commander and rose to the rank of brevet Major-General in the regular army. When the regular army was reorganized after the war he was appointed Lieutenant Colonel of the twenty-third Infantry and given command of the district of Boise, Idaho and was highly commended for bringing to an end the Indian war in the northwest. In 1871 he was placed in command of the Department of Arizona and charged with pacifying the hostile APACHES. His methods in dealing with them and for administering Indian reservations proved successful. When orthodox cavalry operations failed to trap the elusive Apache bands he recruited Apache scouts and formed special columns. He was a strong advocate of the use, care and training of mule pack transport, so essential in that campaign. In

1873 he was promoted Brigadier-General and in 1875 was given command of the Department of the Platte. He played a leading role in the SIOUX War of 1876, serving in the field and sharing the hardships of his troops. Crook has been described as an 'unsoldierly soldier'. He sported a forked beard, and on campaign wore a cork sun helmet and plain canvas suit, and preferred to ride a MULE instead of a horse. He did not swear, smoke, or drink coffee or liquor. His kindly, sympathetic nature made him easy to approach; he was liked and respected by his men and highly regarded by the Indians, who called him 'Chief Grey Wolf'. Honest and just in his dealings with the Indians, they came to trust his word. In 1882 he was sent back to Arizona to deal with hostile Apaches under GERONIMO, whom he induced to return to the reservation, but Geronimo fled and continued his raids. Criticized for his 'mishandling' of Geronimo and his use of Apache scouts, Crook resigned his command and was succeeded by General Nelson A. MILES, who adopted Crook's use of Apache scouts and finally brought Geronimo to heel. In 1886 Crook returned to the command of the Department of the Platte; in 1888 he was promoted to Major-General and given command of the Division of the Missouri. He died in Chicago in March 1890.

On the Border with Crook by J. G. Bourke (New York, 1891);
Campaigning with Crook by C. King (Norman, Oklahoma, 1964);
General George Crook: His Autobiography edited by M. F. Schmitt (Norman, 1960).

89 *General George Armstrong Custer, photograph by Mathew Brady.*

CROW INDIANS

Members of the Siouan linguistic family, the Crow tribe call themselves '*Absaroke*' which means 'crow or bird-people'. They once lived along the MISSOURI RIVER in what is now North Dakota; towards the end of the eighteenth century they migrated to the vicinity of the ROCKY MOUNTAINS and settled along the Yellowstone and Big Horn Rivers in Montana, and still occupy this area today. Formerly an agricultural people, the Crows became equestrian nomads in moving to the plains and took part in the meteoric rise and fall of the rich PLAINS INDIAN culture based on the buffalo and the horse. Like other Plains tribes, the Crows attached great importance to battle and highest recognition came through military valour. Led by noted warriors like Red Bear, they were constantly at war with other tribes — especially the BLACKFEET, SIOUX, and CHEYENNE — for possession of horses and hunting grounds. George CATLIN, the artist who lived among them, described the Crows as 'beautifully costumed' in white BUCKSKIN and the men, mostly six feet tall, were 'very handsome and gentlemanly Indians in their personal appearance'. The Crows were always friendly to the white men and readily joined with U.S. soldiers in fighting their traditional enemies; Crow scouts served General CUSTER in the Indian wars of the 1870s. Today the Crow reservation occupies ancestral land in south central Montana. In 1961 the Crows won a judgement against the Federal Government and won compensation of nine million dollars for lands sold and ceded in the last century.

Traditions of the Crows by S. C. Simms (Chicago, 1903);
Plenty-Coups, Chief of the Crows by F. B. Linderman (New York, 1930);
The Crow Indians by R. H. Lowie (New York, 1955).

CUSTER, George Armstrong 1839-76

As commander of the Seventh Cavalry Regiment, George Armstrong Custer gained international fame by his death and defeat at the hands of the SIOUX and CHEYENNE Indians in the Battle of the LITTLE BIGHORN, Montana, on 25 June 1876. One of the most controversial soldiers in U.S. history he has been described as both hero and villain; a dedicated officer and ruthless Indian killer; a brilliant cavalier to some, a reckless glory hunter to others. He was in truth a paradoxical combination of virtue and vice. A strict disciplinarian with those he commanded, Custer himself was often insubordinate and disobedient to his superiors and was once court-martialled and suspended from rank and command for a year. He neither smoked, drank liquor, nor used bad language; he was, however, an inveterate gambler. He possessed great physical endurance and his men called him 'hard arse' from his capacity to remain in the saddle for many hours. The Indians called him 'Yellow Hair' or 'Long Hair' because he wore his light-coloured hair in the long frontier fashion. He was devoted to his wife Elizabeth ('Libbie') who followed him from one frontier post to another during his service on the plains. Born in Ohio, the great grandson of a Hessian officer named Küster, he graduated from West Point in 1861 at the bottom of his class. Serving with the Federal army in the Civil War he distinguished himself in battle as a cavalry officer and, at the age of twenty-three, was made a brevet Brigadier-General; as the youngest to hold that rank in the American army since the Frenchman Lafayette, he won the sobriquet 'the Boy General'. Then came promotion to brevet Major-General in the regular army and Major-General of volunteers. After the war when the volunteer army was disbanded and the regular army reorganized, Custer was appointed Lieutenant-Colonel and in 1866 was assigned as second-in-command of the newly formed Seventh Cavalry, but as a matter of military courtesy and custom was still addressed as 'General Custer'. Because the colonel never joined the Seventh Cavalry (being kept on detached service) Lieutenant-Colonel Custer remained the active commander of the regiment until his death. He led the Seventh in campaigns against the PLAINS INDIANS and in November 1868 scored a signal victory in the Battle of the WASHITA when he attacked and destroyed a Cheyenne village. In 1874 he led an exploring expedition through the BLACK HILLS of the Sioux Reservation, which resulted in the discovery of gold and contributed largely to the Sioux War of 1876 in which Custer and some 225 under his immediate command were wiped out at the Little Bighorn. In his famous 'Last Stand' Custer achieved an immortality that not even the most spectacular victory could have won him.

My Life on the Plains by G. A. Custer (New York, 1874);
Custer, Last of the Cavaliers by F. Hunt (New York, 1928);
Life of General Custer by M. Ronsheim (Cadiz, Ohio, 1929);
Glory Hunter: a Life of General Custer by F. F. Van de Water (Indianapolis, 1934);
The Custer Myth by W. A. Graham (Harrisburg, Pennsylvania, 1953);
Custer's Luck by E. I. Stewart (Norman, Oklahoma, 1971);
Custer, Man and Myth by M. Anglo (London, 1976).

D

DAKOTA

When Congress created the Dakota Territory in 1861 this vast frontier area of the northern plains embraced the present States of North and South Dakota and much of what is now WYOMING and MONTANA. The two Dakotas did not achieve separate Statehood until 1889. The first white men to visit the Dakotas were French explorers from Canada in the mid-eighteenth century. The land was part of the immense LOUISIANA PURCHASE that the United States bought from France in 1803; in the following year LEWIS AND CLARK explored the Dakotas. In 1832 Pierre Chouteau of the AMERICAN FUR COMPANY established the trading post Fort Pierre, the first permanent settlement in South Dakota, and George CATLIN came to the area to paint the Indians. Of the many tribes that inhabited the Dakotas, the most prominent were the SIOUX, also known as the Dakota Indians. The FORT LARAMIE Treaty of 1868 established a Great Sioux Reservation that included all of what is now South Dakota west of the MISSOURI RIVER. When General CUSTER discovered gold in the BLACK HILLS in 1874, prospectors invaded Sioux territory and this resulted in the war of 1876 in which the Sioux defeated Custer's Seventh Cavalry in the Battle of the LITTLE BIGHORN. The Sioux, however, lost the war and in 1877 gave up the Black Hills. The gold seekers rushed in and the mining towns of DEADWOOD, Custer, Lead, and Spearfish were established. In 1878 came the rush for land known as the Great Dakota Boom and soon both the Black Hills and the plains were occupied by settlers. In the early 1880s two remarkable men came to Dakota Territory to ranch and leave their mark on the land. The Frenchman the Marquis de MORES founded the town of Medora, North Dakota; and Theodore ROOSEVELT (later to become President of the United States) set up the Elkhorn Ranch on the Little Missouri River. In 1947 an Act of Congress established the Theodore Roosevelt National Memorial Park in the Little Missouri Badlands of North Dakota. The two Dakotas, North and South, achieved Statehood on the same day, 2 November 1889. In December 1890 the final flicker of Sioux hostility was ruthlessly stamped out by the army at WOUNDED KNEE Creek in South Dakota.

History of Dakota Territory by G. W. Kingsbury (Chicago, 1915);
Dakota Territory, 1861-1889: A Study of Frontier Policies by H. R. Lamar (Yale University Press, 1956);
Bury My Heart at Wounded Knee by D. Brown (New York, 1971).

90 *The dead Dalton gang; top left, the wounded Emmett.*

91 ∧

92 ∨

91 *Buffalo Bill and the Deadwood coach.*

92 *Breakfast Canyon, Death Valley, California.*

93 *Deadwood in 1876.*

93 ∧

formed a gang and began robbing trains, first in California then in Oklahoma Territory. In February 1891 Grat Dalton was captured but escaped from his escort by jumping from a moving train into a river. The brothers continued holding up trains, then Bob decided on a spectacular raid on Coffeyville in which they would rob two banks at the same time, in the hope of outshining the exploits of Jesse James. The Daltons with Dick Broadwell, Bill Powers (alias Tim Evans), and Bill DOOLIN rode towards the town; Doolin's horse went lame and he did not accompany the others into Coffeyville. While the five bandits were holding up the Condon and First National banks, the town was alerted and as the gang attempted to escape four of them were shot dead in a fierce gunfight with the angry citizens; four of the citizens were also killed and three wounded. The badly-wounded Emmett survived and received a life sentence; he served fourteen years until pardoned. He became a respectable businessman, collaborated in writing the book, *When the Daltons Rode,* and died in Los Angeles in 1937. There were two other Dalton brothers, Frank and Bill. Frank was killed in 1888 while serving as a lawman and Bill, a member of the Doolin gang, was shot dead in 1894 by a deputy marshal.

The Dalton Brothers by 'Eyewitness' (Chicago, 1892, and New York, 1954);
When the Daltons Rode by E. Dalton and J. Jungmeyer (New York, 1931);
A Dynasty of Western Outlaws by P. I. Wellman (New York, 1960).

DALTON BROTHERS

The Dalton brothers — Robert, Grattan, and Emmett — were robbers and killers whose gang came to a bloody end while carrying out a bank raid in the Kansas town of Coffeyville on 5 October 1892. Cousins of the outlaw YOUNGER BROTHERS who rode with Jesse JAMES, the Daltons were born in Cass County, Missouri. In the late 1880s they served short terms as lawmen but were discharged for dubious activities. In 1890 they

DEADWOOD, South Dakota

One of the most famous mining towns of the Old West, Deadwood sprang to life during the gold rush to the BLACK HILLS in the latter half of the 1870s. Laid out in April 1876 in Deadwood Gulch, the town consisted of little more than a single main street of wooden buildings in the familiar frontier style. Deadwood is celebrated as the place where Wild Bill HICKOK met his death in August 1876; he was sitting at a table playing cards in Saloon Number Ten when he was shot in the back of the head by Jack McCall. CALAMITY JANE was another Deadwood character; when smallpox swept the town she is said to have risked her life in tending the sick. Both Calamity Jane and Wild Bill Hickok are buried in Mount Moriah cemetery, overlooking Deadwood. Today, this prosperous town attracts many tourists interested in the Old West.

Deadwood Gold by G. W. Stokes and H. R. Driggs (New York, 1926);
Old Deadwood Days by E. Bennett (New York, 1928);
The Black Hills and Their Incredible Characters by R. J. Casey (New York, 1949).

DEADWOOD STAGE

A CONCORD stage coach made famous by its regular appearances in BUFFALO BILL'S WILD WEST SHOW. Built in 1868 by the Abbott-Downing Company of Concord, New Hampshire, it originally served a stage line operating between DEADWOOD, Dakota Territory and Cheyenne, Wyoming. The coach was attacked by Indians and bandits and, according to legend, on one occasion when the driver was killed, CALAMITY JANE took up the reins and drove the coach to safety. The vehicle was eventually acquired by BUFFALO BILL Cody who featured it in his shows throughout the U.S. and Europe; 'wild' Indians would pursue the coach and Buffalo Bill would ride to the rescue on a white horse. Cody was fond of telling the story that when in London four crowned heads of Europe rode inside the coach while the Prince of Wales sat up front beside Cody the driver. 'You now hold a big poker hand, Cody,' the prince commented wittily. 'Yes', replied Cody 'four kings inside and a royal joker on the box!' Today, a coach claimed to be the original Deadwood stage is a permanent exhibit at the Buffalo Bill Historical Centre, Cody, Wyoming.

DEATH VALLEY

A desert valley in CALIFORNIA near the Nevada border, walled on all sides by mountains. It is the lowest, and in the summer the hottest and driest place in North America. Its highest recorded temperature is 134 degrees Fahrenheit and the average yearly rainfall is less than two inches. The Indians called the valley 'Tomesha' or the 'Ground Afire'. It was named Death Valley by a party of emigrants in 1849 who, seeking a short route to California, struggled through the burning, desolate region and suffered terribly, losing thirteen of the party on the way. Prospectors found silver and other precious metals in the area and each strike gave birth to a new short-lived settlement; Death Valley is famed for its lost mines and ghost towns. Even the discovery of rich deposits of borax, the 'white gold of the desert', failed to support a permanent community. It is a place of stark beauty and strange illusions and, surprisingly enough, abundant wildlife. Death Valley National Monument, established in 1933, covers some 3,000 square miles and is administered by the National Park Service. Stan Jones, a Park Ranger in Death Valley found fame and fortune in 1949 by writing and recording the hit song *Ghost Riders in the Sky;* he went on to compose music for Western movies and became a cowboy film actor.

Death Valley in '49 by M. L. Manley (New York, 1894);
Death Valley by B. Lee (New York, 1930);
Lost Mines of Death Valley by H. O. Weight (Twentynine Palms, California, 1953);
Death Valley Story by F. H. Scott (Santa Ana, California, 1957).

DEER

Deer were widespread and numerous throughout the wilderness of the Old West and provided good meat for the hunter and BUCKSKIN for clothing. The Indians used every part of the deer, from hoof to horns. The American pioneers used deer fat to make candles and soap. Two types of common deer inhabit the West: the whitetail and the blacktail or mule deer. The latter is called the mule deer because of its large ears. The small whitetail *(Odocoileus virginianus)* weighs up to 230 pounds, has small, pronged antlers, and when alarmed its prominent white tail stands erect in warning to its kind. The mule deer *(Odocoileus hermionus)* is bigger, up to 400 pounds, with a handsome spread of forked antlers and a black-tipped tail which is not raised as a warning flag. These deer are still widespread and numerous throughout the West, especially in national parks and wildlife preserves. The deer's natural enemy is the MOUNTAIN LION or cougar.

Mammals of North America by V. H. Cahalane (New York, 1947);
The Deer of North America by W. P. Taylor (Harrisburg, Pennsylvania, 1956).

DENVER, Colorado

Denver was founded in 1858 at the beginning of the PIKE'S PEAK gold rush. At first a mining camp of a few tents and huts it quickly grew into a boom town of 5,000 inhabitants by 1870. It became the chief outfitting centre for miners in

94 *Mule deer.*

95 ∧

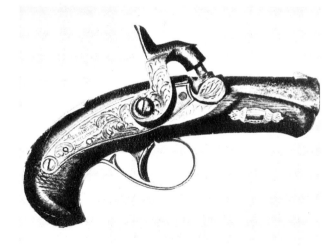

96 ∧

97 ∨

the region and silver and gold from LEADVILLE, Georgetown, Central City and other suburban diggings poured into Denver's busy banks and clearing houses. When Colorado achieved Statehood in 1876 Denver was well established as its capital city. For a time Denver had a private mint which struck ten and twenty dollar pieces with an inscription of Pike's Peak on one side and the name of the mint — Clark, Gruber & Company — on the other side. Bonanza kings, like Horace TABOR of Leadville, invested in Denver real estate and the opulent Tabor Grand Opera House and the luxurious Windsor Hotel ranked with the finest in the nation. Oscar Wilde, Henry Irving, and Lillie Langtry were among the famous who performed at the Opera House. By 1900 bustling Denver had a population of more than 133,000.

Marvels of the New West by W. M. Thayer (Norwich, Connecticut, 1888);
History of Denver by J. S. Smiley (Denver, 1901);
Here They Dug for Gold by G. F. Willison (New York, 1931).

95   *Denver in 1859.*

96   *Derringer .41 calibre of 1855.*

97   *Double-barrelled Derringer made by Remington.*

DERRINGER PISTOL

A small pocket pistol favoured by professional gamblers and 'sporting ladies' of the frontier who did not want to display firearms overtly. This miniature weapon could be easily concealed up the sleeve, in a hat, boot top, or handbag and brought swiftly into action against an awkward customer. Most gunfighters also carried a small hide-out pistol for emergency use; one Arizona lawman was said to carry eleven derringers concealed on his person. Henry J. Deringer, Jr. (1786-1868) was the original maker of these popular pocket pistols and produced the first one about 1825. When other gunmakers began to produce similar models, all pocket pistols came to be known as 'derringers', spelt with a double-r. COLT produced a number of derringer models and REMINGTON manufactured a popular double-barrelled version. The large-bore derringer, varying from .36 to .51 calibre, was deadly only at short range (especially over a gaming table) and varied in size from 3¾ inches to 6 inches overall. It was the ideal weapon for the assassin; John Wilkes Booth murdered President Abraham Lincoln in 1865 with a .44 calibre derringer of the original type.

Henry Deringer's Pocket Pistol by J. E. Parsons (New York, 1952);
Guns of the Early Frontier by C. P. Russell (Berkeley, California, 1957);
Guns of the Old West by C. E. Chapel (New York, 1961).

DIXON, Billy 1850-1913

A frontiersman and scout of wide renown, Billy Dixon was born in West Virginia and went West at the age of fourteen. He became a buffalo hunter and took part in the Battle of ADOBE WALLS in June 1874; during this fight he made his legendary 'long shot' of nearly a mile. With a big SHARPS buffalo rifle he knocked an Indian off his horse at 1,538 yards (182 yards short of a mile) a distance measured exactly by a surveyor some time after the fight. On 12 September 1874 Dixon, another scout and four soldiers were involved in the Buffalo Wallow Fight; after being attacked by about 125 KIOWA and COMANCHE Indians on open prairie near the Washita River, in what is now Hemphill County, Texas, the six men sought protection in a buffalo wallow (a shallow depression made by buffalo). With one man dead and the others wounded, Dixon saved the survivors by bringing a relief force of soldiers. He continued as a scout until 1883, when he homesteaded a claim that included Adobe Walls, where he served as postmaster for twenty years and was the first sheriff of Hutchinson County. Encouraged by his wife Olive, who later became a well-known journalist, Billy Dixon dictated his life to her and the book was first published just after his death.

Life of Billy Dixon by O. K. Dixon (Dallas, 1927);
Death on the Prairie by P. I. Wellman (New York, 1934);
Fighting Indian Warriors by E. A. Brinistool (New York, 1953).

DODGE CITY, Kansas

The most celebrated of the cowboy cattle towns, Dodge City, Kansas was founded in 1872 some five miles west of Fort Dodge, the army post built in 1864. Originally it was a buffalo hunters' town, with millions of buffalo within hunting range, from where 1½ million hides were shipped east on the ATCHISON, TOPEKA AND SANTA FE RAILROAD. After 1875 Dodge became a major railhead cowtown for the cattle driven up from Texas over the long trails; during the cattle boom of the late 1870s and early 1880s Dodge shipped more than 250,000 head a year. The free-spending cowboys attracted professional gamblers, badmen, saloon and brothel keepers and Dodge became a rough town in the best traditions of the Wild West. Lawmen such as Wyatt EARP, Bat MASTERSON, and Bill TILGHMAN were hired to keep the peace. The town's BOOT HILL cemetery gained fame as the last resting place of men killed in brawls and gunfights and buried with their boots on. Dodge City reigned as 'Queen of the Cowtowns' until 1886 when the free range cattle industry came to an end.

Dodge City, the Cowboy Capital by R. M. Wright (Wichita, Kansas, 1913);
Queen of the Cowtowns: Dodge City 1872-1886 by S. Vestal (New York, 1952);
Dodge City: Queen of the Cowtowns by W. S. Campbell (London, 1955);
The Cattle Towns by R. R. Dykstra (New York, 1968).

DOGIE

A dogie was the cowboy name for a motherless calf. However, the term and its origin and its spelling — dogy, doggie, doby — are open to argument. Some believe that dogie derives from the Spanish *dogal*, a halter used by Mexican cowboys to keep a calf from its mother. The generally accepted version is that dogie is a shortened form of 'dough-guts'. When orphan calves were forced to eat grass before they were able to digest it, they developed large bellies similar to a sack of sourdough, hence 'dough-guts', apocopized to 'dogies'. The name was incorporated into the traditional cowboy song *Git along Little Dogies*.

DONNER PARTY

An ill-fated party of emigrants who suffered appalling hardships on their wagon journey to California in 1846-7. Led by George Donner, whose wife and family and the Reed family formed the nucleus of the party, the wagon train of some twenty vehicles and about 100 men,

98 ∧

100 ∨

99 ∨

98 *Front Street, Dodge City, in the 1880s.*

99 *The Donner party struggling over the Sierra Nevada.*

100 *Reward poster for Bill Doolin.*

$5,000.⁰⁰ REWARD

FOR CAPTURE

DEAD OR ALIVE

OF

BILL DOOLIN

NOTORIOUS ROBBER OF TRAINS AND BANKS

ABOUT 6 FOOT 2 INCHES TALL, LT. BROWN HAIR, DANGEROUS, ALWAYS HEAVILY ARMED.

IMMEDIATELY CONTACT THE

U.S. MARSHAL'S OFFICE, GUTHRIE, OKLAHOMA TER.

women and children left INDEPENDENCE, Missouri in April 1846. Badly organized, with overloaded wagons and a late start, they struggled over the OREGON TRAIL to FORT BRIDGER, where they decided to take the little-known Hastings Cutoff route around the south side of GREAT SALT LAKE. After hard travelling across the Nevada desert the party was caught by early snowfalls in the SIERRA NEVADA Mountains and forced to camp at Truckee (Donner) Lake in late October. Here they suffered terribly from cold and hunger and those that survived had to resort to cannibalism, eating those that had died of starvation and exhaustion. During the winter four successive relief parties reached the camp to bring out the survivors (the last in April 1847); when the ordeal was finally over more than half the Donner party had perished.

History of the Donner Party by C. F. McGlashan (Stanford University Press, 1954);
Ordeal by Hunger, The Story of the Donner Party by G. R. Stewart (New York, 1960).

DOOLIN, Bill
1858-96

A bank and train robber who operated in the 1890s . Born on a farm in Arkansas, he worked for a time on a ranch in Oklahoma Territory then turned to crime and joined the DALTON BROTHERS. On the way to rob two banks in Coffeyville, Kansas in October 1892, Doolin's horse went lame and he did not accompany the three Daltons and two other men on the raid, in which four of them were killed and one severely wounded. After Coffeyville, Doolin formed his own gang and carried out a number of bank and train robberies in Oklahoma Territory, Kansas, Missouri and Arkansas. Three famous lawmen, Heck THOMAS, Chris MADSEN, and Bill TILGHMAN were engaged to hunt down Doolin. In December 1895 Tilghman arrested Doolin at Eureka Springs, Arkansas and took him back to Guthrie in Oklahoma; while awaiting trial Doolin escaped from jail and went into hiding. In August 1896 Heck Thomas tracked him down to a farmhouse and lay in wait for the outlaw to emerge. When he did, Thomas ordered him to surrender; Doolin brought his rifle into action and Thomas killed him with a shotgun blast. It seems that Doolin was not a ruthless killer; he is said to have stopped one of his gang from slaying Bill Tilghman, saying, 'Tilghman's too good a man to be shot in the back.'

Oklahoma Outlaws by R. S. Graves (Oklahoma City, 1915);
Outlaw Days by Z. A. Tilghman (Oklahoma City, 1926);
Oklahombres by G. Hines and E. D. Nix (Chicago, 1929).
Bill Doolin, Outlaw O.T. by B. C. Hanes (Norman, Oklahoma, 1968).

E

EAGLE

This noble bird of prey played an important part in American Indian culture and religion. Many tribes had songs and dances based on eagle symbolism. The tail feathers were highly prized as plumes to decorate the war bonnets of warriors and chiefs, and to the SIOUX in particular the number of feathers in a bonnet indicated the wearer's courage in battle. PUEBLO INDIANS captured eagles and caged them, thus providing a living source of feathers which they dyed bright colours. There are two types of eagle indigenous to North America — the bald eagle and the golden eagle. The bald eagle is mostly dark brown with white head feathers, and feeds on fish. The golden eagle is brown with a golden tinge on its head and shoulder feathers, and preys on small mammals and snakes. Both eagles soar on wings with a span of up to seven feet. The bald eagle was adopted by the Second Continental Congress as the American national emblem in 1782 and as such has been imprinted on coins and seals.

The American Eagle by F. H. Herrick (New York, 1934); *American Wildlife* by W. G. Van Name (New York, 1961).

EARP, Wyatt
1848-1929

A gunfighter and sometime peace officer whose legendary reputation as a paragon of law and order was largely manufactured by himself and his biographer Stuart N. Lake, and the television series of the 1950s. Like most Western drifters Earp was an opportunist and his actions were seldom altruistic; he was a cardsharp, bigamist, saloon keeper, and suspected stage robber. Undoubtedly he was also a man of cool courage and gunfighting skill. After working as a freighter and buffalo hunter Earp served as a policeman in WICHITA, Kansas in 1875-6 and then as assistant town marshal of DODGE CITY, Kansas. In Dodge he made friends with Doc HOLLIDAY, a dentist turned gambler and gunman. Earp's supposed exploits in Dodge are mostly fictitious. In December 1879 Wyatt and his brothers and Doc Holliday arrived in TOMBSTONE, Arizona Territory. Wyatt was hired as a shotgun messenger by the WELLS FARGO company and Virgil Earp became the town marshal. Trouble brewed up between the Earp gang and the Clanton-McLaury faction which resulted, on 26 October 1881, in the explosive showdown known as the Gunfight at the O.K. CORRAL. In this celebrated shoot-out that lasted about thirty seconds Billy Clanton, Tom and Frank McLaury were killed, Virgil and Morgan Earp were badly wounded, Holliday was nicked by a bullet, and Wyatt came through unscathed. In November 1881 Virgil was crippled for life when some unknown person fired a shotgun at him. In March 1882 Morgan Earp was killed by a shot in the back while playing billiards in a saloon; Wyatt soon after killed a man suspected of Morgan's murder. Wyatt left Tombstone and drifted around, eventually settling in Los Angeles in 1906. In his old age Wyatt was always looking for a suitable writer to publicize his life story and bring him the fame he craved; and five months before he died

101   *Golden eagle.*

< 102

103 Λ   104 V

he finally found a sympathetic biographer in Stuart N. Lake. Wyatt Earp died aged eighty in January 1929; his controversial biography was published two years later. Virgil Earp's widow, Allie, denounced the book as 'a pack of lies'.

Wyatt Earp, Frontier Marshal by S. N. Lake (New York, 1931);
The Earps of Tombstone by D. D. Martin (Tombstone, 1959);
The Earp Brothers of Tombstone by F. Waters (New York, 1960);
Wyatt Earp: The Untold Story by E. Bartholomew (Toyahvale, Texas, 1963);
Wyatt Earp: The Man and the Myth by E. Bartholomew (Toyahvale, 1964).

ELK
Cervus canadensis

The elk is the second biggest in size of the American deer family; the MOOSE being the largest. Once widely distributed throughout North America the elk, also known by its Indian name of wapiti (white rump), was numerous on the buffalo plains of the Old West until exterminated by white and Indian hunters and now is found in large numbers only in the Rocky Mountains, the national parks, and the wilderness regions of Canada. The Indians hunted the wapiti for its meat, used its hide for clothing and TIPI covers, its teeth for ornaments, and fashioned its large antlers into various tools. Adult males weigh from 500 to 1,000 pounds and sport a wide spread of antlers. During the mating season the bulls blow a loud whistle of defiance, known as a bugle, and fight each other over the cows.

The Deer of North America by W. P. Taylor (Harrisburgh, Pennsylvania, 1956);
The World of the American Elk by J. Van Wormer (New York, 1969).

102   *Wyatt Earp about 1885.*

103   *Ellsworth in 1872; cattle buyers arriving from the East.*

104   *Bull elk in Montana.*

ELLSWORTH, Kansas

A notable railhead cattle town from where the LONGHORNS driven up from Texas over the CHISHOLM TRAIL were shipped east on the KANSAS PACIFIC RAILWAY, that ran through the middle of the town. Ellsworth's role as a major cowtown lasted from 1871 to 1873 and it gained itself a reputation as a wild place. Laid out in the spring of 1867, it was an incorporated third class city by the time the Texas cattle started to arrive. The town boasted the biggest stockyards in Kansas and was mighty proud of the only solid sidewalk — made of limestone rock — west of Kansas City in the plains country; the sidewalk was twelve feet wide and ran the length of the Grand Central Hotel, the favoured house of the Texas cattlemen. Half a mile to the east of the town stood the community of Nauchville, the redlight district. Among the gamblers and other social parasites that came to Ellsworth was the celebrated Ben THOMPSON. He and his brother Bill were involved in a shooting incident in which Bill killed Sheriff Whitney and had to flee town; Ben also left soon after. Legend tells us that Ellsworth had its own kind of Lady Godiva; a dance hall girl called Prairie Rose bet a cowboy 50 dollars that she would walk naked down the main street, and she did, with a revolver in each hand to keep the cowboys at a distance. The financial panic in New York in 1873 brought about a temporary collapse of the cattle trade and marked the end of Ellsworth as a principal railhead town.

Prairie Trails and Cow Towns by F. B. Streeter (Boston, 1936);
Ellsworth, 1867-1947 by G. Jelinek (Salina, Kansas, 1947);
The Cattle Towns by R. R. Dykstra (New York, 1968).

FETTERMAN MASSACRE, 1866

An encounter near FORT PHIL KEARNY, Dakota Territory, between an army column of eighty men led by Captain W. J. Fetterman, in which the column was completely wiped out. At the time, Fort Phil Kearny was being hard pressed by combined SIOUX, CHEYENNE, and ARAPAHO warriors and on 21 December 1866 they attacked a party sent from the fort to bring back logs. Fetterman and his column were sent out to relieve the wood train. His orders from the fort commander, Colonel Carrington, clearly stated: 'Support the wood train, relieve it, and report to me. Do not engage or pursue Indians at its expense. Under no circumstances pursue over the ridge.' Fetterman had little or no respect for the fighting qualities of the Indians. Against Carrington's orders, he rashly crossed the ridge (Lodge Trail Ridge) in a move against the main body of the enemy. According to an Indian account of the fight, Fetterman was drawn into an ambush by a common Indian trick of retreating with a small decoy body into a killing ground surrounded by a larger force. Fetterman fell for the ruse and moved into the trap; none of the column survived the encounter.

My Army Life and the Fort Phil Kearny Massacre by F. C. Carrington (Philadelphia, 1911);
Fort Phil Kearny: An American Saga by D. Brown (New York, 1962);
The Fetterman Massacre by D. Brown (London, 1972).

FISHER, King
1859-84

A Texas gunfighter and desperado, John King Fisher became the leader of a gang of cattle RUSTLERS, killed a number of men, and gained a powerful reputation in Dimmit County, Texas. Despite his criminal activities he nevertheless managed to get himself the office of deputy sheriff of Uvalde County. On 11 March 1884 he met up with Ben THOMPSON, another notorious Texas gunman, and they visited San Antonio for some drink and entertainment. At the Variety Theatre they got into an argument with the owner and in the resulting gunfight King Fisher and Thompson were both shot dead.

King Fisher, His Life and Times by O. C. Fisher and J. C. Dykes (Norman, Oklahoma, 1966).

FLATBOATS

In the main there were three types of flatboat widely used on the Western rivers and streams before the advent of the STEAMBOATS: the primitive raft used by poor emigrants, the mackinaw boat used mostly by freighters, and the keelboat also used by professional rivermen to transport cargo. The emigrant flatboat, roughly constructed to float downstream, was built of rough wood by the pioneer to carry his family, household goods and livestock; it was manoeuvred by poles and a long sweep or oar supported on a forked rest at the stern acted as a rudder. When the emigrants reached their destination the flatboat was broken up to help build a permanent home. The sharp-prowed mackinaw, up to seventy feet long, was powered by oarsmen and steered by a long sweep. The shallow-draught keelboat was powered by oarsmen aided by a large sail. It had a fixed rudder and a capacious cabin. When travelling upstream the keelboat had to be either dragged by ropes or poled against the current. It took a lot of muscle to move a keelboat and their crews were famed for their strength and toughness.

The Keelboat Age on Western Waters by L. D. Baldwin (Pittsburg, 1941);
Life on the River by N. L. Wayman (New York, 1971).

FLATHEAD INDIANS

The name Flathead applied to several different tribes which practised the custom of flattening the heads of their children in infancy. Strangely enough, the tribe known officially as Flatheads — the Salish of Montana — never flattened the head; it is believed they were misnamed because the first white men to visit the tribe found slaves from the north-west with flattened heads among them. The Indians that deformed the heads of their babies were the Chinook of the Columbia River, many of the Vancouver Island tribes, and most of the Salish of Puget Sound and British Columbia. The Montana Flatheads are members of the Salish linguistic stock; originally they were fish eaters, rather than hunters, but in time they acquired horses, made yearly migrations to the buffalo grounds, and took on many characteristics of the PLAINS INDIANS. Today the Salish live on the Flathead Reservation in the Rocky Mountains of Montana.

The Flathead Indians of Montana by H. H. Turney-High (Menasha, Wisconsin, 1937).

FORD, Robert
1861-92

Bob Ford made his mark on the history of the Old West as the man who killed Jesse JAMES. It was his only claim to fame. Bob and his brother Charlie were new recruits to Jesse's gang in 1881 and when a 10,000 dollar reward was offered for Jesse or Frank James, dead or alive, the brothers Ford made a secret agreement with Governor Crittenden of Missouri to assassinate the outlaw chief and collect the reward. On 3 April 1882 the brothers were enjoying Jesse's hospitality at his home in ST JOSEPH, Missouri (where Jesse was living quietly under the alias of Howard) when Bob Ford seized his chance and shot James through the head while his back was turned. For the rest of his life Bob Ford was reviled for the manner in which he had killed the famous outlaw, whose gravestone bore the words. . .'Murdered by a traitor and a coward whose name is not worthy to appear here.' Forced by public opinion to leave Missouri, Bob Ford wandered through the West, taunted by the words of the popular song: 'The dirty little coward, Who shot Mr Howard, Has laid poor Jesse in his grave.' Four years after the death of Jesse James, Charlie Ford shot himself. In 1892 Bob was running a saloon in the mining town of Creede, Colorado, when he was shot dead by Ed Kelley.

The Day Jesse James was Killed by C. W. Breihan (New York, 1961);
The Crittenden Memoirs by H. H. Crittenden (New York, 1936);
A Dynasty of Western Outlaws by P. I. Wellman (New York, 1960);
Jesse James Was His Name by W. A. Settle (Columbia, Missouri, 1966).

105   *Flathead Indians on the move in Montana, by E.S. Paxson.*

109   *Fort Laramie in 1837, by Alfred J. Miller.*

FORT BRIDGER,
Wyoming

A prominent trading post, and later a military fort, built originally in 1843 by Jim BRIDGER, the famous trapper and scout, on Black's Fork of Green River in south-western Wyoming. Favourably situated on the OREGON-CALIFORNIA TRAIL, the post became established as a resting point and supply station for the emigrant wagon trains heading west. Here Jim Bridger used his blacksmith's skill and entertained the travellers with his fund of strange stories. In 1853 the MORMONS, angered by Bridger selling arms to the Indians, raided the fort to arrest him; Bridger fled to the mountains with his family. When Bridger later guided United States troops against the Mormons in 1857, the latter burned the post. It was rebuilt as a U.S. Army fort and served as a stopping point for the PONY EXPRESS and stagecoach lines until eventually abandoned in 1890.

James Bridger by C. B. Alter (Salt Lake City, 1925);
James Bridger: Mountain Man by N. B. Wiltsey (Los Angeles, 1969).

FORT LARAMIE,
Wyoming

An important fur trading post and later a military post at which several Indian treaties were signed. The first post on the site was built in 1834 by fur traders William SUBLETTE and Robert Campbell; it was named Fort William after Sublette, but it

105 V

106   *Robert Ford.*

107   *Flatboat floating down the Mississippi.*

108   *Fort Laramie in 1837, from a painting by A.J. Miller.*

107 Λ

106 Λ   109 V   108 Λ

was known to most as 'Laramie', from the nearby river named after the trapper Jacques La Ramee, killed by Indians on its banks in 1821. In 1826 the post was acquired by the AMERICAN FUR COMPANY and rapidly became one of the major trading centres in the Rocky Mountains. Bands of Indians, seeking trade with white men, camped near the post in large numbers. In 1841 the company replaced the decaying log fort with one made of ADOBE and in that year the post served the first emigrants travelling the OREGON TRAIL; during the next two decades some 200,000 emigrants stopped here on the way west to build new homes in Oregon, California, and Utah. The first band of MORMONS, led by Brigham YOUNG, rested at the fort in 1847 on its way to the Salt Lake Valley. In 1849 the Army bought the post and began erecting other buildings, so that Fort Laramie became a sprawling military post, too large to be walled in but strong enough to deter Indian attack. Here treaties were signed with the Indians in 1851 and 1868. During the period of the PONY EXPRESS in 1860-1 the fort served as one of the relay stations for the express riders. In 1876 General CROOK used the fort as his base for operations against the SIOUX. The post was finally abandoned in 1890 and fell into ruin; in 1938 it became the Fort Laramie National Monument and its buildings were restored to their military appearance in the 1880s.

Fort Laramie and the Pageant of the West by L. R. Hafen and F. M. Young (Glendale, California, 1938);
Fort Laramie by D. L. Hieb (National Park Service Historical Handbook No. 20, Washington, D.C., 1961);
Fort Laramie and the Sioux Indians by R. Nadeau (Englewood Cliffs, New Jersey, 1967).

FORT PHIL KEARNY, Dakota Territory

Built by Colonel Carrington and his troops in 1866 at the foot of the Bighorn Mountains (in what is now northern Wyoming) to protect the BOZEMAN TRAIL, Fort Phil Kearny came under immediate and constant harassment from Sioux chief RED CLOUD and his allies. In December 1866 Captain Fetterman and eighty men rode out to relieve a wood train under attack and were wiped out in the FETTERMAN MASSACRE. With the fort in a state of emergency, Carrington sent two citizen couriers to the telegraph post at Horseshoe Station, about 190 miles away, with messages for his superiors at Omaha and Washington; one of the couriers was John 'Portugee' PHILLIPS, whose ride has been worked into a legend. In August 1867 the Indians attacked a wood-cutting party near Fort Phil Kearny, but the small detachment was armed with the newly-issued SPRINGFIELD breechloading rifles and rapid fire beat off repeated Indian charges in the famous WAGON BOX FIGHT. There were never enough troops at Phil Kearny to mount an offensive against the hostiles, and in 1868 at FORT LARAMIE, the authorities were forced to make a treaty with the Indians, giving them all of what is now South Dakota west of the Missouri River as a reservation. Red Cloud refused to sign the treaty until the troops had abandoned Fort Phil Kearny and his warriors had burned it to the ground.

My Army Life and the Fort Phil Kearny Massacre by F. C. Carrington (Philadelphia, 1911);
Fort Phil Kearny: An American Saga by D. Brown (New York, 1962).

FORT WORTH, Texas

Shortly after the Republic of TEXAS became a State of the Union in 1845, the U.S. Army began to build a chain of forts to protect the border settlements and the emigrants pushing westward. Fort Worth was one of them, established in 1849 by Major Ripley and his company of Dragoons. It was built on the Trinity River, some thirty miles west of the village of Dallas, and named after General W. J. Worth, commander of the Texas Department. Settlements soon sprang up nearby and the army abandoned the post in 1853. Fort Worth became a thriving trading centre and in 1873 was incorporated as a city. When the Texas and Pacific Railroad reached there in 1874 the city became an important railhead for shipping cattle to market. In 1885 Fort Worth had a population of 22,000. Big as it was the place proved too small for the city's ex-marshal Jim Courtright and the gambler Luke SHORT and in 1887 they had a gunfight outside the White

110 *Fort Phil Kearny in 1867.*

111 *Forty-Niners at work in the gold fields of California.*

110 ▼

Elephant Saloon — and by a freak shot, the gambler managed to shoot dead Courtright the gunfighter.

Forth Worth, Outpost on the Trinity by O. Knight (Norman, Oklahoma, 1953);
Cowtown-Metropolis by R. H. Talbert (Fort Worth, 1956).

FORTY-NINERS

The 'Forty-Niners' were the eager fortune seekers who came in their thousands to California during the great GOLD RUSH of 1849. They came from all parts of America, and the world, and by the end of 1849 the population of California had increased by an estimated 80,000. They came by sea to the little settlement of SAN FRANCISCO, quickly transforming it into one of the world's busiest ports, and they came by the overland routes across the United States. Both journeys were long and arduous and many died *en route* of scurvy, cholera and other diseases and misfortunes. Of the 30,000 who travelled overland in 1849 some 5,000 died on the way. All classes and conditions of people flocked to the gold diggings; gentlemen adventurers laboured side by side with ruffians, farmers, sailors, deserters from the army, French peasants, Chinese coolies, and almost every nationality under the sun. It was the greatest gold rush of all time. Virtually all the Forty-Niners came ill-prepared and unequipped only to discover that the cost of simple tools and supplies were skyhigh. Some found fortunes in the gold fields but few managed to keep their riches from the gamblers, robbers, and other unscrupulous opportunists who preyed on the great mass of humanity in the rough and lawless mining camps. Some Forty-Niners gave up digging or washing for gold and waxed rich as merchants and traders, selling goods and services to the miners in exchange for the yellow metal. In 1849 California yielded ten million dollars worth of gold, and hopeful prospectors continued to flood into the land for the next two years.

Experiences of a Forty-Niner by W. C. Johnson (New York, 1892);
The Forty-Niners by S. E. White (New Haven, Connecticut, 1918);
Diary of a Forty-Niner by C. L. Canfield (New York, 1920);
The Forty-Niners by A. B. Hulbert (Boston, 1931);
The Forty-Niners by Time-Life Books (New York, 1974).

FREE, Mickey
*c.*1850-1915

A notable army scout and interpreter who served in the Apache campaigns of the 1880s, Mickey Free was described by Al SIEBER, chief of scouts,

112 ∧

as 'half Irish, half Mexican, and whole son-of-a-bitch'. Born in Santa Cruz, Mexico, Free and his Mexican mother, Jesus Martinez, went to live with Irishman John Ward at his ranch in Arizona, where the boy became known as Felix Ward. When Apaches raided the ranch in 1861 they abducted Felix and he lived with the Indians until he enrolled as an Indian scout at Fort Verde, Arizona, in 1872. Now known as Mickey Free, he served for twenty years as scout, interpreter, and Indian policeman; although his left eye had been gouged out by a deer, he was an excellent tracker and rose to the rank of sergeant of scouts. On his discharge in 1893 he returned to his adopted people, the Apaches, and lived with them on the Fort Apache Reservation until his death.

Mickey Free-Manhunter by A. Kinney Griffith (Caldwell, Idaho, 1969);
Salvador or Martinez? The Parentage and Origins of Mickey Free by A. Radbourne (English Westerners Brandbook No. 175, London, 1972).

FRÉMONT, John Charles
1813-90

Explorer, soldier, and politician, John Charles Frémont earned the sobriquet 'the Pathfinder' for his endeavours in opening up the Far West. Born in Georgia, son of a French *émigré*, he was commissioned a Second Lieutenant in the U.S. Topographical Corps in 1838 and took part in exploring the land between the upper MISSISSIPPI and MISSOURI Rivers. Frémont led five expeditions into the Far West. In 1842, with Kit CARSON as his guide, he crossed the plains and

113 ∧

112 *Mickey Free in 1883.*

113 *Method of trapping beaver under water.*

mountains to southern Wyoming and successfully charted the most favourable route to OREGON. His vivid report of the expedition won him a popular reputation. In 1843-4, again accompanied by Kit Carson, Frémont explored the Great Basin between the ROCKY and SIERRA NEVADA Mountains. The party's return to ST LOUIS in August 1844, after so long an absence in the wilderness, created a sensation. His third exploration, to blaze a new trail to Oregon and

CALIFORNIÁ, turned into a military expedition when his sixty, well-armed frontiersmen aided the American settlers in their Bear Flag Revolt against Mexico; and when the U.S.-MEXICAN WAR broke out in 1846, he and his 'California Battalion' (composed of his hardy explorers and settlers) played a leading role in the conquest of California. His fourth and fifth expeditions were made in 1848-9 and 1853-4 to explore a railroad route across the Rockies to the Pacific. He then pursued his political career and in 1856 was the first presidential candidate for the newly-formed Republican party, losing to James Buchanan, fifteenth President of the U.S. With the outbreak of the Civil War, Frémont was appointed Major-General in the Union Army and given command of the Department of the West, but crossing swords with President Lincoln, he was relieved of his command. From 1878 to 1883 he served as Governor of the Territory of Arizona and died in New York City.

Memoirs of My Life by J. C. Frémont (New York, 1887);
Frémont, the West's Greatest Adventurer by A. Nevins (New York, 1928);
John Charles Frémont by Cardinal Goodwin (Stanford, California, 1930);
Frémont: Pathmarker of the West by A. Nevins (New York, 1961);
The Expeditions of John Charles Frémont edited by D.Jackson and M. L. Spence (Urban, Illinois, 1970).

FUR TRAPPERS

The fur trapping MOUNTAIN MEN played an important role in blazing trails in the Far West in the first half of the nineteenth century. In their constant search for BEAVER, the fur of which was in great demand for the making of beaver hats and fashion wear in America and Europe, the hardy trappers explored vast regions of the uncharted West. The trapper equipped himself with a horse and pack mules for carrying his supplies, and later the beaver pelts, about six double-spring steel traps with chains, a rifle and hunting knife. He then rode into the wilderness following the creeks and streams looking for beaver signs. He set his traps under water, attached by the chains to stakes driven firmly into the stream bottom. He baited his traps with castorum, an oily substance taken from the musk glands of the beaver, then retired until next morning. When the beaver was caught in the trap it drowned. The trapper dragged the carcass out of the water, skinned it with his hunting knife, and stretched the skin over a hoop or framework of twigs to dry. When dry it was folded with the fur turned inwards, and a bundle of up to twenty skins was tightly pressed and corded for transportation on his pack mules. He would take his full load of furs to an agreed rendezvous where the traders and agents of the fur companies awaited the arrival of the trappers.

The Fur Trade and Early Western Exploration by C. A. Vandiveer (Cleveland, Ohio, 1929);
The American Fur Trade of the Far West by H. M. Chittenden (New York, 1935);
This Reckless Breed of Men, the Trappers and Fur Traders of the Southwest by R. G. Cleland (New York, 1950);
Journal of a Trapper, 1834-1843 by O. Russell (Lincoln, Nebraska, 1965);
Firearms Traps & Tools of the Mountain Men by C. P. Russell (New York, 1967).

GALL
c. 1840-94

A war chief of the Hunkpapa SIOUX, Gall played a leading role in the Battle of the LITTLE BIGHORN, 25 June 1876, when the Sioux and their allies defeated General CUSTER and the Seventh Cavalry. He was first named Pizi; as a young and hungry orphan he scavenged the remains of an animal carcass and tried to eat the gall, thus gaining his well-known name. He distinguished himself as a young warrior and hunter and SITTING BULL, Hunkpapa chief and medicine man, adopted him as a brother. He later became Sitting Bull's chief lieutenant. After their spectacular victory at the Little Bighorn, the Sioux scattered before the avenging U.S. troops and Gall fled to Canada with Sitting Bull and his people. In 1880 Gall decided to return to his homeland and was accompanied by a large number of followers. After a final clash with soldiers in Montana in January 1881, Gall surrendered and settled on the Standing Rock Reservation in South Dakota. In 1886 he attended the tenth anniversary of the Battle of the Little Bighorn at the scene of the action and gave an interview describing the battle as he remembered it; his account was published in the *St Paul Pioneer Press* (Minnesota) issue of 18 July 1886. In 1889 Gall was made a judge of the Indian Court at Standing Rock and later accompanied his friend the Indian agent James McLaughlin to Washington on a mission for the Sioux.

My Friend the Indian by J. McLaughlin (Boston, 1910);
Indian Heroes and Great Chieftains by C. A. Eastman (New York, 1918);
Great Indian Chiefs by A. Britt (New York, 1938).

GAMBLING

In every cattle town, railroad and mining camp in the Old West gambling was the chief means of recreation. Card games were the most popular and these included seven-up, black jack, monte, poker, and faro; the latter was known as 'bucking the tiger' to Westerners. Keno (a kind of bingo) and roulette were also played in saloons and casinos. Boom towns attracted professional gamblers, elegant figures in frock coats and a concealed DERRINGER pocket pistol in case of trouble. Gentlemen cardsharps were colourful figures on the big paddleboats that steamed up and down the Mississippi and Missouri and other major rivers of the West; during the 1850s some 2,000 professional gamblers worked the STEAMBOATS on the Mississippi. Most famous Westerners were inveterate gamblers, including

114 *Playing faro in Morenci, Arizona Territory, 1895.*

115 ∧

116 ∨

Wyatt EARP, Bat MASTERSON, General CUSTER, and Wild Bill HICKOK; the latter was killed while playing poker, shot in the back, and the five cards that he held at the time included the ace of spades, ace of clubs, eight of clubs, eight of spades, and these 'aces and eights' became known to poker players as the 'Dead Man's Hand'. Luke SHORT, Ben THOMPSON, and Doc HOLLIDAY were famous professional gamblers.

Forty Years a Gambler on the Mississippi by G. H. Devol (Cincinnati, 1887);
Play the Devil: A History of Gambling in the U.S. from 1492 to 1955 by H. Chafetz (New York, 1960).

GARRETT, Pat
1850-1908

Famed as the lawman who killed BILLY THE KID, Patrick Floyd Garrett also died a violent death, shot in the back on a desert road while urinating. Born in Alabama, son of a wealthy plantation owner, Garrett left home when the family estate was lost after the Civil War. The skinny youth, six feet four inches tall, became a COWBOY in Texas and a BUFFALO HUNTER; in 1877 he shot and killed his first man during an argument. He moved to New Mexico and after working for rancher Pete Maxwell, opened a small restaurant in Fort Sumner, where he became close friends with Billy the Kid. At that time the LINCOLN COUNTY WAR was in progress, a range war between rival cattle interests; the Kid was a leading gunman for one faction but Garrett stayed out of the fighting. When Billy became an outlaw and rustler in Lincoln County, the big ranch owners, especially John CHISUM, wanted him out of the way and the man they chose to do the job was Pat Garrett. He was elected sheriff of Lincoln County on 7 November 1880 and went after Billy. He captured him in December 1880. The young outlaw was tried, found guilty of murder, and sentenced to be hanged on 13 May 1881; but he escaped from jail in April. Garrett went after him again and traced him to the home of Pete Maxwell at Fort Sumner. On the night of 13-14 July 1881 he entered the house and shot Billy by surprise in a darkened room. Garrett was not re-elected sheriff of Lincoln County. He was commissioned a captain in the TEXAS RANGERS, resigned the post in 1885, served several terms as sheriff of Dona Ana County, New Mexico, and in 1901 became the collector of customs at El Paso,

115 *'The Faro Players' by W.L. Dodge.*

116 *Chief Gall, painted by Robert Lindneux.*

117 *Pat Garrett.*

Texas, for four years, then settled on a ranch in Dona Ana County. On 19 February 1908 he was driving his buggy on a lonely desert road; he stepped down to urinate and was shot in the back by a hired assassin. A man stood trial for the murder but was acquitted. Controversy still surrounds the end of Pat Garrett.

The Authentic Life of Billy the Kid by P. F. Garrett (Santa Fe, 1862, Norman, Oklahoma 1954);
Pat Garrett by R. O'Connor (New York, 1960).

GERONIMO
*c.*1829-1909

Warrior leader of the Chiricahua APACHES of Arizona, Geronimo was the last Apache leader to defy the U.S. military. Son of a noted warrior of the Nednis Apaches, Geronimo's tribal name was Goyakla (One Who Yawns); the Mexicans dubbed him Geronimo, or Jerome. His mother, first wife and three children were all killed by Mexicans in a raid on the Apache camp and his hatred of the Mexicans was intense. He then married into the Chiricahua band and became a prominent warrior under the chief COCHISE. Geronimo was of average height, thick-set and of tremendous strength; Charles F. Lummis described him as having 'eyes like two bits of obsidian with a light behind them', and a mouth that was a 'straight, thin-lipped gash . . . without

117 ∨

83726

119 ∧   120 ∨

118   *Geronimo in the 1880s.*

119   *Geronimo in his later years, tamed and top-hatted.*

120   *Ghost shirt of Arapaho.*

one softening curve'. When Cochise died in 1874 Geronimo assumed virtual leadership of the Chiricahuas. In 1876 the U.S. government removed the Chiricahuas from their mountain homeland in south-eastern Arizona to the San Carlos Reservation. But Geronimo remained rebellious and for the next ten years led a small band of hostiles on raids in Arizona and Mexico, leaving a trail of death and destruction. General George CROOK was sent after Geronimo; he enlisted Apache scouts to hunt down his man and in 1883 induced Geronimo to surrender and return to the San Carlos Reservation. But in 1885 Geronimo rejected the captive life and continued his depredations. Crook brought him in again and once more Geronimo fled, bringing about Crook's resignation. General Nelson A. MILES

took his place and throughout the summer of 1886 his troops and Apache scouts hunted Geronimo and his small band of followers. Finally, in September 1886, Geronimo surrendered to Miles and reconciled himself to reservation life. He was converted to Christianity and allowed himself to be exhibited at the St Louis World's Fair, where he sold signed photographs of himself for fifty cents. In 1906 he dictated his autobiography; he died aged eighty of pneumonia at Fort Sill, Oklahoma.

Geronimo's Story of His Life edited by S. M. Barrett (New York, 1906, 1969);
The Truth about Geronimo by B. Davis (New Haven, Connecticut, 1929);
On the Bloody Trail of Geronimo by J. Bigelow (Los Angeles, 1968);
The Geronimo Campaign by O. B. Faulk (New York, 1969);
Geronimo, A Biography by A. B. Adams (New York, 1971).

GHOST DANCE

The Ghost Dance religious cult of the late 1880s was originated by the PAIUTE Indian prophet Wovoka, whose message of hope was enthusiastically received by dejected Indians far beyond the boundaries of Wovoka's NEVADA. His peaceful doctrine promised that the Indian dead would arise, that the white man would go, and that the BUFFALO and other game would once again roam the plains in abundance; by performing the sacred Ghost Dance, Indian life would be restored to its former order and balance. The cult spread like wildfire through the reservations; among its most enthusiastic followers were the SIOUX, who by 1889 were dancing near several South Dakota agencies. It was a simple ritual in which for five consecutive nights, participants joined hands in a circle and shuffled slowly to the left, while chanting special songs of hope and delivery; some danced until they dropped with exhaustion. The dancers usually wore shirts painted with mystic symbols which some tribes believed would be proof against the white soldiers' bullets. The cult was harmless in that it promised things by supernatural, not violent, means, but the authorities became alarmed and feared the ceremony as a preparation for war. Troops were called in to maintain the peace and by the close of 1890 some 3,000 soldiers were in the Sioux country. The culmination of the tension thus created was the Massacre at WOUNDED KNEE in South Dakota in December 1890 in which the army slaughtered some 300 Sioux. It can be said that the Ghost Dance religion also died at Wounded Knee.

The Ghost Dance Religion by J. Mooney (Bulletin 14, Bureau of American Ethnology, Washington, D.C., 1896);
Wovoka by P. Bailey (Los Angeles, 1957);
Bury My Heart at Wounded Knee by D. Brown (New York, 1970).

GIBBON, John
1827-96

A U.S. Army colonel who served in the Indian campaigns after distinguished service in the Union Army during the Civil War. In 1876 he commanded a column of mixed infantry and cavalry in the expedition against the Sioux-Cheyenne forces, which resulted in the crushing defeat of General CUSTER and his Seventh Cavalry in the Battle of the LITTLE BIGHORN. It was the arrival of the Gibbon-General Terry force that lifted the siege of the surviving members of the Seventh Cavalry. In the following year Colonel Gibbon campaigned against Chief JOSEPH and the NEZ PERCÉ and fought a desperate action in the Battle of the Big Hole on 9 August 1877. While the Nez Percé were camped at the Big Hole River, in Montana, Gibbon moved up with a force of some 200 men. He attacked the camp at dawn from three directions and took it within thirty minutes. Then the Indians counter-attacked and drove the soldiers into a defensive position on a wooded knoll. For three days Gibbon (who was wounded) and his men were besieged until the Indians withdrew on the approach of a relief column; and with about half his force dead and wounded, Gibbon was in no condition to pursue the enemy. Promoted Brigadier-General in 1885, John Gibbon retired from active service in 1891.

Battle of the Big Hole by G. D. Shields (Chicago, 1889);
Death on the Prairie by P. I. Wellman (New York, 1934);
The Flight of the Nez Percé by M. H. Brown (New York, 1967).

GILA MONSTER
Heloderma suspectum

With an average length of nineteen inches, the Gila monster is the largest of all lizards in the United States; it is also the only poisonous one. It inhabits the desert regions of the West, namely Utah, Nevada, New Mexico, and in particular the Gila River Valley of Arizona. When the gila monster locks its sharp-fanged jaws into a victim (a rat, ground squirrel, snake) it hangs on like a bulldog; its teeth have grooves through which poisonous saliva — from glands at the roots of the teeth — is transmitted to the victim. The venom of the black-and-orange coloured gila monster is fatal to its natural victims, but rarely to humans, although it would make you sick indeed for several days.

Reptiles of North America by R. Ditmars (New York, 1946).

GLASS, Hugh
? — *c*.1833

A famous mountain man whose remarkable survival after an encounter with a grizzly BEAR is — like John COLTER's run for life — one of the West's great tales of fortitude. It is not certain when Hugh Glass was born or when he died. He is said to have been a pirate with Jean Lafitte and to have lived with the PAWNEE INDIANS. He first came to historical notice in 1823 when he joined

121 ∨

121 *Gila monster.*

122 *Forty-Niners at work in gold country.*

123 *Poster of 1849 advertising passage to California gold fields.*

124 *Hugh Glass fights the grizzly bear.*

125 ∧

126 ∧   127 ∨

ASHLEY's Missouri river fur trapping expedition. He took part in several desperate fights with Indians and gained a reputation among his fellow trappers for courage, integrity, and for his custom of marching and camping at some distance from his colleagues. It was while travelling apart from his fellows that Glass was attacked by a grizzly bear and dreadfully injured. Andrew Henry, the leader of the party, left Glass in the care of two men, John Fitzgerald and the youthful Jim BRIDGER. Believing that Glass must surely die from his terrible wounds the two men abandoned him, taking his rifle and equipment, and reported him dead and buried. Incredibly, Glass managed to survive and slowly regained his strength, living on wild berries and roots, and began to crawl towards Fort Kiowa, more than 100 miles away. It is believed that a band of SIOUX gave him succour and helped him reach the fort. Glass vowed vengeance on the two men who had deserted him but when he caught up with them, having recovered his favourite rifle, he forgave them their infidelity. This epic of endurance, and further adventures, made Hugh Glass a legend among the other mountain men. He is believed to have lost his life in an encounter with Indians on the Yellowstone River in the spring of 1833.

Jim Bridger by J. C. Alter (Norman, Oklahoma, 1962); *Pirate, Pawnee and Mountain Men: The Saga of Hugh Glass* by J. M. Myers (Boston, 1963).

GOLD RUSH

The discovery of gold in CALIFORNIA on 24 January 1848 by James W. Marshall at Coloma on the south fork of the American River, about fifty miles from present-day Sacramento, triggered off the greatest gold rush in history. Marshall was building a sawmill for John A. SUTTER when he found nuggets of gold in the water of the millrace; Sutter wanted the find kept secret for fear that his land would be ruined by a stampede of gold seekers. But the hot news got out and the

125 *Hopeful French peasant lands at San Francisco in 1849, gateway to 'Eldorado'.*

126 *Forty-Niners rounding Cape Horn to California in 1849.*

127 *Charles Goodnight.*

128 *Completion of the first transcontinental railroad at Promontory, Utah, 10 May 1869.*

rush was on. In 1848 the rush was a local one but in the following years thousands of FORTY-NINERS from all parts of the U.S. and the world flooded into California in a mass search for gold. They came by sea to SAN FRANCISCO, transforming the tiny coastal settlement into a booming port, and they came by long overland routes across the United States. Between 1848 and 1852 the population of California increased from an estimated 15,000 to 250,000. The major gold belt was called the Mother Lode, that stretched for 150 miles along the western flank of the SIERRA NEVADA Mountains, in which any steam, canyon, or ancient gravel bed might conceal gold in the form of nuggets, flakes, or dust. The Mother Lode gave birth to many bawling mining camps dubbed with colourful names such as Rough and Ready, Roaring Camp, Fiddletown, Angels Camp, El Dorado, Dry Diggings, Hangtown, Jackass Hill, Bed Bug, Squabbletown, and Slumgullion. At first the gold came relatively easy, in surface diggings or on stream beds. A prospector would 'pan' for gold particles by using a simple wash pan; he would fill the pan with 'pay dirt', then swirl it around in the water, washing out the lighter sand and gravel to leave the heavier gold particles at the bottom. To make the tedious job easier a device called a 'cradle' or 'rocker' was made of wood and rocked by hand to separate the gold from the dirt; the 'long tom' and the sluice were other simple contraptions used for parting the gold from the gravel. In 1849

128 V

California yielded 10 million dollars in gold; this increased annually until the peak year of 1852 in which 81 million dollars' worth was extracted. Then the gold rush went into decline, the easy pickings had gone and the individual prospector gave way to the big mining companies with the mechanized equipment to rip up the earth in huge quantities. Many prospectors found their fortunes in the great California gold rush, but both James W. Marshall and John A. Sutter died poor and ruined by the wild stampede. The gold rush hurried California (acquired from Mexico in February 1848) into the Union as the thirty-first State in 1850, and proved an important catalyst in the development of the Far West.

The Forty-Niners by A. B. Hulbert (Boston, 1931);
Anybody's Gold, the Story of California's Mining Towns by J. H. Jackson (New York, 1941);
Gold Rush Album by J. H. Jackson (New York, 1949);
California Called Them: A Saga of Golden Days and Roaring Camps by R. O'Brien (New York, 1951);
California Gold by R. W. Paul (Lincoln, Nebraska, 1965).

GOLDEN SPIKE,

When the UNION PACIFIC RAILROAD joined rails with the CENTRAL PACIFIC RAILROAD at Promontory, Utah, 10 May 1869 to complete the first transcontinental railroad across the U.S. the marriage was sealed by driving in the last spike, a golden spike. In fact the ceremony involved tapping into position, with a silver sledge, four

special spikes, two made of gold and two of silver. Then came the actual driving of the last spike, an ordinary iron one hammered in with an ordinary sledge by Leland Stanford of Central Pacific and T.C. Durant of Union Pacific; the spike and sledge were wired to the telegraph to signal, at the moment of striking, the great event to the waiting world. First Stanford then Durant swung at the wired spike — and both missed. Nevertheless, the telegrapher sent the signal and two other men drove home the last spike. Then the locomotives — Union Pacific's No. 119 and Central Pacific's 'Jupiter' — advanced until their pilots touched, bottles of champagne were broken, the chief engineers of both railroads shook hands and photographers took their pictures. A telegram sent to the Associated Press stated: 'The last rail is laid. The last spike is driven. The Pacific Railroad is completed. The Point of junction, ten hundred eighty-six miles west of the Missouri River and six hundred ninety miles east of Sacramento — Leland Stanford, Thomas C. Durant.' With the ceremony over, the special spikes of precious metal were quickly removed by officials.

The First Transcontinental Railroad: Central Pacific, Union Pacific by J. D. Galloway (New York, 1930);
Golden Spike by R. M. Utely and F. A. Ketterson (National Park Service Historical Handbook No. 40, Washington, D.C., 1969).

GOODNIGHT, Charles
1836-1929

A pioneer trail driver and cattleman of great renown, Charles Goodnight was born in Illinois and moved to TEXAS in 1846. During the Civil War he served with distinction in the TEXAS RANGERS and took part in many Indian fights. After the war he established a cattle herd in Palo Pinto County, Texas, and in association with cattleman Oliver Loving decided to drive their herds to market in New Mexico. In 1866 they pioneered the GOODNIGHT-LOVING TRAIL, over which Goodnight continued to drive cattle for several years. In 1869 he established a cattle ranch in Colorado and five years later decided to return to Texas. In 1877 he entered partnership with John Adair and developed the great JA Ranch in Palo Duro Canyon, in the Texas Panhandle, into a million acres of land with 100,000 cattle. Goodnight was an innovator. He created the first CHUCKWAGON; designed an improved, safer sidesaddle for women; crossed the hardy Texas LONGHORN with the Hereford to produce excellent beef animals, and conducted experiments in the cross-breeding of cattle and

buffalo, which produced a new type of animal, the cattalo. Goodnight was powerfully built, bow-legged from years in the saddle, and fiery in temperament, with a hatred of hypocrites, liars, and cattle thieves. He died aged ninety-three, leaving a town, a college, and a legend in his name.

Charles Goodnight, Cowman and Plainsman by J. Evetts Haley (Boston, 1936).

GOODNIGHT-LOVING TRAIL

A widely used cattle trail pioneered by Charles GOODNIGHT and Oliver Loving in 1866. Originally it ran from Fort Belknap in Texas to Fort Sumner in New Mexico, twice crossing the Pecos River on the way; a later extension continued north to Denver in Colorado and

129 *The Grand Canyon.*

Cheyenne in Wyoming. The cattle driven over this trail were sold to INDIAN RESERVATIONS, mining camps, and to stock new ranges. The trail ran through COMANCHE country and in 1867 Oliver Loving was wounded in an Indian attack while driving a herd and died soon after.

Cattle Trails of the Old West by J. Potter (Clayton, New Mexico, 1935);
Great American Cattle Trails by H. S. Drago (New York, 1965).

GRAND CANYON

The world's biggest and most spectacular gorge, the Grand Canyon of Arizona is a mile deep, from 4 to 18 miles wide, and 217 miles long. Through it winds the turbulent Colorado River. The river carved the Grand Canyon, working steadily over a period estimated at between 2.6 million and 10 million years. The Canyon is the most awesome example of the power of running water. The NAVAJO, the PAIUTE, the HOPI and other Indians lived and hunted around the Canyon for centuries. The first white men to see the mighty gorge were CONQUISTADORES of Coronado's expedition in 1540. The first expedition to journey down the Colorado River and explore the Grand Canyon was led by Major John Wesley Powell in 1869; Powell described the Canyon as 'the most sublime spectacle on the earth'. It is indeed a magnificent and stunning visual experience. By day and night it presents an endless shifting of colour moods; its buttes blue and purple, its stratified rock walls flashing with ruby and golden lights. In 1919 Congress created the Grand Canyon National Park embracing an area of 1,000 square miles.

The Exploration of the Colorado River and Its Canyons by J. W. Powell (Chicago, 1957);
The Grand Canyon by R. Wallace and E. Haas (New York, 1972).

130 *Construction crews of the St Paul, Minneapolis & Manitoba Railway — forerunner of the Great Northern — in 1887; the men slept in the big dormitory cars.*

131 *Inspection car on Pacific Railway approaching the Great Salt Lake.*

GREAT NORTHERN RAILWAY

One of the five major rail systems that opened up the West, the Great Northern ran from Lake Superior through Minnesota, North Dakota, Montana, Idaho, and Washington to Seattle on the north-west Pacific coast. It did not, however, become known as the Great Northern until 1890. The line had its origin in 1857 when the Minnesota legislature granted a charter to the Minnesota & Pacific Railroad Company to 'construct a railroad in the direction of the Pacific'. But after making only sixty-two miles of railbed the company ran into financial difficulties; in 1862 its rights were acquired by the St Paul & Pacific Railroad Company, which also developed financial problems and in 1878 James J. Hill (1838-1916), a man of immense business acumen and vision, gained control of the company and reorganized it as the St Paul, Minneapolis & Manitoba Railway Company. Under Hill's energetic drive the expansion of the railroad in Minnesota and into Dakota Territory continued at a steady pace and by the close of 1885 the system of main and branch lines had grown to 1,470 miles. Without government land grants and subsidies to help develop his line, Hill worked hard to create traffic and business for his trains and in so doing did much to colonize the northern plains of Dakota. He offered settlers cheap rates of transportation, loaned money to farms, imported purebred livestock, introduced improved strains of seeds, established experimental farms and credit facilities for producers, and he held rail rates at a level which enabled settlers to sell their products competitively in distant markets. By October 1887 the railroad had reached Great Falls in Montana Territory. In February 1890 James J. Hill's newly formed Great Northern Railway company took over the properties of the St Paul, Minneapolis & Manitoba concern and in that year the Great Northern's Pacific coast extension began, over the Rocky Mountains and finally over the Cascade Range in Washington, where the last spike was driven near the present station of Scenic on 6 January 1893.

The Life of James J. Hill by J. G. Pyle (New York, 1917); *The Story of the Western Railroads* by R. E. Riegel (New York, 1926).

GREAT SALT LAKE

This large body of shallow, briny water in north western UTAH, with its 27% saline content, is four to five times saltier than any ocean. It is 75 miles long, 30 miles at its widest point, has an average depth of 10 feet and a maximum depth of 30 feet, and covers an area of 1,500 square miles. It is the most extensive lake of its kind in the western hemisphere. Jim BRIDGER, the roving fur trapper, was the first man to discover Great Salt Lake, in 1824. The lake is fed by four rivers: the Jordan, Weber, Ogden and Bear. What makes the lake so salty? Scientists say the freshwater streams that feed the lake carry minerals and salts from high mountain rocks; and since the lake has no outlet and much of the water evaporates, these elements become trapped and create the saline content. The lake supports little life other than blue-green algae, brine shrimp, and brine flies. However, the irregular shoreline with its extensive mud flats and marshes, as well as the dozen islands that dot the lake, teem with bird life. West of the lake is Great Salt Lake Desert, a vast wasteland of 4,200 square miles, that claimed the lives of many FORTY-NINERS who tried to take a short cut across the desert to the gold fields of CALIFORNIA.

GREELEY, Horace 1811-72

Founder and editor of the New York *Tribune*, Horace Greeley was a keen promoter of Western

132 *Horace Greeley.*

133 *Wild Bill Hickok, a notable gunfighter.*

settlement and he made popular the phrase 'Go West, young man', which succinctly expressed the pioneering spirit of the times. However, contrary to general belief, he did not originate the phrase. It was first used in an article by J. L. B. Soule in the Terre Haute (Indiana) *Express* in 1851 and later adopted by Greeley, who wrote in the *Tribune* editorial of 13 July 1865 — 'Go West, young man, and grow up with your country.' The expression greatly encouraged settlers to go to the West. Greeley himself made a much-publicized trip out West in 1859 and experienced a number of adventures; he was involved in a stagecoach crash that left him with a permanent limp. He backed the founding of a colony in Colorado and in 1870 Nathan MEEKER and fifty families established the prosperous town of Greeley. Through the powerful medium of the New York *Tribune*, Horace Greeley was influential in shaping political opinion in the Northern and Western regions of the United States; in 1872 he was the Liberal-Republican candidate for the U.S. Presidency and was defeated by Grant.

An Overland Journey from New York to San Francisco by H. Greeley (New York, 1860, 1964);
Horace Greeley: Voice of the People by W. H. Hale (New York, 1950).

GRINGO and GREASER

To the Mexican of the Old West the white North American was a 'gringo', a nickname not intended as a compliment. The term derived from the Spanish *griego*, Greek and was used to describe a foreigner who spoke 'Greek' or an unintelligible language and was first mentioned in a Spanish dictionary in 1787. Thus it is not true that the term originated during the U.S.-MEXICAN War of 1846-8 from the song 'Green Grow the Laurels' then popular with American soldiers; it is said that the Mexicans, on hearing the constant repetition of the English words 'Green Grow', began to refer to all Americans as 'gringos'. To the North American of the Old West the Mexican was a 'greaser', a derogatory term that originated in the days when Anglo-American traders bought hides and tallow from the Spaniards in California.

GUNFIGHTERS

The most enduring myth of the Old West is the ritual shoot-out between two gunfighters who, observing the honourable 'code of the West', confront each other in a quick-draw duel in the

132 ∧

133 ∨

accepted Western movie fashion. The quick-draw legend is mostly nonsense; a frontier gunman intent on killing his rival or victim usually did so covertly, by ambush, trickery or surprise. Shooting a man in the back was far more certain than a risky face-to-face encounter. Formidable gunfighters such as Wild Bill HICKOK, Jesse JAMES, Pat GARRETT, and John Wesley HARDIN were all killed by shots in the back, and BILLY THE KID was gunned down by surprise in a darkened bedroom. The heyday of the professional gunfighter (outlaw and peace officer) came between the end of the Civil War and 1890. Cattle towns and frontier settlements employed gunmen of proved ability and steadfastness as peace officers to keep wild cowboys in order and outlaws at bay. Of course, swiftness in bringing a gun into action was important, but deliberation and accuracy were the prime factors for success. According to Wyatt EARP, himself a noted gunfighter, deliberation in a shoot-out was the key to survival; the professional, said Earp, 'took his time and pulled the trigger once'. Although the gunfighter would often use tricks and treachery to gain the advantage, he was usually a man of cool courage, quiet demeanour, and considerable shooting skill. He rarely drew his revolver in company without using it. Bat MASTERSON, another famous gunman, had this to say on the subject: 'Never try to run a bluff with a six gun. Many a man has been buried . . . because he foolishly tried to scare someone by reaching for his hardware. Always remember that a six-shooter is made to kill the other fellow, and for no other reason. Always have your gun loaded and ready, and never reach for it unless you are in dead earnest and intend to kill.' Another Hollywood myth is the low-slung gun holster, tied to the leg, the supposed 'trade mark' of the gunfighter; in the Old West the holster was worn high on the hip. Indeed, some top gunmen, like Wild Bill Hickok did not always use holsters and carried their revolvers stuck into a waistbelt, pirate fashion. The COLT six-shot Peacemaker model which came into general use in 1873 was a favourite weapon of gunfighters; it was finely balanced, ruggedly built, dependable, and fully loaded weighed just over three pounds. A gunfighter would often carry a small DERRINGER pocket pistol concealed on his person for emergency use, and a lawman on duty also favoured a SHOTGUN, one of the most feared weapons of the West. Some gunfighters wore two revolvers, but rarely fired them two-handed in the Hollywood manner; the second gun came into play when the first was empty or had misfired.

Triggernometry by E. Cunningham (Caldwell, Idaho, 1941);
Bat Masterson by R. O'Connor (London, 1958);
The Gunfighter, Man or Myth? by J. G. Rosa (Norman, Oklahoma, 1969).

HARDIN, John Wesley
1853-95

A desperado and gunman credited with killing forty-four men, John Wesley Hardin was born in TEXAS. His father, a Methodist minister, named him after John Wesley, the eighteenth century English evangelist and founder of Methodism. It was hoped that 'Wes' would also become a preacher. But he had a violent temper and at the age of fourteen wounded another boy with a knife; a year later he shot and killed his first man, a Negro. When three soldiers came to arrest him he killed them, from ambush. And so, at fifteen, Wes Hardin became a fugitive with a growing reputation as a gunfighter. In 1870 he was arrested and while on the way to Waco, Texas, to stand trial for murder, he killed one of his escorts and escaped. He then worked as a cowboy, driving cattle up the CHISHOLM TRAIL to ABILENE in Kansas; at that time Wild Bill HICKOK was the town's marshal. In his autobiography, Hardin claims that he made Hickok back down in a confrontation, having got the drop on the marshal with a pistol trick (some historians dispute this incident). Wes did not shoot Hickok and they became quite friendly, until the wild Texan shot a man for no good reason and had to flee Abilene. With the law constantly after him, Hardin traded in cattle and timber, operated saloons, and continued to gamble and argue and kill. The TEXAS RANGERS finally caught up with him in Pensacola, Florida, where he was arrested on a train on 23 August 1877. He was sentenced to twenty-five years in Huntsville Prison, Texas; after several escape attempts he settled down to study theology and law. He was released in 17 February 1894 and granted a full pardon. He opened a law office in El Paso, where he became involved in an argument with policeman John Selman, who shot Hardin in the back and killed him on 19 August 1895.

The Life of John Wesley Hardin by J. W. Hardin (Seguin, Texas, 1896);
John Wesley Hardin by L. Nordyke (New York, 1957).

HAYS, John C.
1817-83

A famous captain of the TEXAS RANGERS, John Coffee (Jack) Hays is best known for several victories over the COMANCHE INDIANS during the years of the Texas Republic (1836-45). Born in Tennessee, he went to Texas as a surveyor and joined the revolution against Mexican rule. A natural leader and courageous fighter, at the age

134 *John Wesley Hardin.*

of twenty-three he was appointed captain of a Texas Ranger company stationed at San Antonio. Jack Hays armed his men with the new COLT REVOLVERS, the early five-shot models; the Rangers used the weapon with great and stunning success, thus assuring the future of Sam COLT, whose later six-shot revolvers helped shape the history of the West. Hays led the first successful mounted action against the Comanches early in 1840 when, with fourteen Rangers, he was attacked by about seventy warriors north-west of San Antonio. The Comanches were accustomed to facing single-shot weapons, and when the firearms were being reloaded the Indians would charge, shooting a blizzard of arrows. But this time, instead of taking up a defensive position, Hays led his men in a spirited charge, taking heavy toll at close quarters with their repeating pistols. Shocked by the fire-power of the new weapon the surviving Comanches fled in terror, leaving 30 dead. In the following year Hays and forty Rangers fought off some 500 Comanches in the Battle of Bandera Pass, inflicting 60 dead or wounded. Jack Hays commanded a regiment of Rangers in the MEXICAN WAR of 1846-8; he later moved to California and became sheriff of San Francisco County and surveyor general of California.

Colonel Jack Hays by J. K. Greer (New York, 1952).

HELENA, Montana

The State capital that started life as a gold mining camp called Last Chance Gulch. In 1864 prospector John Cowan was about to give up his frustrating search for gold when he decided to try one last spot in the foothills of the ROCKY MOUNTAINS, which he named Last Chance Gulch. He found gold and started a rush to the area; a town sprang up and in two years the population numbered 7,500. By 1868 some 16 million dollars, worth of gold had been extracted from the region. As the town prospered on gold and silver, its citizens decided to change the undignified name Last Chance Gulch to Helena. In 1875 Helena became the capital of Montana Territory and retained that status when Montana became a State in 1889. Last Chance Gulch, site of the original gold strike, is now the city's main street and bears the name proudly.

The Montana Frontier by M. G. Burlingame (Helena, 1942).

HICKOK, Wild Bill
1837-76

A gunfighter and lawman of wide renown whose exploits, real and imaginary, have kept writers and film-makers busy for more than 100 years.

135 ▼

Some writers claim he was probably the greatest of the GUNFIGHTERS that roamed the Old West, the 'Prince of Pistoleers'. Hickok himself told Henry M. Stanley (the journalist-explorer) that he had killed more than 100 men, but then Hickok was prone to wild exaggeration of his exploits when the mood took him. James Butler Hickok was a striking figure, six feet tall with shoulder length hair. When not in buckskins he dressed in fashionable city clothes; it was said that, when possible, he bathed every day (an unusual custom among frontiersmen) and that he was quiet and courteous in his manner and speech. In desperate situations he was mostly cool and courageous and, if we are to believe him, he never killed a man except in self defence or in the line of official duty. He usually wore two COLT REVOLVERS stuck into a belt or silk sash, with the butts forward. Born in Illinois, he left home in 1855 to embark on his Western adventures. He became a stagecoach and freight driver and on 12 July 1861 he killed Dave McCanles in a fracas at Rock Creek Station, Nebraska. Some months later he is said to have won his famous sobriquet 'Wild Bill' by stopping a mob, single handed, from lynching a man. He served the Union Army in the Civil War as a scout, wagonmaster, and spy and is credited with all kinds of derring-do. On 21 July 1865 came his celebrated shoot-out with Dave Tutt in the public square of Springfield,

Missouri; he was tried for Tutt's murder and acquitted. The legend of Wild Bill was chiefly created by Colonel George Ward Nichols, whose incredible account of Hickok's supposed exploits, based on an interview with Wild Bill, was published in *Harper's New Monthly Magazine* of February 1867. Hickok was appointed a deputy United States Marshal in 1866, was elected sheriff of Ellis County, Kansas, in August 1869, and also served as town marshal of Hays. In April 1871 he became marshal of ABILENE, the Kansas cattle town; on 5 October he killed gambler Phil Coe in a gunfight and in the same incident accidentally shot and killed his friend, policeman Mike Williams. In 1872 he appeared in a Wild West show and in 1873 joined BUFFALO BILL Cody on the stage in a popular melodrama *The Scouts of the Plains*. In March 1876 he married Mrs Agnes Lake, a women eleven years his senior. Hickok was killed on 2 August 1876 in DEADWOOD, Dakota Territory, shot in the back by Jack McCall while playing poker in Saloon Number Ten. McCall was hanged for the murder in March 1877. Wild Bill was buried at Deadwood.

Wild Bill Hickok — The Prince of Pistoleers by F. J. Wilstach (New York, 1926);
The Real Wild Bill Hickok by W. E. Eisele (Denver, 1931);
Wild Bill and His Era by W. E. Connelley (New York, 1933);
Wild Bill Hickok by R. O'Connor (New York, 1959);
They Called Him Wild Bill by J. G. Rosa (Norman, Oklahoma, 1964, 1974).

135 *Helena, Montana, in the 1880s.*

136 *Wild Bill Hickok.*   136 V

HIDATSA INDIANS

A small tribe of the Siouan language group, the Hidatsa ('People of the Willows') were also known as the Minnetaree. They established a semi-agricultural life near Devil's Lake in North Dakota. Pushed by the SIOUX in the eighteenth century, the tribe moved across the plains to the junction of the Heart and Missouri Rivers. Like their close neighbours the MANDAN, the Hidatsas lived in earth-domed lodges, grew corn, and hunted the buffalo. The Dog Society of the tribe was an important organization of young warriors pledged to bravery in battle and used for tribal police duties. The tribe was visited by LEWIS AND CLARK in 1804, and by Prince Maximilian's party in 1834, when Karl BODMER the artist of the party made a number of paintings of Hidatsa life and customs. George CATLIN also lived with and painted the tribe in the early 1830s. The Hidatsas were almost wiped out by the smallpox epidemic of 1837 which swept up the Missouri and over the plains, killing thousands of Indians. Today, the descendants of the Hidatsas live with the survivors of the Mandan and ARIKARA tribes on the Fort Berthold Reservation in North Dakota.

HOLLADAY, Ben
1819-87

A powerful stagecoach king of the 1860s, self-made millionaire Ben Holladay also owned a Pacific steamship company, a railroad company, and many other business interests. Born in Kentucky, he grew up in Missouri and opened a store there, trading with the Indians and supplying U.S. troops. He prospered as a trader and on 21 March 1862 acquired the property of the bankrupt Central Overland, California and Pike's Peak Express Company. Holladay reorganized, improved and extended the service as the Overland Stage Line, which later became the Holladay Overland Mail and Express Company. By 1866 his coaches were operating over 2,760 miles of Western roads; for carrying the U.S. Mail the Federal Government paid him 650,000 dollars a year. He hired the best drivers, used the best horses and mules, and ran the finest coaches. It was Holladay's custom to make two trips annually over his line, and he travelled in a luxurious CONCORD coach pulled by a spanking team of six matched dapple-grey horses. On one occasion he was held up by a stage robber and relieved of his gold watch and chain and a few hundred dollars from his pocket, but the robber missed Holladay's concealed money belt which contained 40,000 dollars in gold; the incident became his favourite anecdote. On 1 November

137 *Hidatsa warrior in the costume of the Dog Dance, by Karl Bodmer.*

138 *Doc Holliday.*

139 *Ben Holladay.*

138 ∧

137

1866 Holladay sold his stage empire to WELLS FARGO AND COMPANY for 1.5 million dollars in cash and 300,000 in capital stock. He then formed the Northern Pacific Transportation Company, a steamship concern, and in 1868 became the owner of the Oregon Central Railroad Company. In 1873 he ran into financial problems and bond holders took over the railroad and ousted him. Ben Holladay never regained his former business power and died in Portland, aged sixty-eight.

The Overland Mail, 1849-69 by L. R. Hafen (Glendale, California, 1926);
Ben Holladay, the Stage Coach King by J. V. Frederick (Glendale, 1940);
Saga of Big Ben Holladay by E. Lucia (New York, 1959);
Stagecoach West by R. Moody (New York, 1967).

HOLLIDAY, Doc
1852-87

139 ∨

A gambler and gunfighter, John Henry Holliday was a qualified dentist who drilled more torsoes than teeth; he is credited with at least sixteen killings. Born in Georgia, son of a lawyer, he studied dentistry in Baltimore. At the age of twenty-one he developed consumption and was advised to go West where the dry climate would benefit his health. He went to Texas where he killed a man in Dallas and fled. He became a heavy drinker and earned his living as a professional gambler. He was tall and skinny, with fair hair, a pasty face, and cold blue eyes. He had a quick temper and his short life was a succession of violent incidents. Albeit a physical weakling, his skill with firearms made him a dangerous man indeed; he always carried two revolvers and a knife. In 1877 he met the prostitute 'Big Nose' Kate Fisher (or Elder) and thus began a tempestuous relationship (some say they were married). That year Holliday first met Wyatt EARP and they became firm friends. When Doc was jailed for knifing a gambler, Kate freed him by starting a diversionary fire and holding up a guard at pistol point. The couple fled to DODGE CITY, Kansas, where Wyatt Earp was a lawman. Here, Doc saved Earp's life in a desperate situation with a crowd of cowboys. In 1879 Holliday moved with Earp and his brothers to TOMBSTONE, Arizona, and suffered a slight wound in the celebrated Gunfight at the O.K. CORRAL in 1881, a shoot-out between the Earps and another faction. Doc died in the sanitarium at Glenwood Springs, Colorado, in November 1887 at the age of thirty-five after drinking a final glass of whisky. Wyatt Earp, in an article in the *San Francisco Examiner* in August 1896, said this of his friend: 'Doc was a dentist whom necessity had made a gambler; a gentleman whom disease had made a frontier vagabond . . . a long, lean, ash-blond fellow nearly dead with consumption, and at the same time the most skilful gambler and the nerviest, speediest, deadliest man with a six-gun I ever knew.'

The Frontier World of Doc Holliday by P. Jahns (New York, 1957);
Doc Holliday by J. M. Myers (London, 1958).

HOMESTEAD ACT

'I am in favour', said Abraham Lincoln in February 1861, 'of settling the wild lands [of the trans-Mississippi West] into small parcels so that every poor man may have a home.' And on 20 May 1862 President Lincoln signed the Homestead Act which allowed any adult citizen or alien immigrant who was the head of a family, on payment of a ten-dollar registration fee, to claim 160 acres of surveyed and unappropriated public land and after residing upon and cultivating the land for five continuous years, to receive full title to the land on payment of a further small fee. Such homesteads were to be exempt from attachment for debt.

The Lure of the Land: A Social History of the Public Lands by E. N. Dick (Lincoln, Nebraska, 1970).

HOPI INDIANS

Members of the Shoshonean linguistic family, the Hopi are sedentary village dwellers whose name means 'peaceful people'. They are PUEBLO INDIANS and live in pueblos (from the Spanish for town) made of ADOBE and stone on mesas high above the northern Arizona desert; the mesas served as natural fortification against hostile tribes. Hopis have lived in this region for more than 1,000 years. Their villages and lands were, and still are, highly organized under a matriarchal system of family and clan assignment dating back to prehistory. From ancient time the Hopis were agriculturalists, irrigating the desert lands at the foot of the mesas and growing corn, vegetables, fruit, and cotton. The first Europeans to contact the Hopi were members of Coronado's expedition in 1540. In 1598 Juan de Onate, governor and colonizer of New Mexico, entered the Hopi villages and swore the Indians to an oath of fealty to the Spanish crown and endeavoured to convert them to Christianity. However, no active Catholic mission was established until 1629, when four missionaries and twelve soldiers established Mission San Bernadino at Awatobi. Then the Pueblo revolt of 1680 destroyed the precarious

foothold of the missions among the Hopis. The Hopi remained free from outside interference until the mid-nineteenth century when the Americans began to make contact with them; the Hopi Reservation was established in 1882. Highly artistic, the Hopi are renowned for their pottery of exquisitely intricate design, basketry, weaving, carving and silversmithing. As well as being superb dry farmers they are also shepherds and cattlemen. Their rich mythology and folklore are poetic and imaginative; Hopi *kachina* dolls (symbols of human, animal, and plant fertility) and the ceremonial snake dance have become world famous.

The Hopis by W. C. O'Kane (Norman, Oklahoma, 1953);
The Hopi Indians by R. D. Simpson (Los Angeles, 1953);
The Hopi Indians by H. C. James (Caldwell, Idaho, 1956);
The Snake Dance of the Hopi Indians by E. R. Forrest (Los Angeles, 1961);
Book of the Hopi by F. Water (New York, 1963).

HORN, Tom
1861-1903

An army scout, PINKERTON agent, and range detective, Tom Horn is notable in Western history for the controversial trial in Wyoming in which he was found guilty of murdering a boy and was hanged. After distinguished service as a scout in the APACHE campaigns of the 1880s, Horn became a Pinkerton detective from 1890 to 1894 and captured a number of robbers. Then came his year as a range or stock detective. Hired by Wyoming cattlemen to protect their stock against RUSTLERS, Horn rode the range alone, a crack shot with a rifle, tracking down cattle thieves and, it is claimed, killing them instead of arresting them. Although it was never proved that he had shot alleged rustlers, his reputation as a deadly man-hunter was such that by 1898 cattle stealing in Wyoming had been reduced to its lowest ever level. In 1901 Willie Nickell, fourteen-year-old son of Kels Nickell, a sheep rancher, was murdered; it appears that the boy, wearing his father's coat and hat and riding his father's horse, had been shot in error by an assassin lying in wait for Kels Nickell. Rumour pointed the finger at Tom Horn. In 1902 deputy U.S. Marshal Joe LeFors tricked Horn, who was under the influence of drink, into making a private 'confession' to the Nickell murder; while Horn talked about the case in LeFors's office, two witnesses concealed in an adjoining room listened and one wrote down the 'confession'. Horn was arrested and charged with the boy's murder. The trial at Cheyenne, Wyoming, was a controversial one. There was little evidence against Horn but his reputation as a hired killer was damaging. He denied the incriminating statements in the 'con-

140 *Hopi snake dancer.*

141 *Tom Horn.*

142 *Pioneer homestead at Clear Creek, Kansas, in 1867.*

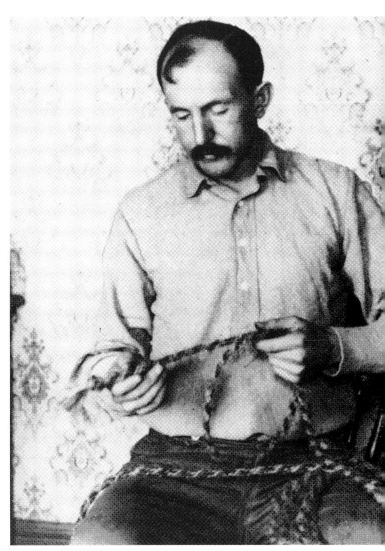

0 ∧   141 ∧   142 ∨

143   *Sam Houston.*

144   *General Oliver O. Howard.*

143 ∧

fession' and protested his innocence of the boy's murder to the last. Found guilty, he was hanged on 20 November 1903.

Last of the Bad Men, Tom Horn by J. Monaghan (Indianapolis, 1946);
The Saga of Tom Horn by D. F. Krakel (Laramie, Wyoming, 1954);
Rifle for Rent by G. Caesar (Derby, Connecticut, 1963).

HORSES

There were no horses in the Americas before the coming of the Spanish CONQUISTADORES in the sixteenth century, who brought with them mounts of fine Arabian stock. At first the Indians were terrified of the strange beasts. Of his conquest of Mexico in 1519-21, Hernando Cortés said: 'After God, we owed the victory to the horses.' Some of the Spanish horses strayed or were turned loose into the wilderness and there they multiplied greatly; to the later Anglo-Americans the wild horse became known as a MUSTANG. The PLAINS INDIANS took to the horse and developed an extraordinary horsemanship, exemplified by the centaur-like COMANCHE tribe of the South-west. The Indians bred special types of horses; the Comanches and KIOWAS favoured the *pinto*, or paint, a two-tone horse with large

145 ∨

144 ∨

patches of white, the NEZ PERCÉ tribe developed the spotted APPALOOSA. The Spanish-Mexicans produced the VAQUERO, the original cowboy, to manage the wild cattle on the great estates. From the vaquero evolved the Texas COWBOY and his cowhorse, a wiry, hardy animal bred from the mustang and other bloodlines; this working mount had an inherent 'cow sense', surefootedness over rugged terrain, and immense endurance. The most highly prized cowhorse was the 'cutting' horse, one trained over a long period to cut out, or separate a particular cow from the herd. Before the coming of the railroad the development of the Old West was dependent on the horse (and the MULE); it pulled the stagecoach, wagon, buggy, and plough, served the trapper and miner as mount and pack animal, did duty as a cavalry horse, and made possible the great cattle industry. The high value placed on horses by Westerners and cowboys made the horse thief the most hated of criminals, and when caught the horse thief usually suffered summary execution.

The Horse in America by J. G. Speed (New York, 1905);
The Western Pony by W. R. Leigh (New York, 1933);
The Horse of the Americas by R. M. Denhardt (Norman, Oklahoma, 1948);
The Indian and the Horse by F. G. Roe (Norman, 1955);
Mustangs and Cow Horses edited by J. F. Dobie (Dallas, 1965).

HOUSTON, Samuel 1793-1863

Frontiersman, soldier, and politician, Sam Houston became the first president of the Republic of TEXAS. Born in Virginia, he grew up in Tennessee and lived for several years with the Cherokee Indians, who adopted him into the tribe and called him 'the Raven'. At twenty he joined the army, fought against the Creek Indians, and resigned five years later. He then studied law and in 1819 was elected Attorney-General of Tennessee; in 1823 he was elected to Congress, as a Democrat, and served two terms; in 1827 he became the Governor of Tennessee. Houston was a big man, six feet two, with a commanding presence, energetic and restless. In 1829, after his first wife had left him, he threw up politics and went to live with the Cherokees in what is now Oklahoma; he established a trading post and took a Cherokee wife. In 1832 he went to Texas and settled there. When the Texans revolted against Mexican rule in 1835, Houston was made commander-in-chief of the rebel army. After the fall of the ALAMO on 6 March 1836 to the army of General SANTA ANNA, president of Mexico, and the subsequent retreat of the Texan forces, Houston managed to keep together a small force of less than 800 men and on 21 April 1836 launched a furious surprise attack on the Mexican army of 1,300 camped on the western bank of the San Jacinto River (near present-day Houston). The Texans completely routed the Mexican army in fifteen minutes, killing 630 and capturing 730, while suffering less than ten dead and twenty-five wounded; Houston himself was shot through the ankle. Santa Anna was captured the next day. With Texas a free and independent republic, Sam Houston was elected the first president and held the position until 1838, and again from 1841 to 1844. When Texas was admitted to the United States in 1845, Houston went as a senator to Washington. Later, when civil war threatened, he was opposed to secession from the Union and in March 1861 refused to take the oath of allegiance to the Confederate government. He relinquished his office and retired from public life.

The Raven: A Biography of Sam Houston by J. Marquis (Indianapolis, 1953);
Sam Houston, the Great Designer by L. B. Friend (Austin, Texas, 1954);
The Autobiography of Sam Houston edited by D. Day and H. H. Ullon (Norman, Oklahoma, 1954);
Sam Houston, American Giant by M. K. Wisehart (Washington, 1962);
Sam Houston and the Cherokees by J. Gregory and R. Strickland (Austin, 1967).

145 *Cowboys breaking in a horse, by Frederic Remington.*

HOWARD, Oliver O.
1830-1909

A general who served on the frontier as a peace negotiator with the Indians and later as commander in campaigns against the hostiles. Oliver Otis Howard commanded Union forces in the Civil War, in which he lost his right arm in the Battle of Fair Oaks, and reached the rank of Brigadier-General in the regular army. In 1872 he was sent to the South-west as peace commissioner to deal with COCHISE, chief of the hostile Chiricahua APACHES, and through patience and understanding managed to conclude a just treaty with Cochise. In 1877 however, when Howard was sent to deal with Chief JOSEPH and the NEZ PERCE INDIANS of the North-west, he displayed little diplomacy or sympathy with the Indian cause and bluntly ordered Joseph to move his people within thirty days from their homeland to a reservation, or be forcibly removed by the army. The situation resulted in the Nez Percé inflicting a crushing defeat on the First Cavalry in the Battle of White Bird Canyon; then Joseph and his people embarked upon their long, fighting journey to reach the sanctuary of the Canadian border. General Howard himself took to the field with a force and pursued the Indians over 1,000 miles. The end came in October 1877, some thirty miles from the Canadian border, when Joseph surrendered to Howard and General MILES. Promoted Major-General in 1886, Howard retired from the army in 1894.

My Life and Experiences Among Our Hostile Indians by O. O. Howard (Hartford, Connecticut, 1907);
Famous Indian Chiefs I Have Known by O. O. Howard (New York, 1908);
Chief Joseph: the Biography of a Great Indian by C. H. Fee (New York, 1936).

HUDSON'S BAY COMPANY

The powerful British enterprise that dominated the fur trade in Canada and the OREGON Country during the eighteenth and nineteenth centuries. Hudson Bay was discovered by the English navigator Henry Hudson in 1610. The Hudson's Bay Company was formed sixty years later when Prince Rupert, cousin of Charles II of England, set about realizing the visions of wealth inspired by the success of Frenchman Pierre Radisson, who had, a few years earlier, brought to Quebec a rich cargo of beaver skins. With seventeen associates

the prince obtained from Charles II a charter, granted on 2 May 1670, giving the 'Governor and Company of Adventurers trading into Hudson's Bay' the sole rights of trade in the unoccupied lands which drain into Hudson Bay. It was many years before the vast extent of this grant was fully realized. In terms of modern geography, the colony known as Rupert's Land embraced the provinces of Ontario and Quebec north of the Laurentian Mountains and west of the Labrador boundary, the whole of Manitoba, most of Saskatchewan, the southern half of Alberta, and a large portion of the North-west Territories. In return for settling and developing the colony, the charter granted the Company a monopoly on the region's natural resources, and powers of government. Over the next century the Company established posts at Hudson Bay and extended its area of operations, obtaining furs from Indians in exchange for trade goods shipped from England. The fur trade was highly lucrative and in 1784 the North West Company was formed in Montreal; the new company disputed the rights of the Hudson's Bay Company and actively opposed it. Forts were built side by side at strategic trading points and the fierce competition led to violence and open warfare until the two companies merged in 1821 under the name and charter of the Hudson's Bay Company. With renewed power the Company expanded its field of operations. In 1823-4 the expedition of Alexander Ross reached the headwaters of the MISSOURI; in 1825-6 Peter Skene Ogden was on the upper waters of the Snake River in southern Idaho, in 1826-7 he was in the valley of the Klamath in northern California, and in 1827-8 he was in Utah, east of SALT LAKE CITY, where the name Ogden City recalls his presence. The Oregon Country became the Company's Columbia District, ruled by the legendary John McLoughlin. Settlement of Oregon began about 1830 when some French-Canadian employees of the Hudson's Bay Company started farms in the Willamette Valley. At that time the Oregon Country — which included the present States of Oregon, Washington, Idaho, British Columbia, and parts of Montana and Wyoming — was divided between Britain and the United States. In 1846 the two nations agreed by treaty on the present boundary line (the Forty-ninth Parallel) that separates Canada from the U.S. When his vast domain became part of the U.S. John McLoughlin became an American citizen. In 1870 the Hudson's Bay Company relinquished its rights to govern Rupert's Land and its extensive territories were transferred to Canada in exchange for £300,000; the Company retained its trading posts and limited lands surrounding them. It continued its fur trading and in the twentieth century diversified into retail

146 *A Hudson's Bay Company trading post in 1845.*

merchandising. Today the Hudson's Bay Company, still in the fur trade, is one of Canada's leading business firms.

Company of Adventurers by L. H. Tharp (Boston, 1946);
The Fur Trade in Canada by H. D. Innis (Toronto, 1956);
The Hudson's Bay Company, 1670-1870 by E. E. Rich (Toronto, 1961).

HUGHES, John R.
1855-1947

A famous captain of the TEXAS RANGERS, John R. Hughes served in the force for twenty-eight years and became something of a legend in the Old West. Born in Illinois, he went to the INDIAN TERRITORY (Oklahoma) and lived with the Indians for several years, learning how to track animals and men. In 1878, working as a cowboy in Texas, he drove cattle up the trail to Kansas. He then started his own horse ranch in central Texas. In 1884 RUSTLERS stole seventy of his horses and he went after the gang alone. He caught up with them in the Texas Panhandle and in the ensuing gunfight four of the six thieves were shot dead and two wounded. Hughes returned to his ranch with most of the stolen horses, having been away just under a year and travelled some 1,200 miles. This incident led him to join the Rangers. He enlisted in Company D, Frontier Battalion, Texas Rangers, in August 1887 and, except for a six month period in 1889, served in the Rangers until January 1915. He was appointed Captain of Company D in July 1893. Hughes was involved in many gunfights with outlaws. He died aged ninety-two a much respected figure.

The Texas Rangers by W. P. Webb (Boston, 1933);
Triggernometry by E. Cunningham (Caldwell, Idaho, 1941).

IDAHO

The first white settlements in Idaho were established by fur traders. In 1809 David Thompson the North West Company erected a building on the shores of Lake Pend Oreille, called Kullyspell House, the first trading post in Idaho. For many years Idaho was part of the OREGON country. The discovery of gold near the present town of Pierce in 1860, and other subsequent strikes, brought a rush of people to the country and in 1863 Idaho Territory was created, a vast tract of land which included all of what is now MONTANA and nearly all of WYOMING. After Montana Territory was organized in 1864 and Wyoming Territory in 1868, Idaho assumed its present size and shape with Boise the capital. The first permanent town was Franklin, in south-eastern Idaho, settled in 1860 by MORMONS; a five-ton steam engine was pulled overland from Fort Benton (Montana) to power a mill in this community. Irrigation in Idaho was pioneered by the people of Franklin. Cattle and sheep flourished on the prairie and Idaho's great forests provided a major lumber industry which increased over the years. As the white settlers moved in, troubles with the Indians began. During the NEZ PERCÉ War of 1877, the warriors of Chief JOSEPH defeated white soldiers in White Bird Canyon, Idaho, and fought off a pursuing force on the Clearwater River; then the Nez Percé crossed the Bitterroot mountains into Montana in their marathon march to escape the U.S. army and reach Canada. In 1878 the BANNOCK INDIANS of Idaho went on the warpath to retain rights on the Camas Prairie. Today, the Nez Percé, Bannocks, and several other tribes live on reservations in Idaho. After being a Territory for twenty-seven years Idaho, with a population of 90,000, was admitted to the Union in 1890. One of the Rocky Mountain States, Idaho is rich in spectacular scenery. Hell's Canyon of the Snake River is the deepest gorge in North America, 5,500 feet deep on the average and 7,900 feet at its extreme. The Salmon River roars over 250 major rapids and through precipitous canyons. The Craters of the Moon National Monument is a strange, stark landscape of volcanic origin.

Idaho in the Pacific Northwest by D. W. Martin (Caldwell, Idaho, 1956);
History of Idaho by M. D. Beal and M. W. Wells (New York, 1959);
Mining Frontiers of the Far West, 1848-1880 by R. W. Paul (New York, 1963).

INDEPENDENCE, Missouri

For a number of years in the mid-nineteenth century the town of Independence, Missouri, served as one of several starting points for thousands of hopeful emigrants to the Far West. Here the WAGON TRAINS were organized and supplied in readiness for the long journey over the OREGON, SANTA FE, and CALIFORNIA Trails. Founded in 1827 on the Missouri River, the town became a centre for Indian and Mexican trade; in the 1840s it became a major outfitting point of departure for the overland emigrants bound for the Promised Land of the Oregon country.

147 *Horsemanship of the Plains Indians, by Frederic Remington.*

148 ∧

INDIAN HORSEMANSHIP

The PLAINS INDIANS were remarkable horsemen, their whole culture and wealth being based on the HORSE and the BUFFALO. In the saddle from early boyhood until old age, they spent every day riding. They hunted the buffalo on horseback, they fought on horseback, they played equestrian games and horse racing was a popular sport. The Indian rode virtually bareback, without benefit of stirrups, keeping his seat by knee pressure, agility, and an inherent 'oneness' with his highly trained mount. The rider did not use bridle and bit in the white man's sense but employed a short rawhide halter tied over the lower jaw of the horse; indeed the horse was so trained that, according to George CATLIN, describing a buffalo chase: 'The Indian has little use for the rein, which hangs on the [horse's] neck, whilst the horse approaches the animal on the right side, giving his rider the chance to throw arrows on the left, which he does the instant when the horse is passing.' The rein was generally used to stop rather than guide the horse. The Plains Indians mostly used a simple

form of pad saddle made from soft tanned skin stuffed with buffalo hair, or a low, forked saddle with a frame of elkhorn. The most celebrated feat of Indian horsemanship was the ability of a warrior to throw himself low on the side of his galloping horse in battle; the COMANCHE was a particular master of this trick, as Catlin describes: 'He is able to drop his body upon one side of his horse at the instant he is passing his enemy, effectually screened from their weapons, as he lies in a horizontal position behind the body of his horse, with his heel hanging over the horse's back; by which he has the power of throwing himself up again, and changing to the other side of the horse if necessary. In this wonderful condition he will hang whilst his horse is at the fullest speed, carrying with him his bow and his shield, and also his long lance of fourteen feet in length, all or either of which he will wield upon his enemy as he passes; rising and throwing arrows over the horse's back, or with equal ease and success under the horse's neck.'

North American Indians by G. Catlin (London, 1844); *North American Indians of the Plains* by C. Wissler (New York, 1927); *The Indian and the Horse* by F. G. Roe (Norman, Oklahoma, 1955).

149 ∧

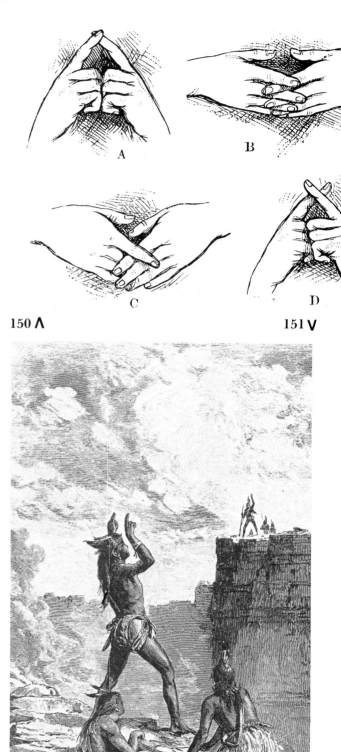

150 ∧

151 ∨

SIGNAL, "WHO ARE YOU?" ANSWER, "PANI."

148 *On a Sioux reservation in the 1880s; note government issue tent and metal cups.*

149 *A Pawnee scout, Rattlesnake, in 1867.*

INDIAN RESERVATIONS

An Indian reservation is an area of land reserved for Indian use. The name comes from the early days of Indian-white relationship when Indians relinquished land through treaty, 'reserving' a portion for their own use. Indian reservations were established in the West by the Federal government in order to control the movements of the nomadic tribes and as convenient places to put Indians removed from their native homelands to make way for white settlers. These reservations were not always the choicest of regions. The Federal government provided food and other supplies to the reservations and appointed an Indian agent to live among the Indians; his duties included dispensing annuities among the Indians in return for their land, to teach them how to farm, to keep white settlers off the land, to restrain traders from cheating the Indians and selling them prohibited alcohol. Some agents were good and able men, others were bad and corrupt. The term 'Indian agent' was abandoned in 1908 and the term 'Superintendent' adopted.

150 *Indian sign language; A illustrates a tipi, B a settlement or town, C a horse rider, and D means a trade or exchange;*

151 *Sign language. The Pani, or Pawnee, were also known as the 'horn people'.*

The Bureau of Indian Affairs, established in 1824, remains the principal Federal agency on the reservation. Modern Indians are not required to stay on reservations and can move about as freely as other Americans.

INDIAN SCOUTS

The Indian-fighting army of the West relied greatly on the services of friendly Indian scouts to guide soldiers through the wilderness, to trail hostile Indians and locate their camps. CROW INDIANS, traditional enemy of the SIOUX, served as cavalry scouts on the North Plains; Crow and ARIKARA warriors did much scouting and fighting for generals CUSTER, CROOK, and MILES in the Sioux War of 1876-7. Major Frank NORTH and his brother Luther raised the famous Pawnee Battalion of Indian scouts that served on the plains in the 1860s and 1870s. When General Crook had difficulty in locating hostile APACHES in the South-west campaigns he hired Apache scouts, realizing that only an Apache could trail another Apache in their arid and mountainous homeland. Indian scouts usually wore a mixture of army uniform and Indian dress.

On the Border with Crook by J. G. Bourke (New York, 1891); *Two Great Scouts and the Pawnee Battalion* by G. B. Grinnell (Cleveland, 1928); *The Crow Indians* by R. H. Lowie (New York, 1955).

INDIAN SIGN LANGUAGE

Because the many different tribes of North America spoke separate tongues the Indians developed a comprehensive method of communication by using hand signs, each expressive sign representing the item or idea it stood for. A few examples are shown in the illustration. The sign for 'buffalo' was made by holding two crooked fingers, representing horns, to the side of the hand. The sign for 'white man' was drawing the index finger across the forehead, indicated a peak or brim of a hat. The sign for 'good' was placing the right hand, palm down, against the left breast, then pushing hand away and upwards. The sign for 'bad' was to hold the clenched right fist against the left breast, then pull downwards, opening the hand fully. Today the sign language is virtually extinct and English has replaced it as the universal tongue of the Indians.

Indian Sign Language by W. Clark (New York, 1885); *Indian Sign Language* by W. Tomkins (New York, 1969).

INDIAN TERRITORY

The Indian Territory, now the State of OKLAHOMA, was established as the new homeland

152 *Indian Wars; Geronimo and three warriors in 1886.*

153 *Indian Wars; 'The Duel' by Charles Schreyvogel.*

of tribes removed by Federal policy from other parts of the United States in the nineteenth century. After the LOUISIANA PURCHASE from France in 1803, the newly acquired land was held in public domain until the 1830s. The western part of the Purchase (west of the State of Missouri and Arkansas Territory) became popularly known as the Indian Territory. It then seemed a remote and isolated part of the nation where Indians could live in freedom, out of the path of advancing white settlement. Accordingly, a Congressional Act of 26 March 1804 authorized the President to negotiate with the eastern tribes to cede their land to the United States in exchange for new tribal lands in the Indian Territory. Under the administration of President Andrew Jackson, removal became Federal policy and the Indian Removal Act of 1830 empowered the President to transfer any eastern tribe to trans-Mississippi regions. While many Indian tribes were moved into Oklahoma, the largest group, about 60,000 people, was that of the Five Civilized Tribes — the Cherokees, Chickasaws, Choctaws, Creeks, and Seminoles; the Civilized Tribes, so-called because of their high degree of cultural development, were resettled between 1828 and 1846 from their lands in the south-eastern U.S. In 1838 the army escorted some 15,000 Cherokees on a forced march of 800 miles, a tragic exodus of suffering and death known as the TRAIL OF TEARS. All of the Indian Territory that lay within the present State

boundaries of Oklahoma was assigned to the Five Tribes, with the exception of the north-eastern corner, which was occupied by a mixed group of Senecas, Shawnees, Quapas and various eastern tribes. In 1866 the U.S. government made the Five Tribes cede the western part of their new land to displaced Indians from Kansas and other States. In 1889 an area of some two million acres in the heart of the Indian Territory, purchased from the Creeks and Seminoles, was opened to white settlement. The next year Congress passed legislation that carved a new Territory of Oklahoma out of the Indian Territory (the latter was never an organized Territory). From 1890 until Statehood in 1907, the area that is now the State of Oklahoma consisted of the remains of the original Indian Territory on the east and the Oklahoma Territory on the west.

Indian Removal by G. Foreman (Norman, Oklahoma, 1932); *The Five Civilised Tribes* by G. Foreman (Norman, 1934); *History of Oklahoma* by E. E. Dale and M. L. Wardell (New York, 1948).

INDIAN WARS 1865-90

Warfare between the Indians of the West and white soldiers and settlers had continued inter-mittently through the first half of the nineteenth century; the final series of clashes and campaigns

153 ▽

came between the end of the Civil War and 1890, a twenty-five-year period in which the Indians fought gallantly to win some battles but were eventually defeated and crushed. Throughout this period of the Indian Wars there was an almost constant succession of small skirmishes and raids by Indian war parties that burned and pillaged, stole horses and cattle, and killed and captured the settlers. They would usually attack suddenly and then disappear. The army would learn of a raid only after it had happened; it would then rush to the scene and take up the trail, sometimes days later. Often the troops were unable to catch the hostiles, for the Indians were considerably more mobile than the American columns. Here, in brief form, are the major campaigns of the period:

Red Cloud's War of 1866-8 was waged by Chief RED CLOUD of the Oglala SIOUX and his allies mainly in protest against the army building forts to protect the BOZEMAN TRAIL, which led through Sioux country to the gold fields of Montana. The Indians constantly harried the trail and the forts, wiping out eighty soldiers in one engagement known as the FETTERMAN MASSACRE. The army lacked sufficient force on the Upper Plains to mount offensive operations and Red Cloud won his war. By the Treaty of FORT LARAMIE in 1868 the government withdrew the garrisons on the Bozeman Trail and abandoned the forts.

The Modoc War of 1872-3 was a campaign launched against the MODOC INDIANS who had left the government reservation in Oregon without permission and returned to their homeland on the California border. The fighting ended in victory for the army; the Modoc leaders were hanged and the tribe returned to reservation life.

The Kiowa-Comanche War of 1874-5 was fought on the Southern Plains and involved 3,000 troops from bases in Texas, New Mexico, and the Indian Territory marching against the hostile KIOWA and COMANCHE tribes in the Texas Panhandle. In September 1874 Colonel Ranald MACKENZIE launched a dawn attack on the Comanches' winter camp in Palo Duro Canyon and destroyed the village, its supplies, and precious horses. With winter approaching, the hostiles surrendered to reservation conditions.

The Sioux War of 1876-7 was a large-scale campaign against the Sioux and CHEYENNES on the Northern Plains which included the battles of the ROSEBUD and the LITTLE BIGHORN. Custer's defeat at the Little Bighorn was the Indians' greatest victory over the U.S. army but it brought relentless military retaliation. The Sioux were scattered; SITTING BULL and his people fled to Canada; CRAZY HORSE was induced to surrender and then killed while in custody. The once-powerful Sioux were broken and placed on reservations.

The Nez Percé War of 1877 resulted when the Nez Percé tribe of Chief JOSEPH refused to leave their tribal lands in Oregon for a reservation in Idaho; the Nez Percé routed an army column sent to remove them and then embarked on a fighting journey of more than 1,000 miles in an attempt to reach the sanctuary of Canada. After a number of running battles Joseph was forced to surrender when only thirty miles from the Canadian border.

The Bannock War of 1878 also came from the refusal of the BANNOCK INDIANS of Idaho to give up their tribal lands; after a final clash with an army column in September 1878 the Bannnocks surrendered.

The Ute War of 1879-80 in Colorado included the murder of Indian agent Nathan MEEKER by the UTE INDIANS, and their successful ambush of Major Thornburgh's command. Like the other hostiles the Utes were forced to accept reservation life.

The Apache War of the 1880s was the last of the major Indian campaigns. Under the leadership of GERONIMO, the fierce Chiricahua APACHES resisted the U.S. military in the deserts and mountains of the South-west for several years until Geronimo finally surrendered in September 1886.

The last battle, if battle it can be called, between the Indians and the U.S. army ended with the brutal massacre of a Sioux band at WOUNDED KNEE in South Dakota in December 1890. The Indian Wars were over.

Indian-Fighting Army by F. Downey (New York, 1944);
Indian Wars of the West by P. I. Wellman (New York, 1953);
Fighting Indians of the West by D. Brown and M. F. Schmidt (New York, 1948);
Great Western Indian Fights by Members of the Potomac Corral of Westerners (Lincoln, Nebraska, 1960);
Bury My Heart at Wounded Knee by D. Brown (London, 1971).

INDIAN WEAPONS

Indian warriors used bows and arrows, war clubs, tomahawks (axes), lances, knives, and small round shields; they also took readily to the white man's firearms. The PLAINS INDIANS bow was short, about three feet long, for easy handling on horseback; it was made of wood, horn or bone and strung with BUFFALO sinews. Arrow heads were of flint, bone, and metal; the shafts were fletched with turkey, owl, or buzzard feathers. The quiver, made of skin, held about 100 arrows; the quiver and bow case were often attached to each other. A COMANCHE could let fly with twenty arrows in the time it took a white man to fire a single-shot musket and reload. War clubs usually had a stone head fixed to a wooden shaft. Tomahawk heads were also made of stone and later metal; the axe was essentially a close quarter weapon but could be thrown from horseback with considerable accuracy. Knives were also used for close quarter combat and for SCALPING the enemy. The Plains Indian circular shield was made of thick buffalo hide, specially cured and toughened; a breastplate of closely threaded buffalo bones was also used for protection. The lance was up to fifteen feet long, its shaft decorated with scalps and feathers. Some fearless warriors rode into battle armed only with a coup stick; to 'count coup' (from the French for blow) or touch an enemy and live to tell the tale was the very highest battle honour among the Plains Indians.

Indians of the Unites States by C. Wissler (New York, 1946); *Indians of the Plains* by R. H. Lowie (New York, 1954); *Indians of the High Plains* by G. E. Hyde (Norman, Oklahoma, 1959).

IOWA

Situated between the MISSISSIPPI and MISSOURI rivers, the State of Iowa is renowned for its agriculture. When the first white settlers came here in the 1830s the land was mostly PRAIRIES, the only strips of forest being found near the rivers. The rich soil produced excellent crops of Indian corn, wheat, rye, oats, buckwheat, and potatoes; pumpkins, melons, fruits and vegetables flourished. Iowa became known as 'the land where the tall corn grows'. Part of the LOUISIANA PURCHASE of 1803, Iowa before 1803 was wholly Indian country and was not open to legal settlement. The Iowa Indians, from whom the State takes its name, inhabited the central area, in the Des Moines River valley; the Sac (or Sauk) and Fox people lived along the Mississippi, and the OMAHA, Oto, and Missouri Indians lived in the western and south-western parts of the country. Iowa's Indian history in the nineteenth century centres mainly upon the Sac and Fox and their leaders Black Hawk, Keokuk, and Wapello. After the Black Hawk War of 1832, the United States purchased a piece of Iowa along the Mississippi and opened it to settlers in June 1833; land-hungry pioneers rushed in to farm the fertile land. Under a treaty of 1842 the Sacs and Foxes ceded all their Iowa lands to the United States. With the subsequent removal of the Indian tribes all of Iowa came under white ownership. Small groups of Sacs and Foxes returned to Iowa over the years and in 1856 the State passed a law

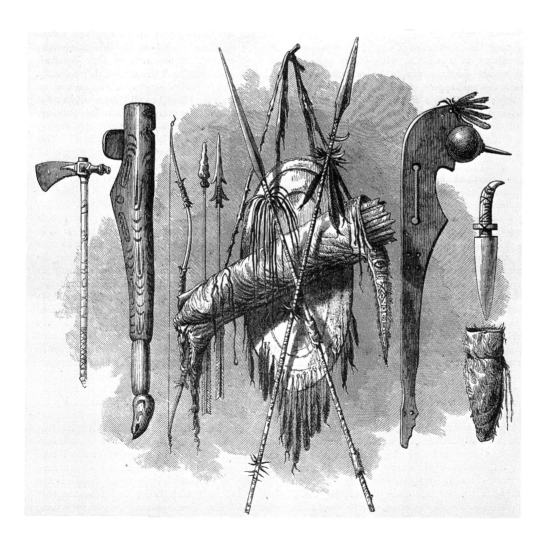

154 *Indian weapons.*

permitting them to remain. The last outbreak of Indian violence in the State was the Spirit Lake Massacre of 1857 when a renegade Sioux and his followers killed 42 whites to avenge the slaying of a relative by a white trader. The Territory of Iowa was created in 1838 and achieved Statehood in 1846, with Des Moines the capital. Council Bluffs, on the Missouri River, became a popular starting point for gold-seeking FORTY-NINERS and emigrants travelling the overland trails to the Far West. By 1870 the population of Iowa had reached more than one million, many being German and Scandinavians.

A History of the People of Iowa by C. Cole (Cedar Rapids, Iowa, 1921);
From Prairie to Corn Belt: Farming on the Illinois and Iowa Prairies in the 19th Century by A. C. Bogue (Chicago, 1963).

J

JAMES, Jesse
1847-82

Jesse Woodson James ranks with BILLY THE KID as the most famous of Western outlaws. Folklore and legend have cast him as a Robin Hood, a good boy forced by circumstances to follow a criminal life. And to some extent this may be true. Born in MISSOURI, son of a Baptist minister, Jesse and his brother Frank (1843-1915) grew up as farm boys. Their mother and step-father held Southern sympathies and during the Civil War their home was raided by Northern militia, who whipped young Jesse and nearly killed his step-father, Dr Samuel. Jesse and Frank joined the Confederate guerrillas of William Clarke QUANTRILL and learned to kill in ruthless company. At the war's end in 1865, Jesse rode in to surrender under a white flag and was shot and seriously wounded by a Union soldier. It is believed that Jesse took part in his first robbery in 1866 when a dozen men held up the bank in Liberty, Missouri. In December 1869 the James brothers were linked to a bank raid in Gallatin, Missouri, by a horse that was left behind and identified as 'the property of a young man named James'. A bank cashier was killed in the raid and a reward was offered for each of the James brothers. In 1873 Jesse and his gang derailed and robbed a train on the Rock Island line near Council Bluffs, Iowa; in the following year they robbed a second train at Gads Hill, Missouri. In June 1874 Jesse married his cousin Zerelda Mimms, who bore him two children. PINKERTON detectives were hired by the railroad companies to hunt down Jesse and his gang, and on a January night in 1875 the agents surrounded the Samuel home, believing Jesse and Frank to be there; they tossed a bomb through the window and the explosion killed Jesse's young half-brother and tore off his mother's right arm. This outrage brought much sympathy for the outlaw brothers. On 7 September 1876 Jesse and Frank in company with the three YOUNGER BROTHERS, attempted a bank robbery at Northfield, Minnesota, and walked into disaster. The alerted citizens opened fire on the raiders; of the eight bandits involved, three were killed and the three Younger brothers were captured. Only Jesse and Frank got clean away to live quietly for several years under assumed names, Jesse as 'J. D. Howard' and Frank as 'B. J. Woodson'. In 1879 they robbed a train, and another one in 1881; in the latter crime a conductor and a passenger were killed. Governor Crittenden of Missouri raised rewards of 10,000 dollars each for the James boys dead or alive. On 3 April 1882 Bob FORD, a new member of the James gang, treacherously shot Jesse dead in the back of the head in his home at ST JOSEPH, Missouri. Frank surrendered six months later; he

155 ∧   156 ∨

REWARD!
- DEAD OR ALIVE -

$5,000<u>00</u> will be paid for the capture of the men who robbed the bank at

NORTHFIELD, MINN.

They are believed to be Jesse James and his Band, or the Youngers.

All officers are warned to use precaution in making arrest. These are the most desperate men in America.

Take no chances! Shoot to kill!!

J. H. McDonald,
SHERIFF

155 *Jesse James.*

156 *Reward poster for the James-Younger gang.*

stood trial and was acquitted. He gave up his criminal ways and lived a respectable life until he died aged seventy-two in 1915.

Life and Adventures of Frank and Jesse James by J. A. Dacus (St Louis, 1880);
Lives and Exploits of the Daring Frank and Jesse James by T. Thorndike (Baltimore, 1909);
The Rise and Fall of Jesse James by R. Love (New York, 1926);
The Complete and Authentic Life of Jesse James by C. Breihan (New York, 1953);
Jesse James was his Name by W. A. Settle (Columbia, Missouri, 1966).

JAYHAWKERS and RED LEGS

The 'Jayhawkers' were Free State men who opposed slavery during the settlement of KANSAS in the 1850s; in particular Jayhawkers were the guerrillas who clashed with the 'Border Ruffians' from pro-slavery MISSOURI during the Kansas-Missouri border warfare of 1857-9 over the slavery question. Both factions were guilty of brutal depredations. Those that supported slavery called the anti-slavery men Jayhawkers, meaning thieves. The term was later applied to Federal guerrilla forces in the Civil War. In time the name ceased to be derogatory and Kansas adopted the nickname 'Jayhawker State'. The 'Red Legs' were also Federal guerrillas from Kansas, raised in the Civil War to combat Confederate guerrilla raids; their name came from the red leggings they wore. BUFFALO BILL Cody and Wild Bill HICKOK were members of the Red Legs.

Civil War of the Western Border, 1854-1865 by J. Monaghan (Boston, 1955);
Kansas: A History of the Jayhawk State by W. F. Zornow (Norman, 1957);
A Frontier State at War: Kansas, 1861-1865 by A. Castel (Ithaca, New York, 1958).

JOHNSON COUNTY WAR 1892

The Johnson County War of WYOMING was instigated by the big cattle men of the powerful Wyoming Stock Growers Association, who raised a force of fifty gunmen, called the Regulators, in order to exterminate alleged rustlers. Trouble had been brewing for some time between the cattle companies and the settlers and small independent ranchers. The cattle boom was over, and the hitherto open ranges were being fenced; there were disputes over the ownership of unbranded cattle, the sale of stock, and cattle stealing. Members of the Association claimed

that Johnson County authorities aided the rustlers and that it was impossible to prosecute them. The final threat to the monopoly of the Wyoming Stock Growers Association was the formation of the rival Northern Wyoming Farmers and Stock Growers Association. The big cattle men decided to invade Johnson County and wipe out the 'rustlers'. They made up a death list of seventy suspects, hired twenty-five gunmen from Texas to aid their local force of Regulators and early in April 1892 the heavily armed expedition, led by cattle man Major Frank Wolcott, set out by train from Cheyenne to hunt down and kill the men they claimed were cattle thieves. They went to the KC Ranch and shot dead Nick Ray and besieged Nate Champion, who held out all day until the attackers set fire to the cabin and forced him into the open where he too was shot dead. News of the outrage reached Buffalo and an army of settlers, 300 strong, led by Red Angus, sheriff of Johnson County, went after the invaders and besieged them in the TA Ranch for three days until the arrival of the Sixth Cavalry ended the battle. Wolcott surrendered to the cavalry colonel and the prisoners were taken to Fort McKinney. However, such was the power and political influence of the cattle companies that the case against the invaders was dismissed.

Cowman and Rustlers: a Story of the Wyoming Cattle Ranges in 1892 by E. S. Ellis (Philadelphia, 1898);
The Longest Rope, the Truth About the Johnson County Cattle War by D. F. Baber (Caldwell, Idaho, 1940);
Frontier Justice by W. Gard (Norman, Oklahoma, 1949).

JOHNSON, 'Liver-Eating' c. 1823-1900

John 'Liver-Eating' Johnson was a huge mountain man who gained his nickname by killing CROW INDIANS and eating their livers in a ritual of revenge. In 1847 on returning to his cabin after a winter's trapping expedition, he found that his pregnant FLATHEAD Indian wife had been murdered by raiding Crows. Johnson, six feet three inches tall and weighing 260 pounds, vowed vengeance against the Crow nation; he determined to kill as many Crows as he could and eat their livers, not as a matter of taste, but to inflict humiliation and to establish his identity as the butcher. It is a point of argument whether he did actually eat the livers or simulate the action. The Crows sent picked warriors to kill him, but he scalped them all and got their livers and became a figure of awesome reputation in the Far West. It is claimed that Johnson killed 300 Crows in his lust for vengeance.

Crow Killer by R. W. Thorpe and R. Bunker (New York, 1969).

JOSEPH, Chief
c. 1840-1904

A famous chief of the NEZ PERCÉ tribe of the North-west, Joseph rose to national fame in the Nez Percé War of 1877. Son of old Chief Joseph, a Christian convert and friend of the white men, Joseph became the tribe's leader while still a young man; not through his prowess as a warrior or hunter, but because of his superior intelligence and remarkable strength of character. In 1855 the Nez Percé ceded a large part of their territory to the United States by treaty and settled on lands in Oregon and Idaho. Joseph's people occupied the ancestral lands of the fertile Wallowa Valley in Oregon. When gold was discovered in Nez Percé country, government agents proposed a

157 *Sheriff Red Angus.*

158 *Major Frank Wolcott.*

159 *Chief Joseph.*

157▼ 158Λ 159 ▼

new treaty which would remove Joseph's people from their valley to a reservation in Idaho. He wanted no part of the treaty but in the summer of 1877 General O. O. HOWARD delivered an ultimatum that all Nez Percé must leave the Wallowa within thirty days or be forcibly removed by the army. The Nez Percé had always been friendly with the white men and Joseph did not want war, but when the situation developed into armed conflict between his warriors and the soldiers, he decided to fight. After defeating a cavalry column sent after them and bringing an angry General Howard into the field with a large force, Joseph and his chiefs decided to seek refuge in Canada, as SITTING BULL had done after defeating CUSTER at the LITTLE BIGHORN. So began the epic flight of the Nez Percé, a fighting march of 1,300 miles across the United States, engaging separate commands of the U.S. Army all the way, and in nearly every instance either beating them or fighting them to a standstill. On 5 October 1877 Joseph and his surviving people were surrounded by fresh troops about thirty miles from the Canadian border. The Nez Percé were exhausted, cold and starving and Joseph surrendered to generals MILES and Howard, delivering his classic speech of the defeated Indian:

'Tell General Howard I know his heart. What he told me before I have in my heart. I am tired of fighting. Our chiefs are killed. Looking Glass is dead. Toohool-hoolzote is dead. The old men are all dead. It is the young men who say yes and no. He who led the young men [Ollokot] is dead. It is cold and we have no blankets. The little children are freezing to death. My people, some of them, have run away to the hills, and have no blankets, no food; no one knows where they are, perhaps freezing to death. I want to have time to look for my children and see how many I can find. Maybe I shall find them among the dead. Hear me, my chiefs. I am tired. My heart is sick and sad. From where the sun now stands, I will fight no more forever.'

Joseph and his people were sent to a reservation in the INDIAN TERRITORY (now Oklahoma) and in 1885 the great chief was sent to Colville Reservation in Washington, where he died in 1904, still an exile from his beloved Wallowa Valley.

Chief Joseph, the Biography of a Great Indian by C. A. Fee (New York, 1936);
Hear Me, My Chiefs by H. R. Sass (New York, 1940);
War Chief Joseph by H. A. Howard and D. L. Magrath (Caldwell, Idaho, 1941);
I Will Fight No More Forever; Chief Joseph and the Nez Percé War by M. D. Beal (Washington, 1963);
Saga of Chief Joseph by H. A. Howard (Caldwell, 1965).

K

KANSA INDIANS

The Kansa (or Kaw) tribe belonged to the Siouan linguistic family and had been long established on the Kansas river when Father Marquette, the French explorer and cartographer, came upon them in 1673. 'Kansa' meant 'wind people'. The tribe paid special attention to the wind's power, which they believed helped warriors setting out for battle. Warfare was the great interest of the Kansa and related tribes, for only by fighting could tribesmen reach high social position. The Kansa did not penetrate far west into what is now KANSAS, but their prairie villages of large, semi-permanent earth lodges became familiar to travellers on the eastern section of the SANTA FE TRAIL during the 1850s. Never very numerous, this hunting and farming tribe was reduced by smallpox and alcohol and degenerated to a poverty-stricken handful. By 1873 the last of their holdings had been sold to the United States and the tribe was removed to the INDIAN TERRITORY (now Oklahoma) where a few hundred Kansa still live.

The Kansa Indians, a History of the Wind People 1673-1873 by W. E. Unrau (Norman, Oklahoma, 1971).

KANSAS

All roads led to, or through, Kansas in the years of the Old West. Texas cowboys drove their LONGHORN cattle up the CHISHOLM TRAIL to the Kansas railheads of ABILENE, NEWTON, ELLSWORTH, WICHITA, and DODGE CITY in the 1860s and 1870s. The SANTA FE TRAIL passed through Kansas to open trade with the Spanish in what is now New Mexico. The OREGON TRAIL crossed the north-eastern section of the State and the land impressed many emigrants who travelled the trail; some stopped and made their homes in Kansas while others returned later to settle on the rich farmlands. In the 1850s 'Bleeding Kansas' was a cockpit of civil conflict over the controversy of slavery. In May 1856 the town of Lawrence was sacked by pro-slavery 'Border Ruffians' from MISSOURI, and anti-slavery Kansas JAYHAWKERS struck back. In January 1861 Kansas entered the Union as a Free State; it was deeply involved in the Civil War, providing 20,000 soldiers for the Northern forces (out of a population of 30,000 men of military age); Lawrence was again sacked, by the guerrillas of W. C. QUANTRILL, in August 1863. In the eighteenth century Spain, France and England all had claims on the Kansas area. The English did nothing to further their claim. French claims were ceded to Spain in 1762 but in 1800 title was returned to France; in 1803 the United States purchased the entire Louisiana territory, which included Kansas, from the French. LEWIS AND CLARK (1804) and Zebulon PIKE (1806) passed through the Kansas area on their exploring expeditions. After the Civil War a series of Indian outbreaks threatened the Western frontier. The tribes were alarmed by the steady encroachment of white settlers. Indian attacks reached their height in Kansas in 1867, when some 130 settlers were killed. Western Kansas continued to have Indian problems until the last Indian raid in Decatur County in 1878. Meanwhile rapid settlement was being made, and the era of the great CATTLE DRIVES came in with the advancing railroads. In 1874 the introduction of Turkey Red Wheat by the Mennonite settlers from Russia was a milestone in Kansas agricul-

160 *Kansa Indians, by George Catlin.*

ture; this hardy winter wheat was ideally suited to crop-growing conditions in the State and provided the early basis for the prominence of Kansas as a wheat producer.

Pioneer History of Kansas by A. Roenigk (Lincoln, Nebraska, 1933);
Kansas: A History of the Jayhawk State by W. F. Zornow (Norman, Oklahoma, 1957, 1971);
Race and Politics: Bleeding Kansas and the Coming of the Civil War by J. A. Rawley (Philadelphia, 1969).

KANSAS PACIFIC RAILWAY

The railway from Kansas City westward was originally chartered in 1855 as the Leavenworth, Pawnee and Western Railroad. But very little construction was done by the contractors. When General John C. FRÉMONT and Samuel Hallett acquired control of the company in June 1863 it was renamed the Union Pacific Railway, Eastern Division, and construction got under way shortly after. In 1867 William F. Cody was hired to supply buffalo meat for the 1,200 workers building the railroad and in an eighteen-month period shot 4,280 of the beasts, thus winning his famous sobriquet BUFFALO BILL. In April 1869 the name of the line was changed to the Kansas Pacific Railway and was completed to DENVER, Colorado, in August 1870. The line carried Texas cattle east from the Kansas cowtowns of ABILENE, ELLSWORTH, and Hays, and brought out many immigrants to settle in the State. In January 1880 the Kansas Pacific lost its separate identity when it was merged with the UNION PACIFIC RAILROAD Company.

The Story of the Western Railroads by R. E. Riegel (New York, 1926);
Union Pacific Country by R. G. Athearn (Chicago, 1971).

KEARNY, Stephen W. 1794-1848

A regular soldier who served for many years on the Western frontier, Stephen Watts Kearny is famous as the commander of the Army of the West in the U.S.-MEXICAN WAR of 1846-8. Born in Newark, New Jersey, he joined the U.S. Army at the start of the War of 1812 and distinguished himself in the Battle of Queenston Heights. From 1819 he served almost continuously on the

161▼

162▼

161 *Kansas Pacific Railway advertisement of the late 1870s.*

162 *Chief Kicking Bird.*

Western frontier, taking part in various expeditions and building a number of forts. At the start of the Mexican War he was given command of the Army of the West and promoted to brigadier-general. Leaving Fort Leavenworth, Kansas, he marched westward with some 2,000 men and conquered New Mexico, of which he was made military governor. Pushing on to California he suffered a setback at the Battle of San Pasqual but eventually marched into San Diego. He then occupied Los Angeles and proceeded to Mexico, where he servd for a time as governor of Vera Cruz. It was in Vera Cruz that he contracted the tropical disease from which he died aged fifty-four.

The Mexican War by O. A. Singletary (Chicago, 1960);
Stephen Watts Kearny: Soldier of the West by D. L. Clarke (Norman, Oklahoma, 1961).

KENTUCKY RIFLE

The 'Kentucky' rifle was the favourite firearm of frontiersmen and hunters in the latter half of the eighteenth century and the first half of the nineteenth century. Its long, rifled barrel produced greater range and accuracy than other contemporary shoulder arms and its small bore — mostly .40 to .45 calibre — required less powder and lead. It was developed and chiefly produced by German and Swiss gunmakers who had settled in Pennsylvania and a more appropriate name would be 'Pennsylvania' rifle. The popular term 'Kentucky' rifle came into being through its association with Daniel BOONE and Davy CROCKETT and others who hunted in the Kentucky country. The rifle had an overall length of between five and six feet, weighed from nine to ten pounds, and was accurate up to 300 yards. It was a flintlock muzzle-loader, the lead ball being wrapped in a greased leather or linen 'patch' and rammed down the barrel, the patch imparting a tight fit to the ball thus ensuring greater muzzle velocity; the patches were kept in a patchbox carved into the rifle's butt and covered with a hinged metal lid. The classic Kentucky was an elegant, handsome weapon; the stock of polished maple wood, the patchbox lid and metal furniture ornate in design. The use of the Kentucky went into decline about 1830, superseded by the PLAINS RIFLE, a shorter more powerful weapon of the percussion type.

The Kentucky Rifle by J. G. W. Dillon (Washington, 1924);
The Rifle in America by P. B. Sharpe (New York, 1938);
Guns of the Early Frontier by C. P. Russell (Los Angeles, 1957).

163   *Typical patchbox decoration on a Kentucky rifle.*

163 ∇

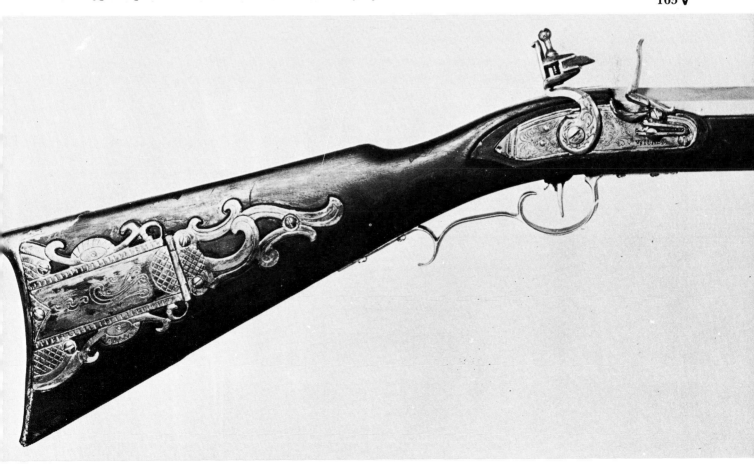

KICKING BIRD, Chief
c.1810-75

A noted chief of the KIOWA tribe, Kicking Bird was the grandson of a Crow Indian captured and adopted by the Kiowa. He distinguished himself as a warrior but later counselled his people to live in peace with the white men. He was one of the chiefs who signed the Treaty of Medicine Lodge in 1867 that settled the Kiowa on a reservation of the INDIAN TERRITORY (Oklahoma). Taunted by younger warriors for his loss of courage, Kicking Bird silenced his critics by leading a raiding party through Texas, beating off an army column sent after him. Having strengthened his leadership he continued to advocate peace. In 1873 he helped establish the first Kiowa school. Despite broken promises by the U.S. government he remained friendly and discouraged many of his people from taking the war path. When the army brought in hostile Kiowas, Kicking Bird was ordered to select those that must go to prison; one of them was medicine man Mamanti, who vowed vengeance against the chief. A little later Kicking Bird died mysteriously from poison.

The Kiowas, Their History and Life Stories by H. D. Corwin (Lawton, Oklahoma, 1958);
The Kiowas by M. P. Mayhall (Norman, Oklahoma, 1962).

164 Λ

KIDDER MASSACRE, 1867

On 29 June 1867 Lieutenant Lyman Stockwell Kidder of the Second Cavalry left Fort Sedgwick, Colorado, with ten men and an Indian guide, Sioux chief Red Bead, to carry dispatches to General CUSTER from General SHERMAN. Custer was in the field campaigning against the SIOUX and CHEYENNE. On the way Kidder and his men were attacked by a large party of hostiles and all were killed. When Custer came upon the scene of the fight he found the bodies of the soldiers horribly mutilated and bristling with arrows; each body pierced by twenty to fifty shafts.

My Life on the Plains by G. A. Custer (New York, 1874).

KING, Richard
1825-85

A powerful cattle baron and founder of the vast King Ranch in Texas, Richard King established a successful steamboat company before turning to the cattle business. Born in New York, he ran away to sea at thirteen and became a cabin boy. In 1847 he went to Texas, bought a small steamer and traded on the RIO GRANDE; in 1850 he went into partnership with Captain Mifflin Kenedy and built up a fleet of some twenty steamboats. In 1852 he decided to establish a cattle ranch and bought 75,000 acres in Nueces County on the coastal plain; he dug wells, purchased LONG-HORNS and horses, and hired Mexican VAQUEROS to ride the range. The ranch prospered and in 1860 Mifflin Kenedy came in as a partner. The King Ranch expanded greatly during the cattle boom of the 1870s and by the time Richard King died in 1885 his empire encompassed 600,000 acres containing 100,000 cattle. The ranch continued to flourish into the twentieth century and today it is the nation's largest cattle ranch, covering a million acres, with branches in Arizona, Pennsylvania, and Australia.

Cattle Kings of Texas by C. L. Douglas (Dallas, 1938);
The King Ranch by R. Lea (Boston, 1957).

KIOWA INDIANS

A small but very warlike tribe of the Southern Plains, the name 'Kiowa' comes from their own word *Kaigwu*, meaning 'principal people'. A tribe of distinct linguistic stock, it was related to the Athapascan Kiowa-Apache group. Originally,

164 *The Kidder Massacre.*

165 *Richard King.*

166 *Kiowa Indians Trailing-the-Enemy and his wife.*

165 ▼

166 ▼

the Kiowa lived in western Montana. According to tradition they left the region over a hunting dispute with another tribe and moved to the BLACK HILLS OF DAKOTA. Here in the early eighteenth century they formed an alliance with the CROW tribe, and the latter's life style changed the Kiowa from small game hunters using the dog TRAVOIS to BUFFALO HUNTERS with large herds of horses. They became typical PLAINS INDIANS, adopting the buffalo-skin TIPI, the annual summer SUN DANCE, and establishing soldier societies. Among the tribes north of Mexico the Kiowa are distinquished for their pictographic records in the form of calendar histories. Towards the end of the eighteenth century the Kiowa were driven south by the SIOUX, finally settling in the area of present western Oklahoma and the Panhandle of north Texas, and west into a part of New Mexico. Having made peace with their one-time enemies, the COMANCHES, around 1790, they established control of the area from the ARKANSAS RIVER to the headwaters of the RED RIVER, and with the Comanches became the masters of the Southern Plains. The Kiowa were among the most hostile and defiant Plains Indians in resisting the movement of white immigration along the overland trails. With the Comanches, they warred upon Texas frontier settlements, extending their raids far south into Mexico. Treaties with the United States, beginning in 1837, had little effect and the tribe remained ,unconquered until the buffalo herds were destroyed. After the Battle of the WASHITA in 1868, the Kiowas, Kiowa-Apaches, and Comanches were forced on to a reservation near Fort Still in the INDIAN TERRITORY (Oklahoma). But Kiowa defiance continued and in 1871, during Kiowa raids into Texas, Chief Satank was killed, and chiefs SATANTA and Big Tree were imprisoned.

The Kiowa Indians, Their History and Life Stories by H. D. Corwin (Lawton, Oklahoma, 1958);
The Kiowas by M. P. Mayhall (Norman, Oklahoma, 1962);
Bad Medicine and Good: Tales of the Kiowa by W. S. Nye (Norman, 1962).

LAND RUSH

At noon on 22 April 1889 the Oklahoma District — two million acres of unassigned land in the heart of the INDIAN TERRITORY, purchased from the Indians in January 1889 — was thrown open to white settlement under the HOMESTEAD ACT. And up to 100,000 eager homesteaders, on the signal to start, rushed in from the border to stake their claim to 160 acres of America's last frontier. They dashed forward on horseback and in wagons in a massed race to claim the best sites and within a few hours 1,920,000 acres were settled in chaotic conditions; by nightfall the newborn Oklahoma City had a population of 10,000 tent dwellers. This was the first of the Oklahoma land rushes, or runs. During the next sixteen years the remaining Indian lands west of the Indian Territory were also thrown open to homesteaders under similar conditions. In the initial settlement of Oklahoma two terms for certain homesteaders came into common use — the 'Boomers' and the 'Sooners'. The Boomers were illegal immigrants who tried to settle in the region in the early 1880s and were driven out by Federal troops; the Sooners were the impatient homesteaders who attempted to pre-empt the official signal that started the rush. In 1907 the Oklahoma Territory (organized in 1890) and the Indian Territory were admitted to the Union as the single State of OKLAHOMA.

History of Oklahoma by E. E. Dale and M. L. Wardell (New York, 1948);
Oklahoma: A History of the Sooner State by E. C. McReynolds (Norman, Oklahoma, 1954);
Frontier Life in Oklahoma by A. B. Wallace (Washington, 1964).

LARIAT

The lariat or lasso is the long rope with a running noose used by cowboys to catch and secure cattle and horses. 'Lariat' is the Americanized form of *lareata*, Spanish for rope, and 'lasso' from the Spanish *lazo* for noose. Actually, the working cowboy has always called the lariat a 'rope' — he does not 'lasso' a cow, he 'ropes' it. When roping on horseback the cowboy throws his noose over the animal's head or feet, then wraps his end of the rope around his saddle horn to anchor it, a technique known as a dally, from the Spanish *da la vuelta*, meaning 'take a turn with the rope'. The Anglo-American cowboys, who inherited many names and phrases from the Spanish-American VAQUERO, mangled the phrase to 'dolly welter', then 'dally'. The rope, loosely coiled, hung from the saddle, close to hand, was an essential tool to the old time cowboy. Apart from roping animals, he used it to form a make-shift corral on the trail, to pull cattle and wagons out of mire, to secure a load on a pack-animal, to haul firewood. The cowboy of the Old West also used his rope to hang horse and cattle thieves. Roping contests form part of the modern rodeo.

Cowboy Life on the Western Plains by E. B. Bronson (New York, 1910);
The Old-Time Cowhand by R. F. Adams (New York, 1971).

LAWMEN

There were various levels of lawmen and peace officers in the Old West: those who held town authority only, those who held county authority, and those with state and nation-wide jurisdiction. Most frontier towns had a town or city marshal, employed by the town council to keep the peace, arrest wrongdoers, and impose fines; the town marshal was usually supported by a body of policemen. The county sheriff was elected to office to enforce county laws and to collect taxes; he was assisted by deputy sheriffs. Although he had a county-wide mandate, the sheriff seldom enforced laws in towns unless requested to by the town marshal or community. Operating on a state-wide level were organizations like the TEXAS

167 *The Oklahoma land rush, by H. Charles McBarron.*

168 ∧

169 ∧   170 ∨   171 ∨

RANGERS and Arizona Rangers acting under the authority of the state governor; U.S. marshals and their deputies also had state-wide, as well as nation-wide authority. United States Marshal was the highest rank of lawman, he alone being appointed to office by the President of the United States. However, the post was generally acknowledged to be a political plum, a reward under the party patronage system; the actual hunting down of outlaws was usually carried out by the deputy marshals, capable men of action experienced in frontier fieldwork. U.S. marshals were mainly concerned with federal crimes, such as the robbing of the U.S. Mail and army desertion, but they could and did assist local law authorities when requested. Another law-enforcement organization which figured large in the Old West was the PINKERTON National Detective Agency, a private, commercial concern that enjoyed federal support in tracking down criminals throughout the United States; in those days the Pinkerton agency was, in effect, the equivalent of the modern F.B.I.

Famous Sheriffs and Western Outlaws by W. M. Paine (New York, 1929);
Frontier Justice by W. Gard (Norman, Oklahoma, 1949);
Great Lawmen of the West by C. W. Breihan (London, 1964);
The Western Peace Officer: A Legacy of Law and Order by F. R. Prasser (Norman, 1972).

172 V

LEADVILLE, Colorado

A boom city in the ROCKY MOUNTAINS, 120 miles south-west of Denver, that grew immensely rich from the silver-lead mines in the district. In 1860 it was a gold camp named Oro City; when the gold ran out in 1867 discovery of extensive silver-lead deposits ten years later created a rush that turned the small town (renamed Leadville in 1878) into a crowded city of 30,000 people by 1879; only DENVER, the State capital, was larger. Its most famous citizen was Horace A. W. TABOR, the poor postmaster whose Matchless Mine made him a silver millionaire and a national figure. Tabor, Leadville's first mayor, built the city an opera house that ranked with the finest in the land; here, in 1882, Oscar Wilde lectured the rough miners on the 'Ethics of Art' and afterwards descended into the Matchless Mine in an ore bucket. From 1879 to 1885 the total product of Leadville mines in lead, silver, gold and other metals amounted to almost 100 million dollars. When the price of silver dropped sharply and the depression of 1893 struck the West, Leadville went into decline and Bonanza king Tabor lost his great fortune. A gold strike in the late 1890s caused some excitement but Leadville's boom days were over.

Silver Dollar: The Story of the Tabors by D. Karsner (New York, 1932);
Here They Dug for Gold by G. F. Willison (New York, 1946).

LEVIS

The durable denim trousers that became popular throughout the Old West were first made and sold by Levi Strauss (1829-1902), a young Bavarian who landed in SAN FRANCISCO in 1850 to seek his fortune in the great GOLD RUSH. He had brought with him a small stock of tough canvas, intending to sell it to miners for tent covers. Instead, he discovered a shortage of hard-wearing trousers in the gold fields and had a tailor make up several pairs from the canvas. The trousers were successful with the miners and the word soon spread that Levi's trousers were stronger than any other. Strauss set up shop in San Francisco and began manufacturing large numbers of the waist-high overalls. He switched from canvas to a tough cotton fabric originally loomed in Nîmes, France, and called *serge de Nîmes;* this fabric, which came to be called 'denim', was supplied to Strauss in a new special indigo blue colour which could be depended upon for unvarying colour quality. The name 'jeans' for blue denims is said to have originated from the trousers worn by Genoese sailors, made from a fabric similar to denim called *genes*. In the late 1860s, to strengthen Levi's trousers, copper rivets were added to pockets and all points of strain; Strauss was granted a patent in 1873 and until it expired his were the only trousers to have copper riveted strength. Levi's ubiquitous denims became the working garb of miners, railroaders, farmers, lumberjacks, oil drillers, and cowboys. Strauss continued at the head of the business until his death in 1902 aged eighty-three. The company became international and today Levis and other types of denim clothes are worn all over the world. Several early pairs of Levis are part of the Americana Collection in the Smithsonian Institution in Washington, D.C.

LEWIS AND CLARK EXPEDITION 1804-6

Directly the United States had acquired the vast Louisiana Territory from France in 1803 (see LOUISIANA PURCHASE), President Thomas Jefferson appointed his private secretary, Captain Meriwether Lewis (1774-1809), to command an expedition to explore the unknown reaches of the MISSOURI RIVER and to find a route to the Pacific Ocean. Lewis chose Lieutenant William Clark

173 Λ

(1770-1838) to share the command and the expedition of some forty men set out from ST LOUIS on 14 March 1804. The party ascended the Missouri in boats into North Dakota and, after travelling 1,600 miles, established winter quarters near a MANDAN Indian village. In the spring of 1805 the party continued its journey, with the addition of French Canadian fur trader Toussaint Charbonneau, hired as guide and interpreter, and his young Indian wife SACAJAWEA and infant son. Sacajawea was a Shoshoni stolen by the Crow Indians and sold to the Mandan as a slave; she was a great help to the expedition, especially in the land of the SHOSHONI, and Lewis and Clark praised her in their journals. The party crossed the ROCKY MOUNTAINS, built canoes and swept down the Columbia River and looked upon the Pacific Ocean on 7 November 1805. They established a camp called Fort Clatsop and wintered on the coast. The homeward journey began in April 1806 and on re-crossing the Rockies the expedition separated into three parties to make a more extensive exploration of the country, descending the Yellowstone as well as the Missouri. They finally returned to St Louis on 23 September 1806, having been given up for dead. The long, arduous journey was a significant one; Lewis and Clark brought back maps of the hitherto unknown region, specimens of strange plants and minerals, accounts of Indian tribes,

the terrible Grizzly BEAR and teeming BUFFALO. They had explored the entire length of the Missouri River, something no man, white or red, had ever accomplished. Their reports made Americans realize what a vast and rich territory had been purchased from France, and this gave stimulus to Westward expansion. Lewis was appointed Governor of Louisiana Territory and died mysteriously in 1809, either by suicide or killing. In 1807 Clark was made superintendent of Indian affairs at St Louis, and in 1813 became Governor of Missouri Territory.

Lewis and Clark Expedition by G. C. Flandraus (St Paul, Minnesota, 1927);
Lewis and Clark by J. Bakeless (New York, 1947);
The Journals of Lewis and Clark edited by B. Devoto (Boston, 1953);
The Field Notes of Captain William Clark (New Haven, Connecticut, 1964);
Meriwether Lewis: A Biography by R. Dillon (New York, 1965).

LINCOLN COUNTY WAR 1878

An armed conflict in Lincoln County, NEW MEXICO, in which BILLY THE KID became a prominent figure, developed from a quarrel between two rival groups of businessmen and ranchers. Major L. G. Murphy, owner of a store, hotel, and other interests headed one faction; he was opposed by Alexander McSween, a lawyer, and his business partner John H. Tunstall, a rancher. McSween and Tunstall were supported by John CHISUM, a powerful cattleman; Murphy was aided by his partners Dolan and Riley and backed by James A. Brady, the sheriff of Lincoln County. Trouble arose through accusations of RUSTLING by Chisum, business rivalry, and a legal issue brought by Murphy against McSween and Tunstall. On 18 February 1878 Tunstall was shot dead by Murphy men and, it is said, Billy the Kid vowed vengeance against the killers of his employer. On 1 April the Kid and his cohorts ambushed and shot dead sheriff Brady and his deputy in the town of Lincoln. A few weeks later a man named 'Buckshot' Roberts was killed in a fight with McSween gunmen. Murphy nows fades from the scene; suffering from ill health he went to Santa Fe where he died in October 1878. George Peppin, sympathetic to the Murphy faction, was made sheriff of Lincoln County and he pressed the action against McSween, which culminated in a three-day gunbattle in the town of Lincoln, starting on 17 July. Peppin with a strong force besieged McSween and his group, which included Billy the Kid, in the McSween home. The battle ended on the night of 19 July when the McSween premises were set on fire;

173 *Meriwether Lewis (right) and William Clark.*

McSween and several others were shot dead as they came out, but the Kid emerged firing his guns, killed one man and made good his escape into the dark. With the chief protagonists now dead and dying the war was virtually over. Major General Lew Wallace took office as Governor of New Mexico on 1 October 1878 and in an attempt to stop the trouble completely he proclaimed an amnesty for all those involved in the bitter feud. But negotiations with Billy the Kid went sour, Chisum turned against him, and the Kid became an outlaw; he was eventually shot dead in 1881 by Pat GARRETT, the new sheriff of Lincoln County, who had not taken part in the 'war'. During the five months of the main conflict — 18 February to 19 July 1878 — nineteen men had been killed in the shooting and many wounded.

Violence in Lincoln County by W. A. Keleher (Albuquerque, New Mexico, 1957);
The True Story of Billy the Kid by W. L. Hamlin (London, 1965);
The Lincoln County War by M. G. Fulton (Tucson, Arizona, 1968).

LITTLE BIGHORN, Battle of the 1876

This fight in the valley of the Little Bighorn River, Montana, on 25-26 June 1876 is the most celebrated of the INDIAN WARS. Contrary to popular belief, General Custer's Seventh Cavalry was not totally annihilated in the battle; CUSTER and his immediate command of about 225 men were wiped out but the rest of the regiment held out in a defensive position until relieved by another column. The Battle of the Little Bighorn was a single action in a concerted campaign involving three separate expeditions against the SIOUX and CHEYENNE. The Seventh Cavalry, numbering some 700 men, located an Indian encampment on the morning of 25 June; it was the largest concentration of Indians ever assembled on the plains, containing about 10,000 to 15,000 Sioux and Cheyenne, with about 3,000 to 4,000 warriors (the figures are often disputed). Underestimating the great strength of the Indians, Custer decided to attack the camp without waiting for the main column, commanded by generals Terry and GIBBON, to arrive. He divided his regiment into three battalions; sent three companies under Captain F. W. Benteen to scout the bluffs to the left, while three companies under Major M. A. Reno and five companies under Custer marched on opposite banks of a small creek toward the Indian village in the Little Bighorn Valley. When near the Little Bighorn, Custer turned north toward the lower end of the Indian camp. Reno, with orders

174 *'Custer's Last Stand' by Otto Becker.* **175** *Longhorn cattle drive, from a painting by Tom Lea.*

from Custer to cross the river and attack, advanced down the Little Bighorn Valley and struck the upper end of the camp. Outflanked by the defending warriors, Reno retreated in disorder to the river and took up defensive positions on the bluffs beyond, where he was soon joined by Benteen and his men. Hearing heavy gunfire from the north, Reno and Benteen assumed that Custer was engaged and set out to join him. An advance company under Captain T. B. Weir marched a mile or so downstream to a high hill, from which the Custer battlefield was visible. By this time, however, the firing had stopped. When the rest of the command arrived on the hill it was attacked by a large force of the enemy, and Major Reno ordered a withdrawal to the original position on the bluffs overlooking the Little Bighorn. Here he was surrounded by an overwhelming enemy force and suffered heavy casualties in the ensuing fight. In the meantime, Custer had ridden into legend. His movements after separating from Reno's battalion are shrouded in mystery. All that is definitely known is that his command, dismounted, was surrounded and destroyed by a mass of warriors. Accounts by Indians who were in the fight vary greatly. The Reno-Benteen defensive position remained under attack until dark on 25 June and on through the following day. The siege was finally lifted with the arrival of the Terry-Gibbon column on 27th June. The

whole affair as far as the Seventh Cavalry was concerned was confusing, chaotic and incredibly messy. In the battle the regiment lost five companies (C, E, F, I, L) that were under Custer; the other seven companies under Reno and Benteen suffered 47 dead and 52 wounded. Indian losses are not known; estimates vary from 100 to 300. Most of Custer's immediate command were stripped, scalped and mutilated, but Custer's body was not treated in this fashion. He had one bullet in the left breast, another in the left temple. In defeating Custer the Indians had gained their greatest and most spectacular victory.

The Story of the Little Bighorn by W. A. Graham (New York, 1926);
Custer's Last Battle by C. F. Roe (New York, 1927);
The Custer Tragedy by F. Dustin (Ann Arbor, Michigan, 1939);
Custer's Fall by D. H. Miller (New York, 1957);
Custers Last by D. Russell (Fort Worth, Texas, 1968);
Custer Battlefield by R. M. Utely (National Park Service, 1969).

LONGHORN CATTLE

The hardy breed that became the foundation stock of the great cattle industry of the South-west in the 1870s and 1880s, the famous Texas Longhorn evolved from the cattle brought to America by the Spanish in the sixteenth century. Wherever the Spanish went in the New World

< 174
175 >

cattle went with them. Indian raids and the open range encouraged many of these animals to escape into the wild; there they increased rapidly and developed the characteristics that enabled them to survive on the hostile ranges of the Southwest. Thus, the longhorn is a distinctly American breed, resulting from natural selection and adaption to environment. The Texas Longhorn was wild and fierce; steers had a horn spread of from three to five feet. The bull, when charging, would turn his head sideways, hooking at his victim with the horn tip. The typical longhorn was big, slab-sided, rawboned and rangy. It has been estimated that as many as six million longhorns were roaming the TEXAS plains at the close of the Civil War. Over the next twenty-five years some ten million longhorns were driven north from Texas over routes such as the CHISHOLM TRAIL and the GOODNIGHT-LOVING TRAIL to railhead towns in Kansas (for shipment east) and the northern ranges. A trail herd usually numbered about 2,500 to 3,000 head, as a larger number was too hard to handle well. When properly managed the longhorns soon became accustomed to the trail and settled down, an aggressive steer taking the lead and usually holding it throughout the journey. Driving longhorns to market developed that special breed of horseman, the COWBOY. Because of the longhorn's wildness, danger of a STAMPEDE was ever present. By 1895 the age of the longhorn was coming to an end as ranchers introduced better strains of beef cattle, Shorthorn and Hereford, and trails were closed as the range was cut up into farms. By 1900 intensive cross-breeding had nearly erased the typical longhorn; it was saved from extinction by government and private endeavour and small herds were settled on wildlife preserves. In 1964 a group of Texas longhorn owners organized the Texas Longhorn Breeders Association of America, and this historic breed is now established with more than 3,000 animals registered.

The Range Cattle Industry by E. E. Dale (Norman, Oklahoma, 1930);
The Trampling Herd by P. I. Wellman (New York, 1939);
The Longhorns by J. F. Dobie (Boston, 1941);
The Chisholm Trail by W. Gard (Norman, 1954).

LONGLEY, Bill
1851-78

A notorious Texas gunman and outlaw, William P. Longley ranks with Wes HARDIN as a ruthless killer, being credited with thirty-two victims. He was sixteen when he killed his first man, a 'bad' Negro, and went on to kill many more blacks. He drifted through the West working as a cowboy, farm hand; a gambler, and for a short time ran a saloon in the BLACK HILLS OF DAKOTA. He was lynched by VIGILANTES as a horse thief; as the mob rode off they turned and fired a ragged volley at the figure hanging from the rope, and one of the bullets hit the rope and weakened it. The weight of Longley's big body, he was over six feet tall and heavy, broke the weakened rope and he escaped with his life. Captured by soldiers he was tried and convicted of the murder of an army quartermaster; he was sentenced to thirty years but while awaiting transfer to the Iowa State Prison he escaped. He continued killing men until he was arrested for the murder of Wilson Anderson, who Longley believed had shot his cousin. He was tried in Giddings, Texas, found guilty and hanged there on 11 October 1878.

Bill Longley and his Wild Career by T. U. Taylor (Bandera, Texas, 1925);
Triggernometry by E. Cunningham (New York, 1934);
Wild Bill Longley: A Texas Hard-Case by E. Bartholomew (Houston, Texas, 1953).

LOUISIANA PURCHASE 1803

When the United States purchased the vast territory of Louisiana from France in 1803 the size of the U.S. was almost doubled by the addition of 875,000 square miles lying between the MISSISSIPPI RIVER and the ROCKY MOUNTAINS. It was one of the world's richest areas, with fertile agricultural lands and great forests. After his failure to suppress the slave revolt in Haiti, Napoleon lost interest in colonies in the New World, and pressure from the U.S. to buy the port of New Orleans, and a coming war with England, decided Napoleon to sell the entire Louisiana territory to the U.S. for the agreed sum of 15 million dollars. A magnificent bargain, but

the U.S. did not have the purchase money and had to borrow it from an English banking firm and a Dutch banking firm at six per cent interest; the total cost of buying Louisiana being nearly 27 million dollars. The treaty of cession was signed in Paris on 2 May 1803 but officially backdated to 30 April 1803; the U.S. took formal possession of Louisiana on 20 December 1803.

Louisiana in French Diplomacy 1759-1804 by E. W. Lyon (Norman, Oklahoma, 1934);
The Man Who Sold Louisiana by E. W. Lyon (Norman, 1942);
Louisiana by E. A. Davis (Baton Rouge, Louisiana, 1961).

176 Λ

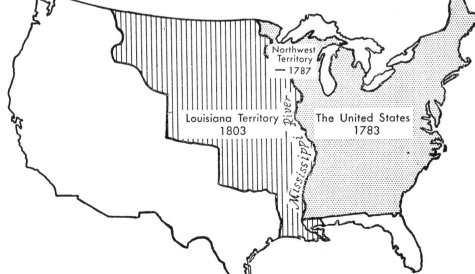

177 V

176 *Bill Longley in 1878.*

177 *The Louisiana Purchase.*

178 *The lynching of Frank McManus in Minneapolis, Minnesota, in 1882.*

178 >

LYNCHING

A lynching in the Old West generally meant the summary execution, usually by hanging, of a person without proper trial or legal process. The term 'lynching' probably derived from the name of Charles Lynch (1736-96), a Virginia justice of the peace who administered rough and ready punishment during the American Revolution. Under frontier conditions, when law enforcement by the proper authorities was weak or non-existent, angry settlers took the law into their own hands. Horse and cattle RUSTLERS, either suspected of stealing or caught committing the crime were often 'strung up' on the spot without benefit of trial. A vigilance committee (see VIGILANTES) was a volunteer and illegal group of citizens formed to wipe out acknowledged criminal activity by direct action. Sometimes prisoners were dragged from jail by a lynch mob and executed. In such situations innocent people were also put to death in the heat of the moment.

McCOY, Joseph
1837-1915

The pioneer cattleman who transformed the tiny settlement of ABILENE, Kansas, into the first major railhead cattle town to ship Texas LONG-HORNS east to the big cities. Joseph Geating McCoy, a livestock dealer from Illinois, came to Abilene in June 1867 and found the prairie hamlet well suited as a cattle-holding and shipping point. He bought 250 acres at the edge of the settlement, erected stockyards, shipping pens, barns, and a big hotel called the Drover's Cottage. He spread the word in TEXAS that he was ready for business and the long CATTLE DRIVES to Abilene began; by the end of 1867 some 35,000 head of beef had been shipped from the growing town on the railroad that in April 1869 became the KANSAS PACIFIC RAILWAY. Abilene boomed as the cattle business expanded. McCoy had made a profitable deal with the railroad but, later, with 200,000 dollars due to him on this account, the railroad abrogated the arrangement and McCoy had to sue for his money. Elected mayor of Abilene on 3 April 1871, McCoy was chiefly responsible for hiring Wild Bill HICKOK as town marshal on 15 April 1871 to control the cowboys and rough element. When Abilene ceased to be a cattle town, McCoy followed the business to WICHITA, Kansas; later he served as an Indian agent and went into politics. He died in Kansas City.

Historic Sketches of the Cattle Trade of the West and Southwest by J. G. McCoy (Kansas City, 1874, Glendale, California, 1940)
Early Days in Abilene by J. B. Edwards (Abilene, 1938);
The Cattle Towns by R. Dykstra (New York, 1968).

McDONALD, Bill
1852-1918

An outstanding captain of the TEXAS RANGERS, W. J. McDonald was widely known as 'Captain Bill'. Born in Mississippi he moved to Texas in 1866. After distinguished service as a deputy sheriff and deputy U.S. marshal he was appointed in 1891 Captain of Company B, Texas Rangers, with headquarters at Amarillo. A most courageous man he was involved in a number of gunfights; perhaps the most noted took place in Hardeman County when he was confronted by three desperadoes led by J. P. Mathews. After taking a shot from Mathews through the lung, the wounded McDonald killed the man. Then the other two opened fire on the ranger, hitting him twice in the left arm and once in the right side; this numbed the fingers of his gun hand and he could not cock the hammer of his single action

179 *Joseph McCoy.*

revolver. So he raised the gun to his mouth and pulled back the hammer with his teeth; this determined action unnerved the two gunmen and they turned and fled. McDonald recovered from his wounds and in 1897 smashed the notorious Bill Ogle gang of San Saba County. McDonald embodied the spirit of the Texas Rangers; it is said that on one occasion when called on to deal with a riot he turned up alone. 'Where are the Rangers?' asked the local authority. 'You ain't got but one riot, have you?' replied Captain Bill. McDonald left the Rangers in 1907 and was appointed State Revenue Collector by the Governor of Texas.

Captain Bill McDonald, Texas Ranger by A. B. Paine (New York, 1909);
The Texas Rangers by W. P. Webb (Boston, 1935).

MACKENZIE, Ranald
1840-89

As Colonel of the Fourth Cavalry, Ranald Slidell Mackenzie was highly successful in pursuing and defeating hostile Indians in the hard campaigns of the 1870s. Arguably a better soldier than his celebrated contemporary George A. CUSTER, Mackenzie eschewed personal glory and shunned publicity; he never wrote for publication and he never permitted journalists to ride with him on

180 ∧

182 ∨

181 ∧

183 ∨

campaign. Therefore he did not achieve the legendary fame of the flamboyant Custer. Born in New York City, eldest son of a famous naval commander, Mackenzie graduated from West Point in 1862 at the top of his class; commissioned Second Lieutenant of Engineers he went straight to the front in the Civil War and served the Union with distinction throughout the conflict. He fought in a number of battles, was wounded six times, was promoted Colonel of Artillery, commanded a cavalry division, and at the war's end held the rank of brevet Major-General. One of his wounds resulted in the loss of fingers and in later years the Indians called him 'Bad Hand'. General Grant, in his memoirs, said of him: 'I regarded Mackenzie as the most promising young officer in the army.' In 1871 as Colonel of the Fourth Cavalry he campaigned in Texas against the fierce COMANCHES and KIOWAS. Restless, tireless, a harsh disciplinarian, he whipped the Fourth into the best cavalry regiment in the army. In September 1874 Mackenzie found the winter camp of the Comanches, Kiowas, and CHEYENNES in a last stronghold, the deep Palo Duro Canyon on the Staked Plains. His surprise attack separated the Indians from their horses and supplies; Mackenzie burned the village and the winter stores and slaughtered more than 1,000 horses, thus depriving the hostiles of mounts and sustenance and forcing their capitulation. After Custer was killed at the LITTLE BIGHORN in June 1876, Mackenzie took part in the large scale operations against the SIOUX and Cheyennes on the Northern Plains. In November 1876 he defeated chief Dull Knife's Northern Cheyennes and destroyed their camp. In 1879 he campaigned successfully against the hostile UTE INDIANS of Colorado. A ruthless, dedicated soldier who never spared himself in the field, Mackenzie drove himself to breaking point. In March 1884 he was retired with the rank of Brigadier-General. Finally, he went insane and died on 19 January 1889 in his forty-eighth year.

On the Border with Mackenzie by R. G. Carter (Washington, 1935);
Ranald S. Mackenzie on the Texas Frontier by E. Wallace (Lubbock, Texas, 1965).

180 *Ranald Mackenzie.*

181 *Chris Madsen.*

182 *Mandan Indian of 1833.*

183 *Bat Masterson.*

MADSEN, Chris
1851-1944

Deputy U.S. marshal Christian Madsen earned his fame in the Old West as one of the so-called 'Three Guardsmen' of Oklahoma Territory, his law officer colleagues being Heck THOMAS and Bill TILGHMAN. Born in Denmark, he fought in the Danish army against the Prussians and later served in the French Foreign Legion. He came to America in 1876, joined the U.S. Cavalry and fought against the Sioux and Cheyennes. He witnessed the fight between BUFFALO BILL Cody and the Cheyenne chief Yellow Hand, in which Cody killed and scalped the Indian. In January 1891 Madsen left the army to become a deputy U.S. marshal in the OKLAHOMA Territory. A relentless manhunter, Madsen, with Thomas and Tilghman, tracked down and broke up the Bill DOOLIN gang. Madsen trailed the most dangerous member of the gang, 'Red Buck' Waightman, until he found him in a lonely cabin; Waightman tried to shoot his way out but was killed in the gunfight. Doolin was eventually killed by Heck Thomas. With the outbreak of the Spanish-American War in 1898, Chris Madsen became quartermaster sergeant of the 'Rough Riders', the cowboy cavalry regiment raised and commanded by Theodore ROOSEVELT. After the war he was appointed deputy U.S. marshal based at Ardmore, Oklahoma Territory, and later served as marshal. Of the Three Guardsmen he was the last to die; Heck Thomas died peacefully in 1912, Bill Tilghman was shot dead in 1924, Madsen died in 1944 aged ninety-two.

Trigger Marshal: The Story of Chris Madsen by H. Croy (New York, 1958).

MANDAN INDIANS

A tribe of the Siouan language group, the Mandans once occupied several villages of fixed earth lodges on the banks of the upper MISSOURI RIVER in North Dakota. A sedentary people, they cultivated maize, beans, gourds, and the sunflower; they also hunted the buffalo, their main source of food and clothing, and fished in the river. Tall, handsome and well-built, the Mandans were fastidious in matters of cleanliness and dress; their skin clothing and buffalo robes, decorated with quills and beads, being among the finest of the PLAINS INDIANS. They were also accomplished in making pottery. Their circular earth-covered lodges were about forty feet in diameter and twenty feet high, the centre of the roof being supported by four stout posts, with an opening in the middle of the roof for the exit of smoke. Largely friendly by nature, the Mandans spent more time on sport and games than warfare; they did, however, have a complex system of military societies. A highly religious people, the Mandans' most important ceremony was the *o-kee-pa*, a ritual of self-inflicted torture and amputation related to the SUN DANCE. Always friendly to the white man, the tribe was visited by LEWIS AND CLARK in 1804, by George CATLIN in 1832, and Prince Maximilian's party in 1833; both Catlin and Karl BODMER produced excellent paintings of the Mandans. In 1837 the tribe, then numbering about 1,600, was drastically reduced by the terrible smallpox epidemic to about 150. In 1870 the surviving Mandans, together with the remnants of the neighbouring ARIKARA and HIDATSA tribes were placed on the Fort Berthold Reservation in North Dakota, where, over the years, the Mandans lost their tribal identity.

Mandan Social and Ceremonial Organisation by A. W. Bowers (Chicago, 1950);
Indian Life on the Upper Missouri by J. S. Ewers (Norman, Oklahoma, 1968).

MANGAS COLORADAS
c. 1790-1863

A prominent chief of the Mimbrenos APACHES, Mangas Coloradas waged war against the whites from 1837 until his death. A powerful giant, six feet six inches tall, his Spanish name meant 'Red Sleeves', from a red flannel shirt he once wore. His implacable hatred of the whites stemmed from a massacre of his people in the Mexican village of Santa Rita del Cobre, instigated by a ruthless American trapper named James Johnson who had invited the Apaches to a feast in the village, then killed some 400 of them with the aid of a concealed cannon in order to collect bounties for Apache scalps offered by the Mexican authorities. Mangas escaped the slaughter and took revenge for the atrocity. In 1851 a party of American gold miners made the mistake of giving Mangas a savage whipping when he visited their camp alone; many innocent white settlers were to die for this humiliation. Mangas formed an alliance with COCHISE, chief of the Chiricahua Apaches, and terrorized the South-west. In 1862 Mangas was wounded in the Battle of Apache Pass in Arizona while fighting the California volunteers under General Carleton. In January 1863 Mangas was captured by U.S. soldiers and shot dead on the pretext that he was trying to escape; a white witness claimed that the chief was provoked by his guards who jabbed him with red-hot bayonets.

Life Among the Apaches by J. C. Cremony (San Francisco, 1868, Glorieta, New Mexico, 1970);
Death in the Desert by P. I. Wellman (London, 1972).

MASTERSON, Bat
1853-1921

A peace officer and gunfighter of legendary reputation, Bartholomew 'Bat' Masterson spent the last twenty years of his life as a popular sports writer on a New York newspaper. As a young professional BUFFALO HUNTER in Texas he had taken part in the Battle of ADOBE WALLS in 1874, in which a small party of hunters beat off a fierce attack by hundreds of Indians. He then served as a scout under General Nelson A. MILES. In 1876 Masterson killed a Sergeant King of the U.S. Cavalry in a gunfight in a Texas saloon. Moving on to DODGE CITY, Kansas, he served as a police officer and became a comrade of Wyatt EARP, Doc HOLLIDAY, Luke SHORT and other celebrated Western characters. In November 1877 he was elected sheriff of Ford County, Kansas, and shortly after captured the noted outlaw Dave Rudabaugh. In April 1878 Bat's elder brother Edward, the marshal of Dodge City, was shot dead by two cowboys; according to his biographer, Richard O'Connor, Bat rushed to the scene and gunned down his brother's killers. In January 1879 Bat was appointed a deputy U.S. marshal; mostly he lived on his wits as a gambler. Later, in Colorado, he became involved in prize fighting, acting as fight promoter and referee. In 1902 he settled in New York City and became a successful sports writer on the *Morning Telegraph;* he died at his desk from a heart attack on 25 October 1921. Masterson was described in a Kansas City newspaper of 1881 as being '. . . a medium sized man . . . his hair is brown, his rather small mustache of the same tint, and his smooth shaven cheeks plump and rosy. His eyes are blue, and gentle in expression, his attire modest but neat, and withal he is about as far removed in appearance from the Bowery frontiersman as one could well imagine. Strange as it may seem, he is grave and quiet in demeanor, and polite to a fault . . . Masterson said he had not killed as many men as was popularly supposed [23] though he had experienced a great many difficulties.'

Bat Masterson; the Dodge City Years by G. G. Thompson (Fort Hays, Kansas, 1943);
Bat Masterson by R. O'Connor (London, 1960);
Spotlight: Bat Masterson and Wyatt Earp as U.S. Deputy Marshals by Z. A. Tilghman (San Antonio, Texas, 1960).

MAVERICK

In the Old West a 'maverick' was an unbranded calf found wandering at large with no apparent owner. It was the general rule that any cattleman who came upon a maverick on his range was entitled to appropriate the stray and mark it with

184 *'Dispute over a Brand' by Frederic Remington.*

185 *Joe Meek.*

186 *Mexican War, the battle of the Resaca de la Palma, 9 May 1846. U.S. Dragoons charge the Mexican lines. Painting by Hal Stone.*

184 ⋀

185 ⋀

186 ⋁

his own brand. There were many disputes over mavericks. The name is believed to have originated from the unbranded cattle owned by Colonel Samuel A. Maverick (1803-70), a Texas lawyer. In 1845 he accepted a herd of cattle as payment of a debt and left them in charge of an idle Negro, who neglected to brand the calves and let the animals roam over a wide region; other ranchers took to adding this unmarked stock to their own herds. In 1853 Sam Maverick sold his herd and range to a rancher called Beauregard, who immediately made claim to all the unmarked cattle on the surrounding range and branded each Maverick animal with the Beauregard symbol. The term 'maverick' spread throughout the cattle country and came into common use, finally gaining dictionary status.

Samuel A. Maverick by I. and K. M. Sexton (San Antonio, Texas, 1974).

MEEK, Joe
1810-75

A notable Mountain Man trapper, Virginia-born Joseph L. Meek went West at the age of eighteen and for a dozen years trapped in the company of such legendary heroes as Jim BRIDGER and Kit CARSON. As brave as any of his hardy colleagues, Meek enjoyed a reputation as a wag and a joker whose sense of humour never deserted him even in the most perilous of situations. He stood over six feet tall, had a jovial, bearded face, and was a splendid story teller. When trapping went into decline in the 1840s, he settled as a farmer in Oregon country and was elected to the legislature. In 1848 he went to Washington to request protection for the American colony in the disputed OREGON territory (in which Britain had an interest) and presented himself — ragged,

187 *Nathan Meeker.*

188 *General Nelson A. Miles.*

189 *The Mexican War, the Battle of Cerro Gordo.*

187 ∧   188 ∧   189 ∨

dirty and lousy — as the 'Envoy Extraordinary and Minister Plenipotentiary from the Republic of Oregon to the Court of the United States'. On making a settlement with Britain, Congress created an Oregon Territory and Joe Meek served for a time as a United States marshal. He died on his farm in Oregon.

Joe Meek, the Merry Mountain Man by S. Vestal (Caldwell, Idaho, 1952).

MEEKER MASSACRE, 1879

The murder of Nathan C. Meeker, Indian agent of the White River Agency in Colorado, and his staff of eight white men by UTE INDIANS on 29 September 1879, caused as much excitement in the United States as had Custer's defeat three years earlier. On the same day as the Meeker massacre, Major T. T. Thornburgh and his command of 150 soldiers were halted by Utes at Milk Creek, some 25 miles from the White River Agency, and besieged for 6 days; Major Thornburgh and 9 soldiers were killed and 43 wounded. Meeker was a conscientious agent with high ideals, but his forceful attempts to turn the free-ranging Utes into farmers caused them to rebel and kill. When the Indians began to show hostility towards Meeker he sent for military aid. In answer, Major Thornburgh marched from Fort Steele, Wyoming, on 21 September. His command was besieged until relieved by a column under General Wesley Merritt. In the meantime, the Utes had killed Meeker and his staff and carried off three women, including Meeker's wife and daughter, who were raped by their captors. The uprising was eventually brought to an end by the efforts of Ute Chief OURAY and the women released. The Utes paid dearly for their violence. Their treaty rights were cancelled; they had to make heavy annuities to the white survivors and to the families of those killed in the massacre, and they were forcibly removed from their ancient tribal lands (12 million acres long coveted by white settlers) to a barren reservation in Utah.

Massacre; the Tragedy at White River by M. Sprague (Boston, 1957).

MEXICAN WAR, 1846-8

The war between Mexico and the United States was the result of the annexation of TEXAS to the U.S. on 1 March 1845. Mexico had protested the annexation of Texas, whose independence she had never acknowledged, and immediately broke off diplomatic relations with the U.S. When Texas was part of Mexico, the southern boundary of the province had been the Nueces River, but on declaring independence in 1836 the Texans had claimed the RIO GRANDE as their boundary. U.S. President James K. Polk sent a representative to Mexico to negotiate for the recognition of the Rio Grande as the southern boundary of the United States; when the Mexicans refused to negotiate, Polk ordered General Zachary Taylor and his army to march into the disputed territory and establish himself on the Rio Grande. The Mexicans viewed this move as an act of war. The first clash occurred on 25 April 1846 when Mexican troops crossed the Rio Grande and defeated an American cavalry patrol; more fighting followed and the U.S. declared war on 13 May 1846. President Polk entered the war with at least one object clearly in view — to seize all of Mexico north of the Rio Grande and the Gila River and westward to the Pacific. The war was mostly fought in Mexico proper but in June 1846 the Anglo-American settlers in the Sacramento Valley of California raised their 'Bear Flag' of revolt and declared California's independence of Mexican rule; they were aided by U.S. army officer John C. FRÉMONT and his small command. The United States won the war and American troops marched into Mexico City on 14 September 1847. Mexico's President SANTA ANNA resigned his office and fled the country. The war was formally ended by the Treaty of Guadalupe Hidalgo signed 2 February 1848. Mexico lost more than a war. By the terms of the Treaty she relinquished all claims to Texas above the Rio Grande, and ceded to the U.S. the lands of New Mexico (including the present States of Arizona, New Mexico, Utah, Nevada, and parts of Wyoming and Colorado) and Upper California (the present State of California). In return for this vast acquisition the victorious U.S. agreed to pay Mexico 15 million dollars. In 1853 Mexico sold another piece of land to the U.S. for 10 million dollars, known as the Gadsden Purchase after James Gadsden who negotiated the settlement; with this purchase the South-western borders of the United States were fixed as they are today.

The War with Mexico by J. H. Smith (New York, 1919);
The Story of the Mexican War by R. S. Henry (New York, 1950);
The Mexican War by O. A. Singletary (Chicago, 1960);
The Mexican War: A Compact History 1846-8 by C. L. Dufour (New York, 1968).

MILES, Nelson A. 1839-1925

An outstanding Indian-fighting general, Nelson Appleton Miles campaigned successfully against various hostile tribes in the 1870s and 1880s. Born in Massachusetts, Miles fought with great distinction in the Civil War on the Union side, being wounded four times and promoted to Major-General of volunteers. After the war he was appointed Colonel of the Fifth Infantry and commanded a column of infantry and cavalry in the Red River War of 1874-5 and defeated the COMANCHES, KIOWAS, and CHEYENNES in the South-west. Intensely ambitious, Miles was determined to reach the highest rank in the army. He was an excellent regimental commander; energetic, flexible in strategy and tactics, aggressive and relentless in pursuit of objectives. In 1876 he played a leading role in the pacification of the powerful SIOUX nation in Montana. In 1877 he pursued the NEZ PERCÉ and forced Chief JOSEPH to surrender. Miles was promoted Brigadier-General in 1880 and commanded the Department of the Columbia until 1885. In April 1886 he succeeded General CROOK as commander of the Department of Arizona; GERONIMO and his APACHES were on the warpath and Miles planned the campaign that eventually defeated the elusive hostiles. Miles established a system of observation posts located on high peaks, connected by the heliograph signalling device, and covering the operational area. He then sent small, mobile columns to intercept any hostiles sighted. Miles again proved successful and Geronimo surrendered to him in Skeleton Canyon, Arizona, on 4 September 1886. For his service in pacifying the Apaches the people of Arizona presented Miles with a sword of honour. Promoted Major-General in April 1890, he assumed personal command of field operations during the GHOST DANCE troubles which culminated in the massacre of Sioux at WOUNDED KNEE in December 1890. Miles viewed this slaughter of men, women and children as an outrageous blunder: he castigated the office responsible and convened a court of inquiry. In 1895 Miles achieved his life's ambition when he became Commanding General of the Army. He died in Washington, D.C. aged eighty-six.

Personal Recollections and Observations by N. A. Miles (Chicago, 1896);
Serving the Republic by N. A. Miles (New York, 1911);
The Unregimented General: A Biography of Nelson A. Miles by V. W. Johnson (Boston, 1962).

MINNESOTA

A land of large PRAIRIES, rolling hills, forests and more than 15,000 lakes, Minnesota is where the MISSISSIPPI RIVER begins its long journey through the United States to the Gulf of Mexico. Organized as a Territory in 1849, Minnesota entered the Union as the thirty-second State in 1858. Much of the land was opened to settlement

by treaties with the Santee SIOUX in 1851; in return for ceding their hunting grounds the Sioux received Federal annuities, supplies, and other considerations, but these benefits were not always regularly delivered, and settlers destroyed most of the Indians' wild game. In 1862 the Santee Sioux perpetrated the great Minnesota Massacre in which hundreds of men, women and children were killed. It began when government provisions were not forthcoming and the hungry Indians went to the Agency and pleaded for food; trader Andrew Myrick was unmoved, saying, 'Let them eat grass or their own dung'. The Santee, led by chief Little Crow, went on the warpath; they looted the Agency store, killed Myrick, stuffed his mouth with grass, and murdered twenty other settlers. The Indians swept through surrounding settlements, killing the men and carrying off the women and some of the children. It has been calculated that 644 white people were slaughtered in the uprising, and when the army moved against the hostiles 757 soldiers were killed in battle. The army subdued the Santee and thirty Indians were hanged in the town of Mankato in December 1862. Little Crow escaped and was shot dead by a settler in July 1863. The government confiscated the Santee annuities and lands and removed all Indians from Minnesota to a reservation in Dakota Territory.

History of Minnesota by W. W. Folwell (St Paul, Minnesota, 1921);
The Indian Wars of Minnesota by L. H. Roddis (Cedar Rapids, Iowa, 1956);
The Sioux Uprising of 1862 by K. Carley (St Paul, 1961).

MISSISSIPPI RIVER

The Mississippi River, the 'Father of Waters', is regarded as the greatest river in North America, the main stem of the Western river system. The exact length of the Mississippi is always arguable; it rises at Lake Itasca in northern Minnesota and flows in wide bends and curves for nearly 2,500 miles to empty in the Gulf of Mexico. Throughout its long journey there are great variations in the river's width and depth. Its principal tributaries are the MISSOURI, the ARKANSAS, the RED, and the Ohio rivers. Altogether there are in the Mississippi system 250 tributaries and their branches; during the steamboat age this vast network of rivers provided some 9,000 miles of navigable waterways. Hernando de Soto is generally accepted as the first white discoverer of the Mississippi; he reached it near the site of Memphis, Tennessee, in May 1541, he died upon its banks and was buried in it. In 1673 the Frenchmen Marquette and Joliet descended the river in canoes as far as the mouth of the Arkansas. In 1681 La Salle, another Frenchman,

190 *Steamboat on the Mississippi.*

followed the river from Illinois to the Gulf of Mexico. It was not until 1832 that the source of the Mississippi proper was discovered by Henry R. Schoolcraft. Throughout the nineteenth century the Mississippi served as the major artery of trade and commerce. Its entire length and tributaries became the waterways for the great surge of Western settlement by FLATBOATS, keelboats, and STEAMBOATS. During the Civil War control of the Mississippi was of vital importance to both sides, and when it came into full possession of the Union forces after the fall of Vicksburg, the Confederacy was split and seriously weakened.

Life on the Mississippi by M. Twain (Boston, 1883);
The Mississippi River by J. Chambers (New York, 1910);
Father Mississippi by L. Saxon (New York, 1927);
Life on the River by N. L. Wayman (New York, 1971).

MISSOURI

For many thousands of settlers, gold seekers, traders, and adventurers, Missouri was the gate-way to the West. The city of ST LOUIS, situated on the MISSISSIPPI RIVER where it is joined by the MISSOURI RIVER, was founded by French fur traders in 1764 and became the headquarters of the Western fur trade. Pioneers congregated at St Louis before starting out across the plains, purchased supplies and outfits, then boarded STEAMBOATS which took them 400 miles up the Missouri to the river bend at the Kansas border. Here, where the Missouri turns north, the frontier towns of Westport, INDEPENDENCE, and ST JOSEPH sprang up. Thousands of wagons bound for Santa Fe, Oregon, and California were moved by steamboat from St Louis to these outposts before rolling westward. Many emigrants settled in Missouri and worked the fertile land, raising large crops of Indian corn, oats, wheat, flax, hemp, and tobacco, as well as large numbers of livestock. Originally part of the LOUISIANA PURCHASE of 1803, Missouri was a slave State until 1865. The question of slavery was a major issue when Missouri applied for Statehood in 1818;

admission to the Union came in 1821 by way of the Missouri Compromise, in which slavery was prohibited in all that portion of the Louisiana Purchase lying north of 36° 30′, excepting Missouri. In the 1850s Missouri became involved in 'border wars' with Kansas, when Missouri 'Border Ruffians' invaded Kansas to aid the establishment of a proslavery government. During the American Civil War of 1861-5 the people of Missouri were bitterly divided in their loyalties; the State was plagued with guerrilla raids and Jesse JAMES, notable son of Missouri, rode with QUANTRILL's outlawed guerrillas. During the brief spell of the PONY EXPRESS, St Joseph served as the eastern terminus, and in 1882 Jesse James was shot dead while living in the town.

Missouri and Missourians by F. C. Shoemaker (Chicago, 1943);
The Missouri by S. Vestal (New York, 1945);
The History of Missouri by D. D. March (Chicago, 1967).

MISSOURI RIVER

The longest river in the United States, the Missouri was the principal route of the early fur traders and the settlers migrating to the West. Known as 'Big Muddy' from the immense amount of soil and sand it carries along, pioneers said the water was 'too thick to drink, to thin to plough'. Rising in the confluence of the Jefferson, Madison, and Gallatin rivers in the Rocky Mountains of MONTANA, the Missouri flows for 2,700 miles through mountains and plains until it joins the MISSISSIPPI RIVER above ST LOUIS. Marquette and Joliet were the first white explorers to discover the mouth of the Missouri, as they came down the Mississippi in 1673. The Missouri made St Louis, founded by the French in 1764, the greatest centre of the fur trade. LEWIS AND CLARK were the first to explore the upper reaches of the river during their expedition of 1804-6. The first steamboat was seen on the Missouri in 1819. For many years the Big Muddy served as a highway to the Far West for fur traders, gold seekers, settlers, and soldiers.

A History of the Missouri River by P. E. Chappell (Kansas City, Missouri, 1905);
Conquest of the Missouri by J. M. Hanson (New York, 1946);
The Fur Trade on the Upper Missouri 1840-1865 by J. E. Sunder (Norman, Oklahoma, 1965).

MOCCASINS

The moccasin, from an Algonquian word for shoe, was the universal footwear of the American Indian. Generally made of soft deerskin, the upper part was usually decorated with porcupine quills and beads. There were different types of moccasins. The PLAINS INDIANS favoured soft tops with soles of hard buffalo hide; the Woodland Indians of the East wore moccasins with soft sole and uppers. The COMANCHES of the South-west had moccasins with high leg tops, more boots than shoes; the APACHES wore similar moccasin-boots, with turned-up toes. Each tribe had its own style of making moccasins and this enabled trackers to identify a tribe by footmarks on the ground. The moccasin was adopted by the MOUNTAIN MEN trappers and other white frontiersmen.

MODOC INDIANS

A small tribe of northern California, the Modocs were hunters, fishers, and warriors; they were also slave traders, capturing the miserable Digger Indians of the California and Nevada deserts and selling them to the wealthy tribes of the north-west coast. In 1864 the Modocs reluctantly ceded their tribal lands to the United States and were moved to the Klamath Indian reservation in Oregon. The Modocs could not live peacefully with the more powerful Klamath tribe and a band of Modocs, under the leadership of Kintpuash (or Kientpoos), better known as 'Captain Jack', left the reservation and returned to their former lands. They refused to go back to the reservation and the army was sent to forcibly remove them; the result was the so-called Modoc War of 1872-3. Captain Jack and his followers took up an almost impregnable position in the Lava Beds on the California-Oregon border; the Lava Beds provided a natural stronghold of contorted masses of solidified volcanic lava, a broken region of natural rock trenches and caves. Here, Captain Jack held off superior forces for months. Finally he and his followers surrendered. Captain Jack and four other Modocs were tried by court martial and hanged at Fort Klamath on 3 October 1873. The survivors of his band were sent to a reservation in the INDIAN TERRITORY of Oklahoma.

Captain Jack, Modoc Renegade by D. P. Payne (Portland, Oregon, 1938);
The Modocs and Their War by K. A. Murray (Norman, Oklahoma, 1959).

MONTANA

A land of mountains and plains, Montana was the hunting ground of the BLACKFEET, SIOUX, CROW and other tribes who lived off the BUFFALO which once roamed the region in their millions. As part of the LOUISIANA PURCHASE, Montana was first explored by LEWIS AND CLARK in 1805-6; they came up the MISSOURI RIVER, crossed the

193∨   91∧   192∧

191 *Marquette and Joliet find the mouth of the Missouri in 1673.*

192 *'Captain Jack', Modoc leader in the war of 1872-3.*

193 *Moccasins of the Plains Indians.*

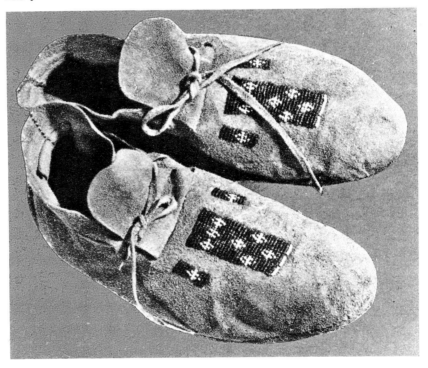

Montana Rockies and pushed on to the Pacific. The Missouri River begins in Montana, at the confluence of the Jefferson, Madison, and Gallatin rivers at Three Forks. Fort Benton, founded as a fur trading post in 1846, was the head of steamboat navigation on the Missouri. In 1862 gold prospectors struck it rich in Bannack, with later strikes in Virginia City and HELENA. Henry PLUMMER, sheriff of Bannack District and the biggest crook in Montana, was hanged in Bannack in 1864 by irate VIGILANTES. In 1863 the BOZEMAN TRAIL was opened from FORT LARAMIE, Wyoming, to Montana; the Sioux, CHEYENNES and Blackfeet attacked the wagon trains moving towards the gold fields and Montana's first army post, Fort C. F. Smith, was established in 1866 on the Bighorn River to protect the travellers. Montana has excellent ranges for raising cattle and in 1866 the first LONGHORNS were trailed up from Texas and Montana's great livestock industry was established. Charles M. RUSSELL, the famous Western artist, was a young cowboy here in the 1880s. In the summer of 1876 Montana attracted

194 ∧

195 ∧

194   *The Marquis de Mores in Dakota Terri-*
tory.

195   *Bull moose.*

196   *Monument Valley, the Mitten Buttes.*

196 ∨

national attention with the defeat of General CUSTER in the Battle of the LITTLE BIGHORN. In 1877 Chief JOSEPH and the NEZ PERCÉ marched from Idaho across Montana in a dramatic endeavour to reach Canada, but the army forced them to surrender in the Bear Paw Mountains, only thirty miles from the Canadian border. Montana became an organized Territory in 1864 with Bannack City its first capital, followed by Virginia City in 1865, and finally Helena in 1875; Montana entered the Union as the forty-first State in 1889. Today, Montana is the home of some 20,000 Indians, including the Blackfeet, Crow, Sioux, and Northern Cheyennes, who live on or near the State's seven reservations which total more than five million acres.

The Montana Frontier by M. G. Burlingame (Helena, 1942); *Montana: High, Wide and Handsome* by I. K. Howard (New Haven, Connecticut, 1943); *A History of Montana* by M. G. Burlingame and K. R. Toole (New York, 1957); *From Wilderness to Statehood: A History of Montana 1805-1900* by J. M. Hamilton (Portland, Oregon, 1957).

MONUMENT VALLEY

Located on the Arizona-Utah border, Monument Valley is part of the NAVAJO Indian Reservation. It is an area of natural sandstone monuments carved and fashioned by erosion over millions of years. Monument Valley, covering 1,500 square miles, is studded with pinnacles, columns, turrets, buttes and mesas of various shapes and sizes, some rising 2,000 feet above the desert floor. These magnificent rocky outcrops have been given names that seem appropriate enough: Totem Pole, Castle, Organ Rock, Mitten Buttes, etc. Film makers like John Ford have incorporated this spectacular landscape in many Western movies, such as *Stagecoach; My Darling Clementine; She Wore a Yellow Ribbon; The Searchers; How the West Was Won;* and *Cheyenne Autumn.* Monument Valley is owned and inhabited by the Navajos; they call it 'Among the Red Rocks'.

MOOSE
Alces americanus

Largest member of the deer family, the moose was hunted by the Indians for its meat and medicine; its ground-up hoofs and antlers being used in various potions for curing sickness. A huge, horse-like animal, often standing seven feet high at the shoulders and weighing anything from 900 to 1,500 pounds, it has remarkable antlers, flattened in a manner known as palmation; each antler is like a broad hand, the palm curved and held upwards, with the edges set with prongs. A bull moose often grows a spread of antlers six feet wide; like all deer, they shed their antlers each year. A semi-aquatic beast, the moose is normally seen alone or in small groups during the summer, frequenting marshy meadows and the margins of lakes and streams, feeding on tree twigs and aquatic plants. The name 'moose' is an Algonquian Indian word meaning 'twig-eater'. Moose often feed while submerged in water. When enraged a bull moose strikes vicious blows with its front feet as well as with its heavy antlers, and is a dangerous foe for man or beast. Moose are rapid runners and have a sharp sense of hearing and smell; nevertheless, Indians, white hunters and sportsmen greatly depleted the moose until the killing was strictly regulated by law. Today the moose population of North America is more than 250,000 and rising; they are found in Montana, Wyoming, Idaho, Minnesota, and are numerous in Alaska and Canada.

The Deer of North America by W. P. Taylor (Harrisburg, Pennsylvania, 1956).

MORES, Marquis de 1858-96

A French nobleman who became a cattle rancher in DAKOTA Territory in the 1880s, the Marquis de Mores founded the town of Medora on the Little Missouri River in Billings County (North Dakota). A restless adventurer, expert horseman and duellist with sword and pistol, de Mores married American heiress Medora von Hoffman in Paris in 1882 and came to New York; Medora's father gave the marquis a 500,000-dollar dowry and a job in Wall Street. He moved to Dakota Territory in 1883, bought a ranch overlooking the Little Missouri and entered the cattle business, establishing a packing plant and a town, which he named Medora after his wife. By the end of 1884 the thriving little town had a population of 251. The aristocratic de Mores made quite an impression on the tough Westerners. When a dispute arose between the marquis and another cattleman, a cowboy named Riley Luffsey threatened to shoot the marquis; the Frenchman killed Luffsey in a gunfight. However, bad management, harsh weather, and other difficulties doomed his cattle enterprise and de Mores quit Dakota in December 1886 and returned to France. Ten years later he was killed by Arab tribesmen in North Africa. Today a bronze statue of the marquis, dressed in cowboy garb, stands in Medora's De Mores Memorial Park.

Marquis de Mores at War in the Bad Lands by U. L. Burdick (Fargo, North Dakota, 1930); *Le Marquis de Mores* by C. Drouler (Paris, 1932); *A Gallery of Dudes* by M. Sprague (London, 1967).

MORMONS

The Mormon settlers came to UTAH in 1847, built SALT LAKE CITY, and tamed the desert, making it blossom like a rose. They were dedicated, disciplined, and industrious pioneers who overcame daunting obstacles to establish their own society and religious freedom. Mormons are members of the Church of Jesus Christ of Latter-day Saints, founded by the prophet Joseph Smith (1805-44) in the State of New York in 1830, and their bible is the Book of Mormon. The Mormon Church grew rapidly. Its members were pious, clannish, self-reliant, good farmers and hard workers. They practised polygamy, and for this and other religious 'deviations' they were persecuted by intolerant non-Mormons, who tarred and feathered and whipped Mormon leaders and burned the homesteads of their followers. After being driven out of Missouri the Mormons established the city of Nauvoo in Illinois; again they were forced to flee and in the violence Joseph Smith and his brother were killed. In 1847, led by the new leader Brigham YOUNG, the Mormons trekked into the wilderness of the Far West in search of Zion, their promised land — and found it in the valley of the GREAT SALT LAKE, a parched and unpopulated land. Immediately they began to irrigate, plant crops, build forts and houses, explore and colonize thousands of square miles of the virgin wilderness. Salt Lake City was their capital and base of operations. During the next few decades tens of thousands of Mormon converts, from Europe as well as the U.S., made the long journey to Utah to settle and cultivate the land. They came by covered wagon and on foot, pulling and pushing hand-carts. In 1850 congress established the Territory of Utah and named Brigham Young as governor. The Mormon colony grew in strength and in isolation and when it began to ignore Federal laws the U.S. government sent an army in the summer of 1857 to enforce Federal authority. Mormon guerrillas delayed and finally halted the army, which went into winter camp near FORT BRIDGER, Wyoming, and negotiations averted a full scale war. During this period of tension and threat of invasion some Mormons committed the MOUNTAIN MEADOWS MASSACRE, in which they wiped out a wagon train of non-Mormon immigrants passing through southern Utah. Although removed from his post as territorial governor in 1857, Brigham Young remained the real master of Utah until his death in 1877. He had directed the founding of more than 350 Mormon communities in Utah, Idaho, Nevada, Arizona, Wyoming and California.

A Comprehensive History of the Church of Jesus Christ of Latter-day Saints by B. H. Roberts (Salt Lake City, 1930);
Desert Saints: The Mormon Frontier in Utah by N. Anderson (Chicago, 1942);
The Mormons by T. F. O'Dea (Chicago, 1957);
The Utah Expedition 1857-1858 by L. R. Hafen and A. W. Hafen (Glendale, California, 1958);
Handcarts to Zion by L. R. and A. W. Hafen (Glendale, 1960).

MOUNTAIN LION
Felis concolor

Also known as the puma, panther, or cougar, the mountain lion ranged wide throughout the Old West, roaming the plains and woods as well as its preferred hunting ground in the high, rocky country. Short-haired and generally tawny in colour the mountain lion has an average body length, excluding its long tail, of five feet and weighs between 100 and 175 pounds. It feeds on small game, DEER, ELK, BIGHORN sheep and domestic livestock, including cattle and horses. It kills its victim by silently creeping close and pouncing suddenly; a single spring of twenty-five feet is not uncommon. It rarely makes an unprovoked attack on man. Hounded by ranchers protecting their livestock and professional hunters after bounty payment, the mountain lion was greatly reduced in settled regions by 1900. Today it is only found in the remote wilderness: the Rocky Mountains, New Mexico, Arizona, western Texas, and western Canada.

Mammals of North America by V. H. Cahalane (New York, 1947);
Wild Animals of North America by National Geographic Society (Washington, D.C., 1960).

MOUNTAIN MEADOWS MASSACRE
1857

In September 1857 a group of MORMONS massacred a wagon train of non-Mormons passing through southern Utah. The band of 140 ill-fated emigrants, known as the Fancher Party, included a number of roughnecks from Missouri. It is claimed that these so-called 'Missouri Wild Cats' sorely provoked the Mormons by trampling crops, killing chickens, insulting their women, and bragging of taking part in the massacre of Mormons in Missouri some twenty years before. On 7 September an Indian war party (incited by the Mormons) attacked and besieged the wagon train at Mountain Meadows. On 11 September a group

197 *Mormon hand-cart emigrants to Salt Lake City.*

198 *The Mountain Meadows Massacre.*

of Mormons, led by John D. Lee, approached the Fancher Party and offered safe passage through the Indians on condition that the emigrants give up their weapons. They agreed; then the Mormons (and the Indians) treacherously attacked the unarmed party, killing them all except seventeen small children. Ostensibly an Indian outrage, the Mormons later purged their collective conscience by bringing John Lee to trial in 1875 and executing him in 1877 on the site of the Mountain Meadows Massacre.

The Mountain Meadows Massacre by J. Brooks (Stanford, California, 1950);
John Doyle Lee: Zealot-Pioneer Builder-Scapegoat by J. Brooks (Glendale, California, 1961).

MOUNTAIN MEN

The hardy fur trappers of the ROCKY MOUNTAINS were known as Mountain Men. In their constant search for untrapped BEAVER streams in the first half of the nineteenth century, they became the first explorers of the unknown regions. The life of a wilderness trapper was a lonely, arduous, and dangerous one; his enemies included Indians, wild beasts, and ruthless rivals. By necessity he

199 *A typical mountain man with packhorse loaded with furs.*

200 *Mountain man trapper, heavily armed, with decorated buckskin coat.*

201 *Osage Indians capturing mustangs, painting by George Catlin.*

202 *Loading mule on the Washburn expedition through Yellowstone National Park in 1870.*

199⋀   200⋁

often lived with the Indians and adopted much of their way of life; he spoke their tongues, married their women, and adopted their buckskin dress and moccasin footwear. They came from Anglo-American, French, and Spanish stock and they used a polyglot jargon known as 'mountain talk'; more savage than civilized, few of them could read or write. Between the 1820s and the 1840s some 600 Mountain Men roamed the Far West, trapping beaver and other fur animals and discovering the land. Once a year this reckless breed of men attended an organized 'rendezvous' in the open country to sell their furs to traders and stock up with fresh supplies. The rendezvous was a wild orgy of drinking, gambling, brawling and fighting, in which most Mountain Men dissipated their hard-earned money; after which they set out on another year's trapping. In later years, when the fur trade declined, a number of Mountain Men, notably Jim BRIDGER, Kit CARSON, Jim BAKER, the SUBLETTE brothers, became famous figures, serving as guides and scouts for government expeditions and emigrant wagon trains, leading the way over trails and routes which they had blazed and pioneered.

The American Fur Trade of the Far West by H. M. Chittenden (New York, 1902);
The Fur Trade and Early Western Exploration by C. A. Vandiveer (Cleveland, Ohio, 1929);
Mountain Men by S. Vestal (Boston, 1937);
This Reckless Breed of Men by R. G. Cleland (New York, 1950);
The Mountain Men and the Fur Trade of the West in ten volumes edited by L. R. Hafen (Glendale, California, 1965-1972).

MULE

As much as the HORSE, the mule played a leading role in the winning of the West. The mule's great strength, endurance, his willingness to accept heavy work, his cheap support and longevity made him a virtually indispensable beast of burden in the Old West, and indeed throughout the United States. Mules pulled WAGONS, stagecoaches, ploughs, canal boats, logs, railway cars, streetcars, and worked on sugar and cotton plantations; they carried stores and ammunition for the army, the tools, grubstakes and hopes of gold prospectors, and were often used as personal mounts, General CROOK and CALIFORNIA JOE Milner preferred to ride a mule instead of a horse. The mule is a hybrid, the offspring of a jackass and a female horse; the hybrid bred from a female ass and a stallion is technically called a hinny, but the term 'mule' is generally used without this distinction. The mule (which is normally sterile) combines the strength of the horse with the surefootedness and docility of the ass. George Washington brought the mule to America, importing prize male and female asses from Spain and Malta in the 1780s to start domestic production of the useful work animal. The coming of the mule gave rise to that foul-mouthed, ill-tempered, whip-cracking character peculiar to the Old West, the mule-skinner (mule driver), who — with the bullwhacker — flourished in the days when millions of tons of freight were hauled over the plains by teams of mules and oxen (see BULLWHACKER).

The Mule by H. Riley (New York, 1867);
The Bullwhacker by W. F. Hooker (New York, 1925);
Wagons, Mules and Men by N. Eggenhofer (New York, 1961).

MUSTANG

The mustangs, or wild horses, that once thrived on the Great Plains of the West were the descendents of the HORSES brought to America by the

201V　　202V

Spanish CONQUISTADORES of the sixteenth century. The word 'mustang' derives from the Spanish *mesteños*, meaning horses that escaped from a *mesta* or group of stockraisers. These horses ran wild and multiplied, the Western plains being natural horse country. They evolved into a hardy, wiry, ill-formed breed of small horses, rarely above fourteen hands high. The mustangs ran in a band, called a *manada*, led by a dominant stallion. The PLAINS INDIANS caught and broke the wild horses for riding and pulling the TRAVOIS. Mustangers were frontiersmen who captured and broke the animals for sale; the cowboy's range pony was usually a mixture of mustang and other breeds. Some uncatchable wild stallions became Western legends, like the pure white 'Ghost Horse' of which many tales are told. The wild horses that survive today are mostly under Federal protection and there are several Mustang associations concerned with preserving the breed.

Mustangs and Cow Horses edited by J. F. Dobie (Dallas, Texas, 1940);
The Wild Horse of the West by W. D. Wyman (Caldwell, Idaho, 1945);
The Mustangs by J. F. Dobie (Boston, 1952);
Mustangs by H. Ryden (New York, 1972).

NAVAJO INDIANS

A large and important tribe of the Athapascan linguistic group, the Navajos (also spelled Navahos) have lived in ARIZONA and NEW MEXICO for centuries. In the seventeenth century they were an aggressive and powerful tribe. They lived by hunting and food-gathering and plundering the villages of the peaceful PUEBLO INDIANS. Later, they acquired horses and sheep from the Spaniards, as well as a knowledge of working with metal and wool.

The Spanish hoped to convert them to Christianity and the peaceful ways of the Pueblos, but the warlike Navajos (who were related to the APACHE people) preferred to raid Pueblo and Spanish villages. By the middle of the nineteenth century Navajo attacks on American settlements led to conflict with United States troops. In 1863 Colonel Kit CARSON was ordered to round up all Navajos and confine them on the Bosque Redondo reservation, New Mexico, where they would be taught a regulated, agricultural life patterned after that of the Pueblo Indians. The Navajos resisted fiercely, led by chiefs such as Delgadito, Barboncito, and Manuelito. Carson was ruthless in his campaign to subdue them; he slaughtered their sheep and horses, destroyed their cornfields and precious peach orchards. Finally the Navajos were starved into submission and 8,000 were taken to the Bosque Redondo. In 1868 the Navajos signed a treaty with the United States that allowed them to return to their old homelands; from this period the pattern of modern Navajo life began to emerge. They settled on their reservation and became excellent shepherds, weavers and silversmiths. Over the years their reservation has been extended and today it covers some 24,000 square miles, the largest INDIAN RESERVATION in the United States. Today, the Navajos number over 100,000 and are perhaps the most prosperous of Indian tribes.

Kit Carson Days by E. I. Sabin (New York, 1935);
The Navajo and Pueblo Silversmiths by J. Adair (Norman, Oklahoma, 1946);
The Navajo by C. Kluckhorn and D. Leighton (Cambridge, Massachusetts, 1951);
The Navajos by R. H. Underhill (Norman, Oklahoma 1956).

NEBRASKA

Throughout the Frontier years Nebraska served as a main corridor to the West; through this territory on the Great Plains passed the OREGON TRAIL, the traditional route of overland migration to OREGON, CALIFORNIA, and UTAH. But Nebraska itself, with its fertile soil and abundance of water, was the goal for many settlers who made the State into a major cattle and agricultural centre. Nebraska became an organized Territory in 1854. This opened lands west of the Missouri, previously reserved for Indians, to white settlement. The HOMESTEAD ACT of 1862 allowed settlers to claim 160 acres of land in eastern Nebraska. Statehood was granted in 1867 with Lincoln the capital. The railroads contributed greatly to the early development of the State; the UNION PACIFIC was completed across Nebraska in 1867, and the lines of the Burlington system criss-crossed most of the State by the 1880s. Many early railroads received State and Federal land grants to offset the costs of construction. These lands were sold to settlers through extensive advertising campaigns, with some companies sending representatives to Europe to encourage immigrants to come to Nebraska. By 1900 most of the State's prime land was settled. At one time about 40,000 Indians inhabited Nebraska, including the SIOUX, CHEYENNE, ARAPAHO, PAWNEE, and OMAHA. By 1876 all the tribes had ceded their lands to the United States. Today, Nebraska's Indian population numbers approximately 15,000. The Platte, Nebraska's main river, empties into the MISSOURI RIVER, which forms the eastern boundary of the State. The wide grassy plains of

203 *Navajo man.*

Nebraska make ideal cattle country; the first Texas LONGHORNS arrived in 1868 and Ogallala became as notorious a cowtown as DODGE CITY, Kansas; by 1872 there were 60,000 head of cattle on Horse Creek, near Scotts Bluff. After the Sioux War of 1876-7 thousands more cattle were driven from Ogallala to the ranges in the northern plains. Today, herds of Hereford and Angus cattle thrive on the nutritious grasslands of the Sand Hills, in the north-central area of Nebraska.

Nebraska: The Land and Its People by A. E. Sheldon (Chicago, 1931);
History of Nebraska by J. C. Olson (Lincoln, Nebraska, 1955);
Union Pacific Country by R. G. Athearn (Chicago, 1971).

NEVADA

The discovery of the Comstock Lode in 1859 brought thousands of fortune hunters into the wilderness of Nevada, then part of Utah Territory. The Comstock Lode, which yielded 300 million dollars in gold and silver in twenty years, gave birth to VIRGINIA CITY and other roaring mining camps. The mining boom and the growing population quickly brought Nevada a separate identity and in 1861 Nevada Territory was created out of western Utah; Statehood came in 1864 with Carson City the capital. A land of barren deserts, green valleys, and snow-covered mountains, Nevada was Mexican territory until ceded to the United States after the MEXICAN WAR of 1846-8. The region was first explored by Jedediah SMITH in 1825 and Joseph WALKER in 1833; John C. FRÉMONT also explored Nevada in the 1840s; he discovered and named Pyramid Lake. The first white community was Mormon Station, settled by MORMONS in 1849, and called Genoa after 1855, a key point on the stagecoach road and PONY EXPRESS. Mining — in gold, silver, and other metals — was Nevada's main industry and source of wealth from 1859 to 1879; thereafter until 1900 cattle and sheep raising took first place. Then new gold, silver, and copper strikes started another boom period. Today, Nevada's many ghost towns, including Virginia City, Austin, Goldfield, Eureka, Rhyolite, and Tonopah, attract thousands of tourists annually. Nevada's Indians included the PAIUTES, SHOSHONIS, UTES, Washoes, and Kosos. The mining boom brought about the end of the traditional Indian way of life. The voracious whites felled the Pinon trees for fuel and destroyed the nut crop; other native food plants were wiped out by the cattle and livestock brought in by the settlers. In the late 1880s Wovoka, a Paiute prophet, started the GHOST DANCE religion that spread like wildfire among the reservation Indians far beyond the boundaries of Nevada and culminated in the disaster at WOUNDED KNEE in 1890. About 4,250 Indians live on reservations in Nevada today.

The Big Bonanza by W. Wright (New York, 1947);
The Nevada Adventure: A History by J. W. Hulse (Reno, Nevada, 1969);
Nevada Ghost Towns and Mining Camps by S. W. Paher (Berkeley, California, 1970);
History of Nevada by R. R. Elliott (Lincoln, Nebraska, 1972).

NEW MEXICO

Land of the PUEBLO INDIANS and the stamping ground of BILLY THE KID and GERONIMO, New Mexico was acquired by the United States after the MEXICAN WAR of 1846-8. The Territory of New Mexico was created in 1850, with Santa Fe the capital, and did not gain Statehood until 1912. Don Juan de Onate took formal possession of the area in 1598 in the name of Spain and began to colonize New Mexico, giving the Indian vilages the saint names which they have today. In 1610 the Spanish established headquarters at La Villa Real de la Santa Fe de San Francisco de Assissi, which became Santa Fe. Famous pueblos of New Mexico include Acoma, the ancient 'sky

city' built on top of a rock 375 feet high, and ZUNI, the largest pueblo in the State. During the American Civil War a Confederate army attempted to seize control of New Mexico and was defeated by a Union force at Glorieta pass in March 1862. The NAVAJOS and APACHES plagued the white settlers of the Territory for many years. In 1864 Colonel Kit CARSON whipped the Navajos and confined them to the Bosque Redondo reservation; Apache depredations in New Mexico ended when Geronimo surrendered in Arizona in 1886. The railroad came to New Mexico in 1879 and the cattle and sheep industry increased. Billy the Kid gained his notoriety through the LINCOLN COUNTY WAR of 1878, a conflict between rival businessmen; Billy was shot dead by Sheriff Pat GARRETT at Fort Sumner in 1881. In March 1916 the little border town of Columbus, New Mexico, came into the news when it was raided and shot-up in 'Wild West' style by Pancho VILLA, the Mexican bandit and revolutionary leader. An American column, including the Seventh and Tenth Cavalry regiments, crossed the border and pursued Villa into Mexico.

New Mexico: A History of Four Centuries by W. A. Beck (Norman, Oklahoma, 1962);
New Mexico: A Pageant of Three Peoples by E. Fergusson (New York, 1964);
New Mexico Past and Present by R. N. Ellis (Albuquerque, New Mexico, 1971).

NEWTON, Kansas

During its brief and violent history as a cowtown in the cattle boom of the 1870s, Newton gained a reputation as one of the roughest, rowdiest spots in the Old West. Founded in March 1871, it became a cattle terminus of the CHISHOLM TRAIL when the ATCHISON, TOPEKA AND SANTA FE RAILROAD reached the town in July 1871; by the end of the year 30,000 head of cattle had been shipped out of Newton. It was a lawless town crowded with saloons, gambling halls, and a brothel district known as 'Hide Park' to accommodate the wild Texas cowboys. The celebrated shoot-out known as 'Newton's General Massacre' occurred in the early hours of 20 August 1871 when a group of Texans opened fire on part-time policeman Mike McCluskie in revenge for a Texan killed by him in a gunfight a few days earlier. McCluskie and four others died in the flying bullets and a number were wounded. In the following months several lawmen tried to bring peace to the town but there were more deaths by shooting. In May 1872 the railroad reached WICHITA, Kansas, which in 1873 replaced Newton as a cattle market and trouble centre. Newton's wild days were over.

Prairie Trails and Cow Towns by F. Streeter (Boston, 1936);
Wild, Woolly and Wicked; the History of the Kansas Cow Towns by H. S. Drago (New York, 1960);
The Cattle Towns by R. R. Dykstra (New York, 1968).

NEZ PERCÉ INDIANS

An important tribe of the Pacific North-west, the Nez Percé were members of the Shahaptian linguistic family. Transformed by the horse from a sedentary fishing tribe to a buffalo-hunting people, they became excellent horsemen and horse breeders, developing the distinctive spotted APPALOOSA horse. The name 'Nez Percé' means 'pierced nose' and was applied to these Indians by early French trappers because of the practice of piercing their noses in order to insert ornaments; however, it has been established that while this custom existed among some neighbouring tribes the Nez Percé were never given to the custom. The first historical mention of the tribe was made by the LEWIS AND CLARK EXPEDITION in 1805, at which time the Nez Percé occupied vast areas of what is now Idaho, Oregon, and Washington. They befriended and guided Lewis and Clark, beginning a tradition of cordiality to white people which continued for many years. In 1855 the tribe ceded much of its territory to the United States and settled on designated lands in Idaho and

204 *Newton, Kansas, in 1872.*

Oregon. With the discovery of gold on Nez Percé land and the resulting influx of white people, a new treaty was proposed to confine them on a reservation at Lapwai, Idaho. The Nez Percé of the Wallowa Valley in Oregon refused to accept the new treaty; they resisted removal and the Nez Percé War of 1877 resulted. A brave, proud, intelligent people, the Nez Percé fought with considerable military skill, defeating a column of soldiers in White Bird Canyon. After a battle near Kamiah, Idaho, the Nez Percé decided to leave the United States and seek refuge in Canada, and under their great chief JOSEPH they set out on a fighting retreat of 1,300 miles, beating off pursuing soldiers all the way. They got to within thirty miles of the Canadian border when, cold, starving and exhausted they surrendered to the surrounding army force in October 1877. The defeated Nez Percé were sent to the INDIAN TERRITORY (Oklahoma). In 1885 Joseph and most of his people were removed to a reservation in the State of Washington. Today the Nez Percé have a reservation in Idaho.

The Nez Percé by F. Haines (Norman, Oklahoma, 1955); *Last Stand of the Nez Percé* by H. Chalmers (New York, 1962); *Nez Percé Indians and the Opening of the Northwest* by A. M. Josephy (New Haven, Connecticut, 1965); *The Flight of the Nez Percé* by M. H. Brown (New York, 1967).

NORTH, Frank
1840-85

Frontiersman and organizer of the famous battalion of Pawnee Scouts, Frank North led his Indian soldiers in several campaigns against hostile tribes in the 1860s and 1870s. Born in Ohio, he went to Nebraska as a youth and there learned the tongue of the PAWNEE and the INDIAN SIGN LANGUAGE, becoming a clerk-interpreter on the Pawnee reservation. Commissioned a captain in October 1864, North was authorized to raise a scout company of Pawnees to serve against troublesome Indians during the Civil War. The company was mustered into service in January 1865, saw action against the CHEYENNE and ARAPAHO, and was disbanded in the spring of 1866. North returned to the Pawnee reservation with his men. Early in 1867, with the rank of major, he was authorized to raise and command a battalion of four Pawnee companies, mainly to protect the construction

205∧   206∨

205 *Looking Glass, a chief of the Nez Percé, about 1875.*

206 *Frank North.*

207 *Construction crew of the Northern Pacific at a bridge crossing Green River in the Cascade Range of Washington Territory in 1886.*

crews of the UNION PACIFIC RAILROAD. Luther North, Frank's young brother, was captain of one of the companies. The Pawnee Battalion proved successful in guarding the railroad and in searching out and punishing hostiles. On 11 July 1869 North and his Pawnees found the camp of Tall Bull, Cheyenne chief, at Summit Springs, Colorado, and led the charge into the village. Frank North killed Tall Bull in the fight, a deed that BUFFALO BILL Cody later took false credit for. Immediately after the Summit Springs fight Frank North was approached by Ned BUNTLINE, the dime-novel writer, who wanted to make him a hero; North rejected the offer and indicated that young Bill Cody might be interested in giving Buntline a story; it was the beginning of the Buffalo Bill legend. In 1876 Frank North and his scouts served under General CROOK and Colonel MACKENZIE against the SIOUX and Cheyenne. The Pawnee Battalion was disbanded in April

1877 and Frank became a partner with Cody in a Nebraska ranch, and later joined Cody's Wild West Show; in the summer of 1884 he fell from his horse during a show and was trampled on, suffering injuries from which he soon died. Luther North lived until 1935.

Two Great Scouts and Their Pawnee Battalion by G. B. Grinnell (Cleveland, Ohio, 1928);
The Fighting Norths and Pawnee Scouts by R. Bruce (Lincoln, Nebraska, 1932).

NORTHERN PACIFIC RAILROAD

Chartered by Congress in 1864, the Northern Pacific Railroad Company was authorized to build from Lake Superior to Puget Sound on the North-west Pacific coast, driving the railroad

207 V

through Minnesota, North Dakota, Montana, Idaho, and Washington. With Jay Cooke and Company as financial agent, construction on the railroad began in July 1870, a few miles west of Duluth, Minnesota. In 1873 the track had reached the MISSOURI RIVER and Bismarck in Dakota Territory; then construction came to a halt as the Great Panic of 1873 brought failure to Jay Cooke and Company and bankruptcy to the railroad. Five years passed before new financing enabled the Northern Pacific's westward march to continue. Henry Villard, head of the Oregon Railway and Navigation Company, purchased control of the Northern Pacific in 1881 and became its president. By July 1881 the railroad had reached Glendive in Montana Territory. During 1882 the company was faced with acute shortages of both labour and materials. The labour problem was resolved by importing 15,000 Chinese coolies; the second problem, caused by a domestic steel shortage, was overcome by importing rails, tie plates, and spikes from England and France. On 8 September 1883 the tracks from the East and the West (the latter of the Oregon Railway and Navigation Company) were joined at Gold Creek, Montana Territory, and former U.S. President Grant drove in the ceremonial last spike. Completion of the Northern Pacific marked the first through route from Lake Superior over the northern plains to the Pacific coast. By energetically advertising and promoting its Federal land grants at home and abroad, and carrying immigrants across America, the Northern Pacific contributed greatly to the settling of the West.

The Story of the Western Railroads by R. E. Riegel (New York, 1926);
Henry Villard and the Railways of the Northwest by J. B. Hedges (New York, 1930).

NORTH WEST MOUNTED POLICE

The red-coated Canadian 'Mounties' played a distinguished role in bringing law and order to the Old West, north of the border. Formed in 1873 as the North West Mounted Police, with a strength of 300, the force was established to suppress the illegal whisky traffic to the Indians,

to collect customs dues, to calm the growing unrest among the Indians and protect them from unscrupulous traders, and in general to patrol the wilderness communities of the North-West Territories (Alberta and Saskatchewan). The force stamped out the whisky traffic and dealt fairly with the Indians. Chief Crowfoot of the powerful BLACKFEET Confederacy summarized the contribution of the N.W.M.P. to the peace of the West with the words: 'The advice given me and my people has proved to be very good. If the police had not come to this country, where would we all be now? Bad men and whisky were killing us so fast that very few of us would have been left today. The police have protected us as the feathers of the bird protect it from the frosts of winter.' Many situations arose to test the new force and foremost of these was the arrival in Canada of SITTING BULL and some 5,000 SIOUX seeking refuge from the United States army after defeating General CUSTER and his Seventh Cavalry at the LITTLE BIGHORN in June 1876. Anxious years followed in which the N.W.M.P. peacefully and tactfully contained the Sioux and preserved the Blackfeet hunting grounds from the newcomers, until Sitting Bull and his people eventually returned to the United States in 1881. The self-reliant red-coated policeman became a legendary figure on the plains, respected and feared by wrongdoers as a brave, dedicated and relentless manhunter. In 1885 the N.W.M.P. played a major role in quelling the Riel Rebellion, an uprising of the Metis and Cree Indians instigated by Louis Riel. In 1886 the strength of the N.W.M.P. was increased to 1,000 and its outposts dotted the territories; no part of the Canadian plains was now beyond the reach of the law. In the Yukon gold rush of the 1890s, the vigilance and determination of the Mounties kept murder and other serious crimes to a minimum in a society where criminals abounded. The policemen also undertook the carrying of mails to the scattered gold camps. In 1904 King Edward VII bestowed the prefix 'Royal' upon the N.W.M.P. and in 1920 its title was changed to Royal Canadian Mounted Police.

The Riders of the Plains by A. L. Haydon (London, 1911);
The Royal Canadian Mounted Police by R. C. Fetherstonaugh (New York, 1940);
The Northwest Mounted Police 1873-1893 by J. P. Turner (Ottawa, 1950);
The Scarlet Force by M. T. Longstreth (Toronto, 1953).

208 *North West Mounted Police town station at Regina in 1895.*

209 *Officers of the North West Mounted Police at Fort Walsh in 1878.*

OAKLEY, Annie
1860-1926

A superb markswoman and star of BUFFALO BILL'S Wild West Show, Annie Oakley was born in Ohio, her full name being Phoebe Anne Oakley Mozee. Brought up on a farm she learned to shoot at an early age, bagging quail and RABBIT for the family pot. She was a dead shot from the start. At fifteen she entered a shooting contest and beat Frank Butler, a noted marksman and travelling showman. A few years later they married and formed an exhibition shooting act. Butler soon realized that winsome little Annie was the main attraction and he became her assistant and personal manager. In 1885 she joined Buffalo Bill Cody's show and became an international star. Cody treated her like a daughter, as did the Sioux chief SITTING BULL when he joined the show, calling her 'Little Sure Shot'. At thirty paces she could slice a playing card held up edgeways by her husband, hit coins tossed in the air, and shoot a cigarette from her husband's lips; she once shot a cigarette from the lips of the German Crown Prince (later Kaiser William II), at his request. By sighting through a hand-mirror she could fire over her shoulder and hit a small target, and she was adept at breaking glass balls tossed into the air, once shattering a record 4,772 out of 5,000 balls. She was just as accurate on the back of a running horse. Annie Oakley was indeed an original and remained one of the main features of Cody's show for seventeen years. She died at Greenville, Ohio.

Annie Oakley — Woman at Arms by C. R. Cooper (New York, 1927);
Little Annie Oakley and Other Rugged People by S. H. Holbrook (New York, 1948);
Annie Oakley of the Wild West by W. Havighurst (New York, 1954).

O.K. CORRAL, Gunfight at the 1881

The most celebrated shoot-out of the Old West took place on the afternoon of 26 October 1881 on Fremont Street, at the rear of the O.K. Corral in TOMBSTONE, Arizona, between the three EARP brothers aided by Doc HOLLIDAY, and the Clanton-McLaury cowboy faction. The gunfight lasted about thirty seconds and when the shooting

210∧

211∨

210 *Annie Oakley.*

211 *Annie Oakley shooting over her shoulder using a hand mirror.*

stopped, three of the Clanton-McLaury party were dead, and Virgil and Morgan Earp were seriously wounded. Bad blood had been brewing for some time between the Earps and the cowboys. Virgil Earp was the town marshal and Wyatt had his eye on the post of county sheriff, then held by John Behan. The brothers Ike and Billy Clanton and Tom and Frank McLaury (sometimes spelled McLowery or McLawry) were known as cattle rustlers. The feud between the two factions reached its climax at about two o'clock on the afternoon of 26 October, when the Earps and Holliday marched along Fremont Street towards the assembled Clanton and McLaury brothers and their friend Billy Claibourne. Intent on a showdown, Virgil Earp had taken the precaution of deputizing his brothers and Holliday. Sheriff Behan tried to stop the fight but was brushed aside by the determined Earps. Eyewitness accounts of the fight differ in many ways. All that is certain is that both sides opened fire at close range and that the McLaury brothers and Billy Clanton were shot dead. Virgil Earp was wounded in the leg and Morgan in the

shoulder; Holliday suffered a slight wound and Wyatt emerged unscathed. Ike Clanton and Billy Claibourne had run away from the fight at the start. The result of the shooting began a controversy that still continues. Some said that the Earps opened fire without just reason, others claimed that the lawman were defending themselves. Wyatt Earp and Doc Holliday were arrested on murder warrants made out by sheriff Behan and Ike Clanton. At the conclusion of the preliminary court hearing in Tombstone, Judge Spicer absolved the defendants of all blame and discharged them. They had, said Spicer, 'been fully justified in committing these homicides; that it was a necessary act done in the discharge of official duty'.

Doc Holliday by J. M. Myers (London, 1957);
The Earps of Tombstone by D. D. Martin (Tombstone, 1959);
The Earp Brothers of Tombstone by F. Waters (London, 1963);
It All Happened in Tombstone by J. P. Clum (Flagstaff, Arizona, 1965).

OKLAHOMA

The State of Oklahoma was formed in 1907 from the INDIAN TERRITORY and Oklahoma Territory. As part of the LOUISIANA PURCHASE, the region that is now Oklahoma was chosen by the U.S. government as a distant enough land in which to

212 *Aftermath of the Gunfight at the O.K. Corral, the bodies of Tom and Frank McLaury and Billy Clanton.*

213 *Map of the Oregon Trail.*

212▼

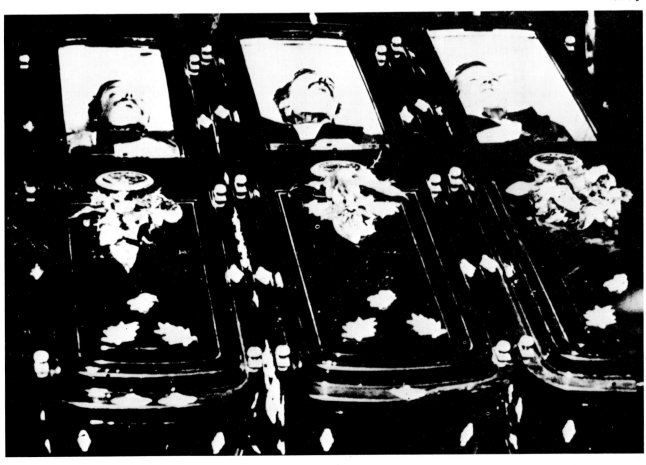

place the many Indian tribes moved from the East under the Indian Removal Act of 1830. The name 'Oklahoma' comes from the Choctaw words *'okla humma'*, meaning 'red people'. The name was first used in 1866 by Allen Wright, principal chief of the Choctaw Nation; in a treaty that year, plans were presented for the organization under one government of all the Indian nations and tribes within the area of the present State. These plans for an Indian State never materialized but the name Oklahoma became popular and was given to the western part of the region when it was opened to white settlers and organized as a separate Territory in 1890. When the U.S. government purchased two million acres of the Indian Territory the region was thrown open to white settlement under the HOMESTEAD ACT. On 22 April 1889 came the first Oklahoma LAND RUSH. Thousands of settlers who wanted 160-acre homesteads on the new land lined up at the borders; when the signal was given at noon they rushed in on horseback, carriage, wagon and on foot to stake claims for their homes. By nightfall tent cities had sprung up from the prairies and six counties were born — Logan, Oklahoma, Cleveland, Canadian, Kingfisher and Payne; Beaver County was added in 1890. The settlers who entered the land before the official signal were known as 'Sooners', and later Oklahoma adopted the nickname the 'Sooner State'. In the 1890s, the last years of the Old West, Oklahoma Territory was the stamping ground of a number of notorious outlaws, including Bill DOOLIN, the DALTON BROTHERS, Little Dick West, and Henry Starr. The Indian nations strived to remain independent of Oklahoma Territory; an attempt for separate Statehood failed in 1905 and in 1907 the two territories entered the Union as the single State of Oklahoma with Guthrie the capital.

History of the State of Oklahoma by L. B. Hill (Chicago, 1908); *Standard History of Oklahoma* by J. B. Thoburn (Chicago, 1916); *Oklahombres* by G. Hines and E. D. Nix (Chicago, 1929); *Oklahoma: A History of the Sooner State* by E. C. Reynolds (Norman, Oklahoma, 1954).

OMAHA INDIANS

Members of the Siouan linguistic family, the Omaha tribe migrated West from Ohio and settled in what is now South Dakota. Their tribal existence centred upon farming, hunting, and warfare. They lived in houses made of earth and sod and used the skin-covered TIPI when they travelled and hunted. In 1802 a smallpox epidemic reduced the Omahas to only a few hundred. The survivors moved farther down the MISSOURI RIVER, where LEWIS AND CLARK visited them in 1804. Omaha hospitality and friendship

213V

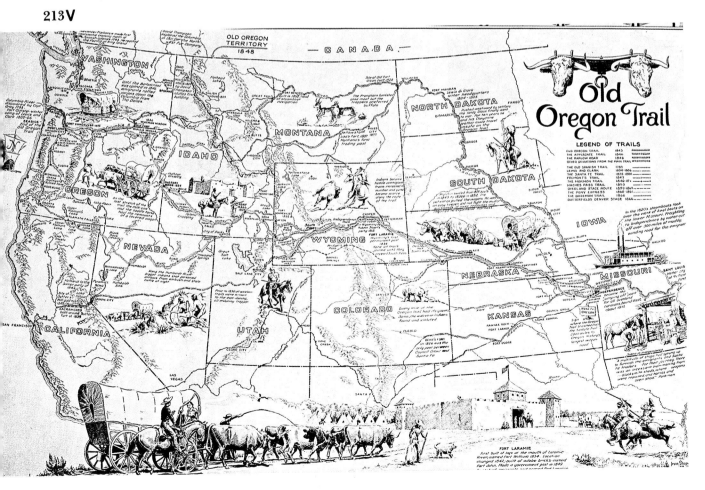

to whites, established during that stay, became a tribal tradition that never changed. In 1854 they ceded all their lands west of the Missouri to the United States and in 1856 the tribe was placed on a reservation of their own choice in north-eastern Nebraska. In 1960 the Omahas, largest of the Nebraska tribes with over 1,000 members, were awarded nearly three million dollars by the Indian Claims Commission as recompense for lands ceded by them under treaties in the past.

The Omaha Tribe by A. C. Fletcher and F. La Flesche (Lincoln, Nebraska, 1972).

OREGON

To thousands of emigrants who travelled the OREGON TRAIL across the Western plains and deserts, the Oregon country seemed to be the promised land, a far place of lush valleys and great forests. And indeed the fertile Willamette Valley was a settlers' dream. In the early years of the nineteenth century Oregon country included the present States of Oregon, Washington, Idaho, and parts of Montana, Wyoming, and British Columbia. The first official exploration of the vast region was that of the LEWIS AND CLARK EXPEDITION of 1804-6. In 1818 Britain and the United States agreed to jointly occupy the Oregon country until it could be equitably divided between them. There followed years of rivalry between American and British fur traders, the latter represented by the powerful and ubiquitous HUDSON'S BAY COMPANY which dominated the Oregon country for some twenty years. To strengthen the U.S. claim to the region, American pioneers began the peaceful settlement of the land; in the early 1840s thousands of pioneers arrived in covered wagons over the Oregon Trail. In 1846 Britain and the U.S. finally agreed on the boundary line — an extension of the forty-ninth parallel to the sea — that separates Canada from the United States. In 1848 Congress established the Oregon Territory. This was reduced by half on the creation of Washington Territory in 1853; Oregon achieved Statehood in 1859. As land-hungry settlers continued to come to Oregon, Indian resentment at the increasing invasion led to attacks on white settlements and missions: these included the murder of Marcus WHITMAN and the destruction of his mission. The discovery of gold caused more Indian trouble. In 1877 the government ordered the removal of the NEZ PERCÉ from their tribal land in the Wallowa Valley, to open it to homesteaders, and this resulted in the Nez Percé War. The Indians were dispossessed of their lands which were rapidly occupied by wheat and cattle ranchers. In 1883 the NORTHERN PACIFIC RAILROAD brought Oregon its first transcontinental rail connection.

History of the Willamette Valley by R. C. Clark (Chicago, 1927);
A General History of Oregon prior to 1861 by C. H. Carey (Portland, Oregon, 1935-36);
Winning Oregon by M. C. Jacobs (Caldwell, Idaho, 1938);
The Old Oregon Country by O. O. Winther (Stanford, California, 1950).

OREGON TRAIL

The first overland wagon route to the Pacific coast along which thousands of settlers rode, walked and suffered on one of the greatest treks in history. Beginning at INDEPENDENCE, Missouri, the Oregon Trail climbed steadily for 921 miles to the South Pass over the Continental Divide, and reached its highest elevation at 8,200 feet a short distance beyond FORT BRIDGER; thence to Oregon City, 2,000 miles from Independence. The arduous Oregon Trail tested the pioneer stock of America; those that survived its difficulties were hardy indeed. The first to use this route to the Far West were the FUR TRAPPERS who roamed the ROCKY MOUNTIANS in the early nineteenth century. During the period from 1834 to 1843 fur traders yielded control of the Oregon country to missionary colonists and farmer immigrants. In 1834 the Reverend Jason Lee led a party over the faintly discernible trail to Fort Vancouver. In 1836 Dr Marcus WHITMAN, a Presbyterian missionary, drove the first wagon to the Columbia River. In 1842 Dr Elijah White led the first large group of settlers over the Oregon Trail. However, the Great Migration of 1843 marked the real beginning of the Oregon Trail, and the thousands of emigrants that followed wore a deeply rutted highway with their covered wagons. From 1849 to 1852 the California gold seekers (the FORTY-NINERS) as well as those bound for Oregon crowded the trail; the CALIFORNIA TRAIL branched off near the GREAT SALT LAKE. In later years stage lines operated over the Oregon Trail and parts of it were used by the PONY EXPRESS.

The Oregon Trail by F. Parkman (New York, 1931);
The Road to Oregon by W. J. Ghent (New York, 1939);
Westward Vision: The Story of the Oregon Trail by D. Lavender (New York, 1963).

OSAGE INDIANS

Members of the Dhegiha group of the Siouan linguistic family, the Osage tribes lived for generations along the river which bears their name in MISSOURI. Here they raised small crops near their villages, taking to the BUFFALO plains of western Kansas for summer hunts. Powerful and well

214 *Ouray, chief of Uncompahgre Utes.*

215 *Commodore Perry Owens.*

216 *Clermont, head chief of the Osage tribe, painted by George Catlin.*

organized, the Osages were respected by whites and Indians alike as formidable foes. About 1820 the tribe moved to Kansas. When George CATLIN, the artist, visited them there around 1835 he reported that Osage men were the tallest Indians in North America, from 6 to 6½ feet in height. Osage scouts served with General CUSTER at the WASHITA in 1868. White pressure against the Osages increased until in 1870 an act of Congress provided for their removal to the INDIAN TERRITORY (Oklahoma), where their descendants live today. When the Indian Territory and Oklahoma Territory were admitted to the Union as a single State in 1907, the Osage reservation was incorporated as the State's largest county. The Osage Indians became the nation's richest tribe after oil was found in Osage County in 1920; all mineral royalties had been reserved for the tribe and its members, numbering approximately 2,100 today, share in the distribution of the tribal income.

The Osages by J. J. Mathews (Norman, Oklahoma, 1962).

OURAY, Chief
c. 1830-80

A prominent chief of the Uncompahgre UTE
INDIANS of Colorado, Ouray (the Arrow) was
always friendly to the whites and amenable to
their demands, but could be a hard bargainer
when the interests of his tribe were concerned. An
intelligent and cultivated man, he spoke both
Spanish and English, and never used tobacco or
alcohol. He became a close friend of Kit CARSON
and in 1867 helped Carson to suppress the
uprising led by the Ute sub-chief Kaniatse. In
1868 he visited Washington and negotiated a
treaty. In 1872 he strongly resisted a government
move to compel his people to give up certain
lands granted to them forever; however, he
accepted a compromise. Because of his absence,
Ouray was unable to prevent the MEEKER
MASSACRE at the White River Agency in
September 1879. But he quickly used his influence to stop the Ute rebellion and secure the
release of white women captives. Despite his
abstemious way of life, Ouray died of inflam-
mation of the kidneys aged about fifty.

The Last War Trail; the Utes and the Settlement of Colorado by
R. Emmitt (Norman, Oklahoma, 1954).

OWENS, Commodore Perry
1852-1919

A famous Arizona sheriff of the 1880s, Owens was
born in Tennessee and named after Commodore
Perry, the naval hero of the Battle of Lake Erie in
the War of 1812. After serving as a deputy sheriff
of Apache County in Arizona Territory, Commodore Perry Owens was elected sheriff of Navajo
County in November 1886. His term of office
coincided with the so-called Pleasant Valley War,
a vicious family feud between the Tewksbury and
Graham clans. Sheriff Owens was unusually brave
and a crack shot. In September 1887 he went
alone to a house to arrest Andy Blevins, who had
killed two Tewksbury men. Inside the house were
three desperate Blevins brothers and a relative
named Roberts: all were armed. In the shoot-out
that followed, Owens shot dead three of the
gunmen and wounded the fourth; he himself
emerged unscathed from the battle. Sheriff
Owens had to shoot some more men before the
Tewksbury-Graham vendetta came to an end.

Great Lawmen of the West by C. P. Breihan (London, 1964).

P

PAIUTE INDIANS

The Paiute tribes ranged through NEVADA, OREGON, CALIFORNIA, UTAH, and ARIZONA. They belonged to the Shoshonean branch of the Uto-Aztecan language stock. White men first found them without established villages and with few possessions; primitive desert nomads, their life was simple and harsh, dominated by the quest for food. They hunted small game, mice, snakes and reptiles, and because they were always digging for edible roots and insects, the whites called them 'Digger Indians'. Jedediah SMITH, the explorer, described them in 1827 as 'the most miserable objects in creation'. They lived in simple brush shelters called wickyups. As a result of their mistreatment by encroaching settlers and adventurers, the Paiutes went on the warpath in 1860. The first clash of the so-called Paiute War was the Battle of Pyramid Lake, in Nevada, when the Indians routed a volunteer force. The settlers immediately called for troops to defend them and soldiers were sent from California. Other fights and raids followed but by the end of 1861 the Paiutes were scattered and defeated. In 1888 a Paiute prophet named Wovoka had a vision and began to preach the message of the GHOST DANCE, a religious cult that spread to other reservation Indians far beyond the boundaries of Nevada. The Ghost Dance movement died when a band of SIOUX believers was massacred by the army at WOUNDED KNEE, South Dakota, in 1890. Today Paiutes live on reservations in Nevada and Arizona.

Life Among the Paiutes by S. Hopkins (New York, 1883); *The Paiute Indians of California and Nevada* by R. Underhill (New York, n.d.); *Indians of the Southwest* by E. E. Dale (Norman, Oklahoma, 1949).

PARKER, Judge Isaac 1838-96

A severe and able Federal judge, Isaac Charles Parker was dubbed the 'Hanging Judge' because of the many men he sent to the gallows. During his twenty-one years on the bench at Fort Smith, Arkansas, 79 convicted criminals were hanged outside his courtroom. Appointed judge of the Western District of Arkansas in May 1875, his jurisdiction extended over the INDIAN TERRITORY (now Oklahoma), a wild and lawless country plagued by outlaws red, white, and black. Parker replaced a corrupt judge at Fort Smith, located on the edge of the Indian Territory, and soon

made his presence felt. He had a gallows built to accommodate twelve men at the same time, and in September 1875 six men were hanged in public view by George Maledon, chief executioner for the Western District of Arkansas. For the first fourteen years of his twenty-one years at Fort Smith, Parker's judgements were final and irrevocable; there could be no appeal to a higher court. Parker was hard on killers and rapists but he was not a cruel and heartless man; he reserved his sympathy for the victim and his family. Most of Parker's critics lived in civilized communities and did not appreciate the raw frontier conditions of the Indian Territory; during Parker's years at Fort Smith, 65 deputy marshals were killed while carrying out their lawful duties. However, the local citizens approved of the Hanging Judge. Belle STARR, the woman outlaw, came before Parker a number of times and in 1882 he sentenced her to a year in jail for horse stealing. Judge Parker, a stern Methodist, was an impressive figure, six feet tall and weighing 200 pounds. He brooked no nonsense in his court. Honest and hardworking, he opened his court at 8.30 a.m. and continued till dark, six days a week. At Fort

217 *Petalesharo, chief of the Pawnee, painted by Samuel Seymour.*

Smith he tried a total of 13,490 cases of which some 9,000 resulted in convictions; he sentenced 172 men to death and 79 were hanged.

Hell on the Border by S. W. Harman (Fort Smith, Arkansas, 1898);
He Hanged Them High by H. Croy (New York, 1952);
The Law West of Fort Smith by G. Shirley (Lincoln, Nebraska, 1968).

PAWNEE INDIANS

An important tribe of the Caddoan linguistic family, the Pawnee occupied much of NEBRASKA when the first white men arrived. The name 'Pawnee' probably derives from the word *pariki* or 'horn', a reference to the curved and stiffened scalp-lock of the warriors. The numerous and powerful Pawnees were divided into four subtribes, each in turn forming bands which kept together in villages ruled by hereditary chiefs. Their culture was the most advanced of any tribe in the area, and was imitated by other groups. Pawnees were good farmers, raising crops of corn, beans, pumpkins, melons and squashes on their rich Platte River lands. For part of the year the tribes left their permanent earth-lodge villages on the Platte for the south-west plains to hunt the

218 *Paiute Indians of Nevada.*

219 *Judge Isaac Parker.*

220 *John 'Portugee' Phillips.*

218∧   219∨   220∨

BUFFALO. The Pawnees were skilled in crafts, medicine, and music and their ceremonial dances and prayers were distinguished for their dignity, rhythm and symbolism. Stars and other heavenly bodies were of special significance to these extremely religious Indians; in particular they worshipped the Morning Star, to which they annually sacrificed a captive Indian maiden until their great chief Petalesharo ended the cruel practice in 1818. The opening of the West brought disaster to the Pawnees; they lost their tribal lands and were struck by white man's diseases. In 1831 a smallpox epidemic killed nearly half the tribe, and in 1849 cholera wiped out another 1,200 of them. Beginning in 1818, the tribe made several treaties with the U.S. and finally ceded all their lands to the government. In 1876, weakened and greatly diminished, the Pawnees were removed to the INDIAN TERRITORY (now Oklahoma). When they were powerful, the Pawnees were constantly at war with surrounding tribes, but they never fought the whites, indeed they aided the settlers and the government against hostile tribes. Pawnee scouts under Major Frank NORTH served with distinction during the Indian campaigns between 1865 and 1885. Today about 1,000 Pawnees are organized under the title 'Pawnee Indian Tribe of Oklahoma'.

Pawnee Hero Stories and Folk Tales by G. B. Grinnell (New York, 1929);
Pawnee Indians by G. E. Hyde (Denver, 1951).

PEMMICAN

A concentrated food product originated by the Indians, pemmican was the preserved meat of the BUFFALO or DEER. The fresh meat was cut into strips and dried in the sun or in the smoke of a wood fire until hard. It was then pulverized and the powder mixed with animal fat; the resulting paste, usually seasoned with wild berries, was packed tight into a skin bag. Pemmican was very nutritious and would keep for several years; it was mainly used during lean winter months and on long journeys. Pemmican became an item of trade between the Indians and white trappers, who found this type of food useful in the wilderness.

PETRIFIED FOREST

The Painted Desert of northern ARIZONA is a strange landscape of curious rock shapes and a brilliant variety of colours. Its most celebrated phenomenon is the Petrified Forest, fallen trees that have turned to stone. Thousands of great logs, sparkling with jasper and agate, lie scattered about; the ground is strewn with broken sections and chips. A petrified log is a treasure chest of gemstones, including quartz crystals, opal, carnelian, onyx, and amethyst. The NAVAJO INDIANS have a legend of a god who went hunting in the forest; when he wanted to make a fire to cook the game he had killed, he found the wood too damp to burn, and in his anger he cursed the forest and turned it into stone. Geologists, however, tell a different story. Millions of years ago these trees were buried in mud, sand, and volcanic ash. Scarcity of oxygen arrested rot and decay. Silica-bearing water penetrated the wood cells and holes in the buried logs; the water evaporated, leaving only the silica in the cell interiors and holes. The wood tissues remained intact and the silica turned into quartz. Over eons of time the petrified trees, entombed in layers of rock, heaved under cataclysmic pressures and cracked and broke into large and small pieces. Wind and water carved away the sandstone and shale surrounding the logs, leaving them on the surface as we see them today. Gemstones have a high commercial value and many petrified logs were destroyed by treasure seekers in the Old West before the government stepped in. The Petrified Forest was made a National Monument in 1906 and a National Park in 1962. Today Federal law prohibits the removal of any petrified wood, no matter how small the piece.

Petrified Forest; the Story Behind the Scenery (available from the Petrified Forest Museum Association, Arizona 86025).

PHILLIPS, 'Portugee' 1832-83

John 'Portugee' Phillips was a frontiersman famed in Western folklore for his remarkable horse ride in winter through hostile Indian country to bring help to besieged FORT PHIL KEARNY, in what is now Wyoming. Legend has it that he rode alone more than 200 miles, fighting off Indians all the way, to reach FORT LARAMIE, where he staggered in on a Christmas night dance. He handed over his vital message then collapsed with exhaustion; outside in the snow, the noble horse that had carried him dropped dead from the great effort. The truth is less romantic or remarkable. Phillips was born in the Azores with the name Manuel Felipe Cardoso. In 1850 he joined the GOLD RUSH to California, changed his name to Phillips, and after many years of prospecting found himself wintering at Fort Phil Kearny in 1866. The fort was under pressure by Chief RED CLOUD and his Sioux. On 21 December 1866 Captain FETTERMAN and a force of 80 men were lured into an Indian trap and wiped out a few miles from the fort. To get news of this disaster to his superiors in Omaha

221 *Polished petrified wood from the Petrified Forest, Arizona.*

222 *Petrified logs of the Petrified Forest, Arizona.*

223 *Fur trappers fighting Indians in the Fight at Pierre's Hole.*

221Λ

222Λ

223V

and Washington, Colonel Carrington, the fort's commander, hired two 'citizen couriers' — John Phillips and Dan Dixon — to carry his message to the telegraph post at Horseshoe Station, some 190 miles away. Both received 300 dollars each for the journey. Most writers tell us that Phillips, setting out *alone*, requested the best horse in the fort and Carrington gave him his Kentucky thoroughbred, Gray Eagle. But Robert A. Murray in his excellently researched article 'The John "Portugee" Phillips Legends, A Study of Wyoming Folklore' points out that an experienced frontiersman like Phillips would have taken more than one horse on such a trip, would have changed mounts on the way at certain posts, and would certainly not have chosen a sensitive thoroughbred for the task. Murray writes that Phillips arrived at Horseshoe Station with Dixon and several others during the morning of Christmas day, and then carried an additional message on to Fort Laramie, forty miles away, arriving there about 11 p.m. that same evening. There is no evidence that his horse dropped dead, or that he was hotly pursued by Indians after leaving Fort Phil Kearny. Phillips later worked as a contractor of government supplies, and died in Cheyenne.

The Army on the Powder River by R. A. Murray (Bellevue, Nebraska, 1969).

PIERRE'S HOLE, The Fight at 1832

A battle between MOUNTAIN MEN and hostile Gros Ventre Indians on 18 July 1832 near the trappers' rendezvous of Pierre's Hole in the Teton Mountains in what is now eastern Idaho. Pierre's Hole was a valley named after a French trapper killed by Indians in 1828 — 'hole' was the mountain man's word for 'valley'; Jackson's Hole was another fur trading rendezvous. The trappers and their Indian allies drove the Gros Ventres into deep, swampy woods where the Indians built a fortification of logs. Bill SUBLETTE was wounded in an early attack on the stockade. The fight continued until dark. At sun rise next morning the trappers rushed the stockade but the Indians had evacuated the place during the night, carrying off their wounded and leaving nine dead warriors and about thirty dead horses. The mountain men suffered five dead trappers, seven friendly Indians, and about a dozen wounded.

Great Western Indian Fights by The Potomac Corral of the Westerners (New York, 1960).

PIKE, Zebulon M. 1779-1813

A soldier and explorer of the West, Zebulon Montgomery Pike led an expedition in 1805-6 which explored the Upper Mississippi but failed to find the true source of the river. Promoted captain, he led a second expedition in 1806-7 to explore the far South-west. In COLORADO he discovered the mountain that came to bear his name — PIKE'S PEAK, and explored the head-waters of the ARKANSAS and RED rivers. In 1810 he published *An Account of Expeditions to the Sources of the Mississippi and through the Western Parts of Louisiana.* As a brigadier-general in the war of 1812, Pike was killed in an explosion while leading an assault on the British fort that protected the town of York (now Toronto), Canada.

The Lost Pathfinder: Zebulon Montgomery Pike by W. E. Hollon (Norman, Oklahoma, 1949).

PIKE'S PEAK

The most celebrated mountain in COLORADO, Pike's Peak figured largely in the gold rush to Colorado in 1858-9, when hopeful prospectors headed West with the slogan 'Pike's Peak or Bust' on their lips or painted on their wagons. The mountain — 14,110 feet above sea level — was first sighted by Zebulon M. PIKE in 1806. It was first climbed by Dr Edwin James in 1820 and was known as James' Peak for some years. But trappers and traders continued to call the snow-covered mountain Pike's Peak and the name became official. When gold was discovered at Cherry Creek in 1858 it started a stampede known as the Pike's Peak Gold Rush; although some seventy miles from the scene of the strike, the mountain served as a landmark and symbol for the gold country.

The Past and Present of the Pike's Peak Gold Regions by H. Villard (Princetown, N. J., 1932); *Colorado Gold Rush* by L. R. Hafen (Glendale, California, 1941).

PIMAN INDIANS

The tribes of the Piman language group — the Pima and Papago — lived in the desert lands of southern Arizona. The Pima ('river people') occupied territory along the Gila River; they irrigated the land and raised crops and cotton. They lived in flat-roofed houses made of cactus sticks and brush often plastered with ADOBE, sun-dried clay. The Pimas were skilled in making baskets and in pottery and because of the hot climate they wore little clothing. To the south of the Pimas, extending into Mexico, lived their close relatives the Papagos ('bean people'), who specialized in raising mesquite beans for food. The Papagos lived in smaller villages than the Pimas and were equally skilled in basketry and pottery. For ceremonial purposes the Papagos made wine from the agave cactus. The lands of these two tribes once covered a vast area of southern Arizona and northern Mexico known as 'Pimeria' to Spanish explorers. The Pima country became U.S. territory in 1853 through the Gadsden Purchase, a region bought from Mexico. Today the Pima and Papago live on reservations in southern Arizona.

The Papago Indians of Arizona and Their Relatives by R. M. Underhill (New York, 1939).

PINKERTON, Allan 1819-84

Founder of Pinkerton's National Detective Agency, Allan Pinkerton was born in Glasgow, Scotland, and emigrated to the United States in 1842. He became the first detective of the Chicago police force and in 1850 established his own private detective agency in the city. The Pinkerton company's trademark was a wide-awake eye with the slogan 'We Never Sleep', which probably gave rise to the term 'private eye' for a private detective. The Pinkerton agents earned a reputation throughout the Old West as determined and efficient manhunters of train robbers, bank bandits, and other villains. In 1861 Allan Pinkerton helped prevent an attempt on President Lincoln's life, and during the Civil War he served as General McClellan's intelligence officer, under the alias of 'Major E. J. Allan', and organized a secret service for the Union Army. After the war he resumed the personal direction of his detective agency and opened branches in New York and Philadelphia. When the RENO BROTHERS committed the first train robbery in the United States, in Indiana in 1866, the Pinkerton agents went after the gang and Allan Pinkerton himself played a leading role in the pursuit and capture of the robbers. The agency became involved in the pursuit of a number of celebrated Western outlaws, including Sam BASS, Rube BURROWS, and Jesse JAMES; during operations against the latter, three Pinkerton agents were shot dead by the James gang. In 1875 Pinkerton detectives surrounded the home of Jesse's parents and, believing the bandit to be inside, threw a 'flare' into the house to illuminate the interior; the device exploded, tearing an arm off Jesse's mother and killing his nine-year-old half-brother Archie. Jesse and Frank James were not in the

house at the time, or had escaped. The incident brought public rebuke of the Pinkerton agency and sympathy for the James boys. When Allan Pinkerton died in 1884 his sons (William and Robert) continued the family detective business; they had also proved themselves to be capable manhunters in the field. Notable Pinkerton agents active in the West included Charlie Siringo, the 'cowboy detective', and the enigmatic Tom HORN. In the 1890s the Pinkerton agency was instrumental in breaking up the WILD BUNCH gang led by Butch CASSIDY. The success of Pinkerton's National Detective Agency was based on its excellent organization, the detailed reports of its agents, and the comprehensive files including the physical data, photographs, criminal records and modes of operation of thousands of known outlaws and fugitives. Today, Pinkerton's Inc. is the world's largest non-governmental force in the field of private investigation and security.

The Pinkerton's, A Detective Dynasty by R. W. Rowan (Boston, 1931);
The Pinkerton Story by J. Horan and H. Swiggett (New York, 1951);
Allan Pinkerton, America's First Private Eye by S. A. Lavine (New York, 1963);
The Pinkertons: The Detective Dynasty that Made History by J. Horan (New York, 1967).

PLAINS INDIANS

The life style of the Plains Indians was shaped largely by the BUFFALO and the HORSE. The buffalo provided meat, clothing, tools, and materials; the horse enabled the Indians to chase and kill the buffalo on the wide open PRAIRIES. The Plains Indians ranged over a geographical area extending from the Mississippi River and northern Texas to the Rocky Mountains and

224 *'The Buffalo Hunt' of the Plains Indians, painted by Charles M. Russell.*

227 *Slow Bull of the Oglala Sioux taking an oath, photograph by Edward S. Curtis.*

224▼

225 *The Pinkerton eye symbol.*

226 *View of Pike's Peak.*

225∧

226∧

227∨

adjacent parts of Canada. There were two distinct types of Plains Indians: the nomadic and semi-nomadic. The nomadic tribes — which included the ARAPAHO, BLACKFEET, CHEYENNE, COMANCHE, CROW, KIOWA, and SIOUX — were purely hunters to whom the buffalo was the staff of life; they lived in portable skin tents or TIPIS and roamed freely, transporting their belongings on the TRAVOIS, a wheel-less framework dragged by dogs and horses. The semi-nomadic tribes — which included the ARIKARA, HIDATSA, KANSA, MANDAN, OMAHA, OSAGE, and PAWNEE — spent part of the year in permanent villages of fixed earth or grass-covered lodges and raised crops; the rest of the year they hunted the buffalo and lived in tipis. The buffalo was vital to the Plains Indians' economy; its meat, fresh or dried, provided a basic diet. Buffalo hides were transformed into tipi covers and robes; rawhide made ropes, buffalo sinews provided bowstrings and thread; bones were carved into tools, horns into spoons, ladles and ornaments; hoofs made glue, and the tail, fixed to a stick, became a fly swish. The Indians had more than 100 uses for the buffalo: nothing was wasted, even the animal's dung, dried hard, was used as fuel for fires. The Indians lived off and worshipped the buffalo, the skull being an important Totem used in religious ceremonies. The SUN DANCE was another sacred ritual. The Plains Indians developed a distinctive art form; tipis, horse-trappings, shields, clothing were decorated with anecdotal paintings of war games or the hunt, or with geometric designs worked into porcupine-quill and bead embroidery. Before the Spaniards introduced the HORSE to America in the sixteenth century, the Plains Indians hunted and travelled on foot. By the mid-eighteenth century the horse had reached the northernmost Plains tribes. The Indians caught and trained wild horses, which had evolved from Spanish strays, and became superb equestrian hunters and fighters; they also acquired the animals through trade and theft and the ownership of horses became a measure of wealth. The warriors sought personal fame and social prestige by prowess in hunting and in intertribal warfare; they raided enemy camps to steal horses or seek revenge. To 'count coup' — to touch an active enemy in combat with the hand or a stick and escape to tell the tale — was the very highest honour; the counting of coup was long remembered and retold at gatherings. The coming of the white settlers and the professional BUFFALO HUNTERS in the latter half of the nineteenth century ended the free life of the nomadic natives. They fought to preserve their hunting grounds but could not stop the westward expansion of white civilization which finally engulfed them. With the buffalo exterminated to the brink of extinction, the Plains Indians had no means of independent sustenance and were confined on government reservations.

Indians of the Plains by R. H. Lowie (New York, 1954);
The Indian and the Horse by F. G. Roe (Norman, Oklahoma, 1955);
Indians of the High Plains by G. E. Hyde (Norman, 1959);
Plains Indian Raiders by W. S. Nye (Norman, 1968).

PLAINS RIFLE

When the frontiersmen emerged form the eastern woodlands into the plains and mountains of the trans-Mississippi West, they required a shorter more powerful firearm than the hunter's traditional KENTUCKY RIFLE; they needed one that

228▼

229▼

was easy to handle on horseback, and with the stopping power to drop the larger animals — the BUFFALO, ELK, and Grizzly BEAR. The Plains rifle was the answer. It lacked the slim beauty of the Kentucky rifle from which it was developed; it was rugged and functional in design, fired by the new percussion system of ignition. The Hawken, made by the Hawken family of ST LOUIS, Missouri, was a popular type of Plains rifle with the hunters and MOUNTAIN MEN of the Far West in the first half of the nineteenth century. Its barrel was some ten inches shorter than the Kentucky, with a larger bore, mostly .45 to .55 calibre, and had an effective range of 350 yards. Ideal for killing buffalo and dropping Indians, the muzzle-loaded Plains rifle remained popular in the West until the coming of the superior breech-loaded rifle.

The Plains Rifle by C. E. Hanson (Harrisburg, Pennsylvania, 1960);
Firearms, Traps and Tools of the Mountain Men by C. P. Russell (New York, 1967).

PLUMMER, Henry
c. 1837-64

A bandit leader who also wore a sheriff's badge, Henry Plummer organized a gang of highwaymen who robbed and murdered with impunity until the outraged people of Bannack District (MONTANA) lynched him and his desperadoes. Handsome, neatly dressed, with good speech and manners, Boston-born Plummer was a plausible personality and arrant opportunist. In 1857 while marshal of Nevada City, California, he killed a man named Vedder when caught in an intimate

situation with the man's wife. Sentenced to ten years in prison, he was soon released on the grounds that he was dying from tuberculosis. He became a gambler and leader of a bandit gang in Idaho; in 1862 he moved to the mining camp of Bannack. Here he mounted a successful campaign to drive out the sheriff and got himself elected to the post. Plummer's gang — known among themselves as The Innocents — imposed a reign of terror on the district, robbing stage-coaches and miners and killing more than 100 people. Plummer himself maintained a masquerade of honesty. Finally the citizens of Bannack and Virginia City organized a Vigilance Committee to rid the district of the bandits. Before he was lynched, one of The Innocents revealed the truth about Plummer and his crooked deputies. The VIGILANTES seized Plummer and dragged him to the scaffold that he had built for legal executions. To the last he tried to bluff his way out of the situation; with the rope around his neck he made the grim jest: 'You are hanging an Innocent man.'

Frontier Justice by W. Gard (Norman, Oklahoma, 1949); *The Vigilantes of Montana* by T. J. Dimsdale (Norman, 1953).

PONY EXPRESS
1860-1

A fast mail service run by relays of horsemen, the Pony Express was created, organized and operated by the freighting firm of RUSSELL, MAJORS AND WADDELL to prove the feasibility of a central route to California — as opposed to the circuitous southern route used by the BUTTERFIELD OVERLAND MAIL stagecoaches —

228 *Henry Plummer.*

229 *Replica of the original Pony Express saddle and mochila.*

230 *Pony Express advertisement of July 1861.*

231 *Pony Express rider pursued by Indians, painted by H.W. Hansen.*

230V

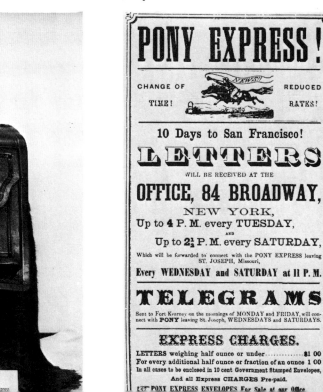

231V

and to secure a lucrative mail contract from the U.S. government. The Pony Express established a string of over 100 relay stations across the West from ST JOSEPH, Missouri, to Sacramento, California, a route of 1,966 miles; purchased 500 of the finest, fleetest ponies and recruited suitable riders — the following notice appeared in a San Francisco newspaper:

> Wanted, Young skinny wiry fellows, not over eighteen. Must be expert riders willing to risk death daily. Orphans preferred. Wages $25 per week. Apply Central Overland Express.

One lad who got the job was fifteen-year-old William F. Cody who later became famous as BUFFALO BILL. The young riders were required to brave many hazards: rugged terrain, foul weather, wild animals, outlaws and hostile Indians. The letters, written on lightweight paper, were padlocked into the four leather pouches of the special saddle cover called the *mochila*, which fitted snugly over the saddle and could be removed instantly; the letters were charged (in the beginning) at 5 dollars per half ounce. Each rider rode a certain distance, exchanging horses on the way, then handed over the mail to the next relay rider; two minutes were allowed for the transfer of the *mochila* and the fresh rider and horse were off at the gallop. The service was inaugurated on 3 April 1860 and the first mail reached Sacramento on 13 April. A fast service indeed for its day, but the electric telegraph was quicker. While the Pony Express raced over the plains a transcontinental telegraph line was being erected, and the completion of the line on 24 October 1861 abruptly ended the life of the Pony Express two days later. Russell, Majors and Waddell had run the service at a loss and it ruined them. During its brief career the Pony Express carried 34,753 pieces of mail (losing only one *mochila*) and galloped a total 616,000 miles, a distance equal to 24 times around the world. Today, the original Pony Express stables building in St Joseph, Missouri, is maintained as a Pony Express Museum.

The Pony Express by A. Chapman (New York, 1932);
The Pony Express Goes Through by H. R. Driggs (New York, 1935);
Riders of the Pony Express by K. B. Carter (Salt Lake City, 1947);
Saddles and Spurs: The Pony Express Saga by R. W. and M. L. Settle (Harrisburg, Pennsylvania, 1955).

PRAIRIES

Extensive tracts of flat, rolling grasslands, generally treeless, the prairies formed the great central plain of North America, from the Great Lakes in the East to the foothills of the ROCKY MOUNTAINS in the West, from Texas to Alberta in Canada. The climate of the prairie (a French word from the Latin *pratum*, a meadow) is generally dry, with most of the rain falling in the summer. Being far from the sea the climate is extreme — very cold winters intensified by the free-sweeping wind, and hot summers. The average rainfall in the eastern prairies is about twice that of the western prairies; as the rainfall increases from the Rockies eastwards, the vegetation of the Great Plains changes from short grass prairie in the west to mixed grass through the middle and to tall grass prairie in the east. The prairies have a rich growth of some 150 grasses, providing fine pasturage and hay for live-stock; hundreds of other shrubs and plants also flourish. Trees are found by streams and rivers. Just 150 years ago millions of BUFFALO roamed these grasslands, hunted by the PLAINS INDIANS. White settlers developed the eastern prairie into the greatest wheatland region in the world, stretching from Texas into Canada. The western prairie was formerly given up almost entirely to raising cattle and horses. In the Old West a prairie fire could be a disaster: whipped by the wind the wall of flames moved swiftly across the open plains consuming crops, cattle, houses, and people. Such a fire could be started by a carelessly attended camp fire, sparks from a locomotive or by hostile Indians. Pioneer farmers used to plough a wide section of land around their property to serve as a firebreak.

Nothing But Prairie and Sky; Life on the Dakota Range in the Early Days by W. D. Wyman (Norman, Oklahoma, 1954);
A Tour of the Prairies edited by J. F. McDermott (Norman, 1956);
The Great Plains by W. P. Webb (New York, 1957);
The Farmer's Frontier, 1865-1900 by G. C. Fite (New York, 1966).

PRAIRIE CHICKEN
Tympanuchus americanus

A plump game bird related to the grouse, the prairie chicken or hen of the Great Plains and grasslands became an important item of food for the settlers and pioneers of the Old West. During the mating season the male birds perform a curious dance and utter a strange booming sound; the Indians adapted these movements for use in a ceremonial dance. The sage-grouse and mountain-grouse, close relatives of the prairie chicken, were also widely bagged for the pioneer pot; the sage-grouse inhabited the dry sage-brush plains of the West. The once abundant prairie chicken was slaughtered on such a massive scale by Westerners, and by professional hunters who shipped them to city markets, that their numbers were drastically reduced.

American Wild Life by W. G. Van Name (New York, 1961).

PRAIRIE DOG
Cynomys ludovicianus

A member of the squirrel family, the prairie dog is a burrowing rodent that once infested the Great Plains in millions. The French-Canadians named it *chien de la prairie* — prairie dog — because its high-pitched yap is similar to that of a small dog. There are seven subspecies of prairie dog, of which the black-tailed type is the most common; an adult varies in length from 11 to 14 inches and weighs between one and three pounds. They live in underground colonies or 'towns' which often spread for miles. They feed almost entirely on grass and plants. In the Old West they were regarded as pests by farmers and ranchers because they ruined grassland, crops, and irrigation ditches, and horses often broke legs by stepping into holes dug by prairie dogs. A gregarious and community-minded creature, it rarely strays far from its burrow entrance. When danger appears, guard dogs bark the alarm and within seconds all have vanished underground. Its natural enemies include the ferret, badger, COYOTE, snakes, EAGLES and hawks. Indians ate the prairie dog and young boys learned marksmanship with bow and arrow in stalking them. Over the years poison and gas have been used on a wide scale to wipe out the prairie dog. Today they are mostly found in protected areas such as National Parks.

Mammals of North America by V. H. Cahalane (New York, 1947).

PUEBLO INDIANS

When the Spanish CONQUISTADORES arrived in what is now NEW MEXICO and ARIZONA in the sixteenth century, they called the sedentary

232   *Prairie chickens.*

233   *Prairie dog at his burrow.*

234   *Taos Pueblo, New Mexico.*

232Λ

233Λ

234 V

natives they met 'Pueblo' Indians, from the Spanish for 'town', because they lived in compact, permanent settlements of stone and ADOBE houses. The Pueblo Indians include the HOPI people of Arizona and the ZUNI of New Mexico. Traditionally, the pueblo was built on a mesa, a high, steep-sided, flat-topped rock formation which served as a natural fortress against marauding nomads. The central mass of the pueblo complex of apartments rose to several stories, the separate levels being connected by removable ladders. The Pueblos were — and still are — skilful dry farmers who irrigated and cultivated the desertlands at the foot of their mesas, growing corn, vegetables and fruits. They have long excelled in making baskets, pottery, textiles, and beautiful jewellery. An extremely religious people, the supernatural influenced everything they did. It was not until 1598 that the Spanish invaders began to influence Pueblo life. Considered subjects of the Spanish crown, they were required to pay taxes in the form of cloth, corn, or labour. Their villages were renamed after Catholic saints and their own ceremonies and religious practices were forbidden in an attempt to convert them to Christianity. In 1680 the Pueblos rebelled against the harsh Spanish rule and, under the leadership of medicine man Pope, drove the Spaniards from New Mexico. Spanish rule did not return until 1692 when the province was retaken by Diego de Vargas. When the Pueblo lands were ceded to the U.S. by Mexico in 1848 the lands were in question for many years thereafter, as Indian holdings were intruded upon by white settlers. In time, however, the Supreme Court confirmed most of the Pueblos' tribally owned lands. Notable Pueblo communities which still exist include the Acoma Pueblo in New Mexico, the ancient 'Sky City' built on a mesa 357 feet high; Acoma — which contends with the Hopi village of Oraibi in Arizona as the oldest continuously occupied town in the U.S. — is famous for its distinctive pottery.

The Taos Pueblo is the northernmost pueblo in New Mexico and is considered the most traditional and native religion dominates all facets of life. Zuni Pueblo is the largest in New Mexico, the only surviving community of the legendary gold-filled Seven Cities of Cibola, the mythical El Dorado sought by Coronado; Zuni is noted for beautiful turquoise, silver and shell-mosaic ornaments.

Desert Drums, the Pueblo Indians of New Mexico by L. Crane (Boston, 1928);
Pueblo Indian Religion by E. C. Parsons (Chicago, 1939);
Revolt of the Pueblo Indians of New Mexico (Albuquerque, New Mexico, 1942);
The Pueblo Indian World by E. L. Hewitt and B. Dutton (Albuquerque, 1945).

Q

QUANAH PARKER
*c.*1845-1911

The greatest of COMANCHE chiefs, Quanah (or Kwahnah) Parker was the eldest son of a chief and a white girl, Cynthia Ann Parker, captured by the Comanches in 1836 when she was nine years old. Tall and powerfully built, Quanah, despite his white blood, had a darker complexion than most of his people; but he had blue eyes instead of brown. In 1860 a force of TEXAS RANGERS and soldiers attacked a Comanche camp and 'rescued' Cynthia Ann, who was now completely Comanche, the wife of a chief and mother of three halfbreed children. Restored to the prominent Parker family of Texas, Cynthia Ann never reconciled herself to the white way of life. She tried to return to the Comanches but the Parkers stopped her; she sank into apathy and starved herself to death. Quanah became a war chief of the Kwahadi band, the fiercest of all Comanches, and fights with settlers on the plains of west Texas were commonplace at that time. In 1867 the Medicine Lodge Treaty assigned the Comanches, and the KIOWAS, Kiowa-Apaches, CHEYENNES and ARAPAHOES to reservations; but Quanah and his band, who had refused to sign the treaty, continued to hunt BUFFALO on the plains and raid settlements. Quanah had a special hatred for the white professional BUFFALO HUNTERS who were wiping out the herds for the price of their hides. In June 1874 he mustered a large war party 700 strong — which included Cheyenne, Kiowa, and Arapaho warriors as well as the Kwahadi braves — and attacked the post at ADOBE WALLS, where some thirty buffalo hunters were quartered. But the post's thick walls and the powerful buffalo rifles of the hunters proved too much for the Indians and after a hard fight they withdrew. Quanah's horse was killed under him and he was lucky to survive the battle. Pursued and pressed by the U.S. Army, Quanah surrendered in the summer of 1875 and quickly adjusted himself to the white man's way. Respected by the army officers as a good fighting man and admired by the Texans, who took a certain pride in him, Quanah became a prosperous businessman with a large house in the INDIAN TERRITORY (now Oklahoma). The Texans called him Quanah Parker and he adopted his mother's surname. Speaking fairly good English and Spanish, he served as leader of the Comanche, Kiowa and Apache confederation, encouraged agriculture and education among the Indians, and served as a judge in the reservation court.

Quanah, Eagle of the Comanches by Z. A. Tilghman (Oklahoma City, 1938);
Quanah Parker: Last Chief of the Comanches by C. L. and G. Jackson (New York, 1963);

QUANTRILL, William C.
1837-65

A Confederate guerrilla leader during the Civil War, William Clarke Quantrill (sometimes spelled Quantrell) was notorious for his general depredations but in particular for the raid on Lawrence, KANSAS, on 21 August 1863 in which he and his men slaughtered the citizens and sacked the town. Born in Ohio, Quantrill was a sometime school teacher then became a drifter and a gambler under the name of Charley Hart; he was involved in horse stealing and several murders. When Civil War broke out he raised a force or irregular horsemen, raiding towns and farms of those in sympathy with the Union, holding up stagecoaches, ambushing Union scouts and skirmishing with enemy militia. In April 1862 the Federal authorities declared Quantrill and his men outlaws. In August 1862 Quantrill was commissioned a captain of partisan rangers and his guerrilla force was mustered into the Confederate Army. A year later he attacked Lawrence with about 450 men, striking at dawn, killing some 150 citizens, and leaving the town in ruins. It must be said that brutal guerrilla warfare was carried out by both sides in the Civil War. In May 1865 while raiding in Kentucky, Quantrill and a small group were attacked by a Federal force; Quantrill was fatally wounded and died several weeks later. His guerrillas included Frank and Jesse JAMES and two of the YOUNGER BROTHERS.

Quantrill and the Border Wars by W. E. Connelley (Cedar Rapids, Iowa, 1909);
Quantrill: His Life and Times by A. Castel (New York, 1962);
The Killer Legions of Quantrill by C. W. Breihan (Seattle, 1971).

QUARTER HORSE

The first breed developed in America, the Quarter horse became popular in the Old West for its speed and agility. The breed originated during the colonial period, in the Carolinas and Virginia where match-racing was the leading outdoor sport. The races were run on village streets and along country lanes and because these horses were seldom raced beyond the quarter-mile they became known as 'quarter horses'. The foundation stock came from Arab, Barb, and Turk breeds brought to North America by the Spaniards; stallions selected from these first arrivals were crossed with mares which arrived from England in 1611. The cross produced compact, heavily muscled horses which could run a short distance faster than any other breed. As the settlers moved West they took the Quarter horse with them; it pulled the ploughs, wagons

235 Quanah Parker.

236 William Clarke Quantrill.

237 The ideal of the American Quarter Horse, painted by Orren Mixer.

237∨   236∧

<235

and buggies of the pioneers. The Quarter, or short horse became established in the South-west in the early part of the nineteenth century and became popular with ranchers and cowboys as a fine ROUND-UP and trail driving horse which possessed a lot of 'cow sense'. The American Quarter Horse Association was established in 1940 to promote and register the breed. Today Quarter horses are popular as working cow ponies and rodeo mounts.

The Horse of the Americas by R. M. Denhardt (Norman, Oklahoma, 1948).

RABBITS

Widespread and numerous throughout North America, the rabbit was meat for everybody's pot in the Old West — trapper, explorer, pioneer family, farmer, cowboy, and Indian. In particular, the HOPI INDIANS of the South-west hunted the animal with a 'rabbit club', a curved stick like a boomerang; skilfully thrown it broke the legs of a running rabbit or knocked it down. Indian boys learned marksmanship with bow and arrow stalking the rabbit, and white youngsters mastered frontier firearms by shooting the fast-moving target. The most ubiquitous rabbit in the United States is the cottontail, a small creature weighing from two to three pounds, so-named from the patch of white hair on the underside of its tail, which bobs and flashes as it runs for cover. Cottontails inhabit prairie land, woods, sagebrush flats, and desert; they eat all types of vegetation and secure most of the water they need from the plants they eat. Although they reproduce rapidly, they are held in check by their natural enemies — bobcats, COYOTES, snakes, and hawks. Their young are born hairless and blind. The black-tailed jackrabbit is also widespread in the West. Larger and faster than the cottontail, it runs by great leaps and bounds, reaching speeds up to 40 m.p.h. The name jackrabbit is short for jackass rabbit, from its large mule-like ears. When living in sagebrush and desert country the jackrabbit is harmless, but in agricultural areas it is a pest, damaging clover, alfalfa, grain, and other crops.

American Wild Life by W. G. Van Name (New York, 1961).

RAIN-IN-THE-FACE
? — 1905

A chief of the Hunkpapa SIOUX, Rain-in-the-Face took part in the Battle of the LITTLE BIGHORN in June 1876 and for many year was credited with having killing General CUSTER. It is believed that Rain-in-the-Face was so named because in a fight during his youth his face was cut and his blood and war paint became streaked so that it looked as if his face had been rained upon. In 1875 he was arrested by Tom Custer, the general's brother, but managed to escape from jail; legend tells that he swore to cut out the heart of Tom Custer and eat it, and did so at the Little Bighorn. When his fighting days were over Rain-in-the-Face joined BUFFALO BILL'S WILD WEST SHOW and, probably for publicity reasons, it was claimed that he had personally killed General Custer.

238   *Black-tailed Jack Rabbit.*

239   *Hopi Indian with rabbit he killed with his curved rabbit stick.*

238∧

239∨

RATTLESNAKES

The rattlesnake was so named because the end of its tail is furnished with hollow, horny segments which, when vibrated, produce a 'rattling' sound. Rattlesnakes — of which there are thirty species — are found only in the Americas; they prefer dry regions and in the United States are mostly found in the arid South-west. The sidewinder (*Crotalus cerastes*) can be found in most desert regions of the West and South-west. It gets its name from its peculiar method of locomotion that enables it to progress in sandy areas; it throws a portion of its body ahead in a loop, thus travelling sideways, like a rolling spring, leaving behind interesting patterns in the sand. All rattlesnakes are venomous but some are more dangerous to humans than others. The most deadly species of the West are the western diamondback (*Crotalus atrox*), the timber rattlesnake (*Crotalus horridus*), the Mojave rattlesnake (*Crotalus scutulatus*), and the western rattlesnake (*Crotalus viridis*). The biggest of these is the western diamondback, found from Texas to California, which grows to a length of some six feet and up to fifteen pounds in weight. The bigger the rattlesnake the more dangerous it is, because size determines its striking distance, the quality and quantity of its venom, and the length of its fangs. When alarmed, or ready to strike, a rattlesnake vibrates its rattles; it lunges forward with its jaws

240▼

open to the fullest extent and drives its long, curved fangs deep into its victim, injecting venom through the hollow fangs. The venom can kill a man. Rattlesnakes are nocturnal, sleeping in the shade during the day and emerging at night. They live mainly on small rodents and the young of larger mammals.

The Reptiles of North America by R. L. Ditmars (New York, 1946);
Rattlesnakes: Their Habits, Life Histories, and Influence on Mankind by L. M. Klauber (Los Angeles, 1956);
Rattlesnakes by J. F. Dobie (Boston, 1965).

RED CLOUD
1822-1909

An eminent chief of the Oglala tribe of the Teton, or Western SIOUX, Red Cloud stands alone in the history of the American West as the chief who won a war — Red Cloud's War of 1866-7 — with the United States. Described by General George CROOK as 'A magnificent specimen of physical manhood, as full of action as a tiger', Red Cloud was a notable warrior and intelligent leader of his people. He was so named because a meteor turned the sky red at the time of his birth. He strongly opposed the government's attempt to construct army forts along the BOZEMAN TRAIL, which ran through the Indian hunting grounds of Wyoming's Powder River country to the newly discovered gold fields in Montana. In the summer of 1865, with a party of Sioux and CHEYENNE, he intercepted the first unit of troops sent out to begin work on the forts and held them captive for several weeks. When commissioners came to treat with the Sioux, Red Cloud refused to meet them. However, in June 1866 he agreed to attend the peace council at FORT LARAMIE in which white negotiators again attempted to get Sioux and Cheyenne permission for passage of emigrants and construction of forts along the Bozeman Trail; but on learning that the government intended to build the forts whether the Indians agreed or not, the angry Red Cloud walked out on the meeting to start his war. He maintained constant harassment of the trail and its three forts; he kept the largest post, FORT PHIL KEARNY under virtual siege and wiped out Captain FETTERMAN and eighty men when they attempted to rescue a woodcutting party under attack near the fort in December 1866. Red Cloud's resolute campaign eventually forced the

240   *Chief Red Cloud.*

241   *Chief Rain-in-the-Face.*

242   *The Sidewinder Rattlesnake.*

241∧

242∨

U.S. government to negotiate and yield to his ultimatum — the complete abandonment of the forts and of all further attempts to open the Bozeman Trail. He refused to sign the treaty until the troops had left the Powder River country and his warriors had burned the forts to the ground. This done, he signed the Fort Laramie Treaty of 1868 which created the vast area known as the Great Sioux Reservation, and agreed to settle peacefully at the Red Cloud Agency in Nebraska. He kept his word and took no active part in the Sioux hostilities of the 1870s. However, he remained a forceful critic of the government and its Indian agents, and his long feud with agent Dr McGillycuddy resulted in the latter deposing him from the chieftainship of his people in 1881. Red Cloud died on the Pine Ridge Reservation in South Dakota.

Fighting Red Cloud's Warriors by E. A. Brininstool (Columbus, Ohio, 1926);
Red Cloud's Folk: A History of the Oglala Sioux by G. E. Hyde (Norman, Oklahoma, 1937);
Red Cloud and the Sioux Problem by J. C. Olson (Lincoln, Nebraska, 1965.

RED RIVER

An important tributary of the MISSISSIPPI, the Red River rises in the Texas Panhandle and flows for some 1,300 miles in a south-easterly direction between Texas and Oklahoma, Texas and Arkansaas, then across Louisiana to join the Mississippi about 250 miles above New Orleans. During the years of the great CATTLE DRIVES north from Texas the Red was one of a number of major rivers to be crossed. In its low condition the sluggish river could be crossed at many points but the most popular place was Red River Station, where a shelving sandbar ran out from the northern bank and when the cattle reached it they could walk across the river. Another popular place was Doan's Crossing. There is another Red River, known as the Red River of the North, that rises in western Minnesota and flows north for some 300 miles, making a boundary between Minnesota and North Dakota, then on through Manitoba in Canada to empty into Lake Winnipeg.

REMINGTON, Frederic 1861-1909

One of the foremost painters and illustrators of the Old West, Frederic Sackrider Remington was born in Canton, New York, and grew up in nearby Ogdensburg. He went to Yale University and studied art for eighteen months. An energetic youth, over six feet tall, he distinguished himself as an inter-collegiate football player and heavy-weight boxer. When his father died in 1880, leaving him a small legacy, he quit college and roamed the West in search of adventure; he worked as a cowboy, prospected for gold, and ran a sheep ranch in Kansas. He began to draw and paint the people, horses, and vigorous scenes of Western life and the Old West dominated his work thereafter. In 1885 he went to New York City to try and sell his illustrations and establish his name; *Harper's Weekly*, one of the leading journals of the day, showed interest in his work and on 9 January 1886 his illustration 'The Apache War — Indian Scouts on Geronimo's Trail' appeared on the magazine's front cover. His success was now assured. His pictures appeared regularly in *Harper's Weekly* and other magazines and he quickly became one of the best known and most highly paid illustrators in the United States. A prolific worker, he turned out hundreds of black and white illustrations, water-colours, major oil paintings, and in 1895 he began to sculpt. In all he produced more than 2,500 drawings and paintings and twenty-five notable pieces of sculpture. His major works in oils and bronze won him international fame and critical acclaim. He died at the peak of his career, aged forty-eight, after an emergency appendec-tomy, on 26 December 1909.

Frederic Remington, Artist of the Old West by H. McCracken (Philadelphia, 1947);
Frederic Remington: Paintings, Drawings, and Sculpture by P. H. Hassrick (London, 1974).

REMINGTON REVOLVERS

The six-shooters manufactured by E. Remington and Sons of Ilion, New York, were widely used in the Old West and rivalled the COLT revolvers in popularity. Founded by gunsmith Eliphalet Remington in 1816, the family business manufac-tured muskets, rifles, shotguns, pistols, farming implements, sewing machines and typewriters. The firm produced its first revolver in 1857, a model designed by Fordyce Beals, a pocket weapon for civilian use. Beals then designed a bigger revolver with a new type of loading lever and cylinder pin and this developed into the Remington Model of 1861, made in .44 calibre for the Army and .36 calibre for the Navy. Further improvements resulted in the New Model Army of 1863, the second most popular revolver in the Civil War; the first being the Colt Model 1860. Remington revolvers differed from the Colts mainly in the solid frame over the top of the cylinder, which gave added strength and a continuous sighting groove. The Remington of

243 *An Arizona Cowboy by*
Frederic Remington.

244 *Longhorn cattle crossing the*
Red River.

244 **V**

1863 was a cap-and-ball percussion weapon (see COLT REVOLVERS) and 172,000 were sold up to 1875, when it gave way to the metal cartridge model. Frank James, brother of Jesse, carried a Remington revolver and extolled the weapon as 'the hardest and surest shooting pistol made'. The firm became the Remington Arms Company in 1888 and introduced its last revolver, a single-action Army model, in 1891, but it was not a success and in 1894 the company abandoned revolvers. Remington also produced a popular range of DERRINGER pocket pistols and the rolling block rifle, a novel type of breechloader.

Remington Handguns by C. L. and C. R. Karr (Harrisburg, Pennsylvania, 1951);
Remington Arms by A. Hatch (New York, 1956);
The Remington Historical Treasury of American Guns by H. L. Peterson (New York, 1966).

245   *Remington New Model Army of 1863.*

246   *Remington New Model Army of 1875.*

245 ∧

246 ∨

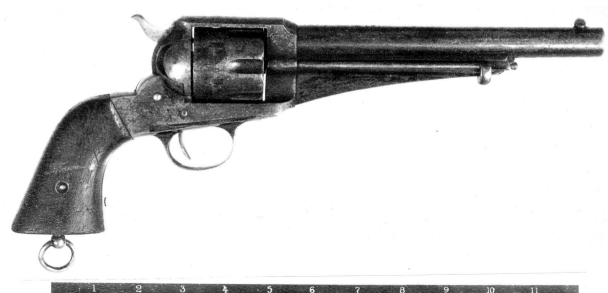

REMUDA

A COWBOY word for the group of saddle horses held ready for use and looked after by the wrangler on a ranch or during a ROUND-UP or CATTLE DRIVE. Working cowboys changed their mounts several times a day; although cow ponies were hardy they would tire after three or four hours of constant activity, and cowboys also used certain horses for particular jobs, such as cutting out cattle from the herd or for roping. The word 'remuda' comes from the Spanish *remudar*, meaning 'to exchange'. The term was mostly used in the South-west: cowboys of the North-west used the word 'cavvy', from the Spanish *caballada* for 'horse herd'. The wrangler was responsible for the remuda at all times; he was generally a youth learning to be a cowboy and he also helped the cook with his chores. Most remudas contained only geldings, as they made more amenable cow horses than stallions or mares.

The Old Time Cowhand by R. F. Adams (New York, 1971).

RENO BROTHERS

The Reno brothers — John, Frank, William and Simeon — led a gang that committed the first train robbery in the United States. On 6 October 1866, a few miles from Seymour, Indiana, they held up a train of the Ohio and Mississippi Railroad and robbed the Adams Express Company car of 10,000 dollars. As protectors of the Adams company, the Pinkerton National Detective Agency went after the bandits. Based in southern Indiana, the Renos headed a large band of outlaws that raided across Indiana, Illinois, Iowa, and Missouri, robbing banks and trains. Allan PINKERTON, founder of the detective agency, went himself into the lion's den and, aided by 'six muscular men', arrested John Reno by a ruse. With brother John sentenced to forty years in prison, the Renos continued their depredations. Finally, Pinkerton and his agents rounded up the brothers and handed them over to the law in New Albany, Indiana. Now that the terrible Renos were confined in jail, the good people of southern Indiana decided to lynch them and on 13 December 1868 the well-organized VIGILANTES burst into the New Albany jail, overpowered the sheriff and his staff, and swiftly hanged Frank, William, and Simeon Reno inside the building.

The Reno Gang of Seymour by R. F. Volland (New York, 1948); *Allan Pinkerton* by A. Lavine (New York, 1963).

REYNOLDS, Charley
c. 1842-76

A notable hunter, army scout and guide, 'Lonesome Charley' Reynolds served under General CUSTER and was killed in the Battle of the LITTLE BIGHORN in June 1876. Believed to have been born in Kentucky, Reynolds was a soldier in the Civil War then became a hunter providing meat

247 V

247 *Warning given by the Southern Indiana Vigilance Committee shortly after the Reno brothers had been lynched.*

248 *Charley Reynolds.*

248 V

for military posts in the Dakota Territory. His nickname 'Lonesome Charley' came from his soft spoken and reserved manner; he did not talk about himself or his deeds. He joined Custer in 1873 and quickly won that officer's respect and admiration, guiding Custer's expedition to the BLACK HILLS in 1874. In the Battle of the Little Bighorn, Reynolds was assigned to Major Reno's battalion and died in the early fighting.

Charley Reynolds by J. E. and G. J. Remsburg (Kansas City, 1931).

RIO GRANDE

The great river of the South-west, the Rio Grande — called the Rio Bravo in Mexico — rises in the San Juan Mountains of Colorado, flows south-east through New Mexico, then divides Texas from Mexico, and enters the Gulf of Mexico after a course of approximately 1,800 miles. Important cities along the river include Albuquerque in New Mexico, El Paso, Laredo, and Brownsville in Texas, and Ciudad Juarez in Mexico. A principal tributary is the Pecos River, which rises in New Mexico and flows through Texas, joining the Rio Grande near Langtry. The establishment of the Rio Grande as the international boundary between the United States and Mexico was a major cause of the MEXICAN WAR of 1846-8. The United States won the war and the Rio Grande was recognized as the boundary between the nations by the Treaty of Guadalupe Hidalgo in 1848.

Great River; The Rio Grande in North American History by D. P. Horgan (New York, 1971).

ROAD RUNNER
Geococcyx californianus

A member of the cuckoo family, the road runner is a curious bird, 'a cuckoo compounded of a chicken and a magpie'. It can fly but prefers to walk or run and can attain a ground speed of 17 m.p.h. It is mainly found in the mesquite and cactus country of the South-west, but it is widely distributed. In the days of the stagecoach and wagon trains the road runner often enjoyed racing ahead of the vehicles for miles; it would then tire of the game, dart to the side of the trail and stand still, as if seeking applause for its performance. It has a white streaked plumage, a prominent erectable crest and a long, expressive tail which, at the end of a run, it sticks up straight to act as a kind of wind brake. It feeds on insects, small rodents, lizards, birds, and snakes. Full grown, the road runner is nearly two feet long. Its

normal call is a soft cooing; when alarmed it clacks its beak and gives out a rattling sound. Its chief enemies are the COYOTE and the bobcat.

American Wild Life by W. G. Van Name (New York, 1961).

ROCKY MOUNTAINS

The great mountain system of western North America that extends from New Mexico to Alaska. The Rocky Mountains include the Bitterroot Range in Idaho and Montana, the Teton Range in Idaho and Wyoming, the Coeur d'Alene Mountains in Montana, the Gallantine Range, the Absaroka Range and the Bighorn Mountains in Montana and Wyoming, the Wasatch Range and Uinta Mountains in Utah, the Front and Sawatch Ranges in Colorado, the San Juan range in Colorado and New Mexico, and the Sangre de Cristo Mountains in Colorado and New Mexico. The highest peaks of the U.S. Rockies are over 14,000 feet, and in COLORADO, where the Rockies attain their most concentrated and imposing mass, there are more than fifty such peaks, the highest being Mount Elbert at 14,431 feet. The Rockies form the Continental Divide in western North America, separating the rivers flowing towards opposite sides of the continent. The mountains are the home of the white-coloured Rocky Mountain goat, the sure-footed BIGHORN, the Grizzly BEAR, the MOUNTAIN LION, and many other animals. It was the abundance of BEAVER in the streams that attracted the MOUNTAIN MEN trappers to the Rockies in the early years of the nineteenth century and these hardy individuals were the real explorers of the central Rocky Mountain West. Official expeditions to the Rockies included those led by LEWIS AND CLARK in 1804-6. Zebulon M. PIKE in 1806-7, and John C. FRÉMONT in the 1840s. Almost all the ranges of the Rockies are rich in precious and useful minerals. There are gold and silver in Colorado, Utah, and the BLACK HILLS of South Dakota, and copper in Montana and New Mexico. Gold strikes in the 1850s and 1860s brought permanent settlement in the Rockies and the establishment of the mountain States.

A Brief History of Rocky Mountain Exploration by R. G. Thwaites (Boston, 1904);
Roaming the Rockies by J. T. Farris (New York, 1930);
Rocky Mountains by H. S. Zim (New York, 1964);
Fourteeners: Colorado's Great Mountains by P. Eberhart and P. Schmuck (Chicago, 1970).

249 ∧   250 ∧   251∨

ROCKY MOUNTAIN FUR COMPANY

A partnership of FUR TRAPPERS and traders founded by William ASHLEY and Andrew Henry in 1822. This company, which later came under the control of famous mountain men Jedediah SMITH, William SUBLETTE, and David Jackson, trapped BEAVER in the central Rockies and originated the rendezvous method of trade in which the trappers gathered to sell their furs to traders at an arranged spot in the wilderness. In 1830 Smith and his partners sold their interests in the company to Jim BRIDGER, Milton Sublette, and Thomas Fitzpatrick, who continued trading until 1834 when the Rocky Mountain Fur Company was absorbed by the AMERICAN FUR COMPANY.

The American Fur Trade in the Far West by H. Chittenden (New York, 1902);
A Majority of Scoundrels: An Informal History of the Rocky Mountain Fur Company by D. Berry (New York, 1961).

252 Λ   253 V   254 V

RODEO

The word 'rodeo' comes from the Spanish *rodear*, to encircle or round up, and in the old South-west it meant the ROUND-UP of cattle. The modern sport of rodeo originated in the 1870s when working cowboys competed among themselves in riding bucking horses. It is claimed that the first organized rodeo took place in Pecos, Texas, in 1883 when cowboys held a rough-riding and cattle-roping competition to celebrate the Fourth of July. The idea caught on and spread throughout the cattle country. So began the multi-million-dollar sport of today, attended by more than ten million spectators annually. There are five standard events in a modern rodeo show: saddle bronc riding, bareback riding, bull riding, calf roping, and steer wrestling. The latter is also known as bulldogging; the rider jumps from his moving horse on to the neck of a running steer, grabs the horns of the beast and, by digging his heels into the ground, brings the steer to a halt, then throws it flat on its side in a matter of seconds. Bulldogging was originated by Negro cowboy Bill Pickett at the turn of the century and he starred in the event in the 101 Ranch Wild West Show, a travelling rodeo that toured the United States and Europe in the years before World War One. Rodeo entered the big league of American sport in 1936 when the present Rodeo Cowboys Association was formed, which brought uniform regulations and professional status to the sport. In saddle bronc riding the contestant, holding the reins with one hand only, must stay in the saddle for ten seconds. In bareback riding no stirrups or reins are used, the rider holds on to a short grip on a leather rigging with one hand and must stay on the horse's back for eight seconds. In bull riding the contestant grips a rope tied around the animal's middle and is required to maintain his seat for eight seconds. In calf roping a rider must throw a rope over the neck of a running calf, then jump down and throw the animal to the ground, crossing and tying any three legs.

The 101 Ranch by E. Collings (Norman, Oklahoma, 1937); *Rodeo* by R. W. Howard and O. Arnold (New York, 1961).

ROMAN NOSE
? — 1868

A war leader of the CHEYENNE, Roman Nose was a great warrior celebrated for his magic war bonnet. Over six feet tall, his Indian name was Woqini, or 'Hook Nose'. Medicine man White Bull made Roman Nose a special war bonnet filled with so many eagle feathers that it trailed to the ground. White Bull instructed Roman Nose that the bonnet would protect him from his enemies' arrows and bullets provided that he obeyed the strict taboos and carried out certain rituals. In September 1865 Roman Nose put his bonnet to the test in a clash with white soldiers in the Powder River county. He recklessly exposed himself to the hottest gunfire, riding to and fro along the line of soldiers. His pony was killed under him but Roman Nose was unscathed. It seemed that his medicine bonnet had saved his life. In September 1868 a large band of Cheyenne and SIOUX attacked a column of scouts under Major G. A. Forsyth, who took up a defensive position on BEECHER ISLAND, in north-eastern Colorado. Roman Nose was not present at the start of the fight as he was undergoing purification ceremonies to restore the protective power of his war bonnet. A few days earlier at a Sioux feast he had broken a taboo of his bonnet by unknowingly eating food touched by an iron fork. However, his warriors implored him, indeed shamed him into joining them in the fight at Beecher Island before his magic had been restored. In his first charge at the frontiersmen, Roman Nose was shot and killed.

Great Western Indian Fights by The Potomac Corral of the Westerners (Lincoln, Nebraska, 1960); *Bury My Heart at Wounded Knee* by D. Brown (London, 1971).

ROOSEVELT, Theodore
1858-1919

Theodore Roosevelt, the so-called 'Cowboy President' of the United States, spent several years in DAKOTA Territory as a young rancher in the 1880s. 'It was still the Wild West in those days,' he wrote, 'the Far West, the West of Owen Wister's stories and Frederic Remington's drawings, the West of the Indian and the buffalo-hunter, the soldier and the cow-puncher.' The Westerners and their rugged country made a deep impression on Roosevelt that coloured the rest of his life. Born in New York City of a wealthy and influential family, he was a sickly child, suffering from asthma and defective eyesight. With great determination he strove to overcome his physical weakness and suceeded: he learned to ride, shoot, swim and box and became an ardent advocate of the strenuous life. After graduating from Harvard in 1880 he entered politics. In September 1883 he visited the Dakota BADLANDS to hunt BUFFALO and other big game and while there purchased the Maltese Cross Ranch.

252 *Bull riding event, modern Rodeo.*

253 *Death of Roman Nose.*

254 *Theodore Roosevelt in his cowboy days.*

Returning to New York he was elected to the State Assembly in November 1883. In February 1884 he was struck by a double tragedy when his mother and wife died. He returned to his ranch in the wilderness and for two years lived the simple life of a frontiersman and cowboy. He bought another ranch, the Elkhorn, on the Little Missouri River and by August 1885 his cattle numbered about 1,600 head. He was in the saddle all day, working with his cowboys on the ROUND-UPS and sharing their hardships on the range. He experienced the dangers of the Western life; riding through a stormy night to break up a STAMPEDE, disarming a drunken desperado, and arresting a band of robbers at gunpoint. Thus did the bespectacled dude from the East win the respect and friendship of the Dakota cowboys he chose to live with. The terrible winter of 1886-7 wiped out Roosevelt's cattle and he suffered great financial loss. He returned to New York to concentrate on politics. He wrote several books about his Western adventures: *Hunting Trips of a Ranchman* (1885); *Ranch Life and the Hunting Trail* (1888); and a history on American Western expansion *The Winning of the West* (1889). When the Spanish-American War broke out in 1898 he raised a regiment of cowboy cavalry, the First U.S. Volunteer Cavalry, known as 'The Rough Riders', and led them to military glory in Cuba. He came back a national hero. In 1900 he became Vice-President to McKinley; when McKinley was killed by an assassin in 1901 Roosevelt became the twenty-sixth President of the U.S.A. He was re-elected in 1904.

Theodore Roosevelt, An Autobiography by T. Roosevelt (New York, 1920);
Roosevelt in the Badlands by H. Hagedorn (New York, 1921);
Ranching with Roosevelt by L. A. Lang (Philadelphia, 1926).

ROSEBUD, Battle of the 1876

A hard fight beteen a column commanded by General George CROOK and a large force of SIOUX and CHEYENNE near Rosebud Creek, Montana, on 17 June 1876. Crook's column consisted of about 1,000 troops and some 300 friendly Indians, CROWS and SHOSHONIS. The hostiles numbered about 1,500. The battle lasted six hours and the fighting line stretched some three miles in length. Finally, the Indians broke off the battle and withdrew. Neither side carried the field conclusively to claim a victory. Crook's official report listed his casualties as 10 killed and 21 wounded, but historians believe they were higher. Hostile casualties are not really known. The Battle of the Rosebud was a milestone in Indian tactics; for the first time a large number of

tribes had combined in a common cause, fighting with unexpected unity and tenacity. Eight days later the combined Sioux and Cheyenne utterly defeated CUSTER and his Seventh Cavalry in the Battle of the LITTLE BIGHORN.

Great Western Indian Fights by the Potomac Corral of the Westerners (New York, 1960);
Frontier Regulars by R. M. Utley (New York, 1973).

ROUND-UP

In the days of the open range cattle wandered freely over a wide area in search of forage. Each rancher claimed a certain area as his range according to the number of cattle he owned and his priority of use. The ranges were not fenced and cattle from different ranches intermingled; the animals were branded to determine ownership. A round-up was the gathering and sorting of the scattered cattle. There were two round-ups a year, in the spring and the autumn. The spring round-up was mainly concerned with BRANDING new calves; unbranded calves kept close to their branded mothers and this signified ownership. Motherless calves or strays were called MAVERICKS. In the autumn or 'beef' round-up the cattle were gathered for the trail drive to market. All cattlemen in the region participated in the round-up, each owner of a herd contributing a number of cowboys and horses. The riders would sweep the country, searching and surrounding the widely scattered cattle and driving them to a point of concentration; here the cattle were separated according to their brands. The round-up was hard work and required all the cowboy's skills in driving out stubborn, half-wild LONGHORNS from brush and broken country, 'cutting out' or separating particular animals, and roping and branding. During the round-up the cowboys slept in the open, tended by a CHUCKWAGON. The coming of BARBED WIRE fences, which enabled ranchers to keep their cattle separated, ended the need for the open range round-up.

The Day of the Cattleman by E. S. Osgood (Minneapolis, Minnesota, 1954);
The Old-Time Cowhand by R. F. Adams (New York, 1971).

RUSSELL, Charles 1864-1926

An outstanding painter of the Old West, Charles Marion Russell was born in ST LOUIS, Missouri, and became a cowboy in MONTANA Territory during the heyday of the open range cattle industry in the early 1880s. He remained a Westerner for the rest of his life. As a working cowboy he was always drawing the animals, people, and scenes around him. He developed a sympathy and affection for the Indians and many of his paintings depict their traditional way of life. A self-taught artist who drew for pleasure with little regard for monetary reward, his professional career as an artist began when he married Nancy Cooper in 1896, who became his business manager, pricing and selling his work. They established a studio-home at Great Falls, Montana, and publishers of magazines and calendars began to buy his colourful illustrations. Like Frederic REMINGTON, he was an artist historian, for he depicted every horse and cattle brand, every item of cowboy and Indian equipment exactly as it was. His work was exhibited at the St Louis World's Fair in 1904 and throughout the United States; in 1914 he held a successful exhibition in London. In 1904 he cast his first piece of sculpture, *Smoking Up*, and completed a total of fifty-three bronzes during his lifetime. He created some 2,500 pictures, mostly with a Montana background, and was at the height of his powers when he died suddenly in his studio home at Great Falls on 24 October 1926. Today his work commands a high premium in the art world.

Charles M. Russell Book: The Life and Work of the Cowboy Artist by H. McCracken (New York, 1957);
Charles M. Russell, Paintings, Drawings, and Sculptures in the Amon G. Carter Collection by F. G. Renner (Fort Worth, Texas, 1966).

256 ∧

257 ∨

255   *'Cowboys of the Bar Triangle' by Charles M. Russell.*

256   *The Round-up.*

257   *Alexander Majors.*

255 ∨

RUSSELL, MAJORS and WADDELL

A large freighting company founded by the partnership of William H. Russell, Alexander Majors, and William Waddell in January 1855. The company secured a two-year contract with the government which gave it a monopoly on the transportation of all military freight west of the Missouri River. Further lucrative government contracts followed and the company prospered greatly. In 1859 Russell, the less cautious of the partners, started an independent venture, the Leavenworth and Pike's Peak Express, a stagecoach line. Without the backing of a government subsidy the line soon ran into financial trouble and it was taken over by Russell, Majors and Waddell and reorganized as the Central Overland, California and Pike's Peak Express. The new company also lost money and in order to prove the feasibility of a central route to California (as opposed to the long, roundabout route then operated by the BUTTERFIELD OVERLAND MAIL) and to win a government mail contract, the partners organized the fast PONY EXPRESS, a spectacular but short-lived mail service that operated from April 1860 to October 1861. The Pony Express made history but no profit; Russell, Majors and Waddell lost heavily on the venture and went out of business.

Empire on Wheels by R. W. and M. L. Settle (Stanford, California, 1949);
War Drums and Wagon Wheels: The Story of Russell, Majors and Waddell by R. W. and M. L. Settle (San Francisco, 1961).

RUSTLERS

Cattle thieves or rustlers were widely active in the Old West when cattle freely roamed the open range. Cattle were branded to signify ownership (see BRANDING). A popular method of stealing was to take big, unbranded calves from their branded mothers and mark them with a different brand. Rustlers also altered the legitimate brand on an animal to form another symbol by applying a running iron, a branding iron with a simple curve at the end. Some rustlers stole calves to build up herds of their own and a number of established ranchers started in this manner. If caught red handed a rustler could expect to be killed on the spot.

S

SACAJAWEA
*c.*1787-1812

The Indian girl who became an American heroine by guiding and aiding LEWIS AND CLARK on their expedition of 1804-6. Sacajawea (also spelled Sacagawea) was born a SHOSHONI; at the age of about twelve she was captured by the HIDATSA, a tribe then living near the MANDAN people at the mouth of the Knife River in North Dakota. The Hidatsas sold her to Toussaint Charbonneau, a French-Canadian fur trader living with the Mandans, who married her according to Indian rites. When Lewis and Clark arrived in the Mandan country they were befriended by the tribe and built Fort Mandan in which they wintered. The explorers hired Charbonneau as interpreter for the rest of the journey and when the expedition continued in April 1805, Sacajawea went with it, her newborn son strapped to her back. If less than the heroine legend has made her, she was invaluable to the expedition as peace envoy and intermediary with Indian tribes. Her most important service came when they reached the land of her people, the Shoshoni. The explorers needed horses to cross the ROCKY MOUNTAINS; Sacajawea persuaded her reluctant brother, a chief, to sell the white men horses and she continued with the expedition to the Pacific Coast and back. Most historians believe that she died of childbirth fever in 1812 at Fort Manuel on the Missouri River; but others claim that she died in 1884 on a reservation in Wyoming. Lewis and Clark spoke highly of her. Sacajawea is honoured by many memorials throughout the West.

Sacajawea, a Guide and Interpreter of the Lewis and Clark Expedition by G. R. Hebard (Glendale, California, 1933); *Sacajawea* by H. P. Howard (Norman, Oklahoma, 1971).

SADDLE, Cowboy

The Western or cowboy saddle is a development of the Spanish war saddle of the CONQUISTADORES. This was based on a wooden frame, or tree, and a high pommel and cantle held the rider in a secure position. The Spanish-Mexican VAQUEROS (early cowboys) modified the war saddle to suit the requirements of cattle ranching; the pommel at the front became a slim horn to which the LARIAT or rope could be attached, and the cantle at the rear was reduced in size for ease of movement. Under American influence in the middle of the nineteenth century the saddle became bigger and heavier, with a stout horn for taking a turn of the lariat to anchor a cow after it had been roped. Spanish names for parts of the Western saddle are still used, such as 'cinch' and 'latigo', straps which keep the saddle in place. The cowboy rode with skill and authority but little finesse, his legs at full stretch, his feet planted firmly in broad, comfortable, leather-clad stirrups; in brush and cactus country the stirrups would be protected by leather hoods or 'taps' (from the Spanish *tapadero*). Every cowboy worth his salt owned his own saddle; he would pay highly for it, for a good saddle would probably serve him well all his working life.

The Cowboy, His Characteristics, His Equipment by P. H. Rollins (New York, 1922).

SAGUARO CACTUS
Carnegiea gigantea

The largest cactus in the United States, the saguaro is found mainly in ARIZONA and northern Mexico. It grows to a height of forty to fifty feet

258 *Sacajawea helps guide the Lewis and Clark expedition.*

259 ∧   260 ∨   261 ∨

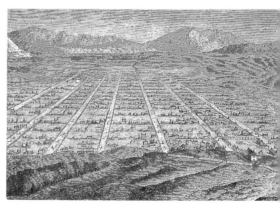

259   *Cowboy saddle.*

260   *Saguaro cactus, Arizona.*

261   *Salt Lake City in 1850.*

and lives to an age of 150 to 200 years. Leafless and spiny, it has a thick green skin that is waxy to retard evaporation and vertically pleated to permit expansion when water is available. During a torrential rain a mature plant absorbs as much as a ton of water. Branches, or arms, begin to develop when the plant is between 16 and 22 feet high. In spring white flowers appear at the tips of the branches and stem; the blossoms mature into red, edible fruit, and in the old days the PIMAN INDIANS ate them fresh and dried, and made syrup from them. The saguaro blossom is Arizona's state flower and in the Saguaro National Monument in southern Arizona these giant cacti stand in forests.

SALT LAKE CITY

The capital of UTAH, Salt Lake City was founded in 1847 by the MORMONS, who had trekked deep into the wilderness to seek refuge from religious persecution. The city stands at the west base of the Wasatch Mountains; it was planned by Mormon leader Brigham YOUNG, even before the advance party arrived in the Valley of the GREAT SALT LAKE, the streets of the settlement were laid out and crops were planted within a few days after the arrival. From a few mud huts Salt Lake City expanded rapidly, growing in size with each arrival of an immigrant wagon train. Its future as a metropolis was assured with the arrival of the railroad in 1869, which brought in Mormon converts by the thousands. The great dome-shaped Tabernacle, capable of seating 5,000, was completed in 1870. With no interior supports, the building was the structural wonder of its day. The six-spired Salt Lake Temple, spiritual hub of the Mormon religion, took forty years to complete — 1853 to 1893.

Salt Lake City by C. D. Harris (Chicago, 1940).

SAN FRANCISCO

Originally a little Spanish settlement called Yerba Buena ('good herb') after a wild plant which grew in the area, the Americans raised the flag over the place on 10 July 1846 during the MEXICAN WAR, and formally named San Francisco on 30 January 1847, after the Mission San Francisco de Asis (Mission Dolores) founded in 1776. In February 1847 a census established the population as 459. San Francisco is located on the tip of a tongue of land between the Pacific Ocean and San Francisco Bay, a land-locked bay connected with the ocean by a narrow channel called the Golden Gate, so named by the explorer John C. FRÉMONT. Early navigators missed the narrow

entrance and so the bay was first seen from the land by José de Ortega of Portolá's expedition of 1769. The bay proper is some 50 miles long, with a maximum width of 13 miles, and depths up to 36 fathoms; it is the largest and most important harbour on the Pacific Coast. The island of Alcatraz, famous for its Federal Penitentiary, is situated near the Golden Gate. The rise of San Francisco as a great seaport began with the discovery of gold in 1848 at Coloma, on the land of John SUTTER. During the GOLD RUSH that followed, thousands of hopeful FORTY-NINERS from all over the world landed in San Francisco to head for the gold diggings and by 1852 the port's population had risen to 35,000. The quickly growing city became a bustling, brawling, lawless place, especially the waterfront area notorious as the Barbary Coast, and during the 1850s several Vigilance Committees were formed to combat crime and many public lynchings were performed in the name of law and order. In the early years a succession of fires razed the crowded wooden buildings; the city was rebuilt again and again and grew into the largest, most commercially important city of the Western United States, with a population in 1870 of 150,000. The city was almost entirely destroyed by earthquake and fire in 1906, but from the ashes arose a new and greater San Francisco.

The Barbary Coast by H. Ashbury (New York, 1936);
San Francisco: A Pageant by C. C. Dobie (New York, 1939);
Golden Gate: The Story of San Francisco Harbour by F. Riesenberg Jr. (New York, 1940);
San Francisco Bay by J. H. Kemble (New York, 1947).

SAND CREEK MASSACRE 1864

On 29 November 1864 Colonel J. M. Chivington, commanding a large force of Colorado militia, launched a suprise attack on a Cheyenne-Arapaho camp, ostensibly peaceful, at Sand Creek in eastern Colorado, and massacred its inhabitants with great brutality. With the Civil War raging and a shortage of troops in Colorado, the Indians had seized the opportunity to raid and kill over a wide area. Local authorities decided to mount a punitive expedition against the Indians and Chivington led a column of undisciplined volunteers. In civil life a Methodist minister, Chivington had a violent hatred of Indians, instructing his men to: 'Kill and scalp all, big and little, nits make lice!' When the column came upon the Indian camp the tipi of Black Kettle, the CHEYENNE chief, was flying the American flag as a token of his peaceful situation; he had been given an assurance (or so he believed) of military protection by the commander of Fort Lyon as long as his people kept the peace.

Chivington ignored the flag; he had come to kill Indians and he attacked. In the barbarous slaughter that followed, the white troops killed fleeing women and children indiscriminately, committing many atrocities and disgusting mutilations in a frenzy of blood lust. Figures differ about the number of Indians killed, and range from 150 to 500: certainly most of them were women and children. The soldiers suffered some 10 dead and 40 wounded. Responsible military leaders deplored the massacre and several commissions were appointed to investigate the affair; all condemned Chivington's action but neither he nor anyone else was brought to trial. General Nelson A. MILES, a notable Indian fighter himself, denounced the Sand Creek Massacre as 'perhaps the foulest and most unjustifiable crime in the annals of America'.

The Sand Creek Massacre by S. Hoig (Norman, Oklahoma, 1961).

SANTA ANNA
1794-1876

The Mexican general and dictator-President who stormed the ALAMO and killed all its defenders in the Texas revolt of 1835-6, Antonio Lopez de Santa Anna played a prominent role in Mexico's stormy history for forty years. He became President of Mexico in 1833. After taking the Alamo he was defeated by Texans under Sam HOUSTON in the Battle of San Jacinto, 21 April 1836, and captured. In 1845 as a result of revolution he was banished from Mexico, but when war broke out with the United States in 1846 he was recalled and appointed *Generalissimo* and provisional President. In February 1847 he was defeated by the Americans in the Battle of Buena Vista, and two months later was again beaten at Cerro Gordo. After the Americans entered Mexico City in September 1847, Santa Anna resigned the Presidency and went into exile in Venezuela. In the following years he returned to Mexico, and was forced to leave, a number of times. In 1867 he went to live in the U.S. Finally in 1874 Santa Anna was allowed to return to Mexico, where he died two years later.

SANTA FE TRAIL

The first of the pioneer roads over which commerce was established between the frontier of the United States, near the MISSISSIPPI RIVER, and the Far West. It was not until Mexico declared her independence from Spain in 1821 that regular trade began to flow over the Santa Fe

Trail. That year William Becknell was the first to take trade goods from MISSOURI to Santa Fe, then in Mexican territory. Becknell established the Santa Fe route. The town of Franklin, Missouri, on the north bank of the Missouri River was the original starting point of the Santa Fe Trail. By 1831 steamboat navigation had advanced so far upstream that a debarkation point was needed closer to the Western frontier. Thus the town of INDEPENDENCE, Missouri, was founded and by 1832 was established as the outfitting station for caravans loading for the trek to Santa Fe. In the beginning the trail followed the ARKANSAS RIVER across Kansas to BENT'S FORT in Colorado, then swung south to Santa Fe. The final and more direct route was known as the Cimarron Cut-Off. The Trail left the Arkansas near present-day Cimarron, Kansas, and drove south-west across the Cimarron Valley to Santa Fe, a total distance of 770 miles. The most dangerous section was the sixty-mile stretch of desert between the ford of the Arkansas and the lower spring of the Cimarron River; there was no drinking water on this parched plain. Hostile Indians were a constant menace to travellers. The completion of the ATCHISON, TOPEKA AND SANTA FE RAILROAD in 1880 ended the importance of the old trail.

The Santa Fe Trail by R. L. Duffus (New York, 1930); *Old Santa Fe Trail* by S. Vestal (Boston, 1939).

SATANTA
c. 1830-78

A chief of the KIOWA, Satanta (also called White Bear) was an accomplished speaker whom white journalists dubbed the 'Orator of the Plains'. He was also a fierce warrior and led many raids against white settlers in Texas and the South-west. Although he signed the Medicine Lodge Treaty of 1867, which confined his people to a reservation in the INDIAN TERRITORY (later Oklahoma), he continued to raid white settlements. In July 1871, Satanta stood trial for murder in Texas and in a speech to the court warned of the consequence if he were hanged: 'I am a great chief among my people. . ..if you kill me, it will be like a spark on the prairie. It will make a big fire — a terrible fire!' The jury of settlers found him guilty and he was sentenced to death, but the governor of Texas took heed of Satanta's warning and the death sentence was

262 ∧   263 ∨   264 ∨

224

commuted to life imprisonment. Two years later he was paroled and continued his raiding. He took part in the attack on the white BUFFALO HUNTERS at ADOBE WALLS in June 1874. Pressed by the military, Satanta surrendered on October 1874 and was imprisoned. Unable to bear life behind bars he sang his death song and killed himself by diving headlong from a high window of the prison hospital.

Satanta, the Great Chief of the Kiowas and His People by C. Wharton (Dallas, Texas, 1935);
Satanta and the Kiowas by F. Stanley (Borger, Texas, 1968).

SCALPING

The taking of an enemy's scalp as a trophy of war was not a custom unique to the North American Indian. Scalping was practised in the Old World by the ancient Scythians, Franks and Visigoths. Before the white man came to North America only the eastern tribes of the Iroquois and Muskhogean scalped their foes; these Indians shaved or plucked most of their hair but let the scalp lock on top of the head grow long as a

265 ▽

challenge to their enemies to try and take it. Scalping was not common practice among the majority of North American Indians. It was promoted and stimulated by the white man; Colonial and United States authorities paid bounties for enemy scalps. During the French and Indian War (1754-63) the French offered rewards for British scalps, and the British paid bounties for the scalps of Frenchmen and their Indian allies. Late into the nineteenth century Mexican and U.S. authorities were paying bounties for Apache scalps. By the time America started pushing West of the Mississippi River, scalping had become widespread among the Indians of the Plains. The scalp — a circular patch of skin and hair on the crown of the head — was usually taken from a dead enemy, but in some Plains tribes a warrior often tried to overpower his foe and scalp him alive. To be scalped alive was a painful experience but not necessarily fatal. Scalping required a knife incision around the scalp lock, which was then tugged and cut away from the head in quick time. The fresh scalp was cleaned and dried, stretched over a small hoop and fixed to a pole, and used in the triumphal

266 ▽

scalp or victory dance. The hair of the scalp was often used to decorate BUCKSKIN shirts, leggings, and other items.

American Indians by W. R. Hagan (Chicago, 1961);
The Sioux — the Life and Customs of a Warrior Society by R. B. Hassrick (Norman, Oklahoma, 1967).

SCHREYVOGEL, Charles 1861-1912

A distinguished artist of the Old West, Charles Schreyvogel mostly painted the U.S. CAVALRY in action during the Indian campaigns of the latter half of the nineteenth centry. Born in New York he studied art in Germany. He made his first trip to the West in 1893 and began to paint his highly accurate historical scenes. He won national recognition overnight with his canvas 'My Bunkie', a major prize winner at the annual exhibition of the National Academy of Design of 1900. The painting depicts a mounted cavalry trooper rescuing his dismounted 'bunkie', or 'bunk mate', in the midst of combat. In all,

265 *Satanta, also called White Bear.*

266 *'My Bunkie' by Charles Schreyvogel.*

267 *Scorpion of Death Valley, California.*

268 *A warrior takes a scalp.*

267 ∧   268 ∨

Schreyvogel produced some 100 paintings and a few bronzes. He died at the height of his fame, of blood poisoning.

The Life and Art of Charles Schreyvogel by J. D. Horan (New York, 1969).

SCORPION

Pioneers in the Old West were wary of scorpions and wisely shook out their boots and clothes before putting them on. Scorpions are widely distributed throughout the United States and are most numerous in the deserts of the South-west, and Mexico. During the day scorpions lie hidden under stones and logs, or in holes, and are rather slow and torpid. They emerge at night to search for food and are very quick and active. They live mainly on small insects and spiders. All scorpions possess a barbed stinger in the tip of their tail, which is the outlet and fang of a poison gland situated at its base. When a scorpion has clutched its prey in its powerful claws, it curves its tail over its head and plunges the paralysing sting into the helpless creature. The poison is sufficient to kill small creatures and to cause man much pain; it may even kill a person who is in a poor state of health when stung. Scorpions can survive many months without food and water.

Poisonous Dwellers of the Desert by N. N. Dodge (Globe, Arizona, 1961).

SHARPS RIFLES

With its large bore and long range the single-shot breechloader developed by Christian Sharps became the most popular BUFFALO killing rifle in the Old West. The classic Sharps was the .45 calibre model using a 120-grain powder charge and a bullet weighing 550 grains; it had tremendous stopping power and a supposed range of 1,000 yards. Sharps later produced a .50 calibre that fired a 140-grain charge and a 700-grain bullet. Christian Sharps (1811-74) patented his newly-invented breech mechanism in 1848, in which the breechblock, operated by lowering the trigger guard, dropped vertically to expose the chamber for loading a cartridge; when the breechblock was closed it sheared off the base of the paper cartridge, thus exposing the powder to the cap flash. It was a simple, sturdy, reliable action that served the various types of Sharps rifles with great success. Sharps won fame in the fighting over the slavery issue in KANSAS in the 1850s. Antislavery preacher Henry Ward Beecher

said that one Sharps rifle contained more moral power 'so far as the slave-holders were concerned than in a hundred Bibles'. And Sharps rifles became known as 'Beecher's Bibles'. The .52 calibre Sharps New Model 1859 and New Model 1863 carbines were highly popular in the Civil War of 1861-5; the Federal government purchased 80,512 for cavalry use, and the Confederates manufactured copies of the Sharps carbine. The big Sharps rifle made an ideal buffalo gun; its strong breech allowed heavy powder charges and its large bullets struck hard. It became the favourite weapon of the professional BUFFALO HUNTERS who slaughtered the vast herds to the edge of extinction. And when the buffalo was gone the single-shot Sharps was no longer required. The Sharps Rifle Company never developed a repeating rifle and went out of business in 1881.

The Sharps Rifle by W. O. Smith (New York, 1943).

SHEEP WARS

Sheep were anathema to cattlemen in the Old West. They claimed the animals ruined the grass by eating it too close and destroyed the roots with their massed, sharp hoofs, creating barren regions on the open range. The COWBOY, the mounted pioneer of the plains, viewed the newly-arrived, pedestrian shepherd with utter contempt. Cowboys said that sheep left a stink on the land and in watering places that upset cattle and horses. Sheepmen argued that sheep and cattle could be raised on the same pasture. The differences of opinion and interests led to violent clashes between the factions. Cattlemen raided sheep herds, slaughtering great numbers of the animals, and sheep ranchers and shepherds were shot. Warfare between cowboys and sheepmen continued for many years, from the 1880s into the early years of the twentieth century. On the Wyoming-Colorado range some twenty men died in the fighting, hundreds were injured, and 600,000 sheep were destroyed; a favourite method of extermination was driving a herd over a high cliff. In Arizona thirty-two men died in the so-called Pleasant Valley War which lasted from 1887 to 1892. But sheep had come to stay, and the cattlemen slowly realized that sheep could be raised with half the effort and twice the profit of cattle and many reconciled themselves to raising both types of livestock. When BARBED-WIRE fences finally ended the open range the sheep-cattle rivalry came to an end.

Sheep by A. B. Gilfillan (Boston, 1929);
Shepherd's Empire by C. W. Towne and E. R. Wentworth (Norman, Oklahoma, 1945).

269 ∧   270 ∨   271 ∨

272 ∨

269   *The Sharps carbine.*

270   *General Philip H. Sheridan.*

271   *General William T. Sherman.*

272   *Luke Short.*

SHERIDAN, Philip H.
1831-88

Appointed commander of the Military Division of the Missouri in 1869, Lieutenant-General Philip Henry Sheridan directed the operations during the period of the most intense Indian campaigns in the West. Born in Massachusetts, he graduated from West Point in 1853 and first saw service along the RIO GRANDE and against the Indians in the North-west. After distinguished service in the Union Army during the Civil War of 1861-5, in which he rose to the rank of Major-General of the regular army, he was made military governor of Texas and Louisiana, where his repressive measures earned him the disapproval of President Andrew Johnson. In March 1869 President U. S. Grant appointed Sheridan Lieutenant-General and gave him command of the Division of the Missouri, to replace SHERMAN who became the Commanding General of the U.S. Army. Sheridan directed forceful campaigns against the PLAINS INDIANS and the APACHES and finally settled them upon reservations. He was ruthless and outspoken in his dealings with the hostile natives. It was he who gave rise to the frontier aphorism — 'the only good Indian is a dead Indian'. When Tosawi, a COMANCHE chief, was presented to Sheridan and introduced himself as: 'Tosawi, good Indian'. Sheridan replied: 'The only good Indians I ever saw were dead.' On another occasion when asked if something should not be done to stop white hunters from wiping out the BUFFALO herds (the Plains Indians' chief means of sustenance) Sheridan answered: 'Let them kill, skin, and sell until the buffalo is exterminated; it is the only way to bring lasting peace and allow civilization to advance.' When sending General CUSTER, one of his favourites, against Black Kettle's CHEYENNE village on the WASHITA, his orders were: 'Destroy their villages and ponies, kill or hang all warriors and bring back all women and children.' In 1884 Sheridan succeeded Sherman as Commanding General of the army. In June 1888 he was made General; he died in August that year.

Sheridan by J. Hergesheimer (Boston, 1931);
Border Command: General Phil Sheridan in the West by C. C. Rister (Norman, Oklahoma, 1944);
Sheridan the Inevitable by R. O'Connor (Indianapolis, 1953).

SHERMAN, William T.
1820-91

As commander of the Military Division of the Missouri, and later as Commanding General of the U.S. Army, William Tecumseh Sherman played a leading role in the final subjugation of the free-ranging Indians of the West. Born in Ohio, his father named him Tecumseh after the great Shawnee Indian chief; he graduated from West Point in 1840 and served in the MEXICAN WAR of 1846-8. In the Civil War of 1861-5 he established his reputation as a successful and relentless general; an advocate of total war he believed in bringing hostilities to a quick end by inflicting the hell of war on the civil population, destroying goods, crops, public buildings, and factories. On his March to the Sea through Georgia in 1864, Sherman burned and destroyed on a sixty-mile-wide front. After the war Major-General Sherman took command of the Military Division of the Missouri and set about pacifying the hostile Indians, who had enjoyed something of a field day while most of the army was involved in the great domestic conflict. In 1866 Sherman was promoted to Lieutenant-General. He viewed the Indians as savages standing in the way of advancing civilization and dealt with them accordingly. But it was not an easy task; the Division of the Missouri contained more than a million square miles of frontier country inhabited by nearly 200,000 Indians. 'Were I or the department commanders to send guards to every point where they are clamored for', said Sherman, 'we would need alone on the plains 100 thousand men, mostly of cavalry.' At that time the total strength of the U.S. Army numbered about 57,000. In 1869 Sherman became the Commanding General of the army and SHERIDAN succeeded him as commander of the Division of the Missouri. In 1871 while on a tour of the West Sherman was involved in a dramatic situation. Reservation KIOWAS had raided into Texas, killing teamsters of a government wagon train. Sherman, visiting Fort Sill, had the responsible leaders — SATANTA, Satank, and Big Tree — arrested in a tense confrontation on the post between armed Indians and soldiers in which only Sherman's coolness prevented an explosion. General Sherman retired from active service in 1883 and died of pneumonia aged seventy-one in 1891.

Sherman: Fighting Prophet by L. Lewis (New York, 1932);
William Tecumseh Sherman and the Settlement of the West by R. G. Athearn (Norman, Oklahoma, 1956).

SHORT, Luke
1854-93

A notable gambler and gunman, Luke Short was a friend of Wyatt EARP and Bat MASTERSON. Born in Mississippi he travelled West as an infant in a wagon train and grew up in Texas. After working as a COWBOY he became a professional gambler and saloon-owner, drifting from town to

273   *Cathedral Peak in the Sierra Nevada Mountains, California.*

274   *Shoshoni Indians.*

275   *Al Sieber (sitting centre) and his Apache scouts.*

273 ∨

274 ∧

275 ∨

town. Slight of figure, five feet six inches tall, he was always elegantly dressed. In TOMBSTONE, Arizona, in February 1881 he had an argument with another gambler, Charlie Storms, and shot him dead. In April 1883, while running the famous Long Branch Saloon in DODGE CITY, Kansas, he had a shoot-out with a lawman and was forced to leave town. However, he returned to Dodge and, backed by Earp, Masterson, and a number of other gunmen, again established himself in the place. In 1887 he was in FORT WORTH, Texas, the owner of the White Elephant Saloon. Here he came into conflict with Jim Courtright, a gunfighter and former marshal of Fort Worth, who demanded protection money from Short. In a final confrontation both men drew guns; Short fired first and wildly, but fortunately for him his bullet hit Courtright's thumb on the gun hand, preventing him from cocking the hammer of his single-action COLT, and before he could switch hands, Short shot him dead. Luke died in bed of dropsy at Geuda Springs, Kansas, at the age of thirty-nine.

Luke Short, Famous Gambler of the Old West by W. R. Cox (London, 1961).

SHOSHONI INDIANS

The most northerly division of the Shoshonean family of the Uto-Aztecan linguistic stock, the Shoshoni (also spelled Shoshone) originally lived in the Great Basin between the Rockies and the SIERRA NEVADA Mountains. The origin of the name 'Shoshoni' is not certain but is thought to mean 'valley dwellers'. The Eastern, or Wind River, Shoshonis left the Great Basin and moved eastward into the plains about 1500, thus acquiring many of the cultural characteristics of the buffalo-hunting PLAINS INDIANS. Hostile tribes, however, drove them back into the ROCKY MOUNTAINS. The northern bands were found by LEWIS AND CLARK in 1805 on the headwaters of the Missouri in western Montana. SACAJAWEA, the Shoshoni girl, helped guide Lewis and Clark through the Rockies. Further west, along the Snake River in Idaho and to the south in Nevada, the Shoshoni tribes were more primitive; the country is extremely barren and large game was scarce. As the nature of the country differed so did the inhabitants. For food they depended mostly on fish supplemented by rabbits, roots, nuts, and seeds and were frequently called 'Digger Indians'; they were also called Shoshokos, or 'Walkers', because they were too poor to own horses. In the north and east the horse and BUFFALO Shoshoni lived in TIPIS. In the sagebrush country to the west they used brush shelters. From their first contact with the white

276 *Sioux chief Sleeping Bull holding captured U.S. Cavalry sabre.*

man the Northern Shoshoni had been generally friendly, especially Chief WASHAKIE and his people, who did much to help white immigrants on their journey West. This friendliness won for Washakie a reservation of his own choosing, the Wind River Valley, a highly-prized section of Wyoming. In 1878 the Federal government moved the Northern ARAPAHOES on to the Shoshoni Reservation as a temporary expedient, and there, despite Shoshoni protests, they have remained permanent residents to this day.

The Shoshonis: Sentinels of the Rockies by V. C. Trenholm and M. Carley (Norman, Oklahoma, 1964).

SHOTGUNS

The double-barrelled shotgun was a popular weapon with saloon-keepers, LAWMEN, and stagecoach guards — the latter use giving rise to the expression 'riding shotgun'. It was the ideal firearm for dealing with a mob, as one blast at close range could knock down a number of men. Shotguns were also widely used by settlers for bagging game. GUNFIGHTERS usually cut, or sawed off, a length of the shotgun barrel for extra spread of buckshot at close range. In a desperate situation a sawed-off shotgun was often more intimidating and effective than a six-shot revolver.

SIEBER, Al
1844-1907

Outstanding chief of scouts during the APACHE campaigns of the 1880s, Al Sieber played an important role in hunting down the elusive GERONIMO. Born in Germany, he came to America as an infant and lived in Pennsylvania. In 1862 he joined the Union Army, was badly wounded at Gettysburg, and served till the end of the Civil War. In 1866 he went West and worked as a prospector in Nevada and California, and as a ranch foreman in Arizona. He gained a reputation as an Indian fighter and was hired by General George CROOK to recruit and lead Apache scouts against the hostile bands. Sieber, six feet tall, was as tough as any of his scouts; he could march sixty miles a day, he survived twenty-nine wounds by bullet or arrow, and was credited with having killed some fifty Indians in combat. He mastered the Apache language and his scouts admired and respected him and were intensely loyal. Sieber and his Apaches were highly successful in tracking down hostiles. After his scouting days were over Sieber continued to work with Apaches, and while in charge of an Indian work-gang he was killed in a construction accident.

Al Sieber, Chief of Scouts by D. L. Thrapp (Norman, Oklahoma, 1964).

SIERRA NEVADA

The great mountain range in eastern California that presented such a formidable barrier to the early settlers on their way to the fertile valleys of central California. The Sierra Nevada — Spanish for 'Snowy Range' — extends from the Tehachapi Pass in the south to the Feather River in the north, a distance of 430 miles. Eleven peaks in the range are over 14,000 feet, the highest point being Mount Whitney at 14,495. The lower slopes of the Sierras are covered with forests of pine, fir, cedar, and oak, and in particular, scattered groves of the world's biggest trees, *Sequoia gigantea,* which attain heights of 300 feet and a base diameter of 30 feet, many of them are 2,000 years old. Sequoia National Park was established in 1890 to preserve these magnificent giants. The fauna of the Sierras include the mountain goat and mountain sheep, the mule deer, and black and brown bears. The discovery of gold in the Sierra Nevada in 1848 started the great California GOLD RUSH. Donner Pass, near Lake Tahoe, was named after the ill-fated DONNER PARTY of emigrants forced to winter in the Sierras in 1846-7. It took the builders of the CENTRAL PACIFIC RAILROAD three years — between 1865 and 1868 — to master the Sierras and join tracks with the UNION PACIFIC in Utah and establish the first transcontinental railway across the United States.

History of the Sierra Nevada by F. Farquhar (Berkeley, California, 1965).

SIOUX INDIANS

The most numerous of the PLAINS INDIANS, the Sioux ranged over a vast area extending from the Minnesota lake country westward to the ROCKY MOUNTAINS, and from the Canadian border to the Platte River in Nebraska. The name Sioux is a French abbreviation of the Algonquin Indian word *Nadowis-sue,* meaning Snake or Enemy; the Sioux called themselves 'Dakota', or 'Lakota' and 'Nakota', depending on the Siouan regional dialect, which means Allies. There were three major divisions. The Eastern or Santee Sioux spoke the Dakota dialect and inhabited the Minnesota area; they were divided into four sub-groups, the Mdewakantonwan, Wahpekute, Sisseton, and the Wahpeton. The Middle or Wiciyela Sioux division spoke the Nakota dialect and lived in eastern South Dakota; they were sub-divided into the Yankton and Yanktonai groups. The Western or Teton Sioux were the largest division and inhabited the high plains of the Dakotas and westward. The Teton — the Sioux prototype most used in portrayals of the North American Indian — included the sub-tribes Oglala, Brule, Sans Arcs, Minnekonjou, Two Kettle, Hunkpapa, and Blackfeet (not to be confused with the Algonquin Blackfeet). Of these the Oglalas were the most numerous and offered the hardest resistance to white invasion. RED CLOUD and CRAZY HORSE were Oglala chiefs; SITTING BULL was a chief of the Hunkpapa. As the nineteenth century began the Sioux had

become the dominant tribe of the Northern Plains. Although habitually at war with other tribes, the Sioux did not actively resist white immigration until the whites began to intrude in great numbers. In 1862 the Santee Sioux went on the warpath in what is known as the Minnesota Uprising (see MINNESOTA); three years later Red Cloud began his war in the Powder River country of Wyoming and in 1866 his warriors wiped out Captain FETTERMAN and eighty soldiers near FORT PHIL KEARNY. In 1876 the Teton Sioux and the Cheyenne defeated General CUSTER and the Seventh Cavalry in the Battle of the LITTLE BIGHORN in Montana. After this last victory the army scattered the Sioux and one by one the chiefs surrendered and settled their people on reservations. In the late 1880s the GHOST DANCE religion spread among the dejected reservation Sioux and the U.S. authorities viewed the peaceful cult as a dangerous movement. In December 1890 troops were sent to intercept a band of Minnekonjou under chief Big Foot camped at WOUNDED KNEE Creek, South Dakota, and the meeting resulted in the massacre of the band. The subjugation of the proud Dakota Indians was now complete. Today the Sioux live mainly on reservations in North and South Dakota.

Red Cloud's Folk: A History of the Oglala Sioux by G. E. Hyde (Norman, Oklahoma, 1937);
A History of the Dakota or Sioux Indians by D. Robinson (Minneapolis, 1956);
The Sioux Indians, Hunters and Warriors of the Plains by S. Bleeker (New York, 1962);
Dahcotah: Life and Legends of the Sioux by M. Eastman (Minneapolis, 1962);
The Last Days of the Sioux Nation by R. M. Utely (New Haven, Connecticutt, 1963).

SITTING BULL
*c.*1831-90

Celebrated chief and mystic of the Hunkpapa SIOUX, Sitting Bull was born in what is now South Dakota. By the time he was twenty he had gained tribal fame as a hunter and warrior. He developed a reputation as a medicine man and believed he had been divinely chosen to lead and protect his people and established himself in this role while still a young man. Always hostile to the whites he was frequently on the warpath. By the end of 1868 nearly half the Sioux had resigned themselves to reservation life, but Sitting Bull remained free with his people in the BUFFALO

country. In December 1875 the Commissioner of Indian Affairs directed all Sioux bands to enter reservations by the end of January 1876 — or be declared hostile. Many bands of Sioux did not meet this deadline and were attacked by U.S. troops. CRAZY HORSE and his Oglala people moved north to join forces with Sitting Bull; by the spring of 1876 some 3,000 Teton Sioux and Northern CHEYENNE warriors had assembled at Sitting Bull's camp in the Valley of the Little Bighorn in Montana. In early June 1876 Sitting Bull subjected himself to the agony of the SUN DANCE, a ritual of self torture, in order to obtain a vision of what lay ahead for the Sioux. He saw a vision of many white soldiers falling from the sky upside down, a prediction of a great victory for the Indians. On 25 June 1876 while Sitting Bull remained in camp making medicine, Crazy Horse and other war chiefs led the allied warriors against General CUSTER and his Seventh Cavalry; Custer and all the men under his direct command were killed. Sitting Bull's vision had come true. This victory, however, brought relentless retaliation from the army and the Sioux were

278 V

277 *Sitting Bull by Robert Lindneux.*

278 *Jedediah Smith.*

scattered; Sitting Bull and his followers fled to Canada and stayed there until July 1881, when he returned to the U.S. and surrendered at Fort Buford, Montana. In 1883 he was placed on the Standing Rock Reservation, South Dakota, and because he continued to regard himself as chief of his people he earned the enmity of Indian agent James McLaughlin. For a year Sitting Bull went on tour with BUFFALO BILL'S WILD WEST SHOW, but most of the 1880s was spent feuding with McLaughlin. When the GHOST DANCE cult reached the Dakota reservations Sitting Bull readily espoused the new religious movement. Fearing that Sitting Bull's active interest in the Ghost Dance might lead to serious trouble, McLoughlin recommended that he be arrested and confined in a military prison. On 15 December 1890 Indian policemen went to take the chief; his followers tried to prevent this and in the struggle Sitting Bull was shot dead by policemen Red Tomahawk and Bull Head.

Sitting Bull: Champion of the Sioux by S. Vestal (Norman, Oklahoma, 1957); *Sitting Bull* by A. B. Adams (New York, 1973).

SKUNK
Mephitis mephitica

The common skunk, a member of the weasel family, is widely distributed throughout the United States and much of Canada. It is notorious for the malodorous liquid it squirts as a means of defence; the stench of this amber-coloured secretion is so nauseous and persistent that most animals stay well clear of the skunk. The secretion is contained in a pair of glands beneath the tail. When alarmed, the skunk ejects the fluid in an accurate double squirt, hitting targets up to twelve feet away. If the liquid touches the eye it can cause severe pain and momentary blindness. Settlers unfortunately infected by skunk secretion claimed that no amount of washing could remove the stench from clothes. About the size of a cat, the skunk was hunted for its valuable fur — black coloured and streaked with white — which was purified by heat for commercial purposes. The chief trader in skunk fur was the HUDSON'S BAY COMPANY.

SMITH, Jedediah
1799-1831

A fur trapper, trader, and explorer, Jedediah Strong Smith was the first American to reach CALIFORNIA overland from the East. Born in New York State, he joined William ASHLEY in the Rocky Mountain fur trade in the early 1820s, and in the search for BEAVER discovered the South Pass through the Rockies in 1824, during which journey he was mauled by a grizzly BEAR. In 1826 Ashley sold his fur business to Smith and two partners. On 22 August 1826 Smith led a party of trappers from the GREAT SALT LAKE (in Utah) to California, via the Mohave Desert and the San Bernardino Mountains, reaching the Mission of San Gabriel (a suburb of modern Los Angeles) on 27 November. On the return journey, Smith crossed the SIERRA NEVADA Mountains and arrived at the Great Salt Lake in June 1827. Both outward and return journeys were marked by extreme suffering and hardship. In July 1827 Smith, with a party of eighteen, set out to retrace the route to California; on the way ten of the party were killed by Indians. On reaching the San Gabriel Mission, Smith had difficulties with the Mexican authorities and spent several weeks in jail. After wintering in the Sacramento Valley, he marched north along the coast to the OREGON country. Jedediah Smith was the first to blaze the overland route from the Great Salt Lake to California, the first explorer of the Great Basin between the Rockies and the Sierra Nevada Mountains. In 1830 he sold his interest in the fur company and entered the Santa Fe trade. On 27 May 1831 he was killed by COMANCHE INDIANS while travelling on the SANTA FE TRAIL. Unlike most MOUNTAIN MEN, Jed Smith was well educated, gentlemanly in manner and speech, and a devout Christian.

Jedediah Smith, Trader and Trail Blazer by M. S. Sullivan (New York, 1936); *Jedediah Smith and the Opening of the West* by D. L. Morgan (Indianapolis, 1953).

SMITH, Tom
c. 1835-70

A marshal of ABILENE, Kansas, 'Bear River Tom' Smith was remarkable in that he kept the peace with his fists instead of firearms. Not much is known of his life before his years out West. He is believed to have been born in New York City, where, it is said, he was a prize fighter and later a member of the police force; while on duty he unwittingly shot a boy and this turned him against the use of guns. He headed West and in 1868 established his reputation as a forceful peace officer at Bear River, Wyoming, one of the mobile towns that followed the construction gangs of the UNION PACIFIC RAILROAD; henceforth he was known as 'Bear River Tom' Smith. On 4 June 1870 he became marshal of Abilene and soon imposed his unusual personality on the wild cowboys who came up from Texas on the long CATTLE DRIVES. A broad-shouldered middleweight, nearly six feet tall, the quiet-spoken Smith carried a pistol but preferred to use his trained prize-fighter fists. When challenged by desperadoes, he took them by surprise and punched them unconscious. A dedicated peace officer, he enforced the ordinance prohibiting cowboys from carrying firearms within the town limits, and brought a fair measure of law and order to Abilene. The gallant Tom Smith was killed on 2 November 1870 while attempting to arrest a settler on a charge of murder.

Heroes Without Glory by J. Schaefer (London, 1968).

SMITH & WESSON REVOLVERS

The revolvers manufactured by Horace Smith and Daniel Wesson were very popular in the Old West. The Smith & Wesson six-shooter of the 1870s differed chiefly from the COLT and REMINGTON revolvers of the time in that it had a tip-up action that allowed the barrel to drop down, ejecting all the spent cartridges cases simultaneously as the cylinder and barrel cleared the frame. In the Colts and Remingtons the empty cases had to be ejected one by one. Smith & Wesson produced their first revolver, a small .22 calibre seven-shot, in 1857. In 1861 they produced a larger model, a .32 calibre six-shot that proved popular in the Civil War. In 1870 came Model No. 3, also known as the American Model, a .44 calibre six-shooter. Major George W. Schofield of the Tenth Cavalry made certain modifications to the .44 American Model and the Schofield-Smith & Wesson was born. The U.S. Army purchased 8,285 of the Schofield Model and WELLS FARGO and the American Express Company armed their guards and agents with the rugged, reliable weapon. Jesse JAMES was just one of many gunmen who favoured the Schofield-Smith & Wesson; Jesse was shot dead in April 1882 by Bob FORD, who used a Smith & Wesson for the treacherous deed. In December 1882 Major Schofield shot himself with one of his own revolvers.

Smith & Wesson Revolvers by J. E. Parsons (New York, 1957); *Smith & Wesson Handguns* by R. C. McHenry and W. F. Roper (Harrisburg, Pennsylvania, 1958).

SOD HOUSES

Settlers on the PRAIRIES lived in houses made of sod, or turf, blocks because there were no forests or stone quarries on the wide open grass plains to provide proper building materials. The best time

279 ∧ 280 ∨

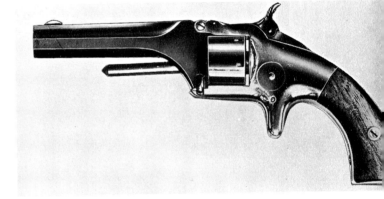

281 ∨

279 *Tom Smith.*
280 *The first Smith & Wesson revolver, 1857.*
281 *Smith & Wesson Model No. 3 of 1870.*

236

282 Λ

283 V

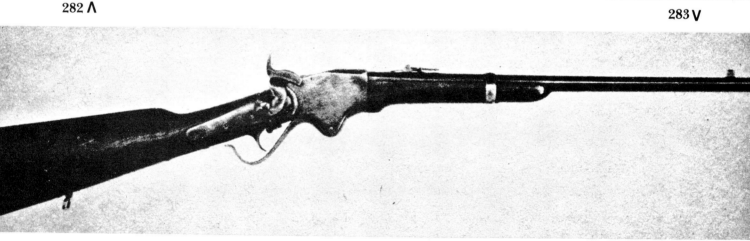

284 V

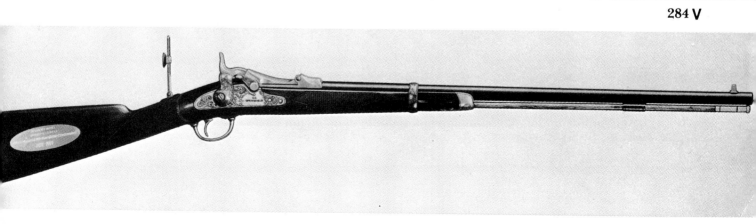

to build a sod house was in the spring when the sod was heavy with grass and wet enough to handle easily. The sod was cut up with a sharp spade into blocks about three feet long and a foot deep, then built up like a brick wall. Door and window frames (made from packing cases or wagon timber) were set into the sod walls. The roof consisted of pole rafters over which was placed a matting of brush covered by prairie hay, then a top layer of sod bricks thinner than those used for the walls; the ridge pole of the roof was supported by thick poles with forks at the top. The cracks between the sod blocks were filled with mud. Such a house was cool in summer and warm in winter but it was a crude structure, dirty and dangerous. In heavy rainfall the roof became heavy with water and collapsed, often killing the occupants under a mass of mud. Another disadvantage of the sod house was its attraction for all kinds of insects, rats and snakes; when the family sat down to eat, insects would fall from the roof into the food. As soon as they were able, settlers built a timber cabin and left the uncomfortable sod house to the livestock.

The Sod House Frontier, 1854-1890 by E. N. Dick (New York, 1931);
Sod House Days by H. Ruede (New York, 1966).

SOUTHERN PACIFIC RAILROAD

Chartered in December 1865 by the California legislature, the Southern Pacific Railroad Company was formed to build a line from SAN FRANCISCO to San Diego, then eastward to meet another projected transcontinental railroad. Owing to financial difficulties the route was amended; San Diego was by-passed and the line did not reach Yuma, on the California-Arizona border, until September 1877. Pushing eastward across New Mexico, the Southern Pacific formed a junction with the Texas and Pacific Railroad at Sierra Blanca, about 100 miles east of El Paso, thus completing another route across the continent — San Francisco to New Orleans. In 1883 the Southern Pacific secured its own line through Texas by acquiring the Galveston, Harrisburg and San Antonio Railroad. Further

282 *A sod house on the Western plains.*

283 *Spencer repeating carbine.*

284 *The 'trapdoor' Springfield rifle, ornate Officer's model.*

285 *Southern Pacific train crossing the Dollarhide Trestle in Southern Oregon, 1882.*

mergers and purchases brought numerous pioneer railroads — including the CENTRAL PACIFIC — under the single banner of the Southern Pacific.

Chapters on the History of the Southern Pacific by S. Daggett (New York, 1922);
Southern Pacific, the Roaring Story of a Fighting Railroad, by N. C. Wilson and F. J. Taylor (New York, 1952).

SPENCER RIFLE

The first successful magazine repeating rifle was patented by Christopher M. Spencer of Connecticut in March 1860 and manufactured by the Spencer Repeating Rifle Company of Boston. The .52 calibre Spencer carbine was the most widely used carbine of the American Civil War. Seven metal rim-fire cartridges were loaded into the tubular magazine in the butt-stock through an opening in the butt-plate; they were fed forward into the breech by a coiled spring. The falling breechblock was actuated by a trigger guard lever, which extracted and ejected the empty case and inserted a fresh cartridge into the chamber. The firing hammer had to be pulled back for each shot. From 1 January 1861 to 30 June 1866 the U.S. Ordnance Department purchased 94,196 Spencer carbines and 12,471 Spencer rifles (civilian purchases pushed the total to 200,000). It was the sustained firepower of the seven-shot Spencer carbine that saved Major Forsyth's command from being overrun by Indians in the Battle of BEECHER ISLAND in September 1868; and the Spencer was used with devastating effect by Custer's Seventh Cavalry

285 ▼

against the Indians at the WASHITA in November 1868. However, the Spencer could not compete with its new rival, the sixteen-shot WINCHESTER Model 1866, which greatly appealed to the civilian market, and the Spencer Repeating Rifle Company went out of business in 1869.

United States Muskets, Rifles, and Carbines by A. Gluckman (Buffalo, New York, 1948).

SPRINGFIELD RIFLES

The single-shot rifles and carbines manufactured by the U.S. Armoury at Springfield, Massachusetts, were standard issue for the army throughout the INDIAN WARS from 1866 to 1890. The muzzle-loaded Springfield rifle had been widely used in the Civil War, and in the years immediately following the war the Ordnance Department, in order to save money, converted 50,000 Civil War muzzle-loaders to breechloaders by the Allin system, devised by E. S. Allin, master armourer at Springfield. The Allin system incorporated a hinged breechblock that could be raised, like a trap door, to expose the chamber and eject the spent cartridge; a fresh cartridge was inserted by hand into the chamber, the breechblock was shut down, and the side hammer cocked for firing. In 1867 the Allin-converted Springfields proved their worth when, newly issued to the troops in the Powder River country, their rapid firepower repulsed and punished the Indians in the Hayfield and WAGON BOX fights. This conversion served the army from 1865 until the adoption of the so-called 'trapdoor' Springfield Model of 1873. After testing more than 100 types of rifles, the Ordnance Board settled for the tried and tested Springfield Allin system. The Model 1873 was a sturdy weapon with a simple mechanism, long range and excellent stopping power; it was superior to most firearms for service in sandy, dusty country as the breechblock and receiver could be easily wiped. The rifle fired a .45 calibre bullet propelled by 70 grains of black powder; the carbine used a .45 bullet and 55 grains of powder. The greatest deficiency of the weapon was that it was a single shot. It was also claimed to have a tendency to jam and this fault received much attention as a possible cause for the crushing defeat of CUSTER and his Seventh Cavalry in the Battle of the LITTLE BIGHORN in June 1876. However, with certain improvements, the trapdoor Springfield continued to serve the regular army until 1892, when the Krag-Jorgensen magazine rifle was adopted. The Springfield was carried by militia units into the Spanish-American War of 1898.

From Flintlock to M-1 by J. W. Shields (New York, 1954); *The Springfield Carbine on the Western Frontier* by K. M. Hammer (Bellevue, Nebraska, 1970).

SPURS, Cowboy

The COWBOY of the Old West was much attached to his spurs. A necessary part of his working equipment, they also served as a flashy insignia of his profession when he arrived in a cattle town after a long trail drive. Some cowboys fixed metal pendants to their spurs to give a pleasant jingle-jangle as they moved. A Western spur is composed of four major components: the metal heel band and shank; the spiked rowel which is attached to the end of the shank; the heel chain that goes under the foot; and the wide leather strap that fastens over the instep. Types of rowels are many and varied, from small star-shapes to the big sunburst kind with huge prongs. A cowboy seldom used his spurs to hurt or lacerate a horse, but merely to prod and signal his well-trained mount into quick action. Sharp rowels were always filed down and blunted.

The Cowboy, His Characteristics, His Equipment by P. A. Rollins (New York, 1922).

ST JOSEPH, Missouri

Situated on the east bank of the MISSOURI RIVER, the town of St Joseph, Missouri, played an important part in the development of the western United States. Here, thousands of emigrant and trade wagons were outfitted for the long trek into the wilderness. St Joseph became the hub of numerous transportation and communications systems involving the steamboat, stage and freight lines, telegraph, railroad, and the PONY EXPRESS, all of which supplied and maintained contact with the West. Founded as a trading post in 1826 and incorporated in 1845, St Joseph became the staging area and starting point for the massive migrations to OREGON and CALIFORNIA in the 1840s and 1850s. In April 1860 the town became the eastern terminus of the Pony Express, linking St Joseph with Sacramento, California. The town continued to prosper and grow and by 1880 the population was some 20,000. In 1882 Jesse JAMES, born in Missouri, was living in St Joseph under the alias of 'J. D. Howard' when he was shot dead in his home by Bob FORD. Today the Jesse James Home and the Pony Express Stables are museums open to the public.

The History of Missouri by D. D. March (Chicago, 1967).

ST LOUIS, Missouri

Founded in 1764 by French fur traders from New Orleans, St Louis became the headquarters of the Western fur trade. Here, William ASHLEY and other leaders of the trade built their homes and directed the activities of the fur trapping MOUNTAIN MEN. Located on a flood-free bluff on the MISSISSIPPI RIVER, convenient to the MISSOURI, Ohio, and other river approaches, St Louis grew into the centre of mid-continental commerce, transportation, and the 'Gateway to the West'. Along the riverfront big STEAMBOATS from the East and South met the smaller riverboats serving the frontier communities and outposts on the upper Mississippi and Missouri rivers. West-bound pioneers congregated at St Louis before starting out across the plains; they purchased supplies and outfits, then boarded steamboats which took them up the Missouri to the Kansas border. Also known as the 'Emporium of the West', St Louis remained the supply base and market place of the frontier for many years. Here emigrants and gold seekers bought tools, wagons, guns, stores, and fur traders, lumbermen, planters, and farmers sold their products. Goods were also manufactured in St Louis, including ploughs, wagons, firearms, and stoves. The business centre grew along the levee, but when the Eade Bridge was completed in 1874 and the railroad came of age, business moved

uptown and the riverfront declined. In 1840 St Louis had a population of 16,469; in 1860 it had risen to 160,773; by 1870 it had reached 310,864. In the 1880s St Louis became a flour-milling centre for the hardy wheat grown on the Western plains. Today a stainless steel arch, 630 feet high, completed in 1965, dominates the riverfront, symbolizing the city's historic role as the 'Gateway to the West'.

Missouri: A History of the Crossroads State by E. C. McReynolds (Norman, Oklahoma, 1962).

STAMPEDE

A stampede or panic flight by massed Texas LONGHORNS on a CATTLE DRIVE was an ever present threat or occurrence. Cowboys dreaded a stampede (from the Spanish *estampida*) because of the time wasted in assembling the herd again, the subsequent loss of cattle, and the damage the milling animals often inflicted on themselves with their long horns. It is said that few cowboys were injured or killed by the rushing cattle. Most

286 ▼

286 *A Cowboy spur.*

287 *St Louis in the 1870s.*

287 ▼

human casualties were caused by lightning or falling horses. Most stampedes occurred at night. The longhorn, because of its wildness, was easily alarmed and quick to move., A sudden clap of thunder or other loud noise, the smell of a WOLF, the bark of a COYOTE, the sound of a RATTLESNAKE, any of a host of things might bring the steers to their feet in fright; the fear spread swiftly and suddenly the herd was running in blind panic. The cattle would run for many miles, with the cowboys riding hard trying to check their flight, until exhaustion brought the animals to a halt. It often took several days to round up the scattered cattle, calm them, and get them on the trail again.

The Longhorns by J. F. Dobie (New York, 1957);
The Old-Time Cowhand by R. F. Adams (New York, 1971).

STARR, Belle
1848-89

A notorious woman outlaw often depicted as a 'bandit queen'. Belle Starr was born in Carthage, Missouri, with the name Myra Belle Shirley, her father John Shirley being a respected businessman who sent his daughter to the Carthage Female Academy. Belle was a plain-faced girl of considerable sexuality. Her first lover was the outlaw Cole YOUNGER, who rode with Jesse JAMES, and he probably fathered her first child in 1866, a daughter she named Pearl. Later, as the common-law wife of bandit Jim Reed she had another child, a boy named Ed. When Reed was killed by a lawman in Texas in 1874, Belle left her children with relatives and became involved with an outlaw gang that operated in the INDIAN TERRITORY (now Oklahoma). In 1880 she 'married' Sam Starr, a Cherokee Indian, and adopted the name Belle Starr which she kept for the rest of her life; their ranch in the Indian Territory became a hideout for prominent outlaws, including Jesse James. In 1883 Judge PARKER sentenced Sam and Belle to a year each in prison for horse stealing. In 1885 Sam Starr killed John Middleton, with whom Belle was having an affair. Her next paramour was an Indian desperado named Blue Duck, who was

288 ∧

288 *St Joseph, Missouri, in 1850.*

289 *Belle Starr and Blue Duck.*

290 *'Cattle Stampede' by Robert Lindneux.*

291 *'In a Stampede' by Frederic Remington.*

290 V   289 ∧   291 V

killed in July 1886, probably by the jealous Sam Starr; six months later Sam was shot dead in a gunfight. Belle then took another Indian lover, Jim July, who managed to outlive her; she was murdered on 3 February 1889 while riding alone, shot in the back by an unknown assassin.

Belle Starr, the Bandit Queen by B. Rascoe (New York, 1941); *Outlaw Queen* by G. Shirley (Derby, Connecticut, 1960).

STEAMBOATS

Before the coming of the railroads, the steamboats played an important role in the development of the West, carrying passengers, pioneers, cargo, and the U.S. Mail up and down the MISSISSIPPI RIVER and its western tributaries the MISSOURI, ARKANSAS, and RED rivers. The Missouri became the principal route for settlers migrating to the West. The first steamboat on the Mississippi was the *New Orleans* in 1811, and in 1819 the first steamboat, the *Independence*, navigated the Missouri; by 1850 more than 1,000 steamboats were active on the Western rivers, transporting over ten million tons of freight annually. Built for shallow inland waters, the boats were flat-bottomed, with huge paddle wheels up to twenty-five feet in diameter. Some boats were propelled by a single paddle wheel at the stern, others had one on either side of the hull; the side-wheelers were faster, more steerable than the stern-wheelers. The typical 'Mississippi' steamboat had several decks. The lower or main deck held the boilers, engines, fuel, and cargo. The second deck contained the main cabin which had passenger staterooms running along each side; the main cabin served as a dining room and social centre. On top of the main cabin sat the texas deck, which held the crew's quarters. It is said the name 'stateroom' originated when one captain named the rooms after every State in the Union, and the State of Texas was left over, so the cabin on the top deck was given the name and the texas deck entered steamboat jargon. Perched high on the texas sat the wheelhouse, from which the boat was navigated by the pilot. Steamboat life enriched American history and folklore with such legendary characters as the slick Mississippi gambler, the wise old river pilot, and the Negro 'roustabout', the deckhand who handled the cargo to the chant of a soulful song, the beginning of the blues. Samuel Langhorne Clemens took his pen name 'Mark Twain' from the two fathom call of the steamboat men. The vessels varied in size and splendour; the big boats of the Mississippi were decorated and equipped like grand hotels and reached a high peak of steamboat Baroque in the 1870s. The captains were fiercely competitive and races between rival vessels were frequent, the most famous being the race between the side-wheelers *Robert E. Lee* and the *Natchez* in June 1870, up the Mississippi from New Orleans to St Louis. The *Robert E. Lee* won the contest, covering the 1,164 miles upstream in 3 days 18 hours and 14 minutes, an all-time record for Mississippi steamboats. By the 1870s the railroads were spreading all over the West and the steamboats, losing trade to the trains, began to fade away.

Steamboats on the Western Rivers by L. C. Hunter (Cambridge, Massachusetts, 1949); *Tales of the Mississippi* by R. Samuel, L. V. Huber, and W. C. Ogden (New York, 1955); *Life on the River* by N. L. Wayman (New York, 1971).

STETSON, John B. 1830-1906

The hatmaker whose famous broad-brimmed, high-crowned felt hats have been won by cowboys and Westerners since the 1870s was born in Orange, New Jersey, into a hat making family and he learned the trade. As a young man, John Batterson Stetson travelled West to cure his ill health. At ST JOSEPH, Missouri, he joined a prospecting party heading for the gold fields at PIKE'S PEAK, Colorado, and there in the ROCKY MOUNTAINS he regained his health. On returning East he settled in Philadelphia, starting a one-man hatmaking business in 1865. He made the hats by hand and sold them to local shops. His business took flight when he created a hat for Western cattlemen, a durable, well-crafted, all-weather felt hat he called 'Boss of the Plains'. It became a bestseller and soon Stetson built a new factory and his Western-style hats became as ubiquitous as COLT revolvers and LEVI trousers. A cowboy's 'John B' was expensive — ten to twenty dollars or more — but it proved an exceedingly useful item of equipment. It sheltered him from sun and rain, helped fend off wind and dust; it was a whip, when needed, to urge on his mount; it slapped lagging cows; in emergency it watered his horses, and at the day's end it fanned his campfire and became his pillow. Eminent Westerners favoured the stylish headgear; BUFFALO BILL Cody always wore a stetson made especially for him, and the Buffalo Bill Hat (No. 1100) was listed in Stetson's illustrated catalogue. Even SITTING BULL was proud of his stetson. In the 1890s the stetson was adopted by Canada's NORTH WEST MOUNTED POLICE. By the time he died in 1906 John B. Stetson's hats were world famous and his company was producing more than two million hats a year.

The Stetson Century, 1865-1965 by the John B. Stetson Company (Philadelphia, 1965).

292　*A cowboy wearing a stetson hat, sketch by Frederic Remington.*

293　*Steamboat* U.S. Oleander *at St Louis.*

292 ⋀　　　　　　293 ⋁

294 Λ   295 V   296 V

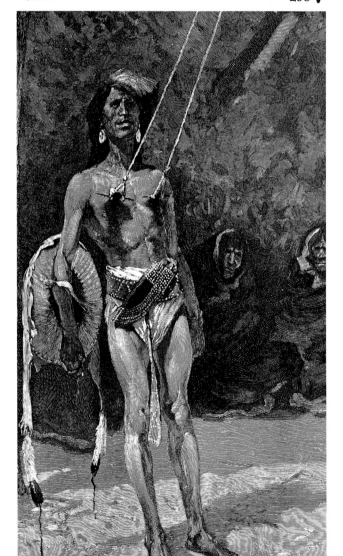

HUTCHINGS'

CALIFORNIA MAGAZINE

| OL. II. | NOVEMBER, 1857. | N |

THE DISCOVERY OF GOLD IN CALIFORNIA.

SUBLETTE, William
c.1799-1845

A celebrated fur trapper and trader, William Lewis Sublette was a leading partner of the ROCKY MOUNTAIN FUR COMPANY in the 1820s. Born in Kentucky of Huguenot parentage, William had four brothers who were also engaged in the fur trade; Milton Sublette, like William, became a prominent figure in the Old West. William and Milton took part in the Rocky Mountain fur expedition organized by William H. ASHLEY in 1823, and in 1828 William Sublette led his own expedition. With his partners Jedediah SMITH and David Jackson, he was the first to take wagons over the perilous trail to the ROCKY MOUNTAINS, and Sublette's Cut-off is named for him. In 1830 he turned to the Santa Fe Trade. In the summer of 1832 he was wounded in the fight between trappers and Indians at PIERRE'S HOLE. In December that year he formed a fur-trading company in partnership with Robert Campbell that lasted until 1842. He then entered politics in Missouri and became a candidate for Congress.

Bill Sublette: Mountain Man by J. E. Sunder (Norman, Oklahoma, 1959).

SUN DANCE

A ceremony of great importance in the PLAINS INDIANS religion, the Sun Dance was an annual ritual performed during the summer and often lasted for eight days. The name derives from the SIOUX version of the ceremony because of the tribal custom of gazing at the sun while dancing. The ritual included secret rites and fasting and was usually climaxed by a form of self-torture, in which the dancers attempted to pull free from skewers which pierced their breast muscles until either the muscles or the skin was torn away. The skewers were attached to ropes secured to a central pole twenty to thirty feet away from the dancer, who would lean with all his weight against the ropes; the participants underwent the ordeal as a demonstration of physical endurance, religious fanaticism, and to experience visions. SITTING BULL subjected himself to the agony of the Sun Dance in 1876 and was rewarded with a vision of Custer's defeat at the LITTLE BIGHORN.

The Sun Dance by G. A. Dorsey (Chicago, 1905); *Red Man's Religion* by R. Underhill (Chicago, 1965); *Sun Dance of the Sioux* by E. A. Milligan (Bottineau, North Dakota, 1969).

SUTTER, John
1803-80

The discovery of gold on the land of John Augustus Sutter in the Sacramento Valley, California, started the great GOLD RUSH of 1849; an unfortunate happening for him. Born in Germany as Johann August Suter, he lived for a time in Switzerland; he emigrated to America in 1834 and settled in California, then part of Mexico. The Mexican governor granted him a large tract of land in the Sacramento Valley, near the junction of the Sacramento and American rivers. Here in 1841 he built Sutter's Fort and established the pioneer colony of Nueva Helvetia (New Switzerland), on which location the city of Sacramento grew. Sutter became a Mexican citizen and prospered; he was influential in local politics and law, rich in cultivated land and live-stock. On 24 January 1848 John Marshall, a carpenter, who was building a sawmill for Sutter, discovered gold in the south fork of the American River. Alarmed that a stampede of gold hunters would ruin his flourishing estate, Sutter swore his workmen to secrecy; but the news leaked out and the gold rush was on. Nine days after the gold find, California became United States territory as a result of the MEXICAN WAR, and Sutter's land title came into dispute under American law. Unable to protect his property from the thousands of invading gold seekers, he saw his land trampled, vandalized, and destroyed. By 1852 he was bankrupt. He spent the rest of his years appealing to State and Federal governments for redress of his losses. In 1864 the California legislature granted him a pension of 250 dollars a month which continued until 1878. He died two years later.

Sutter's Own Story by E. G. Gudde (New York, 1936); *Sutter: The Man and his Empire* by J. P. Zollinger (New York, 1939); *Fool's Gold: A Biography of John Sutter* by R. Dillion (New York, 1967).

294 *Mississippi steamboat 'Mayflower', from an 1865 print.*

295 *Ordeal of the Sun Dance, by Frederic Remington.*

T

TABOR, Horace
1830-99

One of the great silver kings of LEADVILLE, Colorado, Horace Austin Warner Tabor rocketed from humble postmaster to multi-millionaire, then lost his immense fortune and became a post-master again. Born in Vermont, Tabor spent many frustrating years in the Colorado gold fields and in 1878 was earning a modest living in running a store-post office in the mining camp of Leadville. Early that year, in return for a third share of whatever they found, Tabor reluctantly provided two poor prospectors with a grubstake, a small supply of provisions. By an incredible piece of luck the two miners immediately struck a rich deposit of silver ore, and the Little Pittsburg, as it was named, developed into one of the most valuable mines in Colorado, producing 20,000 dollars a week. Within a year Tabor's seventeen dollar grubstake had returned him 500,000 dollars. He sold his interest in the mine to a banking concern for a million dollars and made a further million from shares retained in the Little Pittsburg. He then struck it rich with the Crysolite Mine and the Matchless Mine and his millions increased. Tabor was now a national figure. In November 1878 he became governor of Colorado and five years later a United States senator. He built a grand opera house for Leadville, and later another for the city of DENVER; he surmounted his own bank in Leadville with a huge metal symbol of a silver dollar and coined his own nickname — 'Silver Dollar Tabor'. To combat the lawless element in Leadville he raised and maintained the Tabor Light Cavalry, fifty fighting men in bright uniforms, with himself as general. In the late 1880s the free-spending Tabor experienced financial difficulties; his mines ran out, other projects failed, and he had spent millions on politics. When the world price of silver dropped sharply in 1893, Tabor found himself penniless. He ended his amazing career as a postmaster in Denver with a salary of 3,500 dollars a year.

Silver Dollar: The Story of the Tabors by D. Karsner (New York, 1932);
Silver Kings by O. Lewis (New York, 1947).

TEXAS

Texas has a special place in the ethos of the Old West. Here the American COWBOY was born and flourished in the land of the LONGHORN cattle. Here in 1836 the legendary heroes of the ALAMO fought and perished in the cause of Texas freedom. And the establishment of the RIO GRANDE as the border between Texas and Mexico

297 *Horace Tabor.*

caused the MEXICAN WAR of 1846-8, which resulted in the United States acquiring vast regions of the West from a defeated Mexico. Texas, called the Lone Star State from the single star on its state flag, is a huge country of 275,416 square miles, extending 801 miles from north to south and 733 miles from east to west. Terrain varies from the sub-tropical Rio Grande Valley to the Great Plains in the far north, from the lush pine forests of east Texas to the mountainous trans-Pecos region in the west. The Rio Grande is the longest river in the State, 1,248 miles long, forming the international boundary between Texas and Mexico; other principal rivers include the RED, the Brazos, the Colorado, the Sabine, Nueces, and the Pecos. The name Texas comes from the Indian word *tejas*, meaning friendly. The first white man to explore the region was the Spaniard Alvar Núnez Cabeza de Vaca in the sixteenth century, and the Spanish flag flew in Texas for three hundred years. With the establishment of the Republic of Mexico in 1821, Texas came under Mexican rule. With Mexican permission Stephen AUSTIN brought the first Anglo-American colonists to Texas, the first of many; their numbers grew and they wanted self-government and this desire led to the revolt of 1835, the Texas War for Independence. General SANTA ANNA, President of Mexico, stormed the Alamo, wiped out the garrison, then suffered a crushing defeat by Sam HOUSTON at San Jacinto.

Texas was declared a Republic in October 1836 and Houston became its first president. In 1845 Texas joined the United States; this led to war with Mexico and disastrous results for that country. When the American Civil War broke out in 1861 Texas joined the Confederacy and sent many men into the field. After the war the Texans returned to an impoverished land in which the feral longhorns had proliferated greatly. The northern States wanted beef and Texas began to supply it. In 1867 the first major trail drive north to Kansas opened the period of the long CATTLE DRIVES and the Texas cowboy became a national figure. In 1870 Texas was readmitted to the Union and the Lone Star State, with Austin its capital, began to prosper. In 1901 the gusher at Spindletop oilfield launched Texas into the twentieth century. Today, Texas is America's main producer of oil and natural gas, and remains the leading horse and cattle State.

Texas Cowboys by D. Coolidge (New York, 1937);
Texas: The Lone Star State by R. N. Richardson (Englewood, New Jersey, 1958);
Lone Star: A History of Texas and Texans by T. R. Fehrenbach (New York, 1968);
Texas: A History by S. V. Connor (New York, 1971).

TEXAS RANGERS

The oldest State law enforcement body in the United States, the Texas Rangers were originated in 1823 and formally organized in 1835. When Stephen AUSTIN was colonizing the Spanish province of Texas with Anglo-Americans, he hired a band of horsemen to range over the country to scout the movements of hostile Indians, and this ranging duty gave rise to the Texas Ranger force. During the period of the Republic of Texas, 1836 to 1845, the Rangers became fully established. They were organized into companies with a captain commanding each company. The Rangers were self-reliant individuals who knew no military discipline; they never drilled or saluted their officers, and accepted a leader only if he proved the best in endurance, courage, and judgement. Some notable Ranger captains were Jack Coffee HAYS, Ben McCulloch, Sam Walker, and William 'Big Foot' WALLACE. The Rangers wore no uniform and dressed in frontier style; each man provided his own horse and equipment. What they lacked in military discipline they made up in remarkable riding and fighting ability. They adopted the first COLT revolver and made it famous, using it with devastating effect against the marauding COMANCHES, and carried it with them in the MEXICAN WAR. In 1874 the Rangers were divided into two commands: the Frontier Battalion, which operated against hostile Indians, and the Special Force,

which dealt with rustlers and bandits along the lower RIO GRANDE. After the Indians had been settled, the Rangers concentrated on rounding up Mexican and American desperadoes, such as John Wesley HARDIN and Sam BASS. Famous Rangers of the late nineteenth century included Captain Bill McDONALD, Corporal Jim Gillett, and Captain John HUGHES. The Special Force was disbanded in 1881 and the Frontier Battalion in 1901, when the service was reorganized as the Texas Ranger Force to meet changing requirements. One of the last of the old style Rangers was Captain Frank Hamer, who pursued the outlaws Bonnie Parker and Clyde Barrow to their deaths in 1934. In 1935 the Texas Rangers became the nucleus of the new Texas Department of Public Safety and today the Ranger Force numbers ninety-four officers and men.

Six Years with the Texas Rangers, 1875-1881 by J. B. Gillett (Austin, Texas, 1921);
The Texas Rangers by W. P. Webb (Boston and New York, 1935).

THOMAS, Heck
1850-1912

A deputy U.S. marshal of high repute, Henry Andrew 'Heck' Thomas was one of the celebrated 'Three Oklahoma Guardsmen', the other two being Chris MADSEN and Bill TILGHMAN. Born in Georgia, Thomas saw action as a boy soldier in the Confederate army in the Civil War. Later he served as a policeman in Georgia, then as an agent for the Texas Express Company on the Houston and Texas Central Railway. In March 1878 he foiled an attempt by the Sam BASS gang to rob the express car of 22,000 dollars, and was wounded in the incident. Promoted to chief agent at FORT WORTH, Thomas tried for the post of city marshal in 1882 but failed to get enough votes. In 1886 he was appointed deputy U.S. marshal for the Western District of Arkansas, working out of Judge PARKER's court at Fort Smith, with jurisdiction over the INDIAN TERRITORY and later Oklahoma Territory (both territories entered the Union as the single State of Oklahoma in 1907). In 1890 Thomas shot it out with outlaw Jim July, Indian paramour of Belle STARR, and killed him. In 1892 he led the posse that finally trapped the Cherokee badman Ned Christie, who was killed in the gunfight. In 1893 U.S. Marshal E. D. Nix assigned Heck Thomas, Chris Madsen, and Bill Tilghman to hunt down Bill DOOLIN and his gang. In August 1896 Thomas confronted Doolin and when the outlaw tried to shoot it out, the marshal killed him with a shotgun blast. Thomas and Tilghman ran down Little Dick West, the last of the Doolin gang, and he too was shot dead

299 ∧

298   *Texas Rangers of the
1890s.*

299   *Heck Thomas.*

while resisting arrest in 1898. Grateful citizens dubbed the triumvirate of deputy marshals the 'Three Guardsmen'. Heck Thomas later became the first city marshal of Lawton, and in 1910 he was appointed deputy U.S. marshal for the Western District of Oklahoma, with headquarters in Lawton. He died in 1912.

Oklahombres by G. Hines and E. D. Nix (Chicago, 1929);
Heck Thomas: Frontier Marshal by G. Shirley (New York, 1962).

THOMPSON, Ben
1842-84

A gunfighter and gambler credited with thirty-two killings, Ben Thompson was born in England and grew up in Texas. He was a wild youth. In 1868 he was jailed for two years for shooting a man. In 1871, in partnership with Phil Coe, he

opened the Bull's Head Saloon in ABILENE, Kansas; while Thompson was out of town, Coe was killed by Wild Bill HICKOK in a gunfight. Ben and his brother Billy moved to ELLSWORTH, Kansas, and there in 1873 Billy killed sheriff Whitney; Ben held off the local lawmen while his brother galloped out of town. In 1878 Ben joined the gang of gunmen hired by the ATCHISON, TOPEKA, AND SANTA FE RAILROAD in its 'war' with the Denver and Rio Grande Railroad. In Austin, Texas, he killed the proprietor and bartender of the Senate Saloon, during a gunfight in the establishment on Christmas Eve 1880. He was tried and acquitted of the double slaying and soon after was elected marshal of Austin. On a trip to San Antonio in 1882 he got involved in a gambling argument and shot dead Jack Harris, who had attempted to ambush Thompson; again he was found not guilty of murder. On 11 March 1884 Thompson and his friend John King FISHER were in the Vaudeville Theatre, in San Antonio, when they were both killed in a mysterious outburst of shooting, probably a planned assassination in revenge for Jack Harris.

Ben Thompson: Man With a Gun by F. B. Streeter (New York, 1957);
Ben Thompson: The Famous Texan by W. M. Walton (Houston, Texas, 1958).

TILGHMAN, Bill
1854-1924

A frontier lawman of great renown, William Matthew Tilghman was born in Iowa and became skilled with firearms while still a youth; a buffalo hunter at sixteen he developed into an experienced plainsman and Indian fighter. When his friend Bat MASTERSON took office as sheriff of Ford County, Kansas, in January 1878, Tilghman became his deputy, and later served as marshal of DODGE CITY. Here he established a reputation as a dedicated and fearless peace officer. In April 1889 he took part in the LAND RUSH into the newly-opened INDIAN TERRITORY (which later became Oklahoma) and staked his claim in the tent town that grew into Guthrie; he opened a store in the town and later started a ranch. In 1891 he was appointed a deputy U.S. marshal, and in company with Chris MADSEN and Heck THOMAS, hunted down Bill DOOLIN and his gang; the three deputies became known as the 'Oklahoma Guardsmen'. Elected sheriff of Lincoln County in 1900 he was re-elected in 1902; when his second term ended he announced that he would not run again. In 1904 Tilghman was sent on a special mission into Mexico by President Theodore ROOSEVELT, to bring back the paymaster of a railroad who had absconded with funds. Tilghman accomplished the mission. In 1910 he was elected to the State Senate, then resigned to become chief of police of Oklahoma City. In the summer of 1924, at the age of seventy, he was called out of retirement by the anxious citizens of Cromwell, a rough oil-boom town, to serve as marshal and bring law and order to the place. Tilghman accepted the post and was doing a good job when he was shot dead in the street while disarming a drunk on 1 November 1924.

Marshal of the Last Frontier by Z. A. Tilghman (Glendale, California, 1944);
The Last Frontier Marshal by F. Miller (New York, 1967).

300 *Bill Tilghman when chief of police of Oklahoma City.*

301 *Tipi of the Plains Indians.*

TIPI

From the Siouan word for dwelling or lodge, the tipi (also spelled teepee) was the portable skin tent used by the nomadic PLAINS INDIANS. The tipi is often confused with the wigwam, the latter being the dome-shaped, wood and bark covered lodge of the Algonquian Indians of the north-eastern United States. The tipi was roughly cone shaped, consisting of a framework of long poles tied together at the top, and covered by buffalo hides sewn together. The small entrance was covered by a skin flap, and the top of the tipi was left open to allow the smoke of the fire inside to escape. The tipi could be erected within an hour; when it was dismantled it was carried to the next camp site by TRAVOIS, a drag device made from tipi poles.

The Indian Tipi by R. and G. Laubin (Norman, Oklahoma, 1957).

TOMBSTONE, Arizona

A silver mining town made famous by the Gunfight at the O.K. CORRAL, which took place there in October 1881 between Wyatt EARP and his brothers and the Clanton-McLaury gang. The town came into being with the rich silver strike

300 ▼

made by Ed Schieffelin in 1878. The prospector had been warned by the army that all he would find in the desolate APACHE region would be his tombstone; when news of the strike spread, bringing others, and a town began to grow, it was called Tombstone. Large scale production of silver began in 1880 and during the next twenty years the area yielded some forty million dollars in silver and three million in gold. Tombstone was a rough frontier settlement of miners, gamblers, and outlaws when the Earp brothers arrived there in 1879. Virgil Earp became town marshal. Rivalry between the Earps and the Clanton-McLaury faction resulted in the Gunfight at the O.K. Corral, in which Virgil and Morgan Earp were wounded and three of the opposition were killed. The mines became flooded in the 1890s and were abandoned; Tombstone declined into a ghost town. Today, in a restored condition, Tombstone is a popular tourist attraction; publicized as the 'Town Too Tough to Die', it has museums, a BOOT HILL cemetery, and an annual Helldorado celebration climaxed by a recreation of the Gunfight at the O.K. Corral.

Tombstone's Yesterday by L. D. Walters (Tucson, Arizona, 1928);
Tombstone by W. N. Burns (New York, 1929);
Tombstone: Myth and Reality by O. B. Faulk (Oxford, England, 1972).

301 V

TOTEM POLE

Contrary to popular belief, all Indian tribes did not have totem poles. These tall, carved tree trunks were particular to the tribes of the Northwest Pacific Coast, especially those of British Columbia and Alaska, including the Haida, Tlingit, Tsimshian, and Kwakiutl tribes which had developed a high degree of art and culture. Generally speaking, a totem pole was used by a chief to display his insignia of rank and his distinguished family tree. A totem pole was a spectacular device to proclaim how wealthy, clever, brave, and well bred the owner was. The bigger the pole, the more distinguished the chief; some wealthy chieftains put up totem poles sixty feet high. The cedar poles were carved and painted with human, animal, and legendary creatures representing the family lineage, featuring the chief's mythical ancestors in particular, and the great events in his life. Totem poles were erected in memory of departed chiefs, some actually served as tombs, the body being placed inside. Some tribes, like the Haida, attached totem poles to their houses.

Native Arts of the Pacific Northwest by R. T. David (Stanford, California, 1949);
Art of the Kwakiutl Indians and Other Northwest Coast Indian Tribes by A. Hawthorn (Seattle, Washington, 1967).

302 *Tombstone in the early 1880s.*

303 *Travois of Plains Indians.*

304 *Totem poles of the Haida.*

305 *The Cherokee 'Trail of Tears' painted by
Robert Lindneux.*

304 V   305 V

302 ∧   303 ∧

TRAIL OF TEARS
1838

The 'Trail of Tears' was the forcible removal of the Cherokee Indians, under military escort, from their south-eastern homeland to the INDIAN TERRITORY (now Oklahoma). The Cherokees originally occupied vast areas in what are now the States of North and South Carolina, Virginia, Tennessee, Georgia, and Alabama. The Treaty of New Echota in 1835, signed by a minority of the Cherokee tribe, ceded all their traditional lands to the United States and provided for the Indians' relocation in an area beyond the MISSISSIPPI RIVER, the so-called Indian Territory. The majority of Cherokees oppposed the removal but were forced to make the trek West by General Scott and his soldiers. In October and November 1838, some 15,000 Cherokees began the long march westward, an 800-mile journey, mostly on foot, in winter. Suffering great hunger, disease, and cold weather as a result of inadequate preparation by the Federal agents who guided them, some 4,000 Cherokees perished on the 'Trail of Tears' to a strange land.

Yunini's Story of the Trail of Tears by A. L. Barry (London, 1932);
Indian Removal by G. Foreman (Norman, Oklahoma, 1932).

TRAVOIS

The primitive drag device used by the nomadic PLAINS INDIANS to transport goods, equipment, children and sick persons. Generally, the travois consisted of two long TIPI poles tied together at one end to form a vee-shape: the tied end was secured to a horse or dog which pulled the load. The centre of the dragging ends of the poles was spanned by skins or a 'wickerwork' platform on which was secured the luggage. Small children were carried on the travois in a bentwood cage to prevent them falling off. The making and transporting of the travois were duties of the women.

UNION PACIFIC RAILROAD

One of the great pioneer railroads of the Old West. The Union Pacific Railroad and Telegraph Company was incorporated by Congress in 1862 and authorized to build a line, by the central route, from the MISSOURI RIVER to the western boundary of Nevada Territory, there to join tracks with the CENTRAL PACIFIC RAILROAD, building East from Sacramento, thus completing America's first transcontinental railroad. Union Pacific ground was first broken on 2 December 1863, at Omaha, Nebraska Territory, but owing to financial difficulties it was not until 10 July 1865 that the first rail was laid at the same spot. However, under the leadership of a new group of financiers headed by Oakes Ames and his brother Oliver, the railroad marched west with amazing rapidity, advancing white civilization and the development of the wild country. On the plains the construction crews were much troubled by Indian attacks and General Grenville M. Dodge, chief engineer for Union Pacific, commented that: 'Every mile had to be run within the range of a rifle.' The construction boss, tough Jack Casement, a general in the Civil War, organized his workmen with military precision; the work force consisted largely of Irishmen, many of whom were Civil War veterans. By the end of 1865 forty miles of rail had been completed. During the next year 250 miles were added, and in 1867 a 245-mile advance brought the railroad to the summit of the ROCKY MOUNTAINS. In 1868 the line progressed another 430 miles, and during the first four months of 1869 another 120 miles took the line to Promontory Point, UTAH, where it formed a junction with the Central Pacific, the latter line having pushed farther than originally planned. The ceremony of the GOLDEN SPIKE, driving the final, symbolic spike into the transcontinental track, took place on 10 May 1869. At that time the Union Pacific consisted of a single line from Omaha westward just over 1,000 miles long. It grew rapidly, absorbing smaller lines, building more trackage, and by 1893 the system had expanded to 7,682 miles. That same year, due to financial complications, stiff opposition, and other problems, the railroad was forced into bankruptcy. The property was sold at foreclosure on 1 November 1897 to the newly-formed Union Pacific Railroad Company, which, under the management of E. H. Harriman, developed the system into one of America's great, enduring railroads.

History of the Union Pacific by N. Trottman (New York, 1923); *The Union Pacific Railroad: A Case in Premature Enterprise* by R. W. Fogel (Baltimore, 1960); *Union Pacific: The Building of the First Transcontinental Railroad* by G. Hogg (New York, 1967); *Union Pacific Country* by R. G. Athearn (Chicago, 1971).

UTAH

Utah is the geographical centre of the western United States. Its topography is varied, embracing desert, green valleys, forests, canyons, snow-covered mountains, and the GREAT SALT LAKE. The name Utah comes from an Indian word meaning 'high up'. In northern Utah the Wasatch and Uinta ranges of the ROCKY MOUNTAINS dominate the landscape. Southward is the Colorado Plateau, 5,000 to 6,000 feet above sea level, a land of mesas, buttes, cliffs, and spectacular canyons, such as Bryce Canyon. West of the Wasatch Mountains and high plateaus is the Great Basin, a vast, lonely region reaching westward to the SIERRA NEVADA Mountains. In the context of the Old West, Utah was the land of the MORMONS, who came to the isolated Salt Lake Valley in 1847 to escape religious persecution. Indians had lived in Utah for centuries when the first Europeans arrived in 1776, Spaniards from New Mexico in search of a route to the Pacific Coast. In 1819 British FUR TRAPPERS entered northern Utah, followed in 1824 by American trappers, including Jim BRIDGER, Jedediah SMITH, and Bill SUBLETTE; Bridger is credited with having discovered Great Salt Lake. Pacific-bound emigrants crossed northern Utah during the 1840s but they did not stop. The first white people to settle the land in a serious manner were the Mormons who, under Brigham YOUNG, entered the Salt Lake Valley in July 1847. The industrious Mormons began immediately to irrigate, plant crops, build forts and houses, explore and colonize thousands of square miles of wilderness. Mormon converts arrived by the tens of thousands during the next few decades, scattering across Utah, settling every promising site. In 1849 the independent Mormons organized the State of Deseret but the United States Congress refused to recognize it and in 1850 created Utah Territory, with Brigham Young its governor. Friction between the Mormons and Federal officers led to the so-called Utah War of 1856-8. The joining of the UNION PACIFIC and CENTRAL PACIFIC railroads took place at Promontory Point, near Great Salt Lake, in May 1869, completing America's first transcontinental railroad. Utah's mineral mining boomed in the 1870s and 1880s and in January 1896 Utah became the forty-fifth State of the Union.

History of Utah, 1847-1869 by A. L. Neff (Salt Lake City, 1940); *Desert Saints: The Mormon Frontier in Utah* by N. Anderson (Chicago, 1942).

UTE INDIANS

An important division of the Shoshonean linguistic family, the Utes inhabited the foothills and valleys of the Rocky Mountains of COLORADO, and parts

306 *Ute Indians of Colorado.*

307 *Union Pacific locomotive General Sherman, built 1865.*

307 ∨

30(

of Utah and New Mexico. The Colorado Utes were much influenced by the PLAINS INDIANS' culture, being horseback people who lived in TIPIS and hunted the BUFFALO. The Mouache and Capote bands roamed the eastern face of the Rockies; on the western side were the Weeminuche, Yampa, and Uncompahgre (Tabequache) bands. These five groups, and the Uintah in Utah, formed the powerful Ute empire which early settlers encountered. The Utes have been compared to the Swiss in their almost invincible defence of mountain strongholds; they are thought to be the first tribe north of Mexico to use stone forts in defensive war, and even early Anglo-American military expeditions were to come to grief against them. The Utes made their first treaty with the U.S. in 1849. OURAY, the Uncompahgre chief, favoured peace with the whites and encouraged his people that way; Utes served as scouts and mercenaries with the U.S. military against the Navajos. In 1868 the Utes ceded a large portion of their land to the U.S. in a treaty which confined them to a sixteen million acre reservation in western Colorado. Two agencies were established: one at Los Pinos, the other on the White River. In 1878 Nathan Meeker became the agent of the White River Agency, and he upset the Utes by his forceful endeavour to make them into farmers; the result of the MEEKER MASSACRE, and the Ute War of 1879, in which Meeker and his staff were killed. Because of this uprising most of the Utes were evicted from Colorado in 1881 and placed on a reservation in Utah.

The Last War Trail; the Utes and the Settlement of Colorado by R. Emmitt (Norman, Oklahoma, 1954);
The Utes: A Forgotten People by W. Rockwell (Denver, Colorado, 1956).

VAQUERO

The original North American cowboy, the *vaquero* evolved in Spanish California and Mexico in the eighteenth century. As the *haciendas*, or ranches, became established and the herds of cattle grew, horsemen were needed to look after the animals. Mission Indians and half-breeds were recruited and trained as *vaqueros* (from the Spanish *vaca* for cow) and these humble cow-herders developed traditional skills in managing cattle from horseback. They roped cows with a *reata*, a rawhide rope with a running noose, and they developed gear and equipment to suit their equestrian life. In time the Mexican *vaquero* spread his influence throughout the South-west. It was in the Mexican province of TEXAS that the early Anglo-American COWBOYS adopted and adapted the *vaquero's* skills, equipment, and Spanish jargon. *La reata* was corrupted to LARIAT, *chaparejos* (leather trousers) was shortened to CHAPS, but other words used by the American cowboy remained almost pure Spanish, such as RODEO, REMUDA, BRONCO, corral, hombre, loco (crazy), latigo and cinch (saddle straps). The word *vaquero* was American-ized to buckeroo, a term for cowboy on the northern ranges.

Californios, the Saga of the Hard-Riding Vaqueros, America's First Cowboys by J. J. Mora (New York, 1949).

VICTORIO
c. 1820-80

An aggressive chief of the Mimbreno APACHES, Victorio was a lieutenant of the great MANGAS COLORADAS and became a master of Apache warfare. In 1876 Victorio agreed to settle on the Ojo Caliente reservation in his New Mexico homeland. In the spring of 1877 he and his people were forcibly removed to the undesirable San Carlos reservation in Arizona. In September 1877 Victorio left the hated San Carlos and went on the warpath for three years. He was joined by Chiricahua and Mescalero Apaches and his fighting force numbered about 150 warriors. In New Mexico he stole forty-six horses from the Ninth Cavalry encamped near Ojo Caliente, killing eight soldiers and suffering no losses himself. He then crossed the border into Mexico and ensconced himself in the Candelaria Mountains of northern Chihuahua. When a fifteen-man posse of Mexicans ventured after the outlaw Apaches, Victorio caught the party in a

308 ∧   309 ∨

308 *Vaquero of the early 19th century.*

309 *Victorio, Apache chief.*

310   *A vigilante execution.*

311   *Virginia City in the 1860s.*

310 Λ   311 V

canyon trap and wiped it out; and when a further fourteen Mexicans came in search of the ill-fated posse, Victorio killed them all. He continued raiding back and forth across the border. A price of 3,000 dollars was placed on his head. On 15 October 1880 a special force of Mexican irregulars cornered Victorio and his people in a canyon of the Tres Castillos Mountains in Chihuahua, and eighty Apaches died in the fight, including Victorio.

The Conquest of Apacheria by D. L. Thrapp (Norman, Oklahoma, 1967);
Death in the Desert by P. I. Wellman (London, 1972).

VIGILANTES

In their early years many frontier settlements did not have a regular law enforcement agency. So when flagrant crime threatened to engulf the community its honest citizens formed a Vigilante group, or Vigilance Committee, to deal harshly with the known criminals. Vigilante frontier justice included whipping, banishment, and death, the latter usually by hanging. Sometimes a form of trial was held, more often the suspect was seized and summarily executed; in some cases innocent people were put to death by mistake. In the infant years of SAN FRANCISCO criminal activity became so prevalent and open, and the legal administration so corrupt and ineffective, that in 1851 the city's first Vigilance Committee was organized. Having hanged and punished a large number of leading criminals the Vigilance Committee was disbanded; it was reformed in 1856 to deal with another crime wave. In 1864 Montana vigilantes hanged sheriff Henry PLUMMER, who had used his official position to aid his criminal activities; his gang terrorized the region until the people took the law into their own hands and executed Plummer and many of his desperadoes. When the RENO BROTHERS were caught and held in an Indiana jail in 1868, masked vigilantes burst into the building and hanged the three Renos and another outlaw.

Vigilante Days and Ways by N. P. Langford (Chicago, 1923);
Frontier Justice by W. Gard (Norman, Oklahoma, 1949);
The Vigilantes of Montana by T. J. Dimsdale (Norman, 1953).

VILLA, Pancho
1878-1923

Mexican bandit and guerrilla leader, Francisco 'Pancho' Villa slapped the United States in the face by mounting a surprise raid on the town of Columbus, NEW MEXICO, on 9 March 1916, killing eight American soldiers and ten civilians. In retaliation, President Woodrow Wilson sent General Pershing and a Punitive Expedition into Mexico in hot pursuit of Villa. Born in Chihuahua with the name Doroteo Arango, Villa became a bandit in his youth and adopted the name Francisco Villa from another outlaw. He played a leading role in the Mexican Revolution of 1910-20, winning many victories in the field. For a time Villa, who seemed in line for leadership of Mexico, enjoyed the sympathetic interest of the United States government, who then dropped Villa and supported his rival, Carranza. Villa's resentment resulted in the vengeance raid on Columbus. General Pershing's column, which included the Seventh Cavalry and APACHE scouts, chased Villa deep into Mexico; the Americans captured and killed several of Villa's lieutenants but failed to catch the guerrilla leader. Because of Mexican protests, Pershing's command returned to the U.S. in February 1917. Unable to suppress Villa by force, the Mexican government purchased his retirement from the political arena with a handsome pension and a large estate. Villa was assassinated in 1923 when gunmen ambushed his car.

Viva Villa by E. Pinchon (London, 1933);
Cock of the Walk: The Legend of Pancho Villa by H. Braddy (Albuquerque, New Mexico, 1955);
Pershing's Mission into Mexico by H. Braddy (El Paso, Texas, 1966).

312 *Pancho Villa (left) and his guerrillas.*

VIRGINIA CITY, Nevada

The biggest and most famous of Nevada's frontier mining towns, Virginia City was founded in 1859 when the Comstock Lode, an exceedingly rich silver lode, was discovered. In the resulting rush to the area, amazing fortunes were made and the town boomed into a crowded metropolis with hotels, banks, a stock exchange, churches, an opera house, and a 'Millionaire's Row' of mansions. By 1863 the population numbered 15,000 and rose to an all-time high of 25,000 in 1876. The city boasted five newspapers, including the *Territorial Enterprise*, on which Mark Twain was a reporter. The Comstock Lode got its name from prospector Henry Comstock, who had a share of the claim worked by Peter O'Riley and Patrick McLaughlin; these two men actually discovered the great lode of silver, but Comstock talked so much about 'his' claim that it came to be known as the 'Comstock Lode'. From 1859 to 1882 the mines of the Comstock produced some 400 million dollars in silver and gold. By 1890 the mines became unworkable and Virginia City declined into a ghost town. Today it is a tourist attraction; its historic buildings have been restored and it is claimed that 500,000 people visit the place annually. There is another Virginia City, in MONTANA, founded in 1863 as a gold mining camp. It served as the territorial capital during the boom years of 1865-75. This, too, has been restored as a tourist attraction.

Saga of the Comstock Lode: Boom Days in Virginia City by G. Lyman (New York, 1934);
History of the Comstock Lode by G. H. Smith (Reno, Nevada, 1943);
Mining Frontiers of the Far West, 1848-1880 by R. W. Paul (New York, 1963).

WAGON BOX FIGHT 1867

A sharp engagement between Indians and soldiers, the latter guarding a wood-cutting detail some five miles from FORT PHIL KEARNY, Wyoming (then part of Dakota Territory), on 2 August 1867. The civilian party contracted to supply wood to the fort was escorted by 'C' Company of the Twenty-Seventh Infantry, commanded by Captain James W. Powell, a veteran of twenty years' service. His men were armed with the newly-issued breech-loading SPRINGFIELD rifle, and this weapon saved the day. Some wagons used for hauling the wood to the fort had been removed from their running gear and formed a corral-campsite for the mules, men, and supplies. Several thousand SIOUX and CHEYENNES attacked the wood-cutting party early in the morning and Captain Powell with twenty-seven soldiers and four civilians took up a defensive position behind the wagon box corral. The rapid fire of the breech-loading Springfields (which had recently replaced the slow muzzle-loaders) broke up the massed Indian charges and inflicted heavy casualties. The battle lasted four and a half hours until the Indians were driven off by a relief force from Fort Phil Kearny armed with a howitzer. Of Captain Powell's command, Lieutenant Jenness and five privates were killed,

and two wounded; it appears that civilian casualties were not recorded. Powell estimated Indian losses at 60 killed and 120 wounded.

Great Western Indian Fights by the Potomac Corral of the Westerners (New York, 1960);
The Army on the Powder River by R. A. Murray (Bellevue, Nebraska, 1969).

WAGON, Covered

Wagons were essential to mass migration over the pioneer trails of the Old West. The so-called 'prairie schooner' carried the family furniture, food supplies, cooking equipment, water kegs, and other items necessary for the long journey and the establishment of a home. There was little room left inside the loaded wagon for the family; the men, women and children usually walked beside the slowly moving vehicle, which averaged about two miles an hour in fair going. Only very small children, old women, and the sick rode in the wagon. Generally, the type of vehicle used in the Western migration was based on the large Conestoga wagon developed in Pennsylvania, but was smaller and lighter in order to negotiate

313 *The Wagon Box Fight, 1867. Painted by H. Charles McBarron.*

rough terrain and mountain country. A typical pioneer wagon consisted of an open-topped rectangular wagon box about ten feet long, four feet wide, with sides some two feet high, and a canvas top cover, waterproofed with linseed oil, stretched over a framework of hoop-shaped slats, with drawstrings to close the ends; the four wheels were made of wood strengthened with iron, the front wheels generally smaller than the back wheels, for manoeuvrability. Most immigrant wagons had neither brakes nor springs. The ox — being stronger, cheaper, and easier to maintain than the mule and the horse — was the favoured draught animal. Contrary to popular belief, the ox team was not driven from the front seat of the wagon; yoked oxen had no reins attached, the driver walked beside the beasts, goading and guiding them by shouting and cracking a long whip. And it is doubtful whether the emigrants called their functional wagons 'prairie schooners'.

The California Trail by G. R. Stewart (London, 1965);
Western Wagon Wheels by F. Cambert (Seattle, 1970).

WAGON TRAINS

For reasons of security, efficiency, and companionship, emigrants and freighters to the Far West travelled the overland trails in organized caravans, or trains. Indians rarely, if ever, attacked a large wagon train. These caravans assembled at various outfitting towns in Missouri, such as INDEPENDENCE and ST JOSEPH. The travellers elected a captain and lieutenants, who commanded the column and maintained discipline on the long journey. The wagon trains were guided by MOUNTAIN MEN or other experienced frontiersmen. Whenever a large herd of cattle accompanied a wagon train it was common practice to place the slower moving cows at the rear of the column; the wagons travelled faster but the cattle could catch up after the train had stopped for the day. A wagon train pulled by oxen averaged about ten miles a day (depending on the terrain and the weather); a mule or horse-drawn caravan about fifteen miles a day. When the caravan stopped for the day the wagons were arranged, end to end, in a circular or square compound which served as both corral for the animals and a fortress against Indian attack. The ideal campsite would have a good spring, grazing for the animals, and a generous supply of timber

314 *Wagon train crossing river.*

315 *Joseph Walker and his squaw, from a painting by A.J. Miller.*

316 *Covered wagon of the West.*

for fires and the repair of wagon gear; but such campsites were few and far between. In fair going the 2,000 miles journey from Missouri to the Far West of CALIFORNIA or OREGON country could be made in four or five months; in a wet year the trek might take an extra month. The journey was extremely arduous. To ease the strain on the draught animals, furniture, tools, and other hardware were often abandoned on the way; the overland trails were littered with dead oxen and other livestock, and the graves of pioneers.

The Road to Oregon by W. J. Ghent (New York, 1929);
Westward America by H. R. Driggs (New York, 1942);
The Wake of the Prairie Schooner by I. D. Paden (New York, 1943);
The Overland Trail by J. Monaghan (Indianapolis, 1947).

WALKER, Joseph R. 1798-1876

An eminent mountain man explorer, Joseph Reddeford Walker roamed the Far West for fifty years; he helped establish the SANTA FE TRAIL, discovered the gap in the SIERRA NEVADA Mountains called Walker Pass, and the Yosemite Valley in California. It was said of him that he did not follow trails but made them. Zenas Leonard, a member of Walker's expedition to California in

314 V

315 V

1833 described his leader as 'well hardened to the hardships of the wilderness . . . and to explore unknown regions was his chief delight'. Born in Tennessee, Walker emigrated to MISSOURI in 1819. He matured into a big man, over six feet tall and weighing 200 pounds; he wore his hair long, sported a full beard, and enjoyed the company of Indian girls. After spending a dozen years trapping and trading in the Far West, and serving as the first sheriff of Jackson County, Missouri, he was recruited by Captain Benjamin Bonneville to lead an exploring expedition to California. Walker and his party set out from the Green River (Wyoming) on 24 July 1833; they explored the vast desert region west of the GREAT SALT LAKE (Utah), followed the Humboldt River to its sink (in Western Nevada), then climbed the Sierra Nevadas the hard way, taking almost three weeks to cross the barrier. Walker and his men are believed to be the first to cross the Sierras from the east, and the first white men to see and describe the spectacular Yosemite Valley and the giant redwood trees of California. Walker reached Monterey, on the Pacific coast, in November 1833 and wintered in the California sun. On the return journey, starting 14 February 1834, he searched for an easier way over the Sierras and found a gap (5,245 feet above sea level) at the south end of the range that was later named Walker Pass and served as a point of entry for emigrants into California. Walker's great journey ended at the Bear River rendezvous (Utah) on 12 July 1834. In later years Walker became the first man to guide an emigrant wagon train into California, by way of his pass, and in 1845 he guided FRÉMONT's expedition to California. In the 1850s he served as an army scout and in the early 1860s roamed through Arizona in search of gold. Joe Walker, much respected and admired by all who knew him, died in October 1876 on his nephew's ranch in California.

West Wind: The Life Story of Joseph Reddeford Walker by D. S. Watson (Los Angeles, 1934);
Joseph Reddeford Walker and the Arizona Adventure by D. E. Conner (Norman, Oklahoma, 1956).

WALLACE, 'Bigfoot' 1817-99

A notable Texas Ranger and frontiersman, William Alexander 'Bigfoot' Wallace is a Texas folk hero. Born in Virginia, he went to Texas in 1837 and three years later joined a company of Rangers, under John Coffee HAYS, to help protect the frontier settlements around San Antonio from hostile Indians and outlaws. Later, he served in the MEXICAN WAR of 1846-8 in the Texas Mounted Rifle Volunteers. In 1850 he was given command of his own company of Rangers.

316

Bigfoot was six feet two inches tall and weighed 240 pounds; his boot size is not recorded. He was fearless and survived many fights with Indians and bandits. A genial man when not at war, he was renowned for his story telling. One tale he often related concerned his lone fight with forty COMANCHES. The Indians had stolen some horses and he was trailing them. It was hickory nut time and when Wallace caught up with the Comanches and confronted them, he looked like an enormous Santa Claus. He had taken the precaution of improvising a 'suit of armour' out of hickory nuts; having tied the wrists and ankles of his baggy buckskin shirt and trousers, he had stuffed his clothes with nuts. His hat was also filled with nuts. The Indians fired all their arrows at the strange apparition but the shafts could not penetrate the hickory armour; the Comanches fled in terror leaving the stolen horses behind. When Bigfoot died his fellow Texans honoured him with a burial at the State Cemetery at Austin.

Bigfoot Wallace by S. Vestal (Boston, 1942).

WASHAKIE, Chief
*c.*1804-1900

A prominent chief of the SHOSHONI tribe celebrated for his unwavering friendship and co-operation with white settlers and the U.S. government, Washakie realized early the futility of resisting the white man and the advantages to be gained in siding with him. Born of mixed Shoshoni and FLATHEAD blood, he became a chief of the eastern Shoshoni of Wyoming, often called Washakie's band. He was a great warrior and hunter. The name Washakie has been variously translated but according to most sources it means 'rattler', or 'rawhide rattle', from his practice of using a rattle in combat to frighten enemy horses. Although he delighted in war against traditional enemies, such as the BLACKFEET and the SIOUX, he was always friendly to the whites, helping overland emigrants in many ways; indeed, 9,000 settlers signed a testimony to his kindness. He used his alliance with the whites to great advantage; joining the soldiers to strike at his tribal foes, and using his friendship to gain favourable terms and concessions at the treaty table. Strong minded, positive, and fearless, Washakie ruled his people as an autocrat, and once shot a warrior dead on the

317Λ   318V

317   *'Big Foot' Wallace (right) and General John R. Baylor as they appeared in the 1870s.*

318   *Chief Washakie.*

319   *Battle of the Washita.*

spot for disobedience. When he was about seventy, Washakie sniffed a rumour that the young warriors were questioning his courage and leadership, so he went out on a lone foray and returned with seven enemy scalps to silence his critics. In an 1868 treaty council Washakie secured for his people a reservation of their own choosing, the desirable Wind River Valley of Wyoming, then still rich in BUFFALO. After placing his mark upon the treaty, Washakie said: 'I am laughing because I am happy . . . The Wind River country is the one for me.' Later, however, the government reduced the size of the reservation. Washakie and his warriors served as scouts with the U.S. army in the Sioux War of 1876; for his services, Washakie was presented with an expensive saddle from President Grant. When the old chief died in 1900 at Fort Washakie, Wyoming, he was buried there with full military honours. His people still live in the Wind River country.

Washakie by G. R. Hebard (Glendale, California, 1930).

WASHINGTON

Fur trading companies played a major role in the early economical and political development of the area that became the State of Washington. The first white settlement within the limits of the present State — then part of the vast Oregon country — was Spokane House, established as a fur trading post in 1811 by the North West Company. In 1818 the United States and Britain signed a treaty of joint occupation of the OREGON country which lasted until 1846, when the Forty-ninth parallel was agreed upon as the boundary between the U.S. and Canada. The great migration of American settlers to Oregon started in 1836 and continued through the 1840s; long WAGON TRAINS brought pioneer families and missionaries from the East over the OREGON TRAIL. Marcus WHITMAN established a mission at Waiilatpu, near present Walla Walla, and in 1847 he and his wife were killed by CAYUSE INDIANS and the mission destroyed. This incident and the Indian war that resulted hurried Congress into creating Oregon Territory in 1848, from which Washington Territory was separated in 1853, with Olympia the capital. At that time the white population of Washington numbered 3,964 citizens. The city of Seattle, on Puget Sound, was founded in 1851. The Fraser River gold rush to British Columbia in 1858-9 brought an influx of people and money into the country and by 1870 the population of Washington stood at 23,955. Rich in forests of pine and cedar, the territory became a leading producer of timber. The Columbia River and its tributaries drain the land, and the Cascade Mountain range forms a great barrier between the western and eastern

319 ∨

sections of the State, with Mount Rainier, at 14,410 feet, the highest peak. The present boundaries of Washington were set in 1872 and Statehood was achieved in 1889.

Washington: A History of the Evergreen State by M. W. Avery (Seattle, 1965);
Empire of the Columbia: A History of the Pacific Northwest by D. O. Johansen and C. M. Gates (New York, 1967).

WASHITA, Battle of the 1868

A major engagement of the Indian campaigns in which General CUSTER and his Seventh Cavalry launched a dawn attack against a CHEYENNE village on the Washita River, in the INDIAN TERRITORY (Oklahoma), on 27 November 1868. Custer's regiment was part of a punitive expedition ordered by General SHERIDAN to punish the Indians of the area for recent depredations. Custer marched out of Camp Supply on 23 November; it was bitterly cold. The Seventh charged the sleeping village of Cheyenne chief Black Kettle from four directions, with the band playing the regiment's fighting song 'Garry Owen'. The Indians swiftly overcame their initial surprise and began a spirited defence. A fierce battle developed which the Indians continued from surrounding terrain. By mid-morning Custer learned that this was but one of many villages of Cheyennes, KIOWAS, COMANCHES, and ARAPAHOES extending for miles along the Washita. And indeed, warriors from these other villages were already appearing on the scene. Custer hastened to destroy Black Kettle's village, its food supplies, buffalo robes, and slaughtered some 800 Indian horses. Then, with colours flying and the band playing, Custer pressed on down river as if intending to attack the other villages. When the Indians withdrew to defend these villages, Custer turned about under cover of darkness and made a successful withdrawal to Camp Supply, bringing in fifty-three captive women and children. The Seventh lost twenty-one officers and men killed and a dozen wounded. The Indians suffered about 100 killed, including Black Kettle; the loss of their precious winter supplies and ponies was a particularly grievous blow to the Cheyennes.

Fighting Cheyennes by G. B. Grinnell (Norman, Oklahoma, 1956);
Battle of the Washita by S. Hoig (New York, 1976).

320 *Wells Fargo advertisement of October 1852.*

321 *Grass house of Wichita Indians.*

WELLS FARGO & COMPANY

The leading banking, express forwarding, and stagecoach company of the Old West was originally organized in 1852 by Henry Wells and William G. Fargo, and associates, to serve GOLD RUSH California. The first office was opened in SAN FRANCISCO and by 1856 Wells Fargo was the most important express forwarding company in California. It established a network of offices throughout the West and by 1870 Wells Fargo was the most powerful and efficient company in the field of East-West transportation and communication, having absorbed or forced out of business all its major rivals. In 1880 there were 573 Wells Fargo offices and agents; in 1893 there were 2,829 branch offices. The handsome, ubiquitous CONCORD coaches of Wells Fargo carried treasure shipments, payrolls, passengers, and the U.S. mail over the dusty trails of the West. Gold, valuables, and money were carried in a green-painted strongbox under the driver's seat, protected by a heavily-armed messenger who rode with the driver. The Wells Fargo treasure box became a prime target for highwaymen or road agents; the company's shotgun messengers were renowned for their courage and tenacity in protecting the green box. BLACK BART, the verse-writing bandit, plagued the Wells Fargo company for eight years, robbing twenty-eight coaches before he was finally captured in 1883 by the Wells Fargo chief of detectives James B. Hume.

320 V

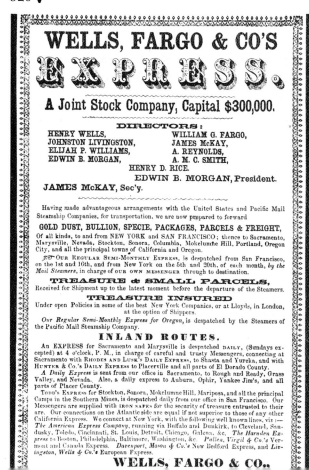

In 1866 the company purchased the HOLLADAY Overland Mail and Express Company, which controlled 2,670 miles of stage lines west of the Missouri River. As the railways spread throughout the West, Wells Fargo cut back its stagecoach operations and acquired railroad rights; in 1888 it established the first transcontinental express via rail. Wells Fargo stopped carrying U.S. mail in 1895 when the Federal Government took over all mail services. Today, the Wells Fargo Company, with its head office in San Francisco, is still in the banking business and operates an armoured car service.

Wells Fargo by E. Hungerford (New York, 1949);
U.S. West: The Saga of Wells Fargo by L. Beebe and C. Clegg (New York, 1949);
Wells Fargo by N. M. Loomis (New York, 1968).

WHITMAN, Marcus 1802-47

A notable Presbyterian medical missionary and pioneer of the OREGON TRAIL, Dr Marcus Whitman worked hard to convert the CAYUSE INDIANS to Christianity and farming. On 29 November 1847 Whitman and his wife Narcissa were killed by the Cayuse. Born in New York, Whitman offered his services in 1834 to the American Board of Commissioners for Foreign Missions, a society supported by several Protestant churches. In 1835 the American Board sent Whitman and the Reverend Samuel Parker to the OREGON country to select mission sites. Whitman returned east to recruit mission workers — the Reverend Henry Spalding and his wife Eliza, William Gray, and Narcissa Prentiss, whom Whitman married in February 1836. Starting out on 31 March, the Whitman-Spalding caravan was notable in the story of the Oregon Trail in that Narcissa Whitman and Eliza Spalding were the first American women to cross the continent overland. Whitman established his mission among the Cayuse at Waiilatpu, and Spalding began his work at Lapwai among the Nez Percé, 110 miles farther east. The Indians proved indifferent to Christian religion, books, and school, and preferred hunting to farming. In 1842 the American Board ordered the Waiilatpu and Lapwai missions to close; convinced the missions should remain open, Whitman returned east to plead their case before the Board. He left Waiilatpu on 3 October 1842 and reached Boston on 30 March 1843. The American Board, moved by his arguments, agreed to rescind its orders. On his trip back to Oregon, Whitman joined the Great Migration of 1843 and gave valuable aid to the wagon train as physician and guide. Despite setbacks and occasional hostility from the Cayuse, the Whitmans refused to abandon Waiilatpu; the mission became an important station on the Oregon Trail. In 1847 white emigrants brought in measles which spread rapidly among the Indians, who had little resistance to the disease. Half the Cayuse died. Mainly because Whitman's medicine had failed to save them, the Cayuse attacked the mission and killed the doctor, his

321 V

wife, a dozen others, and destroyed the mission buildings. The massacre ended Protestant missionary work among the Oregon Indians and led to a war against the Cayuse. Today, the Whitman Mission site, near Walla Walla, Washington, is preserved as a national historic site by the National Park Service, U.S. Department of the Interior.

The Great Command: The Story of Marcus and Narcissa Whitman and the Oregon Country Pioneers by N. Jones (Boston, 1960);
Marcus Whitman, M.D., Pioneer and Martyr by C. M. Drury (Glendale, California, 1973);
Marcus and Narcissa Whitman and the Opening of Old Oregon by C. M. Drury (Glendale, 1973).

WICHITA INDIANS

Members of the Caddoan linguistic family and close relatives of the PAWNEE tribe, the Wichitas hunted the buffalo and grew corn, beans, and melons, and lived in large grass houses. They practised tattooing on the body and face; the men wore a scalp lock, and the women were expert at pottery. Their traditional land was the Wichita Mountains of Oklahoma, but they roamed far. In 1541 Coronado found them living on the ARKANSAS RIVER in what is now Kansas. At the beginning of the nineteenth century they had settled on the RED RIVER. During the American Civil War they returned to Kansas, establishing themselves on the present site of WICHITA, the town named after the tribe. Later, they were removed to the INDIAN TERRITORY, which later became Oklahoma, where a few hundred live today. The Wichita grass house resembled a beehive in shape; it was constructed from a framework of poles bent together at the top, then covered with a thick thatch of grass. The bundles of long grass were laid on, round after round, in single fashion, beginning at ground level, so that each round was overlapped by the next above; the bundles were tied in place with elm bark.

A Guide to the Indian Tribes of Oklahoma by M. H. Wright (Norman, Oklahoma, 1971).

WICHITA, Kansas

A major cattle town of the 1870s, Wichita started life in 1864 as a trading post for the WICHITA INDIANS, who had a village nearby. With the removal of the Indians in 1867 a white settlement developed around the trading post. Wichita was incorporated as a third class city in 1871 and in the following year, when the railroad reached the town, it became a booming railhead of the CATTLE DRIVES from Texas up the CHISHOLM TRAIL. Like other cattle towns, Wichita was a rip-roaring community of saloons, dance halls, GAMBLING houses, and brothels serving the needs of the Texas cowboys. In June 1873 the dance hall run by John 'Red' Beard was the scene of a pitched battle between Custer's Seventh Cavalry and the Texans; the fight started over a girl, fists flew and guns were fired, resulting in one soldier dead and two wounded. Wyatt EARP was one of the many LAWMEN hired to keep the peace in Wichita. By 1874 it was the leading cattle shipping centre, with 200,000 cattle and 2,000 cowboys flooding into the area at the height of the season. Then DODGE CITY took over the role as chief cowtown in Kansas and Wichita, its wild days over, settled down to develop its agriculture and industry and is today the largest city in Kansas.

Wichita, 1866-1883 by R. Long (Wichita, 1945);
The Cattle Towns by R. R. Dykstra (New York, 1968).

WILD BUNCH, The

A celebrated gang of outlaws headed by Butch CASSIDY, the Wild Bunch frequently changed in size and members but its nucleus included Harry Longbaugh, known as the Sundance Kid; Ben Kilpatrick, called the Tall Texan; Harvey Logan, alias Kid Curry, and Bill Carver. Several women were closely associated with the gang, in particular Della Rose, alias Laura Bullion, and Etta Place. Mostly ex-cowboys, the Wild Bunch (so called from their boisterous antics in spending their loot) ranged far and wide throughout the West in the 1890s and into the early years of the twentieth century; they were the last of the old-style, horse-riding outlaws. They stole cattle, robbed banks, and held up trains in Wyoming, Montana, Nevada, Utah, North Dakota, Idaho, and New Mexico. Major robberies committed by the Wild Bunch included holding up the Union Pacific's Overland Flyer at Wilcox, Wyoming, in June 1899, and taking an estimated 30,000 dollars from the express car safe; robbing the First National Bank of Winnemucca, Nevada, in September 1900, of 32,000 dollars; stopping the Great Northern Express No. 3 near the town of Wagner, Montana, in July 1901, and looting 40,000 dollars from the express car. The railway companies posted rewards for the Wild Bunch, and the bandits were pursued by the implacable agents of the PINKERTON National Detective

322   *Wichita, Kansas, in 1878.*

323   *The 'Wild Bunch'. Left to Right, standing, Bill Carver and Harvey Logan; seated, Harry Longbaugh (Sundance Kid), Ben Kilpatrick, and Butch Cassidy.*

322 ∧

323 ∨

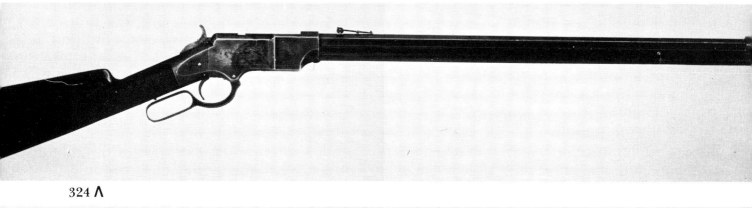

324 Λ

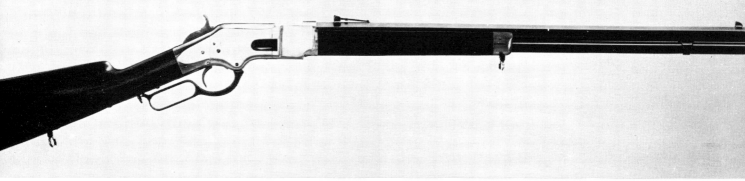

325 Λ

326 Λ 327 V

324 *The Henry repeating rifle, forerunner of the Winchester.*

325 *Winchester rifle, Model 1866.*

326 *Winchester rifle, Model 1873.*

327 *'Flying Hoofs' by Charles M. Russell; gray wolves preying on wild horses.*

Agency, and by special, rail-borne posses organized by the UNION PACIFIC. Under constant pressure the gang scattered. Ben Kilpatrick was caught and sent to prison and was later killed while robbing a train. Bill Carver was shot dead in a gunfight in Texas. Kid Curry was killed in 1903 during a battle with a posse. Butch Cassidy, the Sundance Kid, and Etta Place sailed to South America and continued their banditry there. Etta returned to the U.S. and disappeared; Butch and the Kid are believed to have died in a gun battle with troops in Bolivia or Uruguay in 1909.

The Wild Bunch by J. D. Horan (London, 1960).

WINCHESTER RIFLES

The rifles and carbines manufactured by the Winchester Repeating Arms Company of New Haven, Connecticut, were the most popular multi-shot shoulder arms of the Old West. The Winchester Model 1873, the type usually seen in Western films, was the most widely used, a total of 720,610 being produced up to 1919, when the manufacture of the model was discontinued. Oliver F. Winchester (1810-80), a shirt manufacturer, established himself in the firearms business in 1857 when he purchased the assets of the Volcanic Repeating Arms Company, which had produced pistols and rifles featuring a special repeating mechanism actuated by a trigger-guard lever. Winchester organized a new company called the New Haven Arms Company and made Benjamin Tyler Henry, a highly-skilled gun mechanic, the superintendent of the plant. In 1858 Henry devised a self-contained, metal-cased, rim-fire cartridge and developed a rifle — based on the Volcanic arms system — to fire it. The Henry rifle, with its 15 cartridges housed in a tubular magazine under the barrel, was a successful weapon that led directly to the first Winchester; the gun was operated by moving the trigger-guard lever down and back to its original position, a quick, simple movement which extracted the spent cartridge, carried a fresh shell from the spring-activated tubular magazine into the chamber, and cocked the hammer ready for firing. In 1866 Oliver Winchester reorganized his firearms business as the Winchester Repeating Arms Company and produced a new improved version of the Henry, called the Winchester rifle, Model 1866, which had a more convenient and efficient loading system and a less complicated action. Failing to get military orders, Winchester promoted his rifle in the civilian market and met with considerable success. The second Winchester, the Model 1873, was basically the same as the earlier model but it was stronger, simpler, and lighter. It had a sliding lid covering the ejection port in the top of the frame to keep dirt and water out of the action; the frame and butt plate were made of forged iron (changed to steel in 1881) to replace the brass of the Model 1866, and it used a centre-fire cartridge loaded with a .44 calibre bullet and 40 grains of powder, which gave a substantial increase in range and stopping power over the earlier model's .44 rim-fire cartridge of 28 grains. The Winchester 1873 rifle had a 15-shot magazine capacity, and the shorter carbine carried 12 cartridges; the model was later produced with various barrel lengths and calibres. The quick-firing Winchester, stoutly constructed, easy to use, was the ideal saddle gun; it was never officially adopted by the U.S. military but it enjoyed wide popularity throughout the West with cattlemen, hunters, outlaws, peace officers, farmers, and Indians. Indeed the gun became so popular that in 1878 the COLT company rechambered its successful Peacemaker revolver to take the same .44-40 cartridge used in the Winchester 1873, so that a man need carry only one type of ammunition for both rifle and pistol. Winchester produced further lever-action models, of which the Model 1894, firing a .30-30 cartridge, became the most popular of American sporting rifles, enjoying world-wide sales of nearly three million.

Winchester, the Gun that Won the West by H. E. Williamson (Washington, 1952);
The First Winchester by J. E. Parsons (New York, 1955);
Famous Guns from the Winchester Collection by H. E. Bowman (Greenwich, Connecticut, 1964).

WOLF, The Gray
Canis occidentalis

The slaughter of livestock by the rapacious gray or timber wolf was a constant problem for the settlers and ranchers of the frontier West and they waged a war of extermination against the animal. The gray wolf is larger, more savage than the COYOTE, or prairie wolf, and its loud, prolonged howl is different from the high-pitched call of the coyote. An average adult male has a body length of five feet, stands about three feet high at the shoulder, and weighs in the region of 100 pounds. The colour of the gray wolf ranges from nearly white, through gray to black. The Indians used wolf skins for robes and the head and tail for ceremonial purposes. When the buffalo roamed the plains in millions, gray wolves prowled around the herds, preying on the weak and injured and calves that wandered from the protection of the elders. As the professional BUFFALO HUNTERS wiped out the great herds the wolf turned to the mass killing of cattle, sheep, and horses. The settlers struck back with guns, traps, and poison.

Bounties were offered for dead wolves, professional 'wolfers' were hired to hunt them, and over the years the large wolf population in the West was greatly reduced. Once widespread and numerous throughout North America, the gray wolf today is mostly found in isolated regions, in the ROCKY MOUNTAINS, around the Great Lakes, and in particular in northern Canada and Alaska. It feeds on small mammals, DEER, ANTELOPE, birds, and carrion; in general almost any kind of prey is acceptable to the wolf, even its own kind, if sick or wounded.

The Wolves of North America by S. P. Young and E. A. Goldman (Washington, 1944).

WOUNDED KNEE MASSACRE 1890

The infamous encounter in which a band of Minneconjou SIOUX was slaughtered by the Seventh Cavalry at Wounded Knee Creek, South Dakota, on 29 December 1890 was a direct result of the reservation Indians' adoption of the new GHOST DANCE religion. As the Ghost Dancers grew in numbers, white settlers became alarmed and feared the religious gatherings as a preparation for further Indian hostilities. By the end of 1890 nearly 3,000 troops had been called into the Sioux country to maintain peace. The concentration of soldiers made the Indians resentful and suspicious, and some Sioux bands left their reservations and, although they had not committed any acts of hostility, were immediately branded as 'hostiles'. One such band, 350 strong, was that headed by the Minneconjou chief Big Foot. The Seventh Cavalry, commanded by Colonel James W. Forsyth, intercepted Big Foot's band at Wounded Knee Creek, on the Pine Ridge Reservation. The Indian camp was entirely surrounded by soldiers, and quick-firing Hotchkiss guns on a knoll were trained on the tipis. Forsyth ordered Big Foot, sick with pneumonia, to surrender and his warriors to give up what arms they had. As the soldiers searched the Indians for hidden weapons, the tense situation exploded into terrible violence. Indians and soldiers started fighting and shooting. The artillery opened fire, killing Indians and soldiers alike with explosive shells. The Indians scattered under the hail of shot and shell, pursued by soldiers intent on slaughter. Bodies of women and children were found as far as two miles from the camp, killed in flight after all Sioux resistance had ceased. When the massacre was over some 150 Indians lay dead, including Big Foot and about sixty women and children; many others were wounded and died later. Exact Indian casualties will never be known; one estimate gives the final total of dead as nearly 300. The Seventh Cavalry suffered 25 dead and 39 wounded, most of them victims of their own cannon fire and bullets. General MILES, who was in command of field operations during the Ghost Dance troubles, denounced the incident as a 'melee and a massacre . . . unjustifiable and worthy of the severest condemnation'. He relieved Forsyth of his command and convened a court of inquiry; however, the Secretary of War exonerated Forsyth and restored him to his command. Wounded Knee marked the end of the frontier campaigns against the Indians.

The Wounded Knee Massacre from the Viewpoint of the Survivors by J. H. McGregor (Baltimore, 1940);
The Last Days of the Sioux Nation by R. M. Utley (New Haven, Connecticut, 1963);
Bury My Heart at Wounded Knee by D. Brown (London, 1970).

WYOMING

The land of Wyoming figures largely in the history of the Old West. In the 1820s and 1830s FUR TRAPPERS roamed the region, trapping BEAVER in the mountain country around the sources of the Platte, Green, Yellowstone, and Snake Rivers. In 1825 William H. ASHLEY held the first fur traders' rendezvous on Henry's Fork of the Green River; of the sixteen rendezvous held until the system ended in 1840, a dozen of the meetings were held in Wyoming. The OREGON TRAIL passed through the Wyoming country and emigrants bound for OREGON, CALIFORNIA, and UTAH would stop and rest at FORT LARAMIE and later at FORT BRIDGER, take on supplies and repair their wagons. Fort Laramie became an army post and a number of important Indian treaties were signed there. When the BOZEMAN TRAIL was opened from Fort Laramie to the gold fields of Montana, it ran through the traditional SIOUX hunting grounds of the Powder River country. FORT PHIL KEARNY was built in 1866 to protect the Bozeman Trail and it played a major role in RED CLOUD's War of 1866-8. By the Fort Laramie treaty of 1868 the U.S. government withdrew the troops from the Bozeman Trail and abandoned Fort Phil Kearny, which was immediately burned down by Red Cloud's warriors.

328 *Culmination of the Ghost Dance Religion, the massacre of Sioux at Wounded Knee. Illustration from* The Graphic *31 January 1891.*

329 *The Wounded Knee Massacre; the frozen body of Chief Big Foot.*

328 Λ

329 V

That same year chief WASHAKIE, friend of white emigrants and ally of the U.S. military, secured the coveted Wind River Reservation in central Wyoming for his peaceful SHOSHONI tribe. In July 1868 Congress created the Territory of Wyoming from parts of the Dakota, Utah, and Idaho territories; Wyoming became a State in 1890, with Cheyenne the capital. During the 1870s and 1880s thousands of Texas LONGHORNS were driven into Wyoming and a great open-range cattle industry was established. In 1892 conflicting land and cattle interests resulted in the JOHNSON COUNTY WAR. A ruggedly beautiful country of mountains, green valleys, and sagebrush plains, Wyoming's highest point is Gannett Peak, 13,785 feet, in the Wind River Range. YELLOWSTONE Park, oldest and largest national park in the U.S., has spectacular scenery, high waterfalls and spouting geysers. Wyoming remains very much a cowboy State; its Frontier Days celebration and rodeo, held every summer at Cheyenne, is one of the biggest events of its kind.

Wyoming from Territorial Days to the Present by F. B. Beard (Chicago, 1933);
Wyoming Cowboy Days by C. A. Guernsey (New York, 1936);
Wyoming: Frontier State by V. Linford (Denver, Colorado, 1947);
History of Wyoming by T. A. Larson (Lincoln, Nebraska, 1965).

XIT RANCH

One of the largest cattle spreads of its day, the XIT Ranch covered three million acres of the Texas Panhandle, but it was never a profitable concern. When the Texas State capital in Austin was burned down in 1881 the administration did not have the money to build the grandest capital in the United States, a requirement then demanded by the proud Texans. To raise the money Texas deeded 3,050,000 acres of public land to a Chicago syndicate of financiers and businessmen that built the pink granite structure, started in 1882 and completed in 1888. The syndicate intended to sell off the large tract of land in small portions to farmers. But failing to attract enough buyers, the syndicate decided on the cattle business; in 1885 they fenced the land with 800 miles of BARBED WIRE, stocked it with 150,000 cattle, and hired B. H. Campbell as the resident manager. It was called the XIT Ranch after its brand, which supposedly meant 'Ten in Texas', in reference to the ten counties over which the ranch was spread. Despite its great size the XIT never returned a penny in dividends to its stockholders and in 1901 the ranch was sold up in small lots to farmers, now eager to buy since artesian water had been found on the land.

The XIT Ranch by J. E. Haley (Chicago, 1929);
Cattle Empire: The Fabulous Story of the 3,000,000 Acre XIT by L. R. Nordyke (New York, 1949).

YELLOWSTONE NATIONAL PARK

The oldest and largest national park in the United States, Yellowstone embraces nearly 3,500 square miles of scenic splendour in the north-west corner of WYOMING, edging into Montana and Idaho. Yellowstone is a wilderness of natural wonders: magnificent waterfalls, deep canyons, bubbling hot springs, and gushing geysers. It is immensely rich in wild life — grizzly BEARS, BUFFALO, MOOSE, ELK, fish, and birds. The name Yellowstone comes from an Indian word meaning 'Rock Yellow River', referring to the Yellowstone River which runs through the region. John COLTER, fur trapper and explorer, appears to have been the first white man to see this land of volcanic hot springs and geysers, in 1807-8; his stories were scoffed at as 'Colter's Hell'. Jim BRIDGER, another famous trapper, also caused disbelief when he came back with Yellowstone tales of 'the place where Hell bubbled up'. Two official expeditions, in 1870 and 1871, brought national attention to the wonders of the area and on 1 March 1872 Congress established the Yellowstone National Park (the world's first national park), to preserve its natural state forever from private greed and exploitation, 'dedicated and set apart as a public park or pleasuring ground for the benefit and enjoyment of the people'. Among the scenic wonders are the Grand Canyon of the Yellowstone, sheer cliffs rising 1,000 feet above the river; and the Upper and Lower Falls of the Yellowstone, two beautiful cataracts which plummet a total of 417 feet. Most famous of the park's geysers is Old Faithful, so called because its eruptions never cease; these occur at intervals varying from 33 to 96 minutes, last two to five minutes, and reach heights of 106 to 184 feet. There are bigger geysers but none so regular. Mammoth Hot Springs spills its waters over a series of high terraces, like giant steps, into reflecting pools; there are thousands of other thermal springs, hot pools, and 'paint pot' pools of brilliant blue and green waters.

The Discovery of Yellowstone Park, 1870 by N. P Langford (St Paul, Minnesota, 1923);
The Yellowstone National Park by H. M. Chittenden (Norman, Oklahoma, 1964);
The Place Where Hell Bubbled Up by D. A. Clary (Washington, D.C., 1972).

330 ∧   331 ∨

330 The sudden eruption of a geyser frightens early visitors to Yellowstone National Park.

331 Yellowstone National Park, the Lower Falls, painted by T.H. Thomas in 1888.

332 ∧

333 ∧

334 ∨

335 ∨

332   *Bob Younger.*

333   *Cole Younger.*

334   *Yuma mother and baby in cradle board.*

335   *Brigham Young.*

YOUNG, Brigham
1801-77

Great leader of the MORMONS during the settlement and development of UTAH, Brigham Young was Second President of the Church of Jesus Christ of Latter Day Saints and first governor of Utah Territory. Born in Vermont, Young was baptized into the new faith of Mormonism in 1832. He became a successful missionary of the Mormon church and by 1839 was the senior member of the Quorum of the Twelve Apostles, the administration body which served the Prophet and founder of Mormonism, Joseph Smith. Brigham Young was in Boston when Smith was killed in 1844 during violent anti-Mormon demonstrations in Illinois. Young now established his leadership. With the Mormon community wavering with grief and panic and the church in danger of dissolution, Young assumed command; his courage, strength of will, and powerful personality rallied the Mormons and he resolved to lead them away from the non-Mormon world into the wilderness to find their promised land. The mass migration began in the spring of 1847. Young led his people to the desolate valley of the GREAT SALT LAKE (at that time Mexican territory); on arrival there, in July 1847, he announced 'This is the place.' SALT LAKE CITY was immediately laid out under Young's direction and the Mormon colonizing of Utah began with great energy and determination. Inspired by Young's dynamism and inflexible belief in his people's destiny, the industrious Mormons made the desert bloom and created their promised land. In 1849 these independent settlers petitioned the U.S. Congress to accept the Mormon-governed State of Deseret; Congress denied the petition and in 1850 established the Territory of Utah and Brigham Young was appointed governor. Growing political friction between the Mormons and the Federal government resulted in a U.S. military force marching into Utah in 1857. Full scale war was avoided and Young was replaced as governor by a non-Mormon Federal appointee. Nevertheless, Brigham Young remained the real master of Utah until his death in 1877. A benevolent despot and brilliant organizer, he loved dancing, singing, and the theatre; he hated waste, gambling, and sexual misbehaviour. Polygamy was part of the Mormon creed and Young is credited with as many as twenty-seven wives; he had fifty-six children and left seventeen widows.

Brigham Young by M. R. Werner (New York, 1925);
The Life Story of Brigham Young by S. Y. Gates and L. B. Widstoe (New York, 1930);
Brigham Young, the Man and his Work by P. Nibley (Salt Lake City, 1936);
The Lion of the Lord. A Biography of Brigham Young by S. P. Hirshson (New York, 1969).

YOUNGER BROTHERS

Four outlaw brothers, Cole, James, Robert, and John Younger were born in Missouri, first cousins of Frank and Jesse JAMES. Cole (short for Coleman) and his brother James served with QUANTRILL's Confederate guerrillas in the Civil War. Soon after the war the four Youngers joined with the two James boys and formed a bandit gang, robbing banks, holding up trains, and killing people, for ten years. Cole was the eldest and most impressive of the brothers, a big, handsome man weighing 200 pounds; he is said to have fathered the first child of Belle STARR, the woman outlaw. In March 1874 John Younger was shot dead in an encounter with agents of the PINKERTON National Detective Agency, in which two of the detectives also died. On 7 September 1876 the three Youngers, Frank and Jesse James, and three others attempted to rob a bank at Northfield, Minnesota; the citizens fought back and routed the gang — three of the bandits were killed, the Youngers were all severely wounded and captured, only Frank and Jesse got clean away. Two citizens were shot dead in the Northfield raid. At their trial in November 1876 the Youngers pleaded guilty and were sentenced to life imprisonment; they had taken advantage of the Minnesota law that a person charged with murder who entered a plea of guilty could not be sentenced to capital punishment. Robert died in prison of tuberculosis in 1889. The surviving brothers were both paroled in July 1901 on condition that they did not leave the State of Minnesota. James committed suicide in 1902 over an unrequited love affair. Cole was pardoned in 1903 and returned to his native Missouri where he lived out his life as a popular and respectable citizen, a living legend of the Old West. He died in 1916 aged seventy-two.

The Story of Cole Younger, by Himself (Chicago, 1903);
The Younger Brothers by A. C. Appler (New York, 1955);
The Younger Brothers by C. W. Breihan (San Antonio, Texas, 1961).

YUMAN INDIANS

The major tribes of the Yuman linguistic family include the Yuma, the Mohave, Havasupai, Maricopa, Walapai, Yavapai, and Cocopah. They have lived in the arid south-western part of the United States for centuries, along both sides of the Colorado River in Arizona and California, and the Gila River. A primitive people with little cultural distinction, they farmed the fertile flatlands along the river, gathered wild foods, fished, and hunted small game. They did not construct canoes but made rafts of bundles of reeds tied together. The men often went naked and the women wore a small bark-cloth apron; in particular, the Mohaves were much given to tattooing. The Yumans lived in crude, open-sided dwellings with brush roofs; and, unusual for North American Indians, cremated their dead. The traditional home of the Havasupai is the bottom of an extremely rugged and isolated section of the GRAND CANYON of the Colorado River, about 3,000 feet below the canyon rim. This reservation can be reached only by an eight-mile-long trail from the east and west sides of the Grand Canyon; consequently the Havasupai had little contact with the white men of the Old West. Today the Yuman tribes live on reservations in California and Arizona.

Yuman Tribes of the Gila River by L. Spier (Chicago, 1933); *Indians of the Southwest* by E. E. Dale (Norman, Oklahoma, 1949).

Z

ZOGBAUM, Rufus F. 1849-1925

A leading illustrator of the Old West and military scenes whose work appeared regularly in *Harper's Weekly* during the 1880s. Born in Charleston, South Carolina, Rufus Fairchild Zogbaum studied at Heidelberg University, the Art Students' League in New York City, and under Leon J. F. Bonnat, the French figure painter, in Paris in 1880-2. On his return to America Zogbaum made several trips to MONTANA (and later to the INDIAN TERRITORY, which became Oklahoma) and produced a series of illustrated articles that were published in *Harper's Weekly*; these included 'A Day's Drive with Montana Cow-Boys', 'A Night on a Montana Stage-Coach', 'Across Country with a Cavalry Column', and 'With the Blue Coats on the Border'. In 1888 Zogbaum's book *Horse, Foot, and Dragoons* was published, which contained some of his military illustrations.

Artists and Illustrators of the Old West, 1850-1900 by R. Taft (New York, 1963).

ZUNI INDIANS

A tribe of the Zunian linguistic group, the Zuni live in a famous pueblo, or village, in New Mexico. Like the HOPI of Arizona and other PUEBLO INDIANS, the Zuni have for centuries

336 *A Montana cowboy by Zogbaum, from Harper's Magazine, 1885.*

337 *Zuni Indians performing the Rain Dance, about 1900.*

336 Λ

337 V

inhabited permanent villages made of stone and ADOBE, living mostly by agriculture. The Spaniards were the first Europeans to meet the Zuni, in 1539, drawn to the region by the legend of the Seven Cities of Cibola, supposedly filled with gold. In the following year Coronado visited the Zuni settlement and conquered the people. In 1680 the Zuni participated in the Pueblo Revolt against Spanish rule and since then have managed to preserve their ancient native culture. After the MEXICAN WAR of 1846-8 the Zuni country came under the control of the United States. Today the Zuni Pueblo, about forty miles south of Gallup, New Mexico, is the largest pueblo in the State and the only surviving community of the Seven Cities of Cibola. Skilled in pottery, the Zuni are among the finest jewellery makers in the South-west, famous for their beautiful turquoise, silver, and shell-mosaic ornaments. They are also noted for the Shalako Kachina dance, one of the most spectacular of the Pueblo ceremonial dances.

The Pueblo Indian World by E. L. Hewitt and B. P. Dutton (Albuquerque, New Mexico, 1945);
Zuni Daily Life by J. M. Roberts (Lincoln, Nebraska, 1956).

Alphabetical List of Entries

Pinkerton, Allan
Plains Indians
Plains Rifle
Plummer, Henry
Pony Express
Prairies
Prairie Chicken
Prairie Dog
Pueblo Indians

Quanah Parker
Quantrill, William C.
Quarter Horse

Rabbits
Rain-in-the-Face
Rattlesnakes
Red Cloud
Red River
Remington, Frederic
Remington Revolvers
Remuda
Reno Brothers
Reynolds, Charley
Rio Grande
Road Runner
Rocky Mountains
Rocky Mountain Fur Company
Rodeo
Roman Nose
Roosevelt, Theodore
Rosebud, Battle of the
Round-up
Russell, Charles
Russell, Majors & Waddell
Rustlers

Sacajawea
Saddle, Cowboy
Saguaro Cactus
Salt Lake City
San Francisco
Sand Creek Massacre

Santa Anna
Santa Fe Trail
Satanta
Scalping
Schreyvogel, Charles
Scorpion
Sharps Rifles
Sheep Wars
Sheridan, Philip H.
Sherman, William T.
Short, Luke
Shoshoni Indians
Shotguns
Sieber, Al
Sierra Nevada
Sioux Indians
Sitting Bull
Skunk
Smith, Jedediah
Smith, Tom
Smith & Wesson Revolvers
Sod Houses
Southern Pacific Railroad
Spencer Rifle
Springfield Rifles
Spurs, Cowboy
St Joseph, Missouri
St Louis, Missouri
Stampede
Starr, Belle
Steamboats
Stetson, John B.
Sublette, William
Sun Dance
Sutter, John

Tabor, Horace
Texas
Texas Rangers
Thomas, Heck
Thompson, Ben
Tilghman, Bill
Tipi
Tombstone, Arizona
Totem Pole

Trail of Tears
Travois

Union Pacific Railroad
Utah
Ute Indians

Vaquero
Victorio
Vigilantes
Villa, Pancho
Virginia City, Nevada

Wagon Box Fight
Wagon, Covered
Wagon Trains
Walker, Joseph R.
Wallace, 'Bigfoot'
Washakie, Chief
Washington
Washita, Battle of the
Wells Fargo & Company
Whitman, Marcus
Wichita Indians
Wichita, Kansas
Wild Bunch, The
Winchester Rifles
Wolf The Gray
Wounded Knee Massacre
Wyoming

XIT Ranch

Yellowstone National Park
Young, Brigham
Younger Brothers
Yuman Indians

Zogbaum, Rufus F.
Zuni Indians

Special Colour Photography by
Peter J. Elgar A.I.I.P., A.R.P.S.